FROM CRADLE
TO GRAVE

Joyce Egginton is a professional writer who
has specialized in investigative reporting. She
is particularly interested in the impact of
unusual events upon the lives of ordinary
people, and in the reactions of those caught
up in the drama. This is what attracted her to
the case of Marybeth Tinning.

Born and educated in London, she now lives
in New York. For twenty years she was the
New York correspondent of *The Observer*.

FROM CRADLE TO GRAVE

The short lives and strange deaths
of Marybeth Tinning's nine children

Joyce Egginton

W H ALLEN

Copyright © 1989 by Joyce Egginton
Foreword copyright © 1989 by John L. Emery

First published in the United States by
William Morrow and Company, Inc. 1989

Set in Plantin by Input Typesetting Ltd, London
Printed and bound in Great Britain by
Mackays of Chatham Plc, Chatham, Kent
for the publishers, W. H. Allen & Co. Plc
Sekforde House, 175/9 St John Street, London EC1V 4LL

ISBN 0 491 03824 0 (Hardback edition)
ISBN 0 352 32455 4 (Paperback edition)

In memory of my mother,
Lillian Egginton, who gave me
so much more than life

ACKNOWLEDGMENTS

This book is entirely factual. No pseudonyms have been used, and all the material is based upon my own observations, upon the best recollections of my informants, and upon court testimony. About one hundred and fifty people were interviewed, most of them for several hours at a time, and many of them on several occasions. Some are named in this book; others, at their request, remain anonymous. Their cooperation, patience, and interest in the project were invaluable. My understanding of the medical and psychological aspects of this complex case was greatly helped by a number of experts to whom I am indebted: Dr Stuart S. Asch, professor of clinical psychiatry at New York Hospital—Cornell Medical Center; Dr. Michael M. Baden, director of forensic sciences for the New York State Police; Dr. Janet Christman, pathologist, St. Peter's Hospital, Albany, New York; Dr. Richard Cimma, pediatrician, of East Greenbush, New York; Dr. Jack N. P. Davies, pathologist, of Albany, New York; Dr. Judianne Densen-Gerber, chair of Odyssey Corporation of Connecticut; Dr. Vincent DiMaio, medical examiner for San Antonio, Texas; Dr. John L. Emery, emeritus professor of pediatric pathology, University of Sheffield, England; Dr. David G. Inwood, director of training, Division of Child and Adolescent Psychiatry, Down-State Medical Center, Brooklyn, New York; Dr. Virgil January, behavioral scientist, New York State Police; Dr. Kevin Karpowicz, pediatrician, Schenectady, New York; Dr. Mary Lindsay, child psychiatrist and medical director of the Aylesbury Vale Child Guidance Clinic, Aylesbury, Buckinghamshire, England; Dr. Alan Lobovits, pediatrician, Southborough, Massachusetts; Dr. Roy Meadow, professor of pediatrics and child health, St. James's University Hospital, Leeds, England; Dr. Rudy V. Nydegger, clinical psychologist and professor of psychology at Union College, Schenectady, New York; Dr Michael O'Hara, associate professor of psychology, University of Iowa; Dr. Thomas F. D. Oram, chief of pathology, Ellis Hospital, Schenectady, new York; Dr. Diana Riley, obstetric liaison psychiatrist, Wendover, Berkshire, England; Dr. August C. Schwenk, obstetrician, Schenectady, New York; Dr. Boyd Stephens, medical examiner, San Francisco, California; Dr. Robert L. Sullivan, medical examiner, Schenectady County, New York; and the Reverend Burnham H. Waldo, minister of Centenary United Methodist Church, Greenwich, New York.

I would particularly like to thank those people whose contributions to my research took up an inordinate amount of their time and energies, and who were always cheerfully available to answer my frequent questions: Investigator William W. Barnes, Assistant District Attorney Alan Gebell, Patricia S. McBreen, Suzanne Normington, Dr. Thomas F. D. Oram, Martha Proper, the Reverend Burnham H. Waldo, Cynthia Walter, and various members of the Tinning and Roe families. Marybeth Tinning was given the opportunity to tell her side of the story, but declined.

By no means least, my sincere thanks to my literary agent, Jane Cushman, whose idea it was that I should write this book, and who always made time to listen, advise, and encourage.

—J.E.

CONTENTS

FOREWORD
11

MARYBETH'S BABIES
15

Part One
TAMI LYNNE
19

Part Two
ALL HER CHILDREN
79

Part Three
MARYBETH
209

CONTENTS

Part Four
JUDGMENT
275

INDEX
371

FOREWORD BY JOHN L. EMERY

It is a truism that fact is stranger than fiction. This book is an essay in contemporary journalism concerned with what many saw as a horror story more horrible than that of Jack the Ripper. Joyce Egginton presents us with Marybeth, this woman of today. We see her from childhood until her imprisonment, almost entirely through the eyes and words of the people who formed her world. We are presented also with the people who dealt with her conviction and removal from society; and all these people are described "warts and all". We are largely left to draw our own conclusions and from whatever viewpoint or level we like.

We can read of a trail of baby deaths that occurred in a relatively quiet city in New York's Mohawk River Valley, a city that had grown up with Edison. A series of deaths, of people's complaints followed by the activities of the police that led to her final conviction, a cops and robbers story where everyone knows the villain from the beginning.

We can read this book as a social document of the U.S.A. today. Of the thoughts and actions of people who met and worked with Marybeth, and how they reacted to their knowledge of her babies' deaths. In particular, of the way in which the Reverend Burnham Waldo was almost destroyed in his attempts to help her. How his obviously able pastoral skills and insights into normal bereavement and problems in families were useless tools in the face of Marybeth's personality abnormalities.

This book will also be read, and recommended by psychologists and psychiatrists as a case report of a particular type of Personality Disturbance. An abnormality in development of thought structure of which she exhibits almost all of the classical characteristics – the complete absence of a sense of guilt (a feature that the police used in their manoeuvres to obtain her admission of killing some of her children). We see her inability to make a deep relationship with anyone, her need for immediate self-gratification which led to her repeated debts, having at least a normal level of intelligence; having a short fuse so that most of the people near her treated her with kid gloves; her manipulation of people with no sense of conscience; an amazing facility to tell lies; and all this with the ability to present to the world a high level of social grace and charm so that she superficially appeared to be completely normal. Parts of her mental processes stopped growing while others continued – think of a two-year old and think of the points listed above.

The story can also be read in the framework of north American medical beliefs and organization at this time. Why did nine children have to die before major steps were taken to prevent further deaths? How was she allowed to adopt a child? Not one of the babies who died had an autopsy performed by a pathologist who specialized in baby pathology, and one child had no autopsy at all and yet was signed up as S.I.D.S. My heart went out to Dr. Janet Christman who examined Mary Frances after her death and wanted to record that she had found no anatomical cause for death. She was over-ruled and the death was signed up as S.I.D.S. It is hard to get away from the feeling that if the diagnosis of S.I.D.S. had not been available and thus the deaths tidied away as if of natural causes, then action would have been taken much sooner.

It has been my lot to be concerned with baby murder trials on both sides of the Atlantic and this trial as in so many others, left me in a state of intense frustration due to the way in which the adversarial approach to the medical evidence distorts what little knowledge we have of how babies die. The trial itself seemed to be something of a showpiece. I had seen a national T.V. programme on the family many months earlier where there had been a virtual trial by T.V. with the apparent conviction of the mother. The real trial was set up by the D.A. to be concerned only with the last baby's death, and with the jury having to pretend to a lack of knowledge of the previous deaths. If the trial had been in truth, only concerned with one death, the arguments would have been quite different and simply been as to whether or not the death was a case of S.I.D.S. or not. The arguments would have been largely about the distribution of small bleedings and the pathology of different types of asphyxia over which there are many opinions, the jury would have been very confused and the case would probably have fallen. In the United Kingdom it is extremely unlikely that the mother's confession would have been admitted as evidence in court. I was involved in a somewhat similar situation in England several years ago, of a mother who confessed to smothering three of her children. The judge would not permit her confession as evidence and as there were no fractures and the findings so like those described in S.I.D.S. that the woman was acquitted.

Despite all this, I think that Marybeth almost certainly did suffocate several of these children, but when it comes to the question of an intent to kill we are on much less certain ground. What is equally certain is that if several of these children had been separated from their mother and brought up by a healthy normal woman they would not have died. If we believe this, should we not now take the next step and see why those earlier babies were not adequately investigated? Because quite certainly, some of those earlier diagnoses of S.I.D.S. permitted the later babies' deaths. Where does guilt lie?

Horrible as it may seem, for parents to kill one of their children is not so very uncommon. This occurs today not only in communities where there is limited food such as in Aboriginal tribes of Australia, where, for a woman to have twins is a disaster and so the weakest has to be sacrificed to enable one to survive; but in much more sophisticated communities as in China. There, when families were limited to one child there followed a veritable epidemic of S.I.D.S. among baby girls. I have studied something over 6,000 baby deaths and over 2,000 of these as unexpected deaths. Among the latter there have been many where, like Dr. Janet Christman, I have found no anatomical cause for death. Recently our interest has been focused on families where more than one unexpected death has occurred, and a variety of causes have appeared. There has been a major group where mothers have had a mental abnormality, but these have not always been of the same type. In one family where there were five unexpected deaths, the description of the personality of the mother was remarkably like that of Marybeth.

Marybeth is now in prison, but what have we learned from the Marybeth story? Can we do anything to prevent this happening again in another family? – For the Marybeth situation is only the tip of some iceberg. If in Marybeth's babies someone had found an enzyme system abnormality in one cell that could have been possibly related to the observed raised blood ammonias in several children, by now there would have been several research fellows exploring this in laboratories, probably in many parts of the world and testing all the relatives of Marybeth. But, as the metabolic and the hereditary lines of investigation in her family seem to have drawn little the residue is focused on her mental state. According to Joyce Egginton now that Marybeth is finally out of circulation, that is the end of the story. But surely, should not Marybeth and her history be examined at length by some physicians who specialize in mental diseases related to pregnancy and children, to see if there is some behaviour pattern that could have been spotted before she killed a baby for the second time?

These notes introducing this book have been stimulated not only by the trial but by reading the book. I have approached the story of Marybeth from the viewpoint of a paediatrician, pathologist and a pupil of Anna Freud. Your viewpoint will be different. You will learn something that I have missed. Nine children have died, if these lives had any purpose we should all be able to learn something from them for the benefit of other children. What will you learn?

John L. Emery
Emeritus Professor of Paediatric Pathology,
University of Sheffield

MARYBETH'S BABIES

	BORN	DIED
Barbara	May 31, 1967	March 2, 1972
Joseph	January 10, 1970	January 20, 1972
Jennifer	December 26, 1971	January 3, 1972
Timothy	November 21, 1973	December 10, 1973
Nathan	March 30, 1975	September 2, 1975
Michael	August 3, 1978	March 2, 1981
(adopted)		
Mary Francis	October 29, 1978	February 22, 1979
Jonathan	November 19, 1979	March 24, 1980
Tami Lynne	August 22, 1985	December 20, 1985

Part One

TAMI LYNNE

ONE

No one knows the real Marybeth. She is never the same
person.

— Former colleague

A few hours before she killed her infant daughter Tami Lynne,
Marybeth Tinning bought her a quantity of Christmas presents.
She took her time about it, wandering uncertainly down the
crowded aisles of a discount toy store, picking up an item, turning
it in her hands, then putting it back on the shelf to search for
something better. She also spent more money than her neighbor
and companion Cynthia Walter thought was sensible. "What can
three-month-old babies know about Christmas?" Cynthia argued,
thinking of her own careful budget and of all the holiday expenses.
Ignoring the question, Marybeth bought a musical stuffed animal,
a hand-held water toy, a mobile with bells to attach to the side of
the baby's stroller, a little quilt with colorful objects folded into
the corners, and a second quilt for Cynthia's son, Aaron. Except
for her hesitancy in choosing gifts, there was nothing unusual about
Marybeth's behavior on this evening of December 19, 1985, nothing
to suggest that she was not a rational and loving mother.

Marybeth and Cynthia had babies of the same age and lived next
door to each other, a coincidence which was the basis of their
friendship. During the early summer, in the seventh month of their
pregnancies, they had met for the first time on Michigan Avenue,
Schenectady, the street where the Tinnings and the Walters lived
in upstairs apartments of neighboring two-family houses. Marybeth
made the smiling remark that they both were getting fat. Chatting,
they discovered that their babies were due toward the end of
August. A few days later Cynthia's husband, Mark, was struggling

to carry groceries up the flight of stairs to his front door when Marybeth's husband, Joseph, passed by and offered to help. Mark invited Joe and his wife in for a drink, and this cemented a friendship between the two couples which ended seven months later in overwhelming tragedy.

Cynthia's first impression of Marybeth was that "she seemed very nice. . . . I liked her." Often housebound by the summer heat and by the discomforts of their condition, the two women felt a bond which deepened day by day as they visited each other's homes for coffee and conversation. Otherwise they had little in common. Cynthia, normally a graceful and slender woman with deep dark eyes, who was thirty-one, had grown up in the wild and beautiful countryside of Michigan's Upper Peninsula; Marybeth had never been far from Schenectady, a blue-collar town of 68,000 in the east-central region of New York State. Cynthia was trained for a career as a licensed practical nurse; Marybeth had done a variety of semi-skilled jobs, none of them with many prospects, as a nurse's aide, a waitress, a school bus driver. While Marybeth had insecurities which showed constantly, Cynthia was quietly sure of herself. She was also gentle and caring. It was typical of Cynthia's sensitivity that when she worked full-time, she asked to be transferred from the children's ward because she could not bear to hear sick infants crying in pain, opting instead to nurse some of the most unpleasant cases in geriatrics and intensive care.

She and Mark first met when his work as an instructor in the nuclear industry took him to Michigan. Recently it had brought him back to Schenectady, where they planned to buy a house in Scotia, the suburb where he had grown up. As a wife and mother-to-be Cynthia Walter was clearly devoted, fulfilled, and deeply content, a description which could never have been applied to Marybeth Tinning. But the most dramatic difference of all was the fact that while this was Cynthia's first pregnancy, Marybeth had eight previous children—seven of her own and one adopted—and all of them were dead.

At the time of their first meeting Marybeth was forty-two, pleasant rather than pretty, five feet four inches tall, with a proud way of walking and a figure which returned to enviable shape after every pregnancy. She clearly took trouble with her appearance. When she put on makeup, it was carefully applied: a hint of blush on the cheekbones and just the right amount of gray-blue eye shadow.

Her hair was styled in a shiny blond pixie cut, brushed forward to frame her face and to emphasize the classic shape of her head. It was a face which looked best in profile. Seen from the front, there were the beginnings of harsh lines and small saggings of the chin which would not wear well. Seven months hence, and for a long time after that, the face of Marybeth Tinning—photographed head-on in a variety of unflattering poses—would be all over the front pages of the *Schenectady Gazette* and the nearby Albany newspapers, and strangers would remark to one another that you could see she was a murderer. But that was after some of the facts had become known. The Marybeth who revealed herself to the Walters and to other neighbors on Michigan Avenue was certainly strange at times, but her strangeness seemed no more than the result of having lived through intense tragedy, coupled with a childlike desire to please. She would reach out to new friends like Cynthia with unexpected gestures of generosity—the giving of time and gifts—which were offered with such warmth and affection that it was hard for them not to care about this woman who clearly found them so attractive and needed them so badly.

As they grew to know each other, it became increasingly clear to Cynthia that Marybeth's life had been full of troubles—some very real, some of which may have been exaggerated. The elder of two children Marybeth seemed to feel that she had been mistreated while her brother, Alton junior (known as Buddy in the family), was favored. From the age of six until she married at twenty-three she had lived in the semi-rural community of Duanesburg, about fourteen miles west of Schenectady, in a little house which stood alone halfway up a long winding hill on the outskirts of the village. The isolation and her feeling of having been put upon, rather than the joy of growing up in the green richness of New York's Mowhawk Valley, seemed to stick in her memory. All these years later some of her classmates recalled nostalgic summer days spent playing in the woods, making tree houses, swimming in the creek, but Marybeth spoke instead of staying friendless indoors, her only relief a trip to the grocery store with her parents or, on rarer occasions, to a cinema in Schenectady.

She told Cynthia that her parents sometimes locked her in her room and that once they had gone out and left her there for an entire day. Although her father had been dead for fourteen years, Marybeth seemed to retain a lot of unresolved resentments toward him and toward her mother. Her mother, diabetic and crippled with arthritis, was now living in a Schenectady apartment, and Marybeth often complained about having to do her errands and shopping for her. Cynthia noticed that after a telephone call from her mother Marybeth often seemed upset. But there was a deeper cause for Marybeth's unhappiness, one which made Cynthia's heart ache for her.

"Do you have any more children?" Cynthia had asked shortly after they met.

"I had one son, but he died," Marybeth answered quietly.

To Cynthia, excited about having her first baby, this seemed an unbearable loss. There was more to come. As the friendship deepened, Marybeth confided that not one infant but eight had died. She said that five of her babies had been found dead in their cribs, victims of Sudden Infant Death Syndrome (SIDS). A little girl had had Reye's syndrome. Her one adopted son had been stricken by viral pneumonia. Another baby had been born with cancerous tumors extending from the spine to the brain and had survived only a few days.

Medically, the cancerous tumors did not sound at all correct to Cynthia, but she was so overwhelmed by the sadness of the story and by her embarrassment over awakening so many painful memories that she did not question the description. However, she did ask whether Marybeth and Joe had been tested for genetic incompatibility.

"Oh, yes," her friend replied. "The doctors have done lots of tests. But they couldn't find anything."

As she became more comfortable with Cynthia, Marybeth recounted affectionate little stories about some of her dead children. There was the tale of Barbara, who lived the longest of any, so suddenly stricken by Reve's syndrome at the age of four and three-quarters that beyond a feverish cold, there was no hint of it when Marybeth tucked her into bed one winter evening. According to Marybeth, the last thing Barbara said was, "Mommy, tonight I'm going to see my brother in heaven," referring to two-year-old Joseph, who had died only six weeks earlier. To Cynthia, it sounded as though this story had developed in the fond and fertile imagination of a grieving mother, but along with the unscientific description of congenital cancer she let it go.

Sometimes Marybeth would say that she was afraid something

would happen to this next baby—an understandable remark, except for the way in which it was made.

"It wasn't just that she was being fearful," Cynthia related. "It was as though she was trying to tell me that like all the rest, this baby would not be around for long."

Tami Lynne Tinning was born on August 22, Aaron Walter on August 30. Both were handsome, healthy, full-term babies. Marybeth's choice of a name for her daughter (for it was always Marybeth, not Joe, who decided these things) seemed strangely out of character. Her eight previous children had names which read like a litany of the biblical and classical: Barbara, Joseph, Jennifer, Timothy, Nathan, Mary, Frances, Jonathan, and Michael. Marybeth never mentioned this to Cynthia, but the name of her ninth child had been suggested by another neighbor, Susan Lencewicz, who lived in the house on the other side of the Tinnings. She had an office job, and before her pregnancy Marybeth sometimes baby-sat for Sue's little boy Brian when the regular sitter was not available. Although this was supposed to be on a paying basis, Sue always felt she ended up in her neighbor's debt because Marybeth would spend more than she made from the job buying gifts and treats for Brian. She also fussed over him and made him feel important; whenever he did a drawing at her home she would put it up on her refrigerator.

One day Sue remarked to Marybeth, "If I had a little girl I'd call her Tammy Lynne. I think it's such a pretty name." A few months later Marybeth did just that, with an unusual change in the spelling. Sue took it as a compliment although she wondered why her neighbor never asked if she would mind.

Marybeth did not tell Cynthia of her friendship with Sue although the three families lived side by side. Sue and her husband also had a second-floor apartment, almost identical in design to Marybeth's and Cynthia's. All over Schenectady there are straight streets like Michigan Avenue with turn-of-the-century frame houses set close together, wooden steps up to wide porches, matching balconies at the front of the second stories. The substantial size of these buildings is illusory. They are not, as they might seem, spacious homes for the comfortably off but two-family dwellings, front doors set side by side, a steep flight of stairs behind one of them, a passageway behind the other. From street to street there are subtle differences in the exteriors of these houses, but the arrangement of the apartments hardly varies. Each is set out, railroad style, with a bay-windowed living room at the front, a dining room immediately behind it, and behind that a master bedroom, bathroom and kitchen. Near the kitchen is usually a small room which tenants use as a child's bedroom, as a work space, or for storage.

Schenectady is a company town, its economy largely dependent upon the General Electric plant which sprawls across a broad acreage next to the business area. In more prosperous times the American Locomotive Company also flourished here, and the standard Schenectady apartments were built for blue-collar workers of an earlier generation. Now most of them have a more transient function: they tend to be places where young couples live for a few years, amid unmatched furniture donated by relatives, while they save enough money to buy a house in one of the newer suburban developments.

After almost twenty years of marriage Marybeth and Joe had only recently begun to look for a house of their own. Considering that Joe was well established in a foreman-level job at General Electric, neighbors were surprised that he had been content to rent for so long. They could not believe that the Tinnings were hard up; Marybeth always spent freely on herself and others. Nor was it as though they had been living in the Michigan Avenue apartment for so long that it was too much trouble to upheave themselves. They had moved there only two years earlier, having had at least five previous addresses in different parts of Schenectady. All were rental apartments in two-family houses, so similar in layout that to have lived in one was to have known them all. They had made one attempt to break out of this mold by investing in a trailer in Duanesburg, but it had been destroyed by fire before they could move in. Insurance had compensated for the loss, and they had returned to living in a rented city apartment. These parallel moves were baffling. In a staid industrial community like Schenectady people strive to move up in the world, and they may sometimes be obliged to move down; but there is no apparent reason to move sideways as the Tinnings did, all over town.

There was another peculiarity of their life-style. They were eager to make friends with other couples but seemed unable to sustain more than one such friendship at a time. As Marybeth became closer to Cynthia, her interest in Sue and her husband diminished, and Joe went along with this. Instead of barbecued chicken in the backyard with the Lencewiczes, it became Coke and pizza with the Walters. It was the neighbors, more often than the Tinnings, who initiated these casual get-togethers. Usually Marybeth would accept with enthusiasm, but when a friendship was waning, she made excuses. Joe Tinning, slightly built, slightly bald, and deeply introverted, never had much to say. He could spend a whole evening silently nursing a can of beer in front of someone else's television set. "If you switched it off," one neighbor remarked, "he would just go on sitting there, saying nothing." Marybeth did most of the talking.

Sometimes she would tell him to go home, which he would do, so that she could have a private conversation with Sue or Cynthia—whomever they were visiting. In the kitchen some extraordinary confidences would ensue.

"I have this sister-in-law, Joe's brother's wife, and I don't know why she hates me, but do you know what she said? She accused me of killing some of my children. Sometimes I get these anonymous phone calls, and I'm sure it's her voice, saying I did all kinds of horrible things to them."

Torn between shock and disbelief, Cynthia once offered a practical suggestion. "Why don't you contact the police about these calls?"

"I've tried that already, but it won't work."

"Why not?"

"They said the only way they could do anything would be if I agreed to prosecute."

"So why don't you?"

"I just don't know if I could."

"But you say that the calls are tormenting you. In your place I'd take some action, even if it was against my own sister."

At this point in the conversation (which seems to have taken place, with variations, between Marybeth and several different people) Marybeth would become very quiet. Then in a little girl's whisper she would repeat, "I couldn't possibly do that."

Sue heard an even stranger version of the sister-in-law story. Before Tami Lynne's birth Marybeth waylaid her one day as she was returning home from work.

"I have to talk to you," Marybeth said as she steered Sue into the Tinning apartment. "It's very important."

Sue was used to Marybeth's turning small events into large dramas, and she wanted to get home to cook dinner. But what Marybeth had to relate was so stunning that for a long time afterward Sue was unable to think of anything else.

"My sister-in-law called today. She wanted your name and phone number. She knows I've been baby-sitting for you, and she wants to warn you about me because she thinks I might do some harm to Brian."

There was a sick feeling in the pit of Sue's stomach, and she wasn't sure whether or not it should be there. At that time Marybeth was watching Brian for an hour and a half every day after he got home from kindergarten. She had always been conscientious, affectionate and generous. Sue long remembered, with enormous gratitude, the time when she had gone out for an evening leaving Marybeth in charge of her son. Dennis Lencewicz was out of town, visiting a friend. During the evening there was a telephone message that Dennis's father had suffered a heart attack. Marybeth's reactions were prompt, sensitive, and caring.

She called Dennis, and when Sue came home, Marybeth went with her to join him at the hospital, leaving Joe in charge of Brian. She stayed with Sue and Dennis until they left the hospital at 3:00 A.M. As Sue often told herself, there aren't too many neighbors who would be that considerate.

That was why she didn't know what to do with the story about the sister-in-law's concern for Brian. She tried to shrug it off. In her typically outspoken fashion Sue remarked, "I had to think this sister-in-law was weird, whoever she was." Yet there was a lingering uneasiness. Had this telephone conversation really happened? (In fact, it hadn't.) And why would Marybeth relate it? She was always so eager to be liked. Why would she want Sue to become suspicious of her? Or (Sue wasn't able to put this into words until after Tami Lynne's death): "Was Marybeth trying to tell me something? Was she crying out for help and I didn't undersand?"

Some of Marybeth's stories were so strange that it was easy enough to doubt them. When Sue was first told about the eight dead children, she was very dubious. But over and over Marybeth would describe how her babies had died—except for one of them— and her recollection was always the same. This account was slightly different from the one she later gave to Cynthia; in the version told to Sue, one of the Tinning children had drowned. Marybeth never mentioned her eighth child, Jonathan, and Sue guessed why. Sue had an older son named Jonathan, from a former marriage, and Marybeth was sparing her feelings.

One Mother's Day, before Tami Lynne was born, Marybeth asked Sue to go to the cemetery with her and Joe to tend the children's graves. And there, past any doubting, was evidence of the unlikely saga of Marybeth's motherhood. On the well-kept lawn of the Most Holy Redeemer Cemetery, near a statue of St. Joseph holding the infant Christ, a group of small metal plaques was set flush to the grass. One bore the name of Marybeth's father, Alton L. Roe, the story of his life reduced to a laconic inscription:

NEW YORK PFC 5 AIR FORCE WORLD WAR II.
MAY 12, 1917—OCTOBER 16, 1971.

He had had a sudden fatal heart attack less than three months before the death of eight-day-old Jennifer. She was the third child of Marybeth and Joe, and the first to die. Her grave was next to her grandfather's, marked by a similar plaque with just her name, the word "daughter," and the dates "December 26, 1971—January 3, 1972." The portrait of a little lamb was embossed on the metal in the lower-right-hand corner. Next to this was a joint plaque for Barbara Ann (1967–1972) and Joseph A. Tinning, Jr. (1970–1972), decorated with a picture of St. Joseph and the infant Jesus. The last in the line was Timothy (November 21, 1973—December 10, 1973), with another little lamb.

After Timothy, the Tinnings had given up marking graves, although Nathan, Mary Frances and Jonathan were buried in this same area of the Catholic cemetery on the outskirts of Schenectady. By the time Michael died Marybeth had joined the Protestant church of her in-laws, and he was buried elsewhere in their family grave.

Sue watched while Marybeth and Joe knelt to clean the markers. That Mother's Day there was quite a family gathering at the cemetery: Marybeth's mother, her brother, Alton, and his wife, Sandra. At a time when there should have been togetherness and rejoicing, the sight of this stricken family was almost unbearable. Even Marybeth's father had died before his time. The whole family should have been anywhere but here.

That graveside visit dispelled any doubts of Sue's about Marybeth's lost babies. They certainly had existed. If there had been anything suspect about their deaths, surely the authorities would have raised questions long ago, and Marybeth would not have talked about the tragedies so frankly. She and Joe had moved to Michigan Avenue as a childless couple, and there was no need for them to tell the neighbors anything about their past. The fact that Marybeth volunteered it and paid Sue the compliment of inviting her to share in her grieving removed any cause for suspicion.

Sue was overwhelmed. "God bless you, Marybeth," she said, "that you can still be sane after losing all these children."

But shortly after that, without knowing quite why she did it, Sue found another baby-sitter.

TWO

Only two people know what happened, God and her.
The rest of us can only surmise.

—*Former colleague*

Marybeth seemed very happy with Tami Lynne. She spent hours
playing with her, dressing her up, styling her hair and tying little
ribbon bows in it. In Cynthia's description, this was "a lovely,
lovely little girl." A hospital photograph taken when she was only
a few hours old shows a well-developed infant with a full head of
black hair, a pink-and-white complexion, and a delicately shaped
mouth. All the earlier Tinning babies (except for the adopted child,
Michael) had been either towheaded, as Joe was in childhood, or
strawberry blond, like an infant Marybeth.

Tami Lynne's coloring was unexpected. It also made her special.
To Cynthia, noting Tami Lynne's development alongside that of
her own thriving son, this little girl was so perfectly formed, so
healthy and energetic, and so different from descriptions she had
heard of Marybeth's earlier babies that even if there had been a
genetic problem with the others, it seemed almost impossible that
anything could happen to her.

Marybeth bought a lot of new items for Tami Lynne. Whenever
a child of hers died, it had been her pattern to get rid of everything
which reminded her of its existence, so she was starting afresh for
the ninth time. Sue lent her a bassinet and a few layette items.
Marybeth bought more baby clothes, a crib, a playpen, a changing
table, an infant car seat and a little indoor swing. Some of these
might have been bought or borrowed later as they were needed.
But Marybeth liked to go shopping, Joe was making good money,
and after all they both had gone through, they were surely entitled

[29]

to indulge a baby who, because of Marybeth's age, might well be the last. Or so it seemed to the neighbors on Michigan Avenue.

The daily habit of visiting with Cynthia continued, and after Tami Lynne's birth Sue saw less of Marybeth. There began to be excuses for declining the Lencewiczes' invitations. Tami Lynne was asleep and could not be disturbed. She was awake and cranky. Another time, maybe . . . The coolness was strange after a year and a half of shared confidences. Often in the past Marybeth had told Sue that she was the only person who understood how she (Marybeth) felt about losing her children and that their talks together made her feel better. But now that Sue had less reason to feel sorry for her, was this a friendship which, like some of her earlier ones, Marybeth had used up? She had announced her pregnancy at Brian's birthday party, in her fifth month. Marybeth liked to be the focus of attention, and on this occasion she diverted it from Brian. Sue was impatient about this and about Marybeth's lame explanation.

"I would have told you sooner, but I was afraid you would be mad at me."

"Why should I be mad?"

"Well, my sister-in-law isn't at all happy about me having another baby. She told me so to my face."

"Forget your sister-in-law. I think it's great news. And this time I really hope it will work out for you."

Shortly after this Sue met Carol Tinning, the sister-in-law to whom Marybeth had referred, at Joe's forty-first birthday party. "I liked her," she said. "I couldn't figure what all the fuss was about."

For almost four months after Tami Lynne was born, everything did seem to be working out. Marybeth's pregnancy and labor were normal, and her baby was checked out of hospital in perfect health. Because of the family history, Marybeth's new pediatrician, Dr. Bradley Ford, recommended the use of an apnea monitor, which would sound an alarm if there were a pause in the baby's breathing or heartbeat. To his dismay, Marybeth turned down his suggestion, stating that she did not think a monitor was necessary. (She told Cynthia that she'd had monitors for two of her babies but "they didn't work.") But she was conscientious about taking Tami Lynne to his office for routine check-ups at three weeks old and again at two and a half months. Each time the doctor did a complete physical

examination and found Tami Lynne to be a normal, healthy, matur-
ing infant who gave all the appropriate responses to his tests.

The last of these visits was on October 31, 1985. At that time
Dr. Ford remarked that the baby was making excellent progress
and that, again, he saw no physical problems.

Cynthia Walter, who saw the baby almost every day, had the
same impression. Visiting each other's apartments, the two mothers
would put their babies side by side in the same crib while they
chatted. The development of both infants seemed comparable.
There was only one striking difference. Aaron appeared more contented than Tami Lynne. Maybe, Cynthia thought, this was because
he was breast-fed while Tami Lynne was given formula. Or maybe
Marybeth transmitted some of her own tensions to her daughter.
She seemed to be so insecure, so full of anxieties, always worrying
about her ability to be a good mother.

"If I had been a good mother," she told Cynthia over and over,
"my other babies wouldn't have died."

Cynthia tried to reassure her. "It never crossed my mind," she
said afterward, "that she could have been responsible for those
babies' deaths."

Tami Lynne's crying would usually cease the moment Cynthia
picked her up. She was a baby who loved to be held. Marybeth
did not seem to give her the same feeling of security; in her arms
Tami Lynne's screaming sometimes continued. So it often was
Cynthia who would change her diaper or give her a bottle while
Marybeth looked on.

"She was such a beautiful baby," Cynthia recalled, "that I
quickly grew to love her as though she were my own."

This led to a strange reversal of roles between the two women.
Despite the fact that Marybeth was older and presumably more
experienced in motherhood than Cynthia, it was Cynthia who
attempted to teach her friend the basics of infant care. She was
appalled to learn of Marybeths's habit of making up twenty-four
hours' worth of formula, or even more, and leaving the prepared
bottles on the kitchen counter until they were needed. When told
that the bottles should be refrigerated, Marybeth usually replied,
"They're fine." Leaving them out certainly saved her the trouble
of warming the bottles one at a time.

Marybeth also gave Tami Lynne prepared baby food from its

jar, putting the remainder aside for a later feed. Cynthia pointed
out that each portion of food should be set out on a separate dish;
otherwise some of the baby's saliva could be transferred from the
spoon to the leftover portion, causing bacteria to develop. Marybeth
was not impressed by this information. She also seemed at a loss
to cope with Tami Lynne's diaper rash, one which looked so painful
and long-standing that the tender flesh around the baby's vulva was
an angry crimson. It was the worst diaper rash Cynthia had ever
seen, the kind of rash which is generally associated with failure to
change a baby often enough, and it must have scalded horribly
whenever Tami Lynne urinated. Cynthia urged Marybeth to use
Desitin cream on the baby's diaper area and was amazed that after
nine babies her friend did not seem to know this classic remedy;
also that instead of gently smoothing on the ointment, she plastered
it on in gobs. Yet Marybeth always kept her baby looking clean,
well nourished and prettily dressed.

When Tami Lynne was three months old and it was close to
Christmastime, Marybeth became noticeably tense. She and her
brother's wife Sandra "Sandy" Roe always took turns to hostess
the family Christmas dinner party, which meant cooking a meal for
Marybeth and Joe, Alton and Sandy Roe and their two children,
and Ruth Roe (the invalid mother of Alton and Marybeth). Sandy
usually took charge of the Christmas festivities while it was Marybeth's custom to have the family to her home at Thanksgiving.
This year they had agreed to switch responsibilities, and now it
was Marybeth's turn to cook Christmas dinner.

Day after day she worried about this on the telephone to Sandy.
She couldn't see how she could get the meal ready on time. "Why
did I let you talk me into this?" she asked. "Everyone will arrive
in the morning to watch the baby unwrap her presents. We won't
be done with this until eleven o'clock or so, and then I have to
start cooking dinner. You will all be sitting around getting hungry,
and it will be five or six in the evening before we start eating."

"At her age Tami Lynne won't be opening presents," Sandy
interjected. "You don't even have to wrap them up. You can just
give them to her."

Marybeth still seemed to be overwhelmed by the difficulties. "I
don't know how I'm going to manage," she said. "We haven't put
the tree up yet, and the baby is such a problem. All she seems to
do is cry."

Marybeth was also fretting about the fact that in a few weeks she and Joe would be leaving Michigan Avenue, and right after the Christmas holiday she must start planning the move. After more than twenty years of marriage the two of them had finally made the commitment to buy a home of their own. They had settled on a single-story frame house on a short dead-end street of mostly identical frame houses, about two miles northwest of the town of Ballston Spa. This was a good half hour's drive from Schenectady, in the opposite direction out of town from Duanesberg where Marybeth's brother and Joe's parents lived. There are millions of houses like this in rural areas, built in clusters across the American countryside right after World War II: oblong boxes with the front door set dead center, the living-room window to the right of it, and a smaller kitchen window on the left. The Tinnings' new house had been secured against the weather with white aluminum siding, set off by a black trim. It was moderately priced at $51,500, and they were able to get a $45,500 mortgage. The house was in good shape with possibilities for improvement, and Marybeth was excited about moving. She said she wanted to get away from Schenectady, with all its unhappy memories, and from Duanesburg, where she had grown up. But the prospect of all the work involved dismayed her.

After listening to her sister-in-law's problems, Sandy said, "Stop worrying about it. If it's too much for you, we'll have Christmas dinner at my house. It's no big deal." She had half expected to be stuck with the task. Marybeth always became tense before a family occasion. Sandy remembered this from Joe's birthday party the previous May. She had also observed (although she didn't think of it at the time of this pre-Christmas conversation) that Marybeth also became tense before each of her babies died—at least the four babies Sandy had known since she married into the Roe family. It was almost as though her sister-in-law had some premonition of disaster.

Shopping with Marybeth ten days before Christmas, Cynthia also noticed the tension. It was a Saturday, the two mothers had left their babies at home with their husbands, and they had each decided to buy a fancy silvery ball as a Christmas tree decoration in honor of their new babies. Cynthia had already made her purchase when Marybeth went into a gift shop to pick out hers. Cynthia waited in her car. After a while Marybeth joined her, empty-handed and weeping.

"Why are you crying?" Cynthia asked as her friend got into the passenger's seat.

"I can't decide whether to get that ball for Tami Lynne or not."

"You can't decide? Why ever not?"

"I'm not sure if Tami Lynne would like it."

"Do you like it?"

"Yes."

"Then go back and get it."

"Should I?"

"Yes, I think you should."

Quietly Marybeth responded, "Okay," and went back into the shop.

Cynthia was exasperated. She could not understand why such a simple decision should cause so much trauma. Money did not seem to be the problem; whatever Marybeth wanted she usually bought. Once again Cynthia sat waiting in the car. Soon, smiling brightly like a happy child, Marybeth returned with a small package in her hand.

A few days after this incident Marybeth asked Cynthia if she would help her pick out the rest of Tami Lynne's Christmas presents. Privately wondering why her friend found it so difficult to select a few small toys, Cynthia agreed. They arranged this shopping expedition for the early evening of Thursday, December 19, when Mark would be home to look after Aaron, and Joe's parents could baby-sit for Tami Lynne. Thursday was Joe's regular evening for bowling, an event he hated to miss. It was also an activity he excelled at. In a bowling alley this quiet, unobtrusive man, who had deferred to his wife for so many years that his personality seemed to have been half lost in hers, became a different human being, animated and enthusiastic.

So it happened that on that cold December evening Joe went bowling, his wife went shopping, and the older Tinnings, Joe senior and Edna, made the half hour drive from Duanesburg to Michegan Avenue, Schenectady, to sit with Tami Lynne.

The shopping expedition took a couple of hours, starting around 6.30 P.M. Near the outskirts of Schenectady, in the suburb of Rotterdam, is a small and visibly aging shopping center, predating the designs of modern malls, called Shoporama. There an unprepossessing assortment of shops is grouped around a parking lot next to a narrow and busy highway. The pavement of the parking lot is cracked in places, from time to time some of the stores are vacant, and there is no great feeling of charm, welcome, or prosperity. Softened at this time of year by snow and brightened by Christmas decorations, Shoporama is an unlovely, utilitarian place, offering a miscellany of low-priced goods. But to Marybeth it was comfortably familiar. Over a nine-year period, on and off between babies, she had worked as a waitress at the Flavorland restaurant, which was a prominent feature of Shoporama. (Later it was taken over by the Friendly restaurant chain.) She left the job for the last time after the death of her eighth child, Michael, the adopted son, but still liked to stop at the restaurant for a chat with waitresses who had been her colleagues. This was the plan for Marybeth and Cynthia's shopping expedition: a trip to the Toys for Joy store at Shoporama, followed by a snack at Flavorland.

Toys for Joy was, of course, crowded. Set up like a supermarket, it offered a wide variety of items for children, and six days before Christmas it was like a madhouse. Against a background of piped-in carols, parents and children jostled in the ailes, and there were long, wearying lines at the cash registers. It took Marybeth quite a while to select her purchases. With the hindsight which gives this prosaic expedition a lasting importance, one thinks of her and her friend battling past scores of little children who were shrieking with delight over Shrinky Dinks collector sets, Rainbow Brite dolls, Snoopy jigsaw puzzles and Fisher-Price trucks; on into the infants' section at the back of the store where they were faced with a huge array of crib toys: Blinky Birdies, Hide'n Seek rattles, voice-activated mobiles and music boxes which played Brahms's lullaby while a carousel of little plastic animals moved around and around.

Marybeth couldn't decide what to buy, and Cynthia quickly realized that if she didn't make some suggestions, they would be there all evening. So, one by one, Cynthia picked out a few suitable toys and offered them for her friend's approval. It was a slow and frustrating way to go shopping.

Eventually Marybeth settled for the musical stuffed animal, the hand-held toy, the mobile with bells, and the little play quilt that she was never to give to Tami Lynne, and for a similar quilt for Aaron, which, because of the pressure to return a more expensive gift than she could comfortably afford, was an embarrassment to Cynthia.

At Flavorland the two women sat on either side of a Formica-

topped table and ordered coffee. Cynthia also had a snack. Marybeth did not, and that was unusual. She said she wasn't hungry.

On returning to Michigan Avenue, Cynthia went straight up to
the Tinnings' apartment with Marybeth, planning to visit there for
a short while. Edna Tinning, plump, gray-haired, and grand-
motherly, was sitting in the living room, cuddling Tami Lynne.

"May I hold her?" Cynthia asked, gently taking the baby in her
arms.

This was a question which did not need asking. Almost every
day Cynthia held Tami Lynne, rocked her, fed her, changed her,
making it clear that Marybeth was just as free to be a second mother
to Aaron. Neither she nor Marybeth had ever made the slightest
objection to this arrangement.

Cynthia retained a very clear recollection of Tami Lynne's
appearance and behavior at that time, about 8:30 P.M. on Thursday,
December 19, 1985, and what she noted was to be of crucial
importance. "Tami Lynne was in a very good mood. She was a
very agile little baby, and her arms and legs were going. She cooed
and giggled when I held her up. She seemed so happy."

After watching this for a couple of minutes, Marybeth turned to
her friend sharply. "Give me back my baby," she said in a per-
emptory tone. For a moment Cynthia was stunned. Marybeth had
never spoken to her like that before.

The demand was repeated, just as harshly: "Give her back to
me."

Without a word Cynthia handed Tami Lynne to her mother.
Shrugging, she walked toward the front door. She was offended
and did not mind showing it.

"See you in the morning," she called out as she left.

There are two versions of what happened in the next four hours,
and both of them are Marybeth's. Her in-laws left about 9:30 P.M.,
and Marybeth settled herself in a reclining chair with Tami Lynne
on her lap. For some time she played with the baby. But Tami
Lynne was not as responsive as she had been for Cynthia, and she
fussed when offered a bottle. After fretting and crying for half an
hour, she fell asleep. Then Marybeth got herself ready for bed.

While the master bedroom was at the rear of the apartment,
Tami Lynne's crib was kept in a windowed alcove, about seven
feet by ten, off the living room. In the long, narrow layout of the

Tinning home the two sleeping places were as far apart as it was possible for them to be—the baby at the very front, her parents at the far back. Marybeth's reason for failing to make a nursery out of the little room close to her own, the one that many of her neighbors used as a child's bedroom, was that it was "full of Joe's stuff." At nightime this put Tami Lynne virtually out of earshot of her parents. Since several of their babies were reported to have died in their cribs, without symptoms or warning, this was a curious, if not foolhardy, decision of a middle-aged couple who in some ways seemed to care so desperately, and in others to behave so casually, about rearing their last child.

When Tami Lynne appeared to have settled for the night, Marybeth stretched out on her side of the double bed and dozed until Joe arrived home shortly after 11:00 P.M. They talked together for about ten minutes before he got into bed and fell asleep. There has never been any suggestion that Joe was the worse for alcohol on this or any other occasion, but at the Rolling Greens Bowling Lanes on Hamburg Street it was his habit to join some of his men friends in a few rounds of drinks at the bar before going home. His unvarying order was a black velvet press (a shot of scotch plus a little club soda, with ginger ale sprayed on top) in a tall glass. This could explain why, on that night of December 19, he fell asleep so quickly and slept so soundly as to be unaware of what happened in the next hour or so. It is at this point, with Joe oblivious, that Marybeth's account of the ensuing events takes off in two directions.

In the version she told Joe, Cynthia, and her relatives and other neighbors, Joe was tossing and turning in bed so strenuously that she became increasingly wakeful. She got up, went into the living room and lay on the sofa watching television. After a while she felt sleepy enough to return to bed. Before doing so, she stopped by the alcove to check the baby. Tami Lynne was lying on her stomach, tangled in her blanket. Marybeth turned her over, noticed that there was a spot of blood on her sheet, and that Tami Lynne was very still and not breathing. Marybeth recounted how, in a profound state of shock, she screamed for her husband, called for an ambulance, telephoned for Cynthia, and, while waiting for help, tried to revive her baby by doing the cardiopulmonary resuscitation (CPR) she had learned a few years earlier as a volunteer ambulance driver. But it was too late.

Marybeth told another version of her story, tearfully, when she was questioned by state police officers almost seven weeks later. This was the version which a jury of her peers would eventually judge to be the truthful one. In this account, Marybeth was in bed beside her sleeping husband, just dozing off herself, when she heard Tami Lynne crying. She got up, went to the other end of the apartment, and did what she could to quiet the baby. But nothing seemed to work.

In the loneliness of that midwinter night, faced with a fretful infant, she felt miserable and inadequate. Cynthia's baby hardly ever cried, Sue's little boy hardly ever cried, but her baby cried all the time, or so it seemed to her. She must be doing something wrong. She must be a bad mother. In her confession to the police, Marybeth's feelings of failure and defeat stare painfully through the clumsy prose recorded by an official stenographer. This account gives no indication of what she did, or how long she spent, trying to get Tami Lynne back to sleep. The time Marybeth dozed and the time her baby kept her awake have become blurred and fused in memory. But at some moment between midnight and 1:00 A.M. she went back into her bedroom, saw that Joe was still sound asleep, removed her own pillow from the double bed and took it to Tami Lynne's crib. Then she put the pillow over her daughter's face and held it there long enough to ensure that Tami Lynne would never cry again.

"I did not mean to hurt her," she told the police. "I just wanted her to stop crying."

Marybeth did not panic until later. First, she must have taken time to think through the story she would tell her husband. Having done so, she put her pillow down at one end of the sofa, crumpled it to look as though she had been lying there, watching television . . . and then screamed for Joe.

THREE

She is not much unlike the typical parent, except she
goes one step further.

—*Assistant district attorney*

Cynthia's parting shot, "See you in the morning," became reality
sooner that she had intended. At about 1:15 A.M. she was wakened
by the telephone. It was Marybeth.

"Get over here at once," she said, and hung up. Her voice was
quavery and panic-stricken.

As she flung on some clothes, Cynthia had no doubt about the
reason for the summons: something had happened to Tami Lynne.
After a quick explanation to Mark, she hurried downstairs and out
into the snow, suddenly realizing that she was wearing bedroom
slippers. There was no time to go back. She picked her way through
the snow between the two houses, not caring about the wet chill to
her feet, and tore up the flight of stairs to the Tinning apartment.

A light was on in the dining room, where Marybeth and Joe were
waiting for her.

"Where's Tami Lynne?" Cynthia asked.

Marybeth pointed to the darkened alcove off the living room.

Tami Lynne had been taken out of her crib and was lying next
to it on the changing table. She was on her back with hands
outstretched. She was wearing the warm cotton knit sleeping suit,
white with a multicolored design of clowns all over it, in which she
had been put to bed. She looked innocent and cuddly, except for
the fact that she was very, very still. Suddenly the professional
nurse again, Cynthia noted that her skin was a cyanosed purple,
indicating lack of oxygen, not the grayish shade Marybeth later
described. She could discern no respiration and no pulse, and she

saw no marks on the baby's flesh. Cynthia put her hand under the little body, gently laid it on the floor near the dining room where there was light and space to work, sat beside it, and immediately began cardiopulmonary resuscitation.

Marybeth told her that an ambulance was on its way. She also said that she had tried CPR but there had been no response from the baby. Afterward, when she thought about it, Cynthia was appalled. Anyone who learns the technique of CPR, as Marybeth had done, is taught the life-and-death importance of continuing resuscitation attempts until help arrives, no matter how unresponsive the patient may seem. She knew that if there had been some crisis with her own baby, she would have gone on doing CPR until every last scrap of her energy was spent; that even after she was exhausted, she would have been able to force herself to continue mechanically; that Mark would have been out on the sidewalk so the ambulance driver would not lose a single precious minute by having to search in the dark for the house number.

Instead, she found Marybeth pacing the living room and wringing her hands, while Joe stood there, shaking his head. Marybeth had pulled on navy blue slacks under her short winter nightgown. Joe, surprisingly, was neatly and fully dressed. He had reacted sufficiently to get into some clothes for the trip to the hospital, but in no other way did he seem able to respond to the emergency. There was a delay in the ambulance's arrival, either because Marybeth had given the wrong house number in her panic or because someone on the medical team made a mistake. Cynthia continued her efforts, knowing in her heart they were useless, while Marybeth and Joe watched helplessly.

An ambulance eventually arrived, and paramedics took over the resuscitation attempts. Cynthia stood up, feeling sick and shaken. It kept going through her mind that this could have been her baby; that this was the awful reality of crib death. She had never seen a case of it before, but she thought, This is how it happens. Everything seems normal; you go on a pleasant shopping trip; you come home to a healthy, smiling baby; you put your baby down to sleep . . . and the sleep goes on forever. She wanted to get away from here. She wanted to check on Aaron.

But Joe was asking her something. Marybeth was leaving with the ambulance, and would she follow with him in his pickup truck? Please.

"Yes," she said, "but while you get the truck out, I must go home for a minute to change from these slippers."

She had done all she could for Tami Lynne, and she didn't want to go to the hospital and face the inevitable; but it was impossible to refuse. She wondered why Marybeth and Joe couldn't support each other through this agony without putting her through it, too. If she had not had a baby of her own, it might not have been so difficult, but her emotional involvement—both with Tami Lynne and with her own feelings as a mother—was deep and painful.

Back home, she gave way to hysteria. Alarmed, Mark slapped her to control the sobbing.

"You must pull yourself together," he told her. "For the sake of Marybeth and Joe. They need you."

She was still shaking, silently by now, as she walked out to the truck. "Are you okay?" Joe asked. She nodded.

It was barely a five-minute drive from Michigan Avenue to St. Clare's Hospital on McClellan Street. When Cynthia and Joe walked into the emergency room, Marybeth was giving information to a clerk at the admissions desk. She seemed surprisingly calm.

For a long time the three of them sat in the waiting room while in another part of the hospital doctors tried to revive Tami Lynne. Marybeth did not cry. That surprised Cynthia. Joe was very, very quiet. ("He took this one pretty well," Marybeth remarked to Cynthia when it was all over. "Every other time a baby died he would sit in a corner and turn green.")

Like Marybeth, Cynthia had been brought up as a Roman Catholic and had changed to the Protestant faith as an adult. But at this time of personal crisis, waiting in a Catholic hospital and surrounded by the caring efficiency of nuns, she reacted out of the religious habit of her childhood. She reminded her friend that Tami Lynne had not been baptized and suggested asking for a chaplain. Marybeth agreed, while giving the impression that this was not very important to her.

Several weeks earlier Aaron had been baptized in a Methodist church, and Cynthia had proposed making this a double ceremony by including Tami Lynne. Marybeth declined. She stated that since she and Joe would be moving to Ballston Spa in the new year, she would delay Tami Lynne's baptism until they joined a church there. She did, however, attend Aaron's christening. At that Sunday morning service there was a curious incident which left a lasting impression on another woman in the congregation.

More than twenty-five years earlier this woman had been a classmate of Marybeth's at Duanesburg Central High School. They had not met in the meantime, but she had heard reports of Marybeth's losing all her babies—two or three of them, she thought it was, from congenital heart disease. Now she was suddenly reminded of the tragic story; the blond woman with the baby in her arms, sitting in the Sunday morning congregation, looked so familiar. After the service, as parishioners filed into the church hall for coffee, she went up to Marybeth, touched Tami Lynne fondly, and said, "It's Marybeth Roe, isn't it? Remember me? We were in school together."

There was no response from Marybeth. Embarrassed, the woman walked away. For days afterward she was troubled by this chance meeting: "I remember thinking, That poor little baby may not live much longer. I kept wondering why Marybeth would have another baby. She was old to be bearing children. If there had been a congenital problem with the others, why would she want to put herself through this again?"

In the bleak early hours of morning, with only five days to Christmas, three dejected people sat together in St. Clare's Hospital, waiting to hear whether Tami Lynne could have a very different kind of baptism from Aaron's. Eventually a nun came to them and broke the news that this would not be possible. Tami Lynne was dead.

As they left, Marybeth told Cynthia that she felt too upset to go home; could she come to her apartment for coffee? Joe, however, wanted to go to bed. Cynthia wondered why he couldn't comfort his wife in their mutual bereavement; how, at a time like this, he could feel like sleeping. Had the loss of babies become so commonplace in this household?

As she made coffee for herself and Marybeth, Cynthia worried about the fact that Aaron would soon be waking for his early-morning feed; after this shock she also feared for her ability to feed him. She had always felt comfortable about nursing him in front of Marybeth. But now? With Tami Lynne just dead? Plucking up her courage, she asked whether her friend would find the sight too distressing. No, Marybeth replied. They continued talking as Cynthia's baby nuzzled up to her. Then Marybeth left.

Not long afterward, about 7:30 A.M., Cynthia visited the next-door apartment. She hadn't slept, she couldn't eat, and she felt very groggy. But she wanted to reassure her neighbors that she would be available that day, if needed. She was amazed to find Marybeth and Joe eating breakfast together, talking calmly, apparently enjoying their food.

"If you need me this morning, I'll be at my mother-in-law's," she said. "Then I'll be home this afternoon."

"Okay, I may call you," Marybeth replied. It was said casually, as though this were any normal day.

But a few minutes after Cynthia left, Marybeth began spreading her news. At 7:45 A.M., still in her nightgown, she surprised Sue Lencewicz by running down the stairs, to catch her as she left for work. Sue was standing by her car, replenishing the window-washing fluid before making the fifteen-mile drive to Albany.

"Sue, I've got something to tell you," gasped Marybeth. "I don't want to spoil your day, but I don't want you to hear it from anyone else."

Sue tried not to look exasperated. Her neighbor had waylaid her like this before, usually over trivia, and she did not want to be late for work. She was about to ask whether the confidence couldn't wait until evening when Marybeth blurted out, "Tami Lynne died last night."

Pushing the other woman away from her, Sue screamed, "Not again, Marybeth!" and ran back to her apartment to share the horror with her husband. Dennis worked the second shift at General Electric, 3:00 P.M. to 11:00 P.M., and was still sleeping. Sue woke him up to tell him. He was a shocked as she was.

"You should see what I brought home last night to give Marybeth and Joe for Christmas," he told her. And he showed her a wall plaque with a picture of a baby and what Sue remembers as "a pretty little saying about God having given them the gift of a child." Several hours passed before Sue felt calm enough to go to work.

On that morning of Friday, December 20, Marybeth left a trail of emotional devastation all around Schenectady. She made one phone call after another, with hardly a quaver in her voice. About 8:00 A.M. she called Carol Tinning, the sister-in-law about whom she had complained to Cynthia, and announced flatly, "This is Marybeth. Tami Lynne is dead."

Carol did not wait to hear the rest of the story. She dropped the telephone receiver on the floor, flung herself on the bed, and sobbed and sobbed for hours.

Carol loved babies, but when she married Joe's younger brother, Andy, the two of them made a painful decision not to have a child of their own. Carol had two children by a former marriage, one of them born with cerebral palsy. She had taken care of this helpless son for many years, living with the daily anguish of loving him and wishing he were normal. Doctors advised her that his problems stemmed from a genetic incompatability between her and her former husband. In her marriage to Andy she feared a repetition—especially after seeing Marybeth's babies die, one after another, and being told that this tragedy was also genetic in origin. So in 1977 Carol and Andy adopted a baby girl, whom they named Amanda.

When she was seven and a half years old, Amanda was baptized. Carol arranged a christening party for about forty people at her Schenectady home, and Marybeth chose this occasion, just as she picked Brian's birthday party, to draw all the guests' attention to herself by breaking the news that she was expecting another baby, the baby that was to be Tami Lynne. There was no need for her to make the announcement verbally. Although her pregnancy barely showed, she walked into Carol and Andy's house wearing a vividly patterned, brightly colored maternity dress, a real conversation stopper. As she made this impressive entrance, one woman guest leaned across to her hostess and said, "Oh . . . my . . . God," which must have reflected the thoughts of many other people at the party.

Carol did not hear anyone make a direct comment to Marybeth about her pregnancy. The topic was avoided. But in search of approval and reassurance Marybeth took her sister-in-law into the bathroom, the only place where they could be alone together, and explained (just as she did to Sue Lencewicz), "I was afraid to tell you sooner because I thought you would be angry."

Her voice was almost a whisper, and she was hanging her head like a child.

Carol's response was the same as Sue's. "Why should I be angry, Marybeth?"

"Because I know you don't like me."

There was more to it than that. After losing seven of their own children, Marybeth and Joe had adopted a baby boy named Michael. Unlike most of the Tinning children, he survived babyhood and

FROM CRADLE TO GRAVE

developed into a healthy outgoing toddler. His survival seemed to confirm Marybeth's assertion (and not hers only, since it was also the belief of some of her doctors) that "something in the genes" doomed Tinning babies to die. When he was two and a half years old, Michael developed a mild case of viral pneumonia which should not have been life-threatening. But one morning while in the sole care of Marybeth he also died.

Carol was suspicious about Michael's death; so were others. Doctors, however, ascribed it to natural causes. Almost four years later Carol was incredulous that Marybeth would risk having another baby of her own. Yet here she was at the christening party, diverting attention from Amanda by wearing that flamboyant and unnecessary maternity dress, pleading for her sister-in-law's approval.

In the privacy of the bathroom Carol spoke bluntly: "After losing all those children, I can't think why you would get pregnant again. But let me tell you one thing, Marybeth. Don't you dare let anything happen to this baby."

After Tami Lynne was born, Carol kept in close touch with her sister-in-law. "I knew she was afraid of me, and I figured that if I stayed close to her, she wouldn't risk any harm coming to her child. So I made a vow that I would stick around, and in doing so, I let myself fall in love with Tami Lynne."

Carol's bitter tears on the morning of December 20 were not for Tami Lynne alone. They were for what she felt was her own failure to save this baby, for what she might have done if only she had known—with the certainty which now filled her consciousness— that all those nieces and nephews of hers need not have died.

After devastating Carol with her news, Marybeth telephoned Suzanne "Sue" Normington, a colleague from her waitress days at Flavorland. Sue and her husband were now in business together, running two retail stores. One of them specialized in baby clothes. Marybeth had taken Cynthia there to buy some layette items before their babies were born. Sue had known five of Marybeth's babies and, like Carol, was shocked to see her pregnant again, so shocked that she had found it difficult to serve her. She felt like running away from her own store. "I couldn't deal with the fact that she was going to have another child," Sue explained, "and that this child might die."

After Tami Lynne's birth Marybeth had gone back to Sue's store to buy more clothes. She held the new baby because she loved children and because it seemed the natural thing to do; at the same time she did not want to get emotionally involved. Over the years she had been torn to shreds by the sight of Marybeth's other babies in their open caskets, exquisitely formed and eternally still, like dressed-up dolls in boxes. She could not help wondering whether Tami Lynne would join them.

On the evening of December 19 Sue was shopping in the store named Toys for Joy, this image was not far from her mind, when she saw Marybeth and Cynthia browsing among the baby items. She dodged through the crowd to avoid them.

"I didn't want them to see me," she related. "I didn't want Marybeth to come back into my life."

Shortly after eight o'clock the following morning her telephone rang.

"Sue," Marybeth said in a matter-of-fact tone, "Tami Lynne died last night, and they had to shave her head at the hospital, so I need a lacy bonnet for her funeral. She can wear her little red Christmas dress, but I don't have a bonnet. Could you bring one to me?"

Back when they worked at Flavorland together, Marybeth would ask Sue Normington to do the kinds of favors that none of her colleagues would ask of one another. As they got to know Marybeth, some of the regular customers would make pointed inquiries about why she kept on having babies: Was her husband so irresistible? Why didn't she have her tubes tied? It is the kind of banter, cruel at times, which waitresses in a bustling, family restaurant must learn to deal with. Marybeth was unable to do that. She would turn to Sue to rescue her because of all the waitresses Sue was the least likely to refuse. Sue was kindly, gentle and eminently decent, a dedicated Christian who sincerely tried to practice her faith in her daily life.

At times when the restaurant was crowded and Sue almost run off her feet, Marybeth would ask her, "Would you take this table of mine?" It's a customer who always gives me a hard time." Sue felt she should protect her colleague from the probing, thoughtless questions, but Marybeth never offered to return the favor and serve a table of Sue's.

The two women worked together on and off over nine years, through the lives and deaths of five of Marybeth's babies. Sue could recite their names like a litany: Timothy, Nathan, Mary Frances, Jonathan, and Michael. The only funeral she missed was Mary Frances's, and that was because there was an ice storm and Sue herself was pregnant. Nevertheless, Marybeth made it clear to her that she was disappointed, that she had felt she could depend upon Sue.

After the death of Mary Frances, Sue began to feel uneasy about Marybeth. It was her deeply held conviction that if you can't say something nice about a person, you should keep quiet, but now her conscience was telling her to speak out. Not that she had heard or seen anything to suggest neglect or criminal action. Rather, it was something she knew in her heart. As she expressed it, "You do not hear of God taking baby after baby after baby. Over more than forty years, and that's how old I was at the time, I never heard of such a thing. That's not how God works." There had to be human intervention.

So, after a lot of anguish, Sue called the Schenectady Department of Social Services and suggested an investigation of the Tinning household. "There has to be something in that home which is causing all those babies to die," she said. She was promised that the mystery would be investigated, but she never heard back.

Sue could not bring herself to confront Marybeth directly. "I did not ask her, and I don't think anyone else ever asked her, 'Are you doing anything to those children?' How can you say such a thing? And yet how could I not have said it?"

Sue did not have any lacy bonnets in the shop. They were summer stock, and this was midwinter. She had a ready-made reason to say no to Marybeth, yet she could not bring herself to do this. With five days to Christmas and her own holiday preparations to complete, she drove to one of the big modern shopping malls outside Schenectady and searched the department stores for a baby bonnet. The best she could find was a bonnet with a matching dress which had to be purchased as a set. She took a chance and bought them. Later in the day she delivered them to the Tinnings' apartment.

Marybeth was very appreciative. She was clearly delighted with the outfit. For Sue's benefit, she repeated the story of how she had been unable to sleep the previous night and had lain on the sofa watching television. When she found Tami Lynne dead, she told Sue that she noticed "something on the sheet." She did not explain what the something was, but obviously she meant blood. Her account was very familiar to Sue. There had been "something on the sheet" for Mary Frances's death, for Michael's death, and now for Tami Lynne's.

"If there's a God, he should explain why all this happened," Marybeth added.

Sue knew that there were not many people to whom Marybeth would have made such a remark. "But she made it to me because she knew how I feel about God."

As they talked, Joe was standing just behind his wife with a hand resting lightly on her shoulder. At this point he made his only contribution to the conversation. He agreed that God ought to come up with an explanation.

Afterward Sue kept wondering to herself why she had responded to Marybeth's telephone request. "I didn't want to have any part in it, and yet I went to all that trouble. I suppose I did it for the baby and for Marybeth's mother-in-law and father-in-law, who are very decent, nice people and who would be at the funeral. I also did it for Marybeth because she is a human being and she had lost a child, no matter how. And because she had always felt she could count on me.

"If it were to happen again, I would do it again, not wanting to and yet not being able to refuse."

FOUR

It was the same story with all her babies. There was no illness, no accident. It just happened.

—Hospital physician

While Marybeth was still making telephone calls, Daniel O'Connor and his colleague Joseph Figliola were sitting in a diner on Nott Street, one of Schenectady's main thoroughfares. They worked together as investigators in the vice squad of the city police force, and shortly after 9:00 A.M. on December 20 they had stopped for a coffee break. Suddenly one of their bleepers sounded with a radio message to call police headquarters.

Dan O'Connor, a cheerful, open-faced man in early middle age, looked troubled when he came off the telephone. "Joe, we've got a call to make," he said. "We're going to the D.A.'s office."

The office of District Attorney John Poersch is on the third floor of Schenectady County Courthouse, an imposing stone building on the crown of a hill in the center of town. Like all traditional American courthouses, it is built in Greek Revival style with heavy colonnades and a broad flight of steps to the front entrance. Dan O'Connor raced up the stairs, through the swing doors to the elevator at the back of the hall, and burst into John Poersch's office. It was almost empty. On this Friday before Christmas the district attorney had arranged to take his entire staff to lunch at Luigi's, his favorite Italian restaurant, and it was implicit in the invitation that this was a day when they could slack off.

Of the nine assistant district attorneys, only Stuart Sanders was in his office. Poersch rarely showed up before ten. Sanders, his chief assistant, believed in keeping his office door open so that anyone who wanted to see him could walk in. O'Connor did so, and immediately began talking.

"I just had a tip-off from someone at St. Clare's Hospital. Last night another of Marybeth Tinning's babies died. It's supposed to be a crib death, but she had eight others who died just as suddenly. Some of us in the police thought she may have been doing something to those children way back, when the fourth or fifth died, but we could never get a proper investigation going. Most of the babies were in the ground before we knew they were dead, and then it was too late to get the medical evidence. Some of them weren't even autopsied. I don't want this to happen again. I want to be sure that your office gets on to this case right away."

Sanders had been on the Schenectady district attorney's staff for only a couple of years, and this story of the multiple infant deaths was new to him. So was the name of Marybeth Tinning. But he was struck by Dan O'Connor's extreme concern and by his bizarre tale. Nine babies dead in one family! Even when he worked in a densely populated section of New York City, in the Bronx district attorney's office, Stuart Sanders had never heard of such a thing.

As soon as O'Connor left, Sanders picked up the telephone. First he called St. Clare's Hospital and asked for the attending pathologist, Dr. Young J. Sim. He wanted to make sure there would be an autopsy and that Dr. Thomas Oram, Chief of Pathology and Director of Laboratories at Ellis Hospital, would be present. This request needed to be made tactfully. Schenectady has two general hospitals, St. Clare's and Ellis, and while there is a close relationship between them, there is also a certain rivalry. Ellis is the larger and in some areas better equipped. As a Catholic institution St. Clare's prides itself on its dedicated nursing. Among the populace of Schenectady there is a wide-spread belief that if an ailment requires tender loving care, the patient should check in at St. Clare's; if it becomes life-threatening, he or she might be better off at Ellis.

The pathology departments of both hospitals deal with the day-to-day investigation of unusual deaths. Most of these are from natural causes. A few are accident victims. Fewer still are suicides or homicides. Once in a while a hospital pathologist may be called upon to make a determination which can have far-reaching legal consequences: whether the subject of his autopsy, who appeared to have died naturally, was in fact the victim of another person's plan to commit the perfect murder. Of such stuff are detective novels written. But in real life this happens so rarely that a hospital pathologist can go through an entire career and never meet with such a case.

In real life, therefore, very few pathologists are trained in forensic medicine, the application of medical science to the practice of law. A great many of them would rather not know about it. In an age and a place where medicine is practiced in fear of malpractice suits, few American doctors select the one specialty which will inevitably land them in the witness box, the target of a defense attorney who is out to discredit their testimony.

Dr. Thomas Felix Dennis Oram came out of a different mold. That was the main reason why Stuart Sanders wanted him at Tami Lynne's autopsy. If this case came to a murder trial, he knew that Dr. Oram would not mind testifying and that he made an impressive witness. With his white hair and military bearing, he looked as aristocratic as his name suggested: an Englishman who had been a medical officer in Her Majesty's Colonial Service and who, when he was only in his mid-twenties, had run a hospital in Kuala Lumpur. There he had acquired a great deal of professional experience, along with the necessary diplomatic skills to keep ailing memsahibs in bed while the British Empire crumbled about them. In Malaysia he also served as coroner's pathologist. When he came back to Britain in 1956, he was dismayed to find "a lot of people like me from newly independent countries, flooding the market." He thought of emigrating to Canada but moved instead to Schenectady, lured by a British doctor friend who had recently taken a job at Ellis Hospital. Coming, as Tom Oram did, out of the austerity of postwar Britain, the friend had written enthusiastically: "You would be amazed at the life here. The steaks they serve are as big as toilet seats."

Oram had to start his medical career again at the bottom, on subsistence pay which didn't remotely stretch to steaks. Dispirited, he went back to England after a couple of years but soon decided that Schenectady had more to offer and returned for good. On completing his residency at Ellis, he specialized in pathology. Over the next twenty years he worked his way up to being the most respected and experienced pathologist in the Schenectady area, one of the few who, as part of his British medical education, was also versed in forensic medicine. As Professor of Clinical Pathology at

Albany Medical Center, he had trained many pathologists, including Dr. Sim.

Stuart Sanders was relieved to be told by her that she not only agreed with inviting her former instructor to Tami Lynne's autopsy but had already done so. The autopsy was scheduled for 11:00 A.M. Reluctantly Sanders decided on his next move. He would go to St. Clare's Hospital and watch the grisly event.

It is not common for district attorneys or their assistants to be present at autopsies, but sometimes it is important. When the prosecution of a difficult case is in the offing, a line of research may suggest itself to a legal mind which a medical expert might not consider. Sanders wasn't sure what that might be, but he thought he ought to be there. He asked his investigator William Sanderson to join him, partly because Sanderson had a car and Sanders didn't, but also for moral support.

After the two of them had taken the elevator to the basement of St. Clare's, it crossed Sanders's mind that if patients could see what goes on in the bowels of a hospital, they would never sign themselves in for treatment. He and Sanderson were directed to a windowless room with concrete walls, where they spent the next two hours with Dr. Oram, Dr. Sim, Dr. Oram's assistant, a police photographer, and the body of Tami Lynne Tinning.

It was Sanders's first autopsy, and the sight haunted him for months, returning to his consciousness at moments when he least welcomed it, as when he was relaxing at home with his infant son in his arms. When the time came for Marybeth's trial, a year and a half later, the memory was still so vivid that Sanders avoided going into court when Dr. Oram was testifying, "I didn't want to relive every gory detail," he explained. It was bad enough that he still had the mental picture of that tiny, perfect child lying motionless on a metal table . . . and of what was about to be done to her to determine whether the people of the State of New York had a case against Marybeth Tinning.

Bill Sanderson was struck by the emotional atmosphere in the autopsy room. Later he recalled: "We all knew that eight other children in this family had died, but now we were looking at a baby who seemed so beautiful that it was impossible to imagine anyone wanting to hurt her. Even for Dr. Oram this was a terrible conclusion to reach, and you could tell that he didn't want to come to it. You sat there, not wanting to believe that a mother could kill her

own child, yet in your heart you knew it must have happened. And
without a word being said, you could feel everyone in the room
thinking the same."

Oram was also the father of young children, having married for
a second time in middle age, and although autopsies were routine
to him, he was profoundly disturbed by this one. For months
afterward he worried and conjectured about the threshold between
a mother's civilized tolerance of her child's crying and the mindless
temptation to end it. His present wife, Jo Anne, whom he described
as "very straightforward," had expressed the opinion to him that
under the pressures of daily child care, every mother has a breaking
point. Was Marybeth Tinning one of the few who, on reaching that
point, would react with violence – not intending to do so yet unable
to control themselves?

He also wondered about the severity of postnatal depression
and about stories he heard from medical colleagues concerning
Marybeth's reaction to the first infant death in her family, that of
Jennifer, her third child, who was born and died fourteen Christ-
mases before Tami Lynne's death. Jennifer had had multiple brain
abscesses, apparently from birth, and lived only a week. Attending
doctors believed there was no hope for her from the start. Marybeth
reacted as though she was deeply shaken emotionally but was unable
to express herself through tears. Within two months her two older
children, Barbara and Joseph, had died mysteriously. No one had
made a connection at the time, but was there a link between these
deaths and Marybeth's emotional withdrawal when Jennifer failed
to survive?

There could be no legal action against Marybeth Tinning unless
Oram was prepared to testify that Tami Lynne had died from
unnatural causes. It was an awesome responsibility. "One thing I
learned from this case," he said later, "is something I don't much
like to talk about. An infant has a very small airway, even in
comparison to its size. This makes it very, very easy to stop a baby
breathing without leaving evidence of suffocation. In an older child
you would expect to find signs of a struggle. In a baby, death could
be almost instantaneous." But he was not ready to conclude that
this had happened to Tami Lynne until he eliminated every other
possibility.

Oram had learned the salient facts of the Tinnings' family history when (also with Dr. Sim) he did the autopsy on Michael, their adopted child, almost five years earlier. Before Michael, Marybeth had lost seven of her own children. On the basis of her credible descriptions of how she found them dead or dying, several of the doctors who had been involved in the various deaths hypothesized that this family was afflicted by a rare genetic disease. The most widely held theory among these medical experts was that Marybeth and Joe carried recessive genes which caused inborn errors in metabolism in their offspring.

Michael's death, at the age of two and a half, raised serious questions. He had no blood relationship to the Tinnings and was a sturdy child with a good health record. Marybeth had carried him into her pediatrician's office one winter morning, wrapped in a blanket, with a story that he had a heavy cold and she had been unable to wake him. He was found to be dead. When Oram did the autopsy on Michael, the thought was very much in mind that this might be a homicide. But all he could find wrong with Michael was a mild case of viral pneumonia – not serious enough, he would have thought, to be fatal. In the absence of any other medical finding, and with some misgiving, Oram had certified the cause of death as pneumonia.

He approached Tami Lynne's autopsy with mixed emotions. The question of a genetic disease in the Tinning family was still unresolved. It was hard to believe that a family so afflicted would also have an adopted child die in infancy, but it could happen. It could even be argued that the clearly diagnosed cause of Michael's death – so different from that of the other Tinning babies, most of whom were thought to be victims of Sudden Infant Death Syndrome – lent credibility to the genetic theory.

Later Oram acknowledged, "Right up to the end I was looking for a genetic explanation for Tami Lynne's death. I was quite determined to find something that had been missed when those other Tinning children died. I had heard suggestions that their mother might have been responsible, but I found it hard to believe that any parent would do such a thing. With Tami Lynne it turned out to be the obvious explanation, but none of us wanted to look at it because it was too horrific."

Oram's examination of Tami Lynne showed that this was a well-nourished baby, a little taller and heavier than average with nothing obviously wrong except for a severe diaper rash. This was so bad that at first he considered septicemia as possible cause of death. ("The baby looked as though she had not been changed often enough, and as if the resulting diaper rash had been treated with a whole glue pot of Desitin, causing the skin to fester underneath.") But he found no evidence of septicemia.

With Dr. Sim, he examined the body minutely. Neither of them saw an obvious cause of death. They looked very carefully at the baby's air passages and gastrointestinal tract for possible obstructions but found none. They made the necessary incisions to examine the organs, muscles, bones and brain. They took blood and tissue samples for microscopic examination so that viral and bacterial studies could be done; they arranged for bowel studies, for chromosomic studies to determine any genetic abberation, and toxicological studies to find it there was any trace of poison. "We covered every test known to man," Oram commented. "We even split samples and sent some to a lab in Pennsylvania in order to compare its results with those of the lab technicians at St. Clare's."

The autopsy took two hours. When it was over, Stuart Sanders and Bill Sanderson drove straight to Luigi's restaurant to join their colleagues at the district attorney's Christmas lunch. They were late and felt queasy. When they saw the entrée which had been selected, they felt even worse. It was ziti in tomato sauce. Sanders picked at his portion, pushed the plate away, and hurried back to his office. There was much to be done that afternoon.

His first move was to call in Colleen "Betsy" Mannix, a caseworker in the Child Protective Unit of Schenectady County's Department of Social Services, and Robert Imfeld, an investigator in the juvenile office of the Schenectady Police Department. It was standard practice for Social Services to make an immediate investigation of any complaint of child abuse; when calling upon these families, women caseworkers were usually accompanied by a police officer. Bob and Betsy, as they were known, often worked as such a team.

Sanders briefed them about Tami Lynne's sudden death. Since poison was one of several possibilities being considered, he impressed upon them the importance of looking around the Tinning apartment for any evidence of toxic substances. Subsequently they reported to him that they saw an opened bottle of orange juice on the living-room table, and for a long time afterward Sanders felt chagrined that they had not taken it away with them for analysis. "Some of that juice could have been in the baby's last bottle, and it might have been vital evidence." The omission was understandable. Child abuse cases, such as they were accustomed to handling, rarely ran to murder.

Betsy Mannix and Bob Imfeld arrived at 367 Michigan Avenue at 3:50 P.M. Both Marybeth and Joe were at home. Sitting side by side on the sofa, they struck their visitors as being nervous but cooperative. Betsy, a soft-spoken young woman, with a mass of auburn hair, explained that she had an obligation to investigate Tami Lynne's death and needed to ask some routine questions. Marybeth answered them quietly and without hesitation.

She said that Tami Lynne had no medical problems and seemed fine when last seen alive. On the previous evening, Marybeth fed her before Joe's parents came to baby-sit; noted nothing wrong with the baby when she returned from her shopping expedition with Cynthia; went to bed around the time that Joe came in from bowling but, unable to sleep, got up to watch television; checked Tami Lynne when she was ready to go back to bed about 12:30 A.M. and found her warm but motionless. The story was fluent by now and sounded very plausible. Betsy asked Marybeth if she would sign releases to give her department access to Tami Lynne's medical records, and without hesitation Marybeth agreed. Joe spoke only when he was addressed directly. When asked about his children, he had difficulty remembering how many there had been and who had died from what.

Bob Imfeld was not wearing a police uniform, and at first Marybeth assumed that he, too, was from Social Services. But as she talked with Betsy Mannix, there was a beeping sound from Imfeld's police radio. This was embarrassing; he thought he had turned it off. Immediately Marybeth became nervous and excited.

"You're from the police, aren't you?" she asked. "I know what you are here for. You are going to arrest me and take me to jail."

"No, I'm not here to arrest you," Imfeld replied. "Relax."

Marybeth became even more agitated. Her body shook, and a wild, terrified look came into her eyes. It was a look which Betsy Mannix was to see again on return visits to the Tinning's apartment, one which haunted her for months afterward. Dealing with gruesome cases was part of her everyday experience, but she had never before been frightened by one. Although she did not betray a hint of it, Betsy Mannix eventually became more scared of Marybeth than Marybeth was of her.

But when Betsy made this first visit, Marybeth was clearly terrified. She could not stop shaking. Although no accusations had been made, she asked repeatedly if her visitors were going to take her to jail. Even their reassurances did not calm her.

"Are you sure you haven't come to take me away?" she asked over and over.

Bob and Betsy were struck by this fearful reaction. They also noticed several cardboard boxes in the alcove off the living room, beside the empty crib. Marybeth had been packing the boxes with cleanly folded baby clothes and the unopened Christmas toys as though anxious to put Tami Lynne's belongings out of sight. In fact, she had already asked her in-laws to get rid of them for her.

This removal was accomplished so promptly and effectively that mourners who went to the apartment for a small reception after the funeral saw nothing there to indicate that Tami Lynne had ever existed.

FIVE

Every funeral was a party for her, with hardly a tear shed. After three or four of them, I gave up going.
—*Relative*

The Reverend Roger Day was preparing for Christmas week services at Trinity United Methodist Church when Susan Daly telephoned. The Daly Funeral Home was a respected family business, well known to most of the clergy in town. Susan, the late founder's granddaughter, explained that a baby was being prepared for burial in Schenectady Memorial Park, and the parents wanted him to officiate.

Roger Day recollected having met Marybeth and Joseph Tinning about two weeks earlier, when Cynthia and Mark Walter, regular parishioners of his, brought them to a Sunday service. He had exchanged a few pleasantries with them, remarked on the baby in Marybeth's arms, but sensed they were not interested in joining his church. This had been his first and only meeting with them. He asked Sudan Daly to tell him something about the family and was surprised – almost incredulous – to learn that this was the Tinnings' ninth child to die.

After many years in the ministry Day, a warm and genial man, had learned to view some of the stories he was told with a healthy skepticism. The more he thought about this one, the less likely it sounded. It was his practice to visit a bereaved family as soon as he heard of a death, so that same day, Saturday, December 21, he called at the Tinnings' apartment. On the way there he kept wondering about the situation he was walking into. As he recounted later, "I thought there had to be something wrong, that all those deaths couldn't be natural.

[58]

"I found the parents at home, and I talked to them for some time. They told me, one by one, how all their children died, and they seemed so genuine, so crushed. I thought this must have been some freak tragedy that had happened in their lives, and I felt terribly sorry for them. I offered prayers. And I agreed to do the funeral."

Marybeth, by that time, had become a regular patron of Daly's. Her first contact there had been in October 1971, when her father died. Thereafter, at intervals varying from seventeen days to four years, Daly's had arranged the funerals of Jennifer, Joseph, Barbara, Timothy, Nathan, Mary Frances, Jonathan, Michael, and now Tami Lynne. Some of the Tinning deaths were so close together that in the 1970s Marybeth and Joe were paying installments on three funerals at once. Lawrence H. Daly, owner and manager, would sit down with them in his softly lit reception room, with the linen-weave drapes discreetly drawn and the gentle piped music coming out of the walls ("Greensleeves" plucked on a harp), making arrangements. In soothing tones he would suggest a Babirest casket, a low-cost item made only for infants, with the coffin already encased in the concrete vault required by the cemetery. They would decide on the calling hours (Marybeth always wanted to receive her friends beside an open casket), and when all the details were settled, Larry Daly would inquire, ever so tactfully, how they would like to settle the account. This was the point at which Joe Tinning became involved. Painfully withdrawn, he left the rest of the funeral planning to his wife.

Over the years such an understanding relationship was built up between the funeral parlor staff and the Tinnings that after the fifth or sixth infant burial, Courtland Andrew, a senior staff member at Daly's, was only mildly surprised when Marybeth walked in one day and casually asked him what qualifications she would need to become a funeral director. She lived close to the Daly Funeral Home and would often wave to Larry Daly or to Courtland Andrew as she passed on her way to the shops. Occasionally she would stop by and chat.

Andrew told her about the two-year course at a community college, the year of residency, and the state examinations. He also warned her of the occupational hazards: stomach ulcers and insomnia from the emotional strain and a bad back from the heavy lifting.

"I feel like I own quite a few bricks in this building already,"

Marybeth remarked, in explanation of her interest. But she did not pursue it.

Now she was back again, thoughtfully discussing the family's ninth obituary notice for the *Schenectady Gazette*. It was to be published in both the Saturday and Monday editions to ensure that no one who knew the family would miss it:

TINNING – Tami Lynne, 3½ months, of 367 Michigan Avenue, beloved daughter of Joseph A. and Marybeth Tinning, granddaughter of Mrs. Ruth Roe of this city and Mr. and Mrs. Joseph Tinning of Duanesburg. Survived by several aunts, uncles and cousins. Funeral service 1:30 Monday afternoon at the Daly Funeral Home, 242 Michigan Avenue, with the Rev. Roger Day officiating. Relatives and friends are invited. Calling hours Monday afternoon beginning 12:30. Interment at Schenectady Memorial Park. Memorial contributions may be made to the Sudden Infant Death Syndrome Foundation.

Naming the SIDS Foundation as a beneficiary of Tami Lynne's death was a new twist. Marybeth had asked for contributions to the Arthitis Foundation (a disease which afflicted both her parents) when Barbara died; to the American Heart Fund (her father had died from a heart attack) after the deaths of Joseph, Jennifer and Timothy; and to the St. Clare's Hospital Building Fund for Mary Frances and Jonathan. No memorial contributions had been requested for Nathan. Michael's obituary notice had suggested that money might be sent to the Tinning home, a request which, in the private opinion of Larry Daly, did not look too good in print.

A kindly gray-haired man in middle age, Daly had been around the bereavements of others for more than thirty years, ever since he was in high school and began helping his father in the business. When he was on the job, he assumed, without even thinking about it, a moist look in his light blue eyes and a sympathetic tone of voice which made him every inch the professional undertaker. He saw his work as a genuine public service ("Our job is to care for the needs of the dead, but basically we do everything we can to help the living deal with their grief"). His father had impressed upon him the importance of putting himself in the position of those he was serving, of trying to make things a little easier for them, and he had never forgotten this. Daly felt a special empathy with parents who had lost a child. Only a month after Marybeth's first baby died, one of his own five children slipped on a riverbank while playing behind a relative's house in Massachusetts and was drowned. ("He was a beautiful child, only five years old; I have never stopped thinking of him.") Daly's associate Courtland Andrew had lost a sixteen-year-old daughter. "So we know where these people are coming from, and our hearts go out to them." Daly explained.

Although several years had passed since their own bereavements, both Daly and Andrew still found children's funerals difficult to deal with. "And yet when you have had an experience like this yourself, you are more ready to reach a hand out to the parents," Daly added. "You know their suffering." This may also have made him less ready to recognize that in rare cases there may be child abuse.

"When Marybeth called us about the third funeral, she was distraught," Andrew remembered. "She asked if I would come to pick up her baby. I thought she was talking about the child we buried only six weeks earlier, and that in her grief she was reliving the tragedy. At first I simply didn't grasp that yet another of her children had died."

Some time later the Daly Funeral Home staff became aware of an investigation by the Schenectady police. When nothing came of this, they assumed there was no cause for suspicion.

"Naturally we worried," Larry Daly conceded. "But we felt that the authorities must be keeping an eye on this family. Whenever a Tinning baby died, we assumed they knew about all the others. There was no reason for us to think otherwise. Several of the bodies had been autopsied, and death certificates were issued without delay. We could tell that the babies had been well cared for. There was not a suspicious mark on any of them. Those little children looked perfect. The story we kept hearing from the family was that there was something wrong with the genes.

"These were not rich parents, but the mother would bring in very nice clothing for the funerals and little soft toys to put in the caskets. She was always very tearful when she first came to us about a death. She never looked suspicious or sinister. The whole family seemed very concerned. After the burials they put up grave markers. It was just how you would expect an average family to react to the death of a child. There was nothing out of the ordinary about these deaths in any way, except that there were so many of them."

Later, when Marybeth was arrested for the murder of Tami Lynne, Larry Daly was strongly criticized around Schenectady and even on a local television news program. People said that he should have "done something" long ago, considering that he was probably the only one, outside the Tinning family, with personal knowledge of all nine deaths. Daly took the criticism to heart. "If the authorities were satisfied, what were we supposed to do? Run to the D.A.'s office and say that there just might be some crime here? A client could sue us for that. Our job is to serve the bereaved and serve them well. We cannot be their judge and jury."

From long experience he also knew that the bereaved have a whole spectrum of ways of dealing with loss. Some sob uncontrollably at funerals. Some collapse. Some try to make light of the tragedy by cracking a joke or two, as a cover for the grief which they are unable to express. Some, like Marybeth, go through funeral after funeral in a tearless daze. Hence he was not surprised or suspicious, as some mourners were, to see Marybeth's expressionless reaction to Tami Lynne's open casket – a sight made more poignant by the fact that on that Monday afternoon, the day before Christmas Eve, almost everyone else in Schenectady was preparing to celebrate the birth of a different child. Except for Marybeth and Joe, there was scarcely a dry eye in the Daly Funeral Home as the Reverend Roger Day read the service.

Cynthia sat in the back row against the wall with her head bent low. She could not bear to look at the casket, and she was clutching Aaron as though terrified that he would be taken from her. Over the next few weeks she shared some of these fears with her pastor. "How do I know this won't happen to my baby? How can I ever feel secure again?" She had never worried about the possibility of a SIDS death before; now when her baby slept, she felt compelled to check him every few minutes. Already the anxiety was exhausting her. Having accepted Marybeth's story at face value, just as Cynthia had, Roger Day didn't have the answers. He just hoped, in his fatherly way, that faith and time would heal her anguish.

The last place Cynthia wanted to be that day was at the funeral parlor. "I was a wreck," she related sometime later. "There was this open casket, and I couldn't bear to go near it. I was there to comfort Marybeth, but I was the one who needed comfort. I truly loved Tami Lynne. I had known her from birth. I held that child every day. I fed her. I changed her. Only a few hours before she died, I had her in my arms and she smiled at me. It was like she was my own, and when she died a part of me died with her."

Cynthia was embarrassed about taking Aaron to the funeral parlor. "Some people thought it was tacky for me to come in carrying a baby, but he had to be fed soon afterwards, so I didn't have any choice. Marybeth wanted me there, and this was the only way I could do it."

Several women from the Princetown Reformed Church, near Duanesburg, were at the funeral. Joe's parents, Joe senior and Edna Tinning, had been members there for most of their lives, and encouraged by her mother-in-law, Marybeth had recently taken an interest in the church. At the heart of its social life was a close-knit group of women who organized church suppers, ran bake sales, raised funds, taught Bible class and were ever ready to support one another's families in times of crisis. When tragedy struck a household and prayer did not seem to be enough, the ladies of the Princetown Reformed Church would unfailingly show up with a steaming casserole and a plate of freshly baked cookies.

This was the third Tinning funeral for Sharon Jewett, one of the younger members of the women's guild. At the previous funeral, Michael's, she took charge of setting up the food; this left her with the strange memory of Marybeth saying to her, over and over after the event, "You must have thought badly of me because I was able to eat. You must have thought I didn't care about Michael. You must have thought I was a bad mother to let him die."

Thinking about it afterward, Sharon became increasingly distressed. After Michael's death she made excuses whenever Marybeth offered to baby-sit for her small daughter, without knowing why she made them. She rationalized that this was because of the trauma of having lost her own first baby at the age of two weeks; that despite her faith in God, she feared Marybeth (without meaning to, of course) might bring misfortune on other people's children.

As she dressed for Tami Lynne's funeral, Sharon couldn't stop crying. Almost five years earlier she felt angry at God for allowing Michael to die; now she was angry at herself for the suspicions that had recently begun to creep into her mind. As she wept, she prayed. "I kept asking the Lord to take these terrible thoughts from me." Nevertheless, she couldn't help noticing, as she went to embrace

Marybeth by Tami Lynne's casket, that Marybeth avoided looking her in the eyes.

Sue Normington was another mourner who felt troubled. She had been tormented by terrible thoughts ever since the death of Mary Frances, the sixth Tinning baby. She had acted upon them by asking the Schenectady Department of Social Services to investigate, but that had been almost seven years ago. She had never heard back, and in the meantime, three more babies died. By now she was uncomfortably familiar with the routine of Tinning burials. From her long memory of them, and this went back years before her suspicions were aroused, most of the funerals were in midwinter and Marybeth could be depended upon to wear the same coat, a coat in which she was rarely seen at any other time, gray leather with a gray fox collar. There was always an open casket, sometimes so crammed with toys that there was barely room for the baby. And at the graveside service (Catholic for the first seven children, Protestant for the last two) Marybeth usually said the same concluding prayer.

Two babies ago the Tinning grave site at Most Holy Redeemer Cemetery became filled. So Tami Lynne was buried alongside Michael in the family grave of Joe's parents at Schenectady Memorial Park, a small, tree-shaded cemetery on the same country road as the Princetown Reformed Church. Perhaps because of the ensuing publicity, perhaps because Marybeth had other things to think about, Tami Lynne's name was never added below Michael's on the large bronze marker. TINNING, the marker stated, TOGETHER FOREVER, with a large space left for the names of Joe senior and Edna, and Michael's name in small letters underneath. As Tami Lynne's casket was lowered, it was announced that Marybeth would like to say a prayer, the same prayer that she repeated over Tami Lynne when she tucked her into bed for the last time. Sue knew what to expect. It was the same last prayer that Marybeth claimed to have said to several of her babies, just before they mysteriously died. Marybeth stepped forward and recited in a small, clear voice:

> "Now I lay me down to sleep.
> I pray the Lord my soul to keep;
> If I should die before I wake,
> I pray the Lord my soul to take."

SIX

There is nothing built into the system to prevent child abuse. Something has to happen before action is taken.
—*Social worker*

Several caseworkers had questioned Marybeth over many years of lost babies, but Betsy Mannix was the most persistent. She returned to the Michigan Avenue apartment on the afternoon of December 26, unannounced, with a male colleague from Social Services. At this interview a calmer Marybeth confided to Betsy that she was troubled by the way she had reacted at their previous meeting. She was not alluding to her fear of being arrested but to the fact that Betsy had not found her in tears. Throughout the interview she kept asking Betsy whether she thought badly of her because she had not been tearful. Marybeth explained that although she had not wept at that time, she was very upset about the death of her baby. She wanted this clearly understood. She implied that her behavior of the previous week was not an expression of her true feelings but the result of being numbed by shock. She seemed overly concerned about Betsy Mannix's opinion of her and eager to present herself as a caring mother.

Marybeth added that she had discussed her unresponsive reaction with her husband, and he agreed that they both might be helped to recover from the tragedy if they went for counseling. Betsy told her that this could be arranged, but Marybeth did not pursue the offer.

Over the next few weeks Betsy interviewed many people who were familiar with different aspects of Marybeth's life and personality. She spoke to doctors, relatives, and neighbors. She reviewed medical records of the eight other Tinning babies who

[65]

died. Every one of these deaths had been noted in the obituary
column of the *Schenectady Gazette*, and as the number mounted so
had the incidence of telephone calls to the Department of Social
Services. It is the lot of small-town newspapers that most readers
scan the paid death notices before looking at the main news. Consequently a paragraph in small type recording the passing of yet
another of Marybeth's babies screamed out to every Schenectady
citizen who knew the name Tinning just as loudly as if it had been
emblazoned across page one.

Sue Normington was only one of many people who drew the
department's attention to the strange circumstances of death after
death—all of them unexpected, most of them discovered by Marybeth alone. After the first three or four deaths it became almost
routine for a few concerned neighbors to place anonymous calls to
the child abuse hot line as soon as they read the latest obituary.
The publication of Tami Lynne's death notice precipitated more
of these calls than any of the previous deaths. As a result, Betsy
Mannix knew she would be involved in the investigation before
Stuart Sanders called her into the district attorney's office. One of
the mandates of her department was that every complaint of child
abuse must be followed up immediately.

Very little is known about how Schenectady's Department of
Social Services responded to earlier complaints. In order to protect
the privacy of those who are being investigated, the department
maintains strict confidentiality of its files. Often there is good reason
for this. Some complaints might be mischievous. Some families
who are being helped might be irrevocably hurt by publicity. But
in the case of Marybeth Tinning, Social Services guarded what it
knew about her with such zeal that when she was on trial for the
murder of Tami Lynne, and Betsy Mannix was subpoenaed by the
prosecution, a Social Services attorney tried to argue that because
hers was privileged information, Miss Mannix should not be
required to testify. Although this argument was overruled by the
judge, the contents of a large manila envelope which Betsy brought
into court, presumably containing details of Social Services' confidential knowledge of Marybeth, were not revealed. Hence the case
presented to the jury hinged upon medical and legal technicalities
and gave no hint of the forces which shaped Marybeth's complex
personality. Those who had to determine her fate had to create
their own uninformed picture of her.

Richard Stazak, commissioner of Social Services, upheld the argument for confidentiality on grounds that this was an immutable rule designed to protect clients. He persisted in this stand even after the department's most notorious client, Marybeth Tinning, had been found guilty of murder. His response to inquiries from the media continued to be: "Our attorneys in the New York State Social Services Department have told us that it is not possible for us to discuss this case because of the confidentiality of records." Stazak conceded that "our refusal to answer press inquiries has created a lot of difficulties for us, but it is not something we are doing on our own."

Over the years some notations in the Tinning file would have been routinely removed. It was the department's long-standing practice (again to protect the innocent) to destroy details of child abuse complaints which were deemed to be unfounded. Once it was determined that there were no grounds for action, a complaint would be erased from the department's computer. So when concerned citizens called the child abuse hot line about the deaths of Jonathan, Mary Frances, Michael, and Tami Lynne (as is known to have happened), there would have been no flashing signals from the computer to indicate that the Tinning name had been there before. Although callers mentioned the other deaths, there would not have been any records available for comparison. Every complaint would have been investigated in isolation from the rest.

There was another problem. Sudden unexplained infant deaths were outside the department's everyday experience. Caseworkers from its child protective agency were trained to deal with child abuse, not to look for murder cases. And except, perhaps, in the case of Michael, who was reported to have sustained a facial bruise in a fall, there was never any suggestion that Marybeth's babies were mistreated in their lifetimes. On the contrary, all of them were clean, well nourished, healthy, even indulged. But by the time they came to the attention of Social Services, they were dead. Reputable doctors had already certified the causes of death, and they were classic: Sudden Infant Death Syndrome; Reye's syndrome; acute pulmonary oedema; cardiopulmonary arrest; viral pneumonia. What was there to question? Any caseworker who called on Marybeth would have found a grieving mother and an empty crib. In such a sensitive situation it would have seemed heartless to probe.

And yet . . . as baby after baby died, there developed a widening network of Schenectady citizens who watched helplessly for news of the next birth, convinced that a death would soon follow. The word would go around when Marybeth had another baby, and over the ensuing weeks the *Schenectady Gazette*'s obituary column would be the focus of even more attention than usual. Neighbors would wonder aloud to one another, "How long will this one last?" in tones ranging from disbelieving horror to black humor. There was nothing built into the system to avert the tragedy, not when the mother had all the outward signs of normality and caring, not when doctors repeatedly found unremarkable explanations for these remarkable deaths. There was only the hope that next time, maybe, it might be possible to gather enough evidence to confirm or deny the mounting suspicions.

One of the most anxious Marybeth watchers was Dr. Kevin Karpowicz, a Schenectady pediatrician who first encountered Marybeth when he was a resident at Albany Medical Center. This is a research institution to which the Schenectady hospitals send their most baffling cases, one of which was Marybeth's seventh natural child, Jonathan. At the age of four months he was admitted to the center in a fatal coma for which there was no clear cause, except for the obvious finding that he had suffered a lack of oxygen. Extensive tests were made in search of some metabolic disorder, but none was found. Some of the Albany doctors thought that an attempt might have been made on Jonathan's life and reported their suspicions to the New York State Department of Social Services. But there was no hard evidence to back them up, and when Jonathan died without regaining consciousness, the medical center listed the cause of death as cardiopulmonary arrest.

Several aspects of the case troubled Dr. Karpowicz. One was the flaw in the system which pressures doctors to name a cause of death when they cannot be positive. Part of this, he thought, was a pressure from within themselves, the need to come up with some kind of answer rather than admit they did not know. Part of it was a pressure from the system in which they functioned. In providing an answer, no matter how indeterminate, they precluded any possibility of future investigation. "When the people at Social Services see a normal diagnosis, they are not going to start looking for child abuse," Karpowicz argued. "But if there were an undetermined diagnosis, the case could be reopened for a full investigation at any time."

At the time of Jonathan's death it was not customary for Social Services to report whether, or how, a complaint was followed up. "We were never told if any action had been taken," one of the Albany Medical Center doctors commented. "There was this little conspiracy of silence. You felt you had dumped your complaint into a big black hole." In Jonathan's case, confidential information filed at the State Social Services office in Albany, the city where he died, is unlikely to have been shared with the county office in Schenectady, the town where the family was rearing yet another baby.

In the absence of information from the department itself, there were inevitable suspicions about how Social Services dealt with hot line complaints. Many of the callers drew attention to the previous deaths. But whether this was noted or followed up was never told to them.

After he had settled into his own pediatric practice in Schenectady, Dr. Karpowicz became a champion of the rights of children and served as a consultant to the Schenectady Department of Social Services. His job was to examine children who were suspected victims of abuse. In this role he had no direct contact with Marybeth Tinning, but he tried to keep up with what was happening to her. After his frustrating experience with the death of Jonathan he was dismayed, a year later, to hear that Michael was reported to have died of pneumonia.

"I have never seen pneumonia kill a healthy child of two and a half years old," he asserted. But there was nothing to be done. There had been an autopsy, and these were the findings. Karpowicz was also very skeptical of the theory that a genetic disease affected the Tinnings' natural-born children. He argued that "statistically it is almost impossible for all of them to have had the same recessive gene." He also thought that natural causes were unlikely. "It is extremely rare for a healthy baby to die. In seven years of private practice I have seen about twenty-five hundred children. Only four have died, and all of them had problems from birth."

When Michael died, Dr. Karpowicz alerted Schenectady's Department of Social Services, but again he was frustrated. "I told them that this was not an ordinary case, that it was one of many, and they began to look into it. But then they got a report from the medical examiner's office that Michael had died from natural causes."

Karpowicz was convinced that this was another large gap in the system. "Any time an infant dies there should be an adequate investigation. The autopsy itself may not prove the cause of death. In Schenectady the medical examiner reviews reports of autopsies, and if he is not satisfied, he can demand an inquiry. If he could have plugged into a computer and found the whole list of Tinning children, something would surely have been done sooner. But whenever a death in the Tinning family was brought to his attention, it was done on an individual basis. Sometimes there weren't even autopsies."

Five years after his frustration over Jonathan's death and four years after Michael's, Karpowicz was at a Schenectady nursery school when he saw Marybeth again. She was driving a school bus, and she was pregnant. His heart sank. This time he determined to do everything he could to save this baby and, if he could not, to see justice done.

When Tami Lynne was born, he urged Marybeth's pediatrician, Dr. Bradley Ford, to recommend putting the baby on an apnea monitor – a device which would sound an alarm if there was any change in her heartbeat or breathing. Dr. Ford followed this advice, but Marybeth did not. Karpowicz also spoke of his concern to the emergency room staff at St. Clare's. So, when Tami Lynne was brought in lifeless, the hospital authorities were suspicious enough to file a formal complaint with Social Services. So did Karpowicz. He also informed the district attorney's office at about the same time that Dan O'Connor showed up there. And when the obituary notice was published in the following morning's *Schenectady Gazette*, the staff that manned the child abuse hot line received call after call after call.

It fell to Betsy Mannix to try to fit the pieces of the jigsaw together, at least so far as her department was concerned. Some were irrevocably lost. But she was able to track down medical records, look at them for the first time as an entity, and search for a common factor. Poisoning was one of the first theories to be considered. So was suffocation by a plastic bag. Both possibilities were later rejected by medical experts. Betsy also tried to build up a picture of Marybeth Tinning, the kind of person she was and the forces which had shaped her. She researched the family history and talked to people who had known Marybeth over the years. Betsy put all her energies into this, and the task took over her life. At her first meeting with Marybeth she had a gut feeling that this woman was guilty, yet right up to the end she did not want to believe that a mother could kill her child. In her seven years of dealing with child abuse cases she had always felt this inner conflict. As she put it, "when you see bruises on a child, there's always a part of you which wants there to be an innocent explanation, like a fall downstairs."

Betsy was also haunted by a fear that this very fertile woman might get pregnant again, and she was determined that no more of her babies should die. She thought about little else yet was constrained from talking about the case to friends because the information she was gathering was confidential. The only place where she could discuss it was at meetings of the Tinning Task Force, a group that was put together in the district attorney's office. There medical, legal, and police experts met frequently to share the results of their continuing research into the death of Tami Lynne.

Inevitably politics became involved. Earlier in 1985 the New York State Police had formed a forensic sciences unit whose expertise was available to any police department in the state. The unit was put together by Colonel Henry F. "Hank" Williams, commander of the state police's Bureau of Criminal Investigation, in the realization that many local police departments lacked the resources to do complex investigations of bizarre homicides, major disasters, and questionable or unattended deaths. This was no criticism of small-town police departments, simply a recognition of their inevitable limitations. Williams thought that their capability to solve unusual crimes could be enormously improved if they could call upon the experience of some of the best criminologists in the country.

An impressive panel of experts was assembled. Some of them were from other states, and all of them had worked on investigations of international importance, from the assassination of President John F. Kennedy to the identification of Nazi war criminals. The team included forensic pathologists, forensic dentists, anthropologists, a behavioral scientist, a psychiatrist, a forensic artist and a photogrammetrist. This unique unit was soon to be envied and copied by state police forces across the country. Yet despite the richness of its talent, there was an initial reluctance on the part of some of New York's local police departments to "call in the state" on a baffling case, as thought this were an admission of their own failure.

Within the Schenectady Police Department Dan O'Connor pressured for help from the state unit. The lack of an official inquiry into the deaths of Marybeth's babies had been a frustration to him for years, ever since he first heard about the Tinning family from a former police colleague, John Zampella. Zampella had known of Marybeth since 1972, when her first three children died within a two-month period. He was told about this by his wife, who was friendly with a former neighbor of the Tinnings. After the fourth death, at St. Clare's Hospital in December 1973, he did some investigating and found that several nurses suspected that Marybeth might have done something to cause the deaths, but they did not know what. In every case death had already been ascribed to natural causes, and it was Zampella's impression that none of the doctors was prepared to question a colleague's medical judgment.

By the time Marybeth's sixth natural child, Mary Frances, died in February 1979, Dan O'Connor was John Zampella's partner. Both men heard some distressing stories from nurses at St. Clare's who were suspicious about the condition in which Mary Frances was brought to the hospital. Together they went to the district attorney's office and appealed for an investigation, but they were told there was not enough evidence for an official inquiry.

When Zampella retired, he urged Dan O'Connor to keep track of Marybeth. O'Connor was more than willing. With young children of his own, he couldn't bear to think of anyone harming a baby. One of his many frustrations on this case was that there was no mechanism for the police department to be informed when yet another Tinning child died. If the police heard about it at all, it was by chance, from an ambulance driver, a nurse or from somebody's neighbor, and by that time a hospital doctor or the medical examiner's office had already certified a cause of death. Once that happened, it was virtually impossible, in the small-town atmosphere of Schenectady, to upset the medical authorities by demanding a re-assessment of the case. But when Tami Lynne died, a member of the St. Clare's Hospital staff called a relative in the Schenectady Police Department. That relative, remembering O'Connor's concern about previous Tinning deaths, sent the message to O'Connor in the Nott Street diner which sent O'Connor scurrying to Stuart Sanders in the district attorney's office and Sanders to the autopsy which would provide evidence for an investigation none of them would ever forget.

When the Tinning Task Force was hurriedly assembled in the district attorney's office, there was some initial buck-passing. For all the years of inaction, various participants blamed doctors, Social Services, the district attorney's staff, the police, and the medical examiner—particularly the medical examiner, Dr. Robert L. Sullivan.

In major cities the medical examiner is a full-time official with a staff of his own. Neither the city of Schenectady, nor the whole of Schenectady County was large enough to merit this. Two alternative systems had been tried over the years, but each had its failings. Initially every town in the county had its own health officer, one of whose jobs was to investigate unusual deaths. Any deaths which seemed questionable would be referred to the coroner, who had jurisdiction over the entire county. He was a publicly elected official who did not have to be a doctor; traditionally he was often a funeral director who was assisted by a coroner's physician. Since patronage was often involved, the system became highly political. Schenectady County dispensed with it in the 1960's, opting to have a medical examiner instead.

Dr. Sullivan had held this post since 1968, almost from the time it was created, covering the fourteen-year span of all nine Tinning deaths. It was a part-time job with two part-time assistants, all three of them local physicians in private practice, with one or the other of them on call for twenty-four hours a day. Any unusual death was supposed to be reported to the examiner on duty, and it was up to him to decide whether or not to order an autopsy. For suspected suicides, homicides, and fatal accidents the need for autopsies was obvious. But the sudden death of an infant was often a borderline case, and only four Tinning deaths—including that of Tami Lynne—were even reported to the medical examiner.

It was also Dr. Sullivan's responsibility to review all autopsy reports from the Schenectady hospitals, although pathology was not his speciality. He was a cardiologist with a full-time private practice, and his assistant medical examiners had unrelated specialties of their own. But when others on the Tinning Task Force started hurling accusations, he honorably took the blame—not only for himself but also for a former assistant who had neglected to pass on to him a report of Timothy Tinning's death, at the age of three weeks.

Timothy was the fourth of Marybeth's children to die and the first to come to the attention of the medical examiner's office. Lacking the report of his death, Sullivan did not hear of any death in the Tinning family until that of Nathan, the fifth child. "If I had known about Timothy, perhaps I would have looked harder at Nathan," he admitted.

Three and a half years after Nathan, Mary Frances died. At that time both Dan O'Connor and John Zampella remembered Dr. Sullivan's being present when they went to see District Attorney Poersch in his office to urge an inquiry into Mary Frances's death. The two police investigators made the point that this was the sixth Tinning baby to die in suspicious circumstances. However, a careful autopsy showed no unusual findings, and the police officers were told that there was not enough evidence for a criminal investigation.

Jonathan's death, the seventh, was not reported to Sullivan's office or to the district attorney because it happened in Albany, outside their jurisdiction. Again there were suspicions and a detailed autopsy, but insufficient evidence to suggest attempted murder.

The next Tinning death to be brought to Sullivan's attention was Michael's, apparently of viral pneumonia. Sullivan accepted the hospital diagnosis but noted in the report: "This is the seventh [*sic*] child death in the family in the last ten years. This is the only adopted child. The autopsies of others showed some to have a known cause of death, and some did not. Wide investigation and work-up included genetic studies which were negative. At this autopsy the illness showed acute pneumonia. The family history is bizarre."

There it was left until Tami Lynne died almost four years later. "At the time I did what I thought was the correct thing to do," Dr. Sullivan commented. "But I should have pushed harder, especially after I knew about Nathan. As I look back, the main problem is that different persons or agencies knew about every one of these deaths, but there was no centralized collection of information. Nobody wants to take the blame and probably no one person or agency should. It was all of us together—the medical examiner, Social Services, the hospital staffs, the record keepers. All these people knew. And all of us failed."

Bringing in the New York State Police after Tami Lynne's death would mean showing up these inadequacies. Among Schenectady's public officials there was some resistance to the suggestion, especially from the district attorney's office. Nevertheless, Schenectady's police chief, Richard Nelson, conceded that it would be irresponsible to pursue the investigation unaided. On January 2, 1986, two weeks after Tami Lynne's death, Nelson telephoned Captain Gerald E. Looney of the state police's Bureau of Criminal Investigation and asked for help. Looney consulted with his superior, Colonel Williams, who was on sick leave. Williams had become terminally ill with cancer, but he was so eager to put his new forensic sciences unit to work on this intriguing case that he dragged himself out of bed for a strategy meeting. He was concerned that all the unit's resources should be made available, that nothing should go wrong, nothing be forgotten. He may have had one of those premonitions which people have when their time is running out because it soon became clear that the death of Tami Lynne Tinning would be the unit's first big murder investigation.

Part Two

ALL HER CHILDREN

SEVEN

She was craving for love, and having babies fulfilled that need in her.

—Her mother-in-law

Individually and collectively everyone who researched the deaths of the Tinning babies—police, doctors, investigators in the district attorney's office—came to the same conclusion: that Jennifer's death changed Marybeth irrevocably. This baby's failure to survive was the beginning of the catalog of nine infant deaths, all of them in unusual circumstances. Yet every one of these cases was examined in isolation from the rest, sometimes in ignorance of the family history, often by hospital staff members who had never treated a Tinning baby before. Not until the ninth death, Tami Lynne's, did any of the experts try to solve the mystery by putting together all the babies' medical reports and looking for common factors. Only then did they also look at the personality of the mother and the way she reacted to repeated bereavements. When they finally did this, a pattern began to emerge.

It began right after Jennifer's death, which was different from all the others. She had hemorrhagic meningitis with multiple brain abscesses, an infection which appeared so early in life that it was believed to have developed in the uterus. Marybeth's description of the cause of death, that the baby was "full of cancer", was inaccurate but conveyed the hopelessness of her condition. Jennifer lived for only a week and never left St. Clare's Hospital. Consequently Marybeth was never suspected of being in any way responsible.

Every one of the eight subsequent babies was healthy at birth, flourished for a time, then died unexpectedly. The fatal symptoms always appeared when Marybeth was alone with the child. Her initial reaction was that of any caring mother: a desperate call for a doctor or an ambulance, an anguished account of how she had found the baby motionless in its crib, or how it had gone into convulsions, or how it had made "a funny gurgling sound" and immediately expired. Despite her limited understanding of the technicalities, her early training as a nurse's aide made her a better medical witness than most mothers, and her descriptions fitted the visible symptoms. As time went on, some doctors and nurses suspected that Marybeth knew more than she was telling, but they could never find enough evidence to face her with the question, "Did you do anything to this child?"

The doctors she saw in emergency rooms were different every time, and all of them found her credible. When she rushed into one of these rooms with a limp body in her arms, the urgency was to try to revive the child, not to waste time checking for signs of abuse or delving into family history. These heroic but futile resuscitation attempts inevitably left marks on the infant's body. Afterward it would have been difficult, if not impossible, to distinguish these marks from any bruises which may have been there already.

Whenever a baby died, doctors were naturally reluctant to ask questions; it would have seemed heartless to interrogate parents who were already overwhelmed by grief. There were also answers of a sort within the medical profession. Between 1970 and 1980, when the first seven Tinning children died, two theories about the cause of inexplicable deaths in childhood became widespread among pediatricians. In babies it was Sudden Infant Death Syndrome, popularly known as SIDS or crib death; in older children it was Reye's syndrome. One or the other of these diagnoses seemed to fit what was known about most of the Tinning children, but in light of later medical understanding both terms were overused. Although more is now known about SIDS than when several of Marybeth's babies were believed to have died of it, the syndrome remains a medical mystery. In a classic case an apparently healthy baby a few months old is found dead in its crib for no apparent reason; the mechanism in the brain which tells the lungs to breathe has unaccountably stopped functioning. There are several theories on why this happens but no clear cause. Rarely doctors find a congenital abnormality; usually they find nothing. All kinds of unexplained infant deaths tend to be described as SIDS cases, although some of them may merit further examination. To say that an infant was a SIDS victim is like saying that an adult died of heart failure. It is not a diagnosis. But since healthy and cherished babies do die of what (for want of a clearer definition) is known as SIDS, hospital staffs of the 1970's were hesitant to put tough questions to traumatized parents in search of some dubious alternative. A growing awareness of child abuse has since made them bolder.

Reye's syndrome used to be a rare disease of childhood which flared into an epidemic in the early 1970's, It is always serious and often fatal. Symptoms appear when a child already has a viral infection: the body temperature soars, and there is inflammation of the liver and brain which can cause vomiting, seizures, and wild, irrational behavior. Researchers found that Reye's syndrome could be triggered by the administration of aspirin to a child who already has a high fever, a discovery which caused pediatricians across the country to warn parents against the use of "baby aspirin." This virtually ended the epidemic. But it was at its height when doctors concluded that Reye's syndrome was responsible for the deaths of Barbara Tinning at the age of four and a half and her little brother Joseph, "Joey", when he was two.

These were Marybeth's first two children, born in 1967 and 1970. They were blond and sturdy, with a strong likeness to their parents and the contented demeanor of children who felt loved and secure. "Marybeth really appeared to cherish them," an acquaintance observed. "They were always clean, neat, immaculately dressed, and just beautiful."

At that time the family was living in half of a two-family house on Second Avenue, in a lower-middle-class neighborhood of Schenectady known as Mount Pleasant. It was an old, rather dreary section of town only a short walk from the General Electric plant where Joe worked. He and Marybeth seemed typical of other young couples in the area, still in their twenties, having babies, struggling to make ends meet, hoping to move to a larger place. This was their situation in the spring of 1971, when Marybeth became pregnant with Jennifer.

It was not an easy pregnancy. All through that summer she felt weak and sick, unable to care for Barbara and little Joey or to do her housework. Her mother was severely arthritic, almost crippled by the disease, and could not help her. So her mother-in-law, Edna Tinning, stepped in and took care of her grandchildren for weeks on end.

In mid-October, when Marybeth was in her seventh month her father, Alton Roe, Sr., died suddenly. At the age for fifty-four he had a severe heart attack while on his job at the General Electric plant. He was rushed to the hospital, where he had another heart attack and died within a few days. This was a terrible shock to the Roe family and Marybeth was grief-stricken. At the wake she sat in the reception room at the Daly Funeral Home—the place where she was to become a familiar client—and wept bitterly. Ten weeks later, on December 26, she gave birth to Jennifer. After so much stress Edna Tinning was not at all surprised when her daughter-in-law lost the baby. She remarked, "Marybeth had known for months that there was something wrong with that child."

Within the family Marybeth seemed to take Jennifer's death more calmly than she had taken her father's. But at St. Clare's Hospital some of the medical staff described her reaction as bizarre. When asked if she would like to hold the tiny body, she took it into her own hospital bed and drew a sheet over the two of them. This symbolic act was elementally maternal, a sharing in the death of this flesh of her flesh which could not survive. Yet even beyond this extravagant gesture of grief, Marybeth's demeanor was troubling. A nurse who was on duty at the time described her as "a very disturbed person." This observation was not noted in the medical records. Nor does psychological support seem to have been provided for Marybeth in her emotional crisis, despite the fact that she was going home to care for two small children. Another decade was to pass before a few maternity hospitals began pilot programs to help mothers through the grief of losing their babies. Before then there was a widespread attitude that the less the tragedy was talked about, the sooner a woman was likely to get over it. More than fifteen years later, in prison for murdering Tami Lynne, Marybeth recalled how she felt when Jennifer died. "There was nothing to help me," she stated firmly. "Nothing."

The coincidence of the two Christmas deaths, Jennifer's and Tami Lynne's, the first and the last, made it seem as though this tragic phase of Marybeth's life, the loss of all her babies, had come full circle. There was even a symmetry about it, as though it might have been planned. At that first funeral, in the first week of the

new year, there was tremendous sympathy for her. Setting a pattern
for all the funerals that were to follow, Jennifer's coffin was left
open until the burial service, displaying the heartbreaking sight of
a tiny baby in a long white christening gown. By this time Marybeth
had better control of herself. There was a dazed, glazed look in her
eyes, and she wept a little—more, women friends noted, than at
subsequent funerals but not as much as they themselves wept. "If
this had been my baby," one woman commented afterward, "I
would have buried her quietly and cried forever." Marybeth did
neither. But still recovering from childbirth, she must have felt
wretched.

Joe Tinning also had difficulty expressing his grief. He was reared
in a devoutly Protestant family where life's disasters were seen as
the inscrutable will of the Almighty. One day they would be
explained; in the meantime, they were to be accepted with unques-
tioning stoicism. In the face of tragedy, therefore, Joe was always
stone-faced and withdrawn. He was staunchly loyal to his wife even
under provocation (and there was much of this in their marriage),
but he seemed unable to express his emotional support for her in
any way except by being physically there. In that he never failed.

At Jennifer's funeral friends and relatives made the usual soothing remarks about how much little Barbara and Joey would be a
comfort to the two of them. These were more than just trite condolences. Although some neighbors thought of Marybeth as "strange,"
all of them believed her to be a good mother who truly loved her
children. And with their light blond hair, good looks and evident
intelligence, these were youngsters to be proud of. It was therefore
a tremendous shock to the Second Avenue neighbors when, only
seventeen days after Jennifer's death, Joey suddenly died, to be
followed less than six weeks later by Barbara.

Both children were stricken by inexplicable symptoms which
rapidly became fatal. Both were reported to have had seizures when
they were at home with Marybeth. She took each child to Ellis
Hospital's emergency room twice (avoiding St. Clare's, where Jennifer died, although it was closer), and on the second visit each
child was past saving. But no connection seems to have been made
between these two similar and mysterious deaths. Nor do the Ellis
Hospital authorities appear to have noted their proximity to the
loss of Jennifer, if indeed, they knew about her death.

Joey became ill during the week of his second birthday. Marybeth took him to Ellis Hospital with a story that he had had a seizure and choked on his own vomit. He was kept under observation in the children's ward for a few days, but nothing was found wrong with him. Only a few hours after he was sent home Marybeth brought him back to Ellis's emergency room dead. She said he had complained of feeling sleepy, so she put him down for a nap. When she went to check on him, she found he had turned blue and was tangled in his sheet. These were the same words that she would use fourteen years later to describe the fatal condition in which she found Tami Lynne.

Doctors at Ellis Hospital speculated that Joey might have had Reye's syndrome, but avoiding a positive diagnosis, they recorded the cause of death as cardiorespiratory arrest, which simply meant that he had stopped breathing. There was no autopsy.

Joey died on January 20, 1972. On the evening of March 1, after allegedly telling her mother that she would soon see her little brother in heaven, Barbara was also stricken. Again Marybeth rushed to Ellis's emergency room. She related that shortly after being put to bed, Barbara had developed stertorous breathing and gone into convulsions. Marybeth was urged to leave the child in the hospital overnight, but she insisted on taking her home. Later that evening she brought Barbara back to the emergency room unconscious. Barbara was resuscitated and put in the intensive care unit, where she remained in a coma and died the following day. Her death was not reported to the medical examiner, although there was a hospital autopsy. Because of evidence that Barbara had been feverish as well as having convulsions, it was concluded that she died from Reye's syndrome. At that time medical knowledge of the syndrome was sketchy. Fourteen years later doctors on the Tinning Task Force and state forensic team took another look at the medical records of Barbara and Joey and came up with a different possibility. They thought that neither child's symptoms were what had since been defined as "classic Reye's" and that both could have been suffocated.

If this happened, there would have been a struggle—especially from a child of Barbara's age. One of the team's medical experts speculated: "She may have been mildly ill to begin with, probably with something like a feverish cold. If there was an attempt to smother her, even a sick child of that age would not die quietly. She would have fought back and gained some consciousness. If the attempt continued, she would have had anoxic convulsions and then gone into a coma." Joey's death could have followed a similar pattern.

Ellis Hospital's chief pathologist, Dr. Thomas Oram, pulled Barbara's autopsy report out of his department's files and looked at it in the light of this possibility. He observed: "At the autopsy we found fatty changes in the liver and an edematous brain. These changes seemed consistent with what we knew about Reye's syndrome at that time, but we now know that these changes in Reye's are somewhat different from those found in Barbara. When she died, no one thought of suffocation as a possibility. We now know that the anoxia caused by suffocation will produce a fatty liver. We did not know it then. We knew that Reye's syndrome starts with nausea and vomiting, followed by convulsions, liver failure, coma, and death. And in our ignorance of this new disease, we thought that's what we saw in Barbara."

According to the recollection of a relative, Marybeth had punished Barbara on the evening that she was taken ill. The child had gone to visit neighbors and fussed about returning home when her mother insisted. There were tears and a tantrum, and Barbara was sent to her room. Shortly after that episode Marybeth reported finding her in a convulsion. Fourteen years later Marybeth remained adamant in her insistence that she had done nothing to harm Joey or Barbara.

Right after Barbara's death, the third within two months, there was a great deal of gossip among the Tinnings' Mount Pleasant neighbors. Some of them wondered if the children had been given an undetectable poison. "Her story didn't sound right to me," one woman said. "I saw two normal children who had never been sick rushed to the hospital almost dead. I saw Barbara playing in the backyard only a few days before she died, and she looked fine. Marybeth said that Joey suffocated because he got tangled up in his sheet. Two-year-old children do not tangle in sheets. Barbara and Joey never had anything wrong with them, except once in a while they might have had little runny noses. Nothing more. I had my suspicions about what might have happened, but there was nothing I could do because I didn't have proof."

Barbara and Joey were buried alongside Jennifer and Marybeth's father. Marybeth was dry-eyed at their funerals despite the open caskets. Again the neighbors commented to one another. "I don't know how anyone can bury children that small and not shed a tear," one woman remarked. "God, if they were mine, someone would have to put me away."

When Easter came, a month after Barbara's death and two and a half months after Joey's, Marybeth related a strange story. She told relatives that she found Easter gift baskets on her porch, left by neighbors for the two dead children. "I did not believe it," Marybeth's sister-in-law Carol Tinning said flatly. Others wondered. If the neighbors were unaware of the deaths, this was merely a misplaced act of kindness. But since they all knew, it seemed an intolerably cruel and insensitive gesture. Did the incident happen only in Marybeth's troubled mind? Or were distressed neighbors trying to convey their suspicions? If so, why would Marybeth recount the incident except to pass that message on to her family?

In any event, shortly after Easter she and Joe moved away from Mount Pleasant and rented the ground-floor apartment in a house on Cleveland Avenue, in the Bellevue section of Schenectady. This was only a mile from their last home, but it was a fresh start in a neighborhood where they were not known. They had barely settled when for the first time, they came to the attention of Schenectady's Department of Social Services.

The contact was made by Marybeth. On July 3, 1972, four months after Barbara's death, she telephoned the department to say that she would like to be a foster mother.

EIGHT

What could I do? I couldn't prove anything. I didn't see
anything. I had no evidence. But I knew.

— *Neighbor*

Marybeth and Joe were frank about the recent loss of their three
children. They told a Social Services caseworker that their baby
died of cancer and the two older ones of Reye's syndrome (which
the caseworker noted, incorrectly, was "a disease that cannot be
diagnosed"). They talked about their emotional need to fill this
sudden great gap in their family and said they would like to have
a foster child of between five and ten years old. "Mrs. Tinning feels
she has a lot of love to give a child," the caseworker wrote in her
report. "Mr. Tinning feels cheated of the short time he had his
own children and feels it would be good for his wife to care for a
foster child."

Marybeth was very convincing. Citing her earlier experience as
a nurse's aide on the pediatric ward at Ellis Hospital, she said she
had always been drawn to children who needed help. After her last
child died, she thought of working full-time but decided she would
rather stay at home and be a mother.

The caseworker was clearly overwhelmed by sympathy for Marybeth. There is an artlessness about her report which suggests that
she did not ask probing questions. She described her new client as
a very warm and outgoing woman who was not yet ready to adopt
but who had "a calm and determined attitude about having other
children." Joe impressed her as a man with "a very quiet manner"
who "seemed anxious to be honest." She noted that it was initially
Marybeth's idea to take in a foster child; her husband was more
hesitant because he wanted to be certain that they were doing this

for the right reasons. "He said he had to be sure he was doing it to help a child, not just to fill a gap."

The caseworker added: "She did most of the talking. She seemed compelled to describe what happened to her children and did this with a great effort to keep from crying. She said the boy had not been ill but had a convulsion at home and died a few hours later in hospital. The girl had not been ill either. She played outside in the afternoon, visited friends in the evening, became convulsive and was rushed to hospital where she lived a few hours."

The conversation passed on to what would be expected of Marybeth and Joe as foster parents. Their questions seemed naïve. What food should they give a foster child? Could they go out for an evening and leave a sitter in charge? This "friendly and compatible couple," as the caseworker described them, seemed pathetically anxious to do the right thing.

The worker was worried that the Tinnings might be emotionally hurt by having to give up a foster child at some future date. Her report did not reflect any concern for how a child might fare in this home, so recently devastated by grief that (as she noted) Marybeth had been taking tranquillizers.

After producing glowing references from friends and from the pastor of the Princetown Reformed Church, which Joe's parents attended, the Tinnings were approved as foster parents. Social Services arranged for a little boy named Robert to be sent to their home in the fall of 1972, but if he ever went there, it was for such a short time that none of Marybeth's friends or relatives can remember him. However, a Social Services official sent an appreciative letter to the Tinnings in January 1973, thanking them for having Robert. "We do realize that we ask foster parents to perform the impossible, but your efforts to achieve this were outstanding," the letter stated. Subsequently the Tinnings took in a little girl of about ten years old.

Joe soon became very attached to her. She reminded him of Barbara. He rarely spoke of his feelings, but he seemed to have more difficulty accepting Barbara's death than that of any other child, perhaps because she lived the longest. For a long time after she died, whenever he visited the home of Marybeth's brother and his wife, Alton and Sandy Roe, he made the mistake of calling their small daughter Barbara instead of Linda. Joe tried hard not to let his own emotional needs get in the way of being a foster father, but at times his desire to be a parent overwhelmed him.

Marybeth struck the Social Services caseworker as a woman of unusual emotional strength. There is now no way of telling whether this was her demeanor at that time, whether the worker was ingenuous or Marybeth dissembling. But in 1972 Schenectady's caseworkers were not required to have any formal training in psychology or social science; all that was expected of them was a college education and a willingness to learn on the job. The one who interviewed Marybeth seems to have let admiration of her client cloud her objectivity. But there was another Marybeth, timid and traumatized, who in that same period of time tried to find another way of filling the emotional gap in her life—and who made a very different impression.

A few weeks before her first visit to Social Services she applied for a job as a waitress. Rather, her mother, Ruth Roe, applied for her. The Roes had been regular customers at the Flavorland restaurant in the Shoporama center on Altamont Avenue ever since it opened in 1968. Ruth and her husband had often lunched there and sometimes Marybeth and her children had gone with them. They were all so familiar that several waitresses knew them by name and made a point of offering personal condolences when first Alton Roe died, then Jennifer, Joseph and Barbara Tinning.

"It got so difficult," one waitress remarked. "You can say you're sorry about the first death, and maybe about the second, but when a woman has lost her father and three children, sorry means nothing."

Soon after Barbara's death Mrs. Roe asked the Flavorland manager, Raymond Crofts, if he would give Marybeth a job. Mrs. Roe explained that some regular employment would help take her daughter's mind off her troubles, give her something to do. Although he had a lot of sympathy for Marybeth, Crofts was reluctant to hire her.

"I felt she was not emotionally stable enough to be dealing with the public on a regular basis," he said. "She seemed distraught and withdrawn. You could tell by her facial expression."

Crofts had ample opportunity to observe this. After Barbara died, Marybeth came to Flavorland almost daily, often alone, and sat at the long counter over a cup of coffee, looking terribly depressed. "It was weird," a waitress recalled. "She was not crying; she had no expression; her face was just a blank. We all thought it was shock and that she would break down later. She kept asking us if we thought she could get a job here. She seemed to want this so badly." But she lacked the initiative to make a formal application.

Shortly after Crofts refused her, he was transferred to another of the several Flavorlands in the Schenectady area. Several waitresses who felt sorry for Marybeth urged the new manager to hire her. "Maybe you could give her something part-time," one of them pleaded. Out of pity he did.

Being a Flavorland waitress was a convenient, even prized job for married women of Marybeth's background. Restaurants in this chain were friendly, family-style places whose menus were a permutation on hamburgers, fried chicken and ice cream sundaes. Working conditions were clean and cheerful. With tips, the pay was good. And the working hours could be adjusted to suit a woman's family needs; she could work days or evenings, as much as full-time or as little as one day a week. Marybeth had just settled into a schedule of three afternoons a week when she presented herself to Social Services as a prospective foster mother.

The difference between the two Marybeths—she who had seemed like a poor risk as a waitress and she who, only a few weeks later, impressed the caseworker with her calm and assertive manner—was remarkable. Neither the social worker nor the prospective employer appears to have gained any insight into the other side of her character. Both felt pity for her, and she seems to have known intuitively how to win their sympathy. At Social Services it was her quiet courage which impressed. At Flavorland she capitalized on the tragedy of her lost children, who were remembered fondly by the staff. Barbara and Joey had impressed all the waitresses with their good looks and mannerly behavior. They were not pesky, like some children who came to the restaurant, running around between the tables, spilling food on the floor, emptying the ketchup bottles. Marybeth's youngsters were thoughtful and obedient, and she was always attentive to them.

"We all understood when she came to work at Flavorland and acted a little strange," one waitress observed. "If I had lost three children in two months, I think I would have been in a mental home. It was amazing to me that she could function at all."

She soon became quite good at the job—quick on her feet and pleasant to customers most of the time, but occasionally short-tempered and erratic. After all she had been through, these lapses were understood and readily forgiven. One thing about her, however, struck her colleagues and customers as very strange indeed. She came to work one day with her appearance drastically changed. She had shaved off her eyebrows and drawn heavy pencil lines in a different place.

This was not a conventional style of makeup. It was ugly and bizarre, and the pencil lines kept changing. Some days they were thick zigzags. Some days there would be large, round blobs above the inner corner of each eye, trailing upward to an exaggerated arch. Sometimes she also used bright lipstick to change the shape of her mouth. The effect was striking enough to be the talk of the restaurant. Customers began to describe Marybeth as the "waitress with the eyebrows." Her colleagues discussed among themselves how to tell her what a mess she was making of her appearance. Finally one of the older waitresses spoke to her bluntly: "Being the big mouth that I am, I told her she looked like a jerk. 'If you are going to put eyebrow pencil on,' I said, 'you had better do it right. The way you have it looks terrible.' "

Marybeth let her naturally dark eyebrows grow back. But there were days when she would come to work with her light brown hair dyed a carroty red or strawberry blond. She told the Cleveland Avenue neighbors that she was pregnant when she wasn't and wore maternity dresses when there was nothing to be concealed. A few women spoke to Joe about this strange behavior but he did not seem unduly concerned. He said his wife was having emotional problems because she wanted another baby so badly. Leave her alone, he advised, and she will be all right.

This was the story of Marybeth's life. Ever since childhood her difficulties were pushed aside by people who, for a variety of reasons, chose to ignore them. She had never really succeeded at anything, and when she cried out for attention, she was isolated. As a child she felt unwanted; as a mother she failed. When, too late to help her, a New York State police psychologist tried to make sense of the pieces of her existence, he came to the conclusion that Jennifer's death was the catalyst which made all the subsequent deaths inevitable, considering the fact that for some deeply buried reason—possibly that of having been an abused child herself—this was a deeply troubled woman who did not know how to manage a nurturing relationship.

And yet all the signs were apparent when Jennifer died: the craving for attention, the ways in which she invited it by the first of many stagy funerals and, when that attention diminished, the renewed attempts at motherhood, real, by proxy or pretended. Between babies there were the painted eyebrows, the orange hair, the everyday events turned into melodrama, the telling of incredible stories in which she was the heroine or the victim—and through it all, the longing to be loved, admired, pitied, or at least noticed. At no time did the people close to her understand. They lacked the insight to empathize with her emotional needs or to challenge her lies. In all the tenuous ways they tried to help her they usually did the wrong thing for the right reason. When she tried to look dramatic, they told her she looked like a jerk. Or they left her alone, thinking that if her problems were ignored, they would go away. Yet Marybeth constantly invited these negative reactions by choosing inappropriate ways of drawing attention to herself.

Early in 1973, when she was thirty years old, she became pregnant for the fourth time. Immediately she lost interest in her foster child and insisted on sending her back to Social Services. Her relatives were shocked by the speed with which she got rid of the little girl. "Joe would like to have kept her, but that child went out of the house so fast when Marybeth got pregnant," his brother, Andy Tinning observed. Indeed, the child's existence in the Tinning home was so short-lived that years later no one in the family could remember her name. At Social Services a note was appended to the Tinnings' file stating that "due to the physical condition of the foster mother it was decided that this home would be closed."

The Flavorland waitresses gave Marybeth a baby shower. She had given away all her earlier children's belongings, a gesture which seemed understandable at the time, but was compulsively repeated after each successive death. Even before the funeral arrangements were complete, Marybeth washed and stacked the baby clothes and had them removed from her home, along with the infant furniture. Her need to get rid of these things as fast as possible seemed overwhelming. Every time she began another pregnancy she started buying new layette items with the eagerness of a woman having her first baby.

For the birth of her fourth child Marybeth consulted Dr. Grace Jorgensen, an obstetrician who had not seen her before, and arranged to have her baby at Bellevue Hospital, a fashionable maternity home on the outskirts of Schenectady. Her former obstetrician, Dr. August Schwenk, had refused to care for her any longer. Years later Dr. Schwenk gave his reasons: "After the death of Barbara I had the firm conviction that she was killing her children. I did not face her with it because I had no proof. In today's legal climate, if you face a patient with mere suspicions, the next thing you know is that there will be a lawyer camped on your front porch, waiting to sue you. It's an extremely bad situation. But Marybeth was certainly cognizant of the fact that after the third child died, a number of doctors were concerned about what was happening. I think she also knew that I felt there was something grossly wrong. There was a lot of discussion with pediatricians and obstetricians who were involved in the case, but we could not come up with proof. We wondered who we could go to with our speculations. There was no one, because all we had were speculations and clinical impressions, and they don't count for anything in law."

At Bellevue Hospital Marybeth gave birth to Timothy on the morning of November 21. She had a quick, uncomplicated delivery. The baby was full-term but small, five pounds nine ounces, and slightly jaundiced. Marybeth was advised to leave him in the hospital for a few extra days so that the jaundice could be treated, but she rejected the advice and took him home with her when he was only forty-eight hours old. Despite the mild jaundice, the doctor who checked Timothy before he left Bellevue gave him a good report. By all accounts he was a beautiful baby. Carol Tinning was struck by his blond likeness to Joe's younger brother, Andy, whom she was soon to marry. For years afterward she would say that of all Marybeth's babies, Timothy was her favorite.

With tremendous sadness, Carol could not help comparing him with Joel, her own son by her former marriage. "From the first moment I held him I knew something was wrong with Joel. Before anyone told me he had cerebral palsy, I knew he wasn't right. Mothers have a feeling about these things. And I had a feeling about Timothy as soon as I held him in my arms. I knew that this was a perfectly healthy baby."

Marybeth seemed proud of him. Years later a neighbor still remembered how nicely she dressed him, in a blue knitted suit and bonnet. He lived only three weeks. On December 10 Marybeth took him, dead, to the emergency room at Ellis Hospital. She said she found him like that in his crib, and a doctor who knew nothing of the family history certified the cause of death as Sudden Infant Death Syndrome. Timothy was the third Tinning child to be brought dying or dead to Ellis Hospital in less than two years. it should have caused consternation there. Officially it didn't. Unofficially an emergency room nurse reported to a doctor that she suspected Marybeth of killing her children. Allegedly the doctor told this nurse to keep quiet and mind her own business. The story cannot be fully confirmed because the doctor has since died.

But if the nurse's suspicion over Timothy's death had led to a thorough investigation into the deaths of Joey and Barbara, the rest of this story might have been very different.

Timothy's was the first Tinning death to be reported to the medical examiner's office. There, too, the system had its inadequacies. For reasons which were never explained the assistant medical examiner who was informed of the death neglected to make a report to his superior, Dr. Robert Sullivan. Consequently no autopsy was ordered for Timothy. So when Police Investigator Zampella tried to do some research into Timothy's death, he could get nowhere because there were no medical grounds for a police investigation. So far as the official records were concerned, Timothy died naturally of SIDS.

Carol Tinning gave a graphic account of his funeral: "Marybeth was dry-eyed, without even a trace of sadness. I believe Joe felt something, but he didn't show it. We are talking about the fourth child, dead, and there was Marybeth calmly putting a little toy in his coffin before they closed it. Most women would have jumped off the bridge. But all the attention was on her, and she seemed to be enjoying it. When we got back to her home after the funeral, she was going around quite calmly, making sure everyone had something to eat. It was like party time. I went to the bathroom and could not stop crying. Andy found me there, and I told him that something was very wrong with this family. Everybody seemed so happy, and nobody was dealing with the fact that this baby had died. So we left. And that was the end of Timothy."

A few weeks later Carol invited Joe and Marybeth to her home for a meal and a game of cards. She had a pretty little house, a legacy from her first marriage, in the semirural Coldbrook section of Schenectady, a home which Andy had begun to share with her. She was marrying into a family with a lot of strained relationships, and her invitation was an attempt to make things better. She felt very sorry for Marybeth and Joe in their loss of four children, and she wanted to show them kindness. There were stresses between Andy and Joe which were causing them to drift apart, and she wanted to see the brothers on close terms again. She was also in the painful position of feeling that her husband-to-be's parents did not fully approve of her. As a divorced woman with two children, one of them severely handicapped, she was not the wife they would have chosen for Andy. Indeed, it was her understanding that "they already had a girl picked out for him at church." They were dedicated Protestants, and Carol was a lapsed Catholic. She was also a few years older than Andy. Given all these differences between her in-laws' background and hers, she knew it was asking a lot to be accepted by them. But by nature she was warm and giving, and her years of struggle as a single parent had made her forthright and feisty. She tended, therefore, to face her difficulties directly and to speak her mind. It made her an unusual addition to the introverted Tinning family. She wanted to get along with them and went out of her way to make friends with Marybeth although this was not a woman she would have chosen as a friend.

Even before Timothy's funeral there were things about Marybeth which troubled Carol, but at first she kept quiet about them. The two of them had barely met when Marybeth asked if she could take Joel, then aged twelve, on a shopping expedition to Schenectady's Mohawk Mall. At the time Joel was in leg braces, walking with difficulty. When she brought him back to Carol's house, Marybeth related that she had been stopped by three strangers in the mall, all of whom assumed this was her son, all of whom said in effect, "Aren't you wonderful to keep him at home, considering the shape he is in?"

Carol thought this an unlikely story. No stranger had ever made such a comment to her, not since Joel was born, yet Marybeth claimed to have heard it three times in as many hours.

On the evening of the card party Carol and Marybeth left their handbags on the stairs while they sat around the dining-room table. There were forty dollars in bills loosely stuffed into Carol's bag, an amount which she remembered exactly because she was living on a tight budget and it was all she had to last the week. When she went to buy groceries the next day, all this money had gone. She suspected that Marybeth had transferred it to her own purse and confronted her new sister-in-law when they next met.

"How could you think I could do such a thing?" Marybeth responded. "If anyone took the money, it was your daughter."

Carol was outraged. She knew that Carol junior would not dream of stealing from her handbag. But she could prove nothing.

Shortly after this Marybeth was involved in another episode concerning missing money. On May 1, 1974, she reported to the police that her Cleveland Avenue home had been burglarized. At that time she was treasurer of the bowling club to which Joe belonged, and she claimed that the club's funds, a few hundred dollars in cash, had been stolen. Joe's bowling ball and some of his bowling shirts were also missing, along with some small items of Marybeth's jewelry. The apartment was a mess. The refrigerator had been emptied onto the kitchen floor, and the contents of a fish tank were spilled across the living-room carpet. But there were no signs of forced entry. The bowling equipment was subsequently found off a quiet street in the suburb of Rotterdam, a little more than a mile from the Tinnings' home in the direction of Duanesburg. The missing money was never traced. After two police officers questioned Marybeth, they recommended dropping the investigation. According to their report, they "came to the conclusion that the woman was mentally unstable and that there was a possibility she may have done this herself." At Schenectady's police headquarters it was assumed that she had staged the burglary to cover up the loss of the bowling club funds, for which she was probably responsible.

Money had become a source of bitter quarrels between Marybeth and Joe. He complained that she spent it as fast as he made it. He would hide the checkbook from her; she would find it and take checks from the middle or back of the book; he would write checks which he thought were covered, then be embarrassed to find they weren't. Such were the stories which circulated among relatives and friends.

Waitresses at Flavorland saw a different side of Marybeth. There she counted her tips carefully and hoarded them frugally. "That's a nice one for the college fund," she would say when a customer had been unusually generous—provided, of course, she had a child alive at the time. But when out shopping, she could be a compulsive spender, buying several versions of the same item, never quite satisfied that she had chosen well enough. She bought more sheets and towels and china than she could ever use. One Christmas she gave Carol two sweaters and a camera when any one of these gifts would have been considered generous. Her other sister-in-law, Sandy Roe, had an even stranger experience with her.

"Marybeth was always borrowing my one white slip," Sandy recalled. "After this had been going on for some time, Buddy and I had a joint garage sale with her and Joe, and she put in a big box full of slips, brand-new with the price tags still on them. There were long slips, half-slips, regular-length slips, white and all colors. I asked why she borrowed mine when she had so many. She said it was because she didn't like any of her own."

Some of Marybeth's spending money came from the insurance checks which were paid out when each child died: about a thousand dollars apiece in funeral benefits. This was more than enough to cover the Daly Funeral Home's bill, but Marybeth believed the insurance money was hers to spend. This pattern of her spending the insurance money while Joe met the funeral expenses out of his paycheck seems to have continued for child after child. After the fifth death Sandy remembers being told by Marybeth, "We just got the check for Nathan, so I'm going out to buy new drapes and wallpaper."

Despite his forbearance, Joe Tinning seems to have had his breaking points. Over the years the stresses in his marriage were obvious to several sets of neighbors. In the shared old houses of Schenectady, with the walls not soundproofed and the buildings close together, it was hard to have a marital argument in privacy, and the Tinnings' arguments were louder than most. Early in their marriage one neighbor remembers hearing Marybeth's hysterical screams on several occasions.

"They were really bloodcurdling," she related. "Once or twice I rang her doorbell because I was afraid Joe might be killing her although his voice was never raised. One of them would come to the door as though nothing had happened. And if I saw Marybeth next day, she would never mention it." Ten years and three addresses later other neighbors were telling similar stories.

In the spring of 1974 Joe and Marybeth had several arguments about money. There was the matter of Carol's missing forty dollars and its chilling effect upon the fragile relationship between the two brothers. There was the mysterious burglary which had deprived the bowling club of its funds. What Joe said to Marybeth about all this, or she to him, can only be conjectured. But Joe seemed troubled. One day he remarked to Andy that lately his food had been tasting bitter, and he could not understand why.

Alarmed, Andy advised his brother to put his next home-cooked meal in a package and send it to a laboratory for chemical analysis. Andy was suspicious that Marybeth might be trying to get her own back. He knew she had been prescribed Valium and speculated that she might be crushing some of it into her husband's food. Joe seemed unable to consider this possibility. He laughed and said he felt sure there was nothing to worry about.

At Andy's initiative the two brothers had begun meeting for meals in a local diner. "There had been the argument about Marybeth taking Carol's money, and we had drifted apart," Andy explained. "I wanted to get a relationship going again with Joe." Although he was three years younger, Andy was taller and more outgoing than his brother; also, in his choice of Carol (to whom he was clearly devoted) he was the one who had moved much farther away from the circumscribed atmosphere of their shared childhood.

This led to a role reversal between the brothers, with Andy feeling protective of his older sibling. Concerned about Joe's safety, he urged his brother to leave Marybeth. As Andy saw it, this marriage was headed for disaster—of a kind, perhaps, which did not bear thinking about—and Joe should get out of it before there were any more children. Joe, however, seemed paralyzed into inaction by a dictum of their mother's ("Tinnings don't get divorced") and by a strong sense of duty to his wife.

Their conversation was repeated over many shared meals. Andy felt he was getting nowhere. Eventually he said in exasperation, "My God, Joe, then at least have a vasectomy!"

Joe promised to consider the suggestion.

NINE

Joe would never say a word against Marybeth in public because of the way he was raised. He was brought up to be unassuming and respectful. How could he speak out against a woman who already had everyone's sympathy because she had lost her children?

— *Duanesburg resident*

Carol, meantime, was preoccupied with worries of her own. Her son, Joel, needed to be dosed with phenobarbital to prevent seizures; also, his asthma attacks had become so severe that frequently he had to be rushed to hospital for adrenaline shots. One day Carol called the Draper Pharmacy on Guilderland Avenue for a renewal of the phenobarbital prescription, but before she was able to pick it up, there was another asthma emergency. Hurriedly she telephoned her brother-in-law's home, which was only a block from the drugstore, to ask if Joe or Marybeth would pick up the prescription before the store closed for the night. She promised to collect the pills from them later in the evening (as it turned out, this was not possible) or early next morning.

At about 3:00 A.M. Carol was wakened by the telephone. Marybeth's voice screamed in her ear, "Joe's dead!"

Struggling into consciousness, Carol asked, "What do you mean, Joe's dead?"

Marybeth was sobbing and agitated. It was impossible to get a coherent statement out of her.

"We'll be right over," Carol told her.

Carol and Andy would never forget the next few hours. "Before we rushed out of the house, I had to wake my daughter to tell her to watch Joel," Carol related. "Then we got in the car and drove to Cleveland Avenue like madmen. Joe was unconscious on the bedroom floor, his face was a bluish purple, and the sheets were wound around him as though he had rolled over and over as he fell

[99]

out of bed. There was grape juice splashed all over the room, and Marybeth standing in the corner. All she kept saying was: 'I didn't do it, I didn't do it.'

"She was fully dressed. But she had not called the ambulance or the police. We did that. She just went on standing there, repeating that she didn't do it and pleading with us not to tell her mother.

"The police were there in five minutes. They did mouth-to-mouth on Joe while we waited for the ambulance. I had to leave the room, I was so upset. I took her into the living room and said, 'Marybeth, what have you done?'

"She said, 'I didn't do it.' She was frightened, but she did not cry.

"We got to Ellis Hospital just in time to save Joe's life. The doctor told Andy, 'Your brother has had a lethal dose of phenobarbital.' There were about seventy pills in Joel's prescription, and they were all gone. I said to the doctor that we were sure Joe had not done this to himself. Andy also explained how Joe complained of his food tasting bitter. But no one questioned Marybeth because Joe did not want to press charges."

Ellis Hospital staff treated this as an attempted suicide, offered some therapeutic counseling, and released Joe after a few days. In the hospital he was asked how he had come to take so much phenobarbital. He said he could not remember. This was undoubtedly true; such a heavy dose of a barbiturate would have caused amnesia. Joe was also asked if he had any worries. He volunteered that he was having a hard time making ends meet and that all his four children had died. These seemed reasons enough for a man to get so depressed that he might want to do away with himself. Joe said nothing to correct this impression. He chose to accept the stigma of attempted suicide rather than implicate his wife. Marybeth's main concern seemed to be that her mother might find out about the incident. When her brother learned of it, she pleaded with him not to tell her.

Joe returned to living with Marybeth. He seemed unable to contemplate any alternative. Eleven years later, when police began their inquiries into the death of Tami Lynne, he was asked why he stayed with a wife who tried to kill him. It was an informal question, put by a happily married investigator who found the situation beyond his credulity. The investigator remembered the substance of Joe's reply although he forgot the exact words. It was that he

(Joe) had learned that if he did nothing to upset Marybeth, it wasn't likely to happen again. From 1974 until her imprisonment in 1987 it must therefore be assumed that Joe Tinning lived in uneasy compliance with his wife's wishes, being careful not to cross her, never questioning her self-appointed right to make decisions for the two of them, going short of money while she spent it, enduring ridicule from those who thought him spineless, even fathering babies that she passionately desired and he feared for . . . and always afraid for his own safety.

Only on rare occasions would some hint of his antagonisms surface. Once on a visit to her brother's home in Duanesburg there was a family argument which became so explosive that Marybeth became hysterical. Alton slapped her. Joe did not attempt to intervene. Afterward he took Alton to one side.

"I'm glad you did that," he said. "I never could. But she has had it coming to her for a long time."

Alton felt a lot of sympathy for his brother-in-law. Before he met Sandy, he had gone through an unhappy first marriage, and there was no doubt in his mind what Joe should do.

"After she tried to kill you, you have to be crazy to stay with her," he said. "Joe, if it was me, I'd send her down the road. I've sent one down the road myself. Joe, do what you have to, but you are welcome at my house anytime."

"I don't know," Joe replied. "Something's got to be done, I guess."

That was his only comment on the situation. As Alton remarked, "Joe was never much of a one for talking."

Carol was more openly impatient of her brother-in-law's docility. She was also very angry at Marybeth. But she promised herself, for Andy's sake, that she would try to keep her feelings to herself and maintain some semblance of family accord. So, reluctantly, she invited Joe and Marybeth to another supper party at her house.

From the outset she realized it was not a good idea. Everyone was tense—she most of all. They were again sitting around the dining table playing cards when Carol felt she had to speak her mind. "Things were brewing in me," she explained. Interrupting the game, she asked Marybeth to go with her to the master bedroom. There she stood face to face with her sister-in-law, glaring.

She was a few inches taller than Marybeth, and with her mane of auburn hair and her eyes glinting she could look very intimidating.

"There are a few things I want to say to you," she said, backing her sister-in-law into a corner of the bedroom. "I believe you did something to Joe that night he almost died. I know you stole my money. I don't believe your house was robbed. I think you did it yourself. And God knows what else you have done. There's something wrong with you, Marybeth."

She was shouting now, and her voice carried into the dining room. Joe heard it but went on sitting there.

"It's true, isn't it?" Carol went on.

Marybeth began to sob.

"Tell me you did it," Carol insisted. "Tell me you took my money."

Still pinned in the corner, Marybeth continued to weep. Finally she whispered, "Yes, I took the money. But that's all. I didn't do anything else."

Now that her daughter's honesty was no longer in question, Carol spoke more gently. "You need help, Marybeth. Losing so many babies must have had its effect on you. There's no way you can go through all that and still be normal. But there are doctors who can help you."

Marybeth said nothing, and Carol took her silence for assent. If she did not act immediately, the opportunity might be lost forever. Joining the two men, she announced, "Marybeth has agreed to see a psychiatrist, and we are going to St. Clare's to find one. Right now."

Through all her accusations it never occurred to Carol that her sister-in-law might have had anything to do with the deaths of her children. The idea was too monstrous to cross her mind. She thought that Marybeth's recent problems stemmed from grief which she had never allowed herself to express, as evidenced by her detached, dispassionate behavior at Timothy's funeral. This was the only time Carol had seen it; she had not known Marybeth when the first three children died. The professional help which she envisaged for her sister-in-law was some form of grief therapy, and a Catholic hospital seemed to be the place to find it.

It was 10:00 P.M. when the four of them arrived at St. Clare's. Carol told a doctor in the emergency room that they needed to see a psychologist or psychiatrist that night. She also promised her

sister-in-law that she would stand by her. Marybeth's name was
called, and she was directed to another room. Carol, Joe and Andy
waited in the lobby for a very long time. Eventually one of them
went to find out what had happened to Marybeth.

"She had given us the slip," Carol reported. "She wasn't seeing
a doctor. She had gone to the telephone and called Joe and Andy's
parents and asked them to pick her up. God knows what she told
them. We did not see them come in, but they took her home while
we went on waiting. Can you imagine a thing like this happening
in a family and it not even being discussed?"

Whatever the motive of the senior Tinnings may have been, it
was certainly not to spite their sons. Theirs was a family of deep,
unspoken loyalties. But there was also a fundamentalist distrust of
the kinds of doctors who played around with people's minds. And
there was Edna Tinning's strong attachment to Marybeth, whom
she had grown to love as the daughter she'd never had.

Carol, who would never fill that role, was disgusted with the
whole business. It was bad enough to be marrying into a family from
whom she already felt outlawed. Her attempt to help Marybeth had
merely made her own situation more difficult. She decided to give
up trying and put her energies into her new marriage.

Marybeth's life went in another direction. After Timothy's death
she had returned to Flavorland and was putting in longer hours.
Among the waitresses there was a camaraderie which flourished in
the cheerful, gossipy atmosphere of the place, and she enjoyed this.
It was there she met Sue Normington and several others who
became, if not friends, close acquaintances. Working the evening
shift together, they got to know one another's husbands, since most
of these men would stop by for coffee while they waited to take
their wives home. Joe was judged to be "an okay guy, quiet but
nice."

"He would not talk," one waitress observed. "He would order
his coffee, and you would say, 'Hi, Joe,' and he would nod, but
not say anything. I think he was afraid of Marybeth."

Her employers found her to be a bit tense and jittery but always
willing to work late, come in on her day off, pitch in where she
was needed. "She did not take criticism well, but she could do
a phenomenal job," said Michael Hovey, one of the Flavorland

managers. At one point he selected her to help in a staff training program.

Sara Barker, the cook at the Shoporama Flavorland, shared his opinion. "Marybeth was a good worker," she said. "She did her job well. She was attentive to her customers and had good rapport with them. As a colleague she was strange, but she was okay."

The strangeness was noticed by all the restaurant staff. Other waitresses, who had a closer view of her than her employers, noticed that she could be impatient and snappy with customers for no apparent reason. She would lose out on tips because of this, then feel resentful that her colleagues were making more money. A successful waitress has to be consistently cheerful and willing, no matter how terrible she may feel. Marybeth was not always able to do that, but she appears to have tried.

One way in which the strangeness manifested itself was remarked upon by everyone who came in contact with her: She rarely looked another person in the eye. She would hold a conversation with her head turned away, staring in another direction. Or she would have a blank look. At times she seemed to be in her own dream world.

"She was a very unusual person," one waitress remarked. "She would never talk about anything deep, only trivial things."

Customers were curious about her. "Is that the Marybeth who lost all the babies?" they would ask her colleagues. And sometimes: "Why would she go on having them?" That was when Sue Normington stepped in, all kindness and concern, and served these inquisitive customers to spare Marybeth from dealing with them.

At break time Marybeth often sat alone in the little room at the back of the restaurant, reading pulp fiction. Horror stories were her favorite, and next to them romance. She liked books by Stephen King ("the indisputable king of horror," in *Time* magazine's description) and she was particularly fascinated by a novel by Mary Higgins Clark, *Where Are the Children?* She kept a copy in her locker.

It was an unlikely tale to appeal to a bereaved mother. Other women in her situation would have found it too painful. But in some abstruse way Marybeth seems to have identified herself with the tragic heroine of the story, a lovely and intelligent young woman named Nancy Harmon. Like Marybeth at that time, the Nancy of the novel had borne four children. When the story begins, two are already dead, and she has been unjustly charged with their murder.

Released on a legal technicality, she has fled from a life of fear and repression with the children's father, has remarried happily, and is living in New England town where no one knows her story. Or so she thinks. But one winter day the small son and daughter of her second marriage disappear while playing by a lake. The unsolved mystery of the two earlier deaths is resurrected, and again Nancy is suspected of killing her children.

She becomes so distraught that she half believes herself responsible. She is innocent, of course. But in the unraveling of the mystery there are dark hints of the children's being sexually abused by a man who is half maniac, half monster. There is a strong sense of Nancy's feeling not only misunderstood but abandoned. The one adult upon whom she could depend, her mother, dies in a way that was not as accidental as it seems at the time, just when Nancy needs her most. This leaves Nancy cruelly alone and vulnerable.

She is vindicated in the end, but up to the final chapter the evidence against her continues to mount. The blurb on the novel's paperback version sums up her situation: "Again Nancy could see the accusation in everyone's eyes. Yet how could she protest that she loved her children . . . that she would never do them harm . . . that some unknown person had performed this second monstrous act of evil . . . How could she say she was innocent when she no longer could be sure of it herself?"

Did Marybeth feel that this described her situation? Was she, too, aware of the growing, silent suspicions of others? Were there suggestions of sexual abuse buried in her own background? Did the sudden, unexpected death of a parent—in her case, her father—leave her feeling as abandoned as the fictional Nancy Harmon? And did she feel in some arcane way that "some unknown person" had caused her children to die?

One of the older waitresses—the same waitress who was bold enough to tell Marybeth about her artificial eyebrows—had a theory about this: "Maybe it's like in that movie *The Three Faces of Eve*. Maybe Marybeth Tinning is one person, and there is this other person, also part of her, who killed her children."

This woman (an ex-waitress by this time) was so fearful of what she knew, and how publication of this knowledge might affect her family, that even after Marybeth had been convicted of murdering Tami Lynne, she insisted on remaining anonymous. Interviewed at her home—a cozy mixture of early American style furniture, hooked rugs, chintz upholstery and crocheted afghans—she told of a remarkable incident which had haunted her for more than twelve years.

"I have nothing to gain by telling this story," she said. "If Marybeth gets free, I could have a lot to lose because I think she can be a very, very dangerous person. But it haunts me. It has been like a cancer growing in me for years.

"Only a few months after Marybeth lost Timothy I noticed that she had started getting a stomach. My break time did not coincide with hers very often, but that evening it did. We would get half an hour off, never more than two of us at the same time, and we would sit in this back room where the supplies were kept. There was a small table with three chairs. Most of the time when Marybeth had a break, she would go to her locker and take out this book, *Where Are the Children?*, and she would sit reading it. How long can it take a person to read a book? Yet it seemed like she always kept this one in her locker, and it seemed like forever she was reading the same book. She had just taken it out of her locker when I had the nerve to ask her, 'Marybeth, are you pregnant again?' At first she denied it. Then she admitted she was. And she said, 'Don't tell anybody.' Then she did something very weird. There were just the two of us in the back room. She bent down and more or less whispered in my ear, 'And God told me to kill this one, too.'

"I looked at her like I didn't hear right. I said, 'What?'

"And she said, 'It has to be done.'

"When she talked to you, she would sometimes have a glassy, staring look, but that night she was way off in a twilight zone. Her being in a kind of trance was not unusual, but she was a little more out of it that time than I had ever seen her. Then she turned around and did not say another word to me. She just sat at the table and started reading that book.

"I was dumbfounded. I thought she was crazy, but I didn't think she meant what she said. I thought that losing all those babies had affected her mind and she needed help. I told it to the other girls, and they thought the same. One of them said, 'She's really sicko.' We made light of it, but it stuck in our minds. And we all thought that as she got more advanced in her pregnancy, she would come out of it."

She seemed to do so. She continued working and even organized another house move during this, her fifth pregnancy. The move suddenly became necessary because the Cleveland Avenue landlord had given Joe notice, making it clear that he wanted his apartment back as soon as possible. The landlord did not state his reasons, but it was obvious to him that Joe understood them. The alleged burglary of a few weeks earlier had caused some minor property damage, but the landlord was even more concerned about the police's conclusion that Marybeth had staged the robbery. He did not want any more trouble of that kind.

The Tinnings' next home was the second-floor apartment in a two-family house at 341 McClellan Street, near the center of town. It was another typical Schenectady dwelling, built about the turn of the century, more gracious than most and on the same street as two buildings where Marybeth was becoming increasingly familiar: the Daly Funeral Home and St. Clare's Hospital. In this new location she was a five-minute walk from either one.

Sara Barker, the Flavorland cook, remembers nothing different about Marybeth's fifth pregnancy from the others she observed. "Whenever Marybeth was pregnant, she was never excited. She never showed any highs or lows. She never complained. She never took time off until the baby was almost due. Afterwards she would come back to work like it was nothing."

Nathan was born on Easter Sunday, March 30, 1975. As usual, Marybeth brought her new baby to Flavorland to be admired. Still nervous about that whispered confidence in the back room, the older waitress remarked to Marybeth, "Maybe his being born at Easter is an omen that nothing will happen to this one."

Twelve years later, sitting at home in her rocking chair, this former colleague recalled how Nathan looked that day: "I can still see his face. I can still see his darling little face. His hair was so blond, and with those big blue eyes and the smile he was the most perfect specimen of a little baby boy. He was just beautiful."

She was wrong about the Easter Sunday omen: Nathan died suddenly at the age of five months. What did she think when that happened?

"I was confused," she said. "I was very confused. I was suspicious, but I was trying to talk myself out of it. It tears me apart that I saw all this happening and did not want to believe it. Now I'm angry at her for what she did and at the authorities for allowing it to go on. I'm also angry at myself for being so stupid and so gullible that I believed all the stories she told us. Most of those who knew her at work are angry, too, but not as angry as I am— maybe because of what she said to me that time in the back room. And I shall always remember those babies, those beautiful babies. You and I would die for our babies. But all she did was knock them off, one by one."

TEN

By the time Nathan died we had forgotten how many babies she had. We really lost track.
—*Flavorland waitress*

A few years later Marybeth had difficulty recalling which baby was Nathan and which was Timothy. Was it Nathan who died in his crib and Timothy in the car, or was it the other way around? Or were they both crib deaths? And when did they happen? She had to be reminded before she could get the record straight.

When Marybeth eventually confessed to killing Tami Lynne, she also admitted to having suffocated Timothy and Nathan. "I had two children who died because I put a pillow over their face as I did with Tami," she told police. "I did this because I felt I was not a good mother. I felt I was not a good mother because I lost the other children." At the time she told nobody, not even Joe, what she had done.

She explained that every one of these three babies was crying when she suffocated it and that she used her bed pillow or a cushion. "I held it over his face until he was quiet. And then called for help. Called an ambulance."

She said she suffocated Timothy when he was in his crib making "funny sounds, gurgling sounds" because he had a cold.

"And that, did that upset you?" she was asked by New York State Police Investigator Joseph V. Karas twelve years later.

"Yes," she replied.

"And how did it make you feel?"

"I mean, whatever I did just did not turn out right."

It was a harsh judgment to make on herself only three weeks

after Timothy's birth. She was unable to remember whether the ambulance took this baby to St. Clare's Hospital or to Ellis.

Her recollection of Nathan's death was much more vague.

"I want to ask you about Nathan," Investigator Karas continued.

"They were all the same," Marybeth responded.

"Tell us about Nathan. As best you remember, please."

"I don't remember."

"Marybeth, did you have a son Nathan?"

"Yes."

"When was he born?"

"I can't remember."

"You don't remember?"

"I can't remember."

"Do you remember when he died?"

"No, please."

"I have to ask you. Try to get a hold of yourself."

"No."

"Do you remember how he died?"

"The same way as Tami."

"And where did that happen?"

"At home."

"Who was there?"

"I don't—Joe, I guess. I don't know."

"And you?"

"Yes."

"Anyone else?"

"I don't think so. I can't remember."

"Did you put a pillow over his face?"

"Yes."

"Were you alone?"

"I can't remember."

"Would you remember if anyone else was with you?"

"I don't think so. I don't know. I don't know."

This, her initial recollection of Nathan's death, was wrong in almost every detail. Nathan did not die at home. On September 2, 1975, she took him out with her in the car. Halfway through the afternoon she ran into the Flavorland restaurant on Balltown Road and asked for help. She said that Nathan had stopped breathing. The manager, Michael Hovey, was her new boss. Marybeth had transferred to this smaller, newer store in the fashionable suburb of Niskayuna when she returned to part-time work after Nathan's birth. At that time she had wanted to work the day shift, and there were no daytime vacancies at the Shoporama Flavorland.

Hovey and one of the waitresses ran out to her car, where they found Nathan unconscious. While the waitress telephoned for the rescue squad, Hovey laid the baby on the hood of Marybeth's car and gave mouth-to-mouth respiration.

"I could not tell if he was alive or not," Hovey recalled. "I did not want to lose any time by taking him indoors. The rescue squad was there in minutes, and they rushed him to St. Clare's."

He recalled that Marybeth was very agitated. "But I cannot remember what she said. My attention was on the baby."

The waitress, who was a friend of Marybeth's at that time, was able to observe her more closely. "When Marybeth came into the store, she sought me out. She was panicky, but she had a stupid smirk on her face, and she did not look me in the eye. I asked her what happened, and she said she was out shopping and had stopped at the vegetable place on Route One-forty-six when Nathan made this funny gurgling sound. She thought he was dead. So did I. When I saw him, his lips and his nails had started to turn bluish.

"I asked her why she had driven so far for help. The vegetable stand was two or three miles away, and she could have stopped at any house along the road and telephoned for an ambulance. She said she drove to our store because she did not know what else to do."

It was a lame explanation. By now Marybeth had become familiar with the routine of calling for an ambulance or rushing to a hospital emergency room. Why did she lose precious time by pulling off the road at Flavorland?

"I believe I know why she ran into the store that day," her former friend said, long afterward. "I think she wanted me to see Nathan like that. She knew I thought he was a cute baby, and I believe she wanted to hurt me. She was not devastated by what had happened to him. I was."

Nathan was blue and lifeless when he was brought into St. Clare's emergency room. He was almost certainly brain-dead. In some slender hope of his survival he was put on a pulmonary life support for a short time, but he never regained consciousness.

Ten years later, when she made her confession, Marybeth thought she had smothered Nathan at home, in his crib, the same

way she admitted smothering Timothy and Tami Lynn. Only when
Investigator Karas prodded her memory did she recall driving with
her unconscious baby into the Flavorland parking lot.

"Think about Nathan for a minute, and think about driving the
car up Balltown Road," Karas reminded her. "Did that happen in
the car?"

"Yes," she agreed.

"And you took him to Flavorland?"

"Flavorland parking lot."

"You went inside and used the phone or something."

"Got help."

"This baby died at St. Clare's."

"Yes."

"Where was the baby in the car while you were driving along?"

"In the car seat."

"Next to you?"

"Yes."

"And the pillow was on your bed at home?"

"No."

"Where was the pillow?"

"I had a littler pillow."

"Okay, can you tell me about the pillow? Was it a color? Did it
have a color or stitches or something?"

"It was just a sofa pillow."

"A sofa pillow that you kept in the car?"

"Yes."

"What did you do with it?"

"I put it on his face."

"While he was seated in the car seat?"

"While he was asleep but crying."

"In his sleep?"

"He was crying."

"How long did you hold it over his face?"

"Until he stopped crying."

"How long would you say that was?"

"I don't know."

"Was that in '75 right after he was born?"

"I don't remember the year. I might remember the year."

"Do you remember how old he was?"

"Just a few months."

Even the way she told it this second time, it was an improbable story. When Marybeth was tried for the murder of Tami Lynne, part of her defense was that the police investigators had put words into her mouth. Outside the courtroom one of the defense's expert witnesses argued to reporters that no one could drive a car with one hand while smothering a baby with the other; he insisted that this discrepancy alone made her entire confession questionable.

But there was a different discrepancy which the police did not pick up. Nathan was not beside Marybeth in her car. He was strapped in an infant car seat which had been set on the rear seat. That is how Michael Hovey and the waitress found him. If Marybeth did put a pillow over his face, she could not have done this while she was driving because Nathan was not at her side, as she said he was. He was beyond her reach. So she must have done it earlier, perhaps when she stopped at the vegetable stand. Perhaps even before she left home.

Another overlooked factor was that because of the family history, Marybeth's pediatrician, Dr. Dominick Mele, had ordered an apnea monitor for Nathan. In the Schenectady area in 1975 this was an unusual precaution. Marybeth would have been shown how to give rescue breathing and cardiopulmonary resuscitation if any change in the baby's breathing pattern had caused the monitor's electronic alarm to go off. This alarm—a beeping sound with flashing lights—would come from the square metal box whose wires had to be attached to the infant's body by adhesive pads. For an infant who was thought to be at risk from SIDS, a physician would undoubtedly insist upon this monitor's being in constant use for the first few months of life.

If Nathan's breathing had stopped while he was in his crib at home, as was Marybeth's spontaneous recollection ten years later, she would have had to answer some tough questions from Dr. Mele about why he was not on the monitor. But if the baby was with her in a car, she had an acceptable response. How could a mother cope with that contraption when she had to strap her baby in a car seat and bundle him in outdoor clothes? From her first introduction to the apnea monitor, Marybeth resisted using it. She argued that it was not necessary when she was watching Nathan and that if she used the machine at night, that was good enough. But her friends worried and wondered.

Nathan's death remains one of the biggest mysteries of this mys-

terious case. The blueness of his lips and fingernails indicated that
he had been deprived of oxygen for several minutes, perhaps a lot
longer. Could Marybeth have suffocated him at home, then put
him in the car? Is that why she told first one story and then another
about where and how she put a pillow over his face? And if she
wasn't responsible for his comatose state, why didn't she try to
revive him instead of losing vital time by driving him to Flavorland?
Her excuse, that she didn't know what else to do, sounded
inadequate.

A passage in the novel that Marybeth was reading so avidly, Where
Are the Children?, *described the murderer's thoughts after he had
abducted Nancy Harmon's small son and daughter:*

> *The boy was a threat. If he escaped, it would be the end. Better
> to finish with them both; better to do what he'd done before. In
> an instant he could remove the threat—seal off air so that lips and
> eyes and nostrils were covered—and then in a few hours—when
> the tide was high toss their bodies into the churning surf. No one
> would know. . . .*

Nathan's death was reported to Schenectady's medical examiner,
Dr. Robert Sullivan. One of Dr. Sullivan's assistants handled the
case and ordered an autopsy, which was performed at St. Clare's.
Nathan was found to have no congenital anomalies, and the pathologist determined that he died from acute pulmonary oedema. But
this is not a cause of death; it is simply a condition which is found
when the lungs are congested. And lungs can be congested for a
variety of reasons, suffocation among them.

The autopsy was clearly limited in scope. It was done by a
pathologist who was not familiar with the family history, and it
merely provided a clinical finding to put on the death certificate.
In this examination there seems to have been very little attempt to
understand why a healthy baby should suddenly die. Nor did the
assistant medical examiner question the inconclusive findings of the
St. Clare's pathologist.

By now enough obituary notices had appeared in the *Schenectady
Gazette* for a growing number of citizens to have become morbidly
intrigued by the case. Because Joe's immediate relatives were the

only Tinnings in town, the local obituary scanners were spared any problems of identity when the name appeared yet again among the paid announcements. Some people, strangers to the family, had begun to follow the drama from death to death, like episodes of a mystery serial. From Nathan's funeral on, they began to stop by the Daly Funeral Home for the wake before the funeral mass.

Sara Barker, one of several Flavorland staff to attend Nathan's funeral, remembered the scene clearly: "There was this poor baby in a little white coffin, and Marybeth sitting there with Joe. He looked a little more strained than she did. She was the focus of everyone's attention because she was this poor grieving mother. People who did not know her and who were inquisitive came and shook her hand and hugged her, then left. Some would be weeping and almost hysterical. But I didn't see Marybeth shed a tear.

"After the funeral, when she got back to work, she seemed to enjoy talking about it all. Other than that, she behaved like this was just another occurrence. I never saw one ounce of regret."

It troubled Marybeth's colleagues that the baby photographs which she put on the staff bulletin board in her children's lifetimes remained there after their deaths. Most of the waitresses were mothers, and these reminders of babies they had known and hugged were unbearably tragic. Yet they felt they could not hurt Marybeth by asking her to remove the pictures. After Nathan's death one waitress did venture to ask her why she went on having babies.

Her reply was quoted around the Flavorland kitchen: "Because I'm a woman, and that's what women are supposed to do."

Publicly Marybeth's colleagues sympathized with her. But privately, from this time on, some of them began to make periodic calls to the newly formed Child Protective Unit of Schenectady's Department of Social Services.

A few others in Schenectady were beginning to share their suspicions. One of these was Moira Coons, who lived across the street from the Tinnings' last home on Cleveland Avenue. She had personal knowledge of Timothy's birth and death, and she had heard of the deaths of Jennifer, Joseph and Barbara from a friend who was related to one of Marybeth's former neighbors on Second Avenue. She knew, therefore, that some of the Second Avenue neighbors had speculated that the first three children might have been poisoned. This suspicion was strengthened by the gossip

which Moira had heard about Marybeth's attempt to poison Joe.
"I'm sure she could have convinced him that she didn't mean it,
that she wasn't in her right mind after losing Timothy, and that it
wouldn't happen again," Moira commented.

Marybeth was heavily pregnant when she left Cleveland Avenue,
so it was natural for Moira Coons to join the obituary watchers.
After reading of Nathan's death, she decided to call on Bernard
"Barney" Waldron, the Schenectady County sheriff. She knew him
personally because he lived in her neighborhood, but this gave her
no special advantage. Almost everyone in the Schenectady area
knew Barney Waldron.

The sheriff's office is in the center of town, in the same building
as the county jail, conveniently linked by a second-floor pedestrian
bridge to the County Courthouse. Barney, a man of rangy build
with silver gray hair, was generally available to all comers. He was
a retired police officer who had been elected and reelected sheriff
on the basis of his convivial, easygoing, accommodating personality.
What he lacked in administrative ability was amply compensated
with personal charm. Although, on a steady basis, more prisoners
escaped from the Schenectady County Jail than any other in New
York State, Barney always had plausible explanations which exoner-
ated his staff and himself, coupled with a winning way of putting
them across. As a colleague observed, "He always caught the
escaped prisoners, even if it took a year or two."

He was a consummate politician with a fund of slyly funny stories
about his Democrat opponents and a reputation for showing up at
every politically important wake in town. Consequently Barney
Waldron knew the Schenectady undertakers better than they knew
one another. At one point he went so far as to make Larry Daly
one of his honorary deputy sheriffs.

It is understandable that Moira Coons should have gone to the
sheriff's office with her concerns about Marybeth Tinning. But it
was predictable that nothing would come of this meeting. Many of
the sheriff's staff members were underpaid part-timers, fully occupied with patrolling the county and running the jail. Although
Barney Waldron had the authority to organize a criminal investigation, he had neither the public funding nor the expertise to carry
one out. He was also astutely aware of the political consequences
of spreading himself too thin. Arresting the citizens of Schenectady
was simply not in Barney Waldron's line; indeed, most law enforce-

ment officials who were associated with him would have been hard put to remember when it last happened.

Several years later Moira recalled her conversation with him: "I told Barney I thought it looked suspicious for all these babies to be dying. It was so abnormal. So I said to him, 'You must know the people at Daly's, the funeral parlor. Wouldn't it be a good idea to find out if something fishy is going on?'

" 'Well,' he said, 'if you think so, Moira, why don't you do a little research?'

"I said, 'Are you kidding, Barney? It would be so much easier for you to go to Daly's.' "

She added: "He had to know Larry Daly. Everybody knows Larry. And if you're a political figure like Barney, you go to a wake every time somebody's brother-in-law's cousin dies. But Barney did not follow through on this, and neither did I. Now I feel very badly about it."

At the time of Marybeth's trial in 1987 Barney Waldron was asked about his conversation with Moira Coons. He said he had no recollection of it and doubted that it had taken place.

ELEVEN

When people became suspicious of her, it was always
her reaction to move away from them and go on to
someone else.

—Social worker

The Tinnings' latest move, during Marybeth's pregnancy with
Nathan, was the start of an unexpected new friendship. Pressured
by the Cleveland Avenue landlord to find another apartment, they
answered an advertisement in the *Schenectady Gazette*. Over the
telephone a meeting was arranged with Charles Ray, the owner of
341 McClellan Street. As he let the Tinnings into his house one
evening after work, Marybeth exclaimed in surprise, 'Oh, my God,
it's the mailman!'

Chuck Ray, a letter carrier for the U.S. Postal Service, always
stopped at the Shoporama Flavorland for his midday break. He
and Marybeth had been on first-name terms for some time without
knowing much about each other. Chuck was a warmhearted extrovert, tall and good-looking, the kind of man who with very little
encouragement will tell his life story frankly and in detail. Marybeth
always had a ready smile for such good-natured customers. Now
she was surprised to discover another side of him, that of an astute
property owner.

Early in their marriage Chuck and Janet Ray took out a mortgage
on the McClellan Street house, living in one of its apartments and
renting the other. After a few years they moved to the home they
really wanted, an attractive, modern house surrounded by trees in
the semi-rural community of Guilderland, about three miles south
of Schenectady. Instead of selling the McClellan Street property,
they kept it as an investment. It was important to Chuck to have
dependable tenants, and he was prepared to sacrifice some of his

rental income to get them. Joe Tinning and his pregnant wife struck him as just the kind of people he was looking for, and he agreed to let them have the upstairs apartment for about two-thirds the rent they might have been charged elsewhere. He had no idea that their last landlord had given them notice, let alone the reason why. On the basis of what he already knew of Marybeth, he saw no need to ask for references.

Joe arranged the move around the time that Marybeth was in hospital giving birth to Nathan. Chuck Ray loved children, so after church one Sunday morning he took Janet and their two small daughters to McClellan Street to see the new baby. This was their only glimpse of him. Five months later, while Chuck was out of town doing two weeks' service as a naval reservist, Nathan died.

Again Chuck and Janet stopped by their old house, this time to offer condolences. In appreciation of their kindness Joe invited the Rays to a General Electric staff outing. They reciprocated by taking the Tinnings to some post office social functions. This led to the two families' going on joint camping trips – south to the Catskills and farther afield to the shores of Maine and Massachusetts. The Rays already owned a family-size trailer. The Tinnings bought a smaller, secondhand one. Over several vacations they had some good times together.

As a boy Joe had gone on camping trips with his parents, but this was a new experience for Marybeth, and she was nervous about it, "One time we took a hiking trail and came to a place where we had to climb some rocks," Chuck recalled. "She kept saying she couldn't do it, even though I was telling her, step by step, where to put her feet." He was surprised at how little self-confidence she had.

It was the Rays' impression that their new friends had a caring and comfortable marriage in which Marybeth was dominant. She could be demanding and petulant, and she hated to be teased; but they forgave her idiosyncrasies because of all she had suffered. She told them that before Nathan she had lost her father and three children in a sixty-day period. Actually it happened over six months. She never mentioned her fourth baby, Timothy. They thought Nathan was the fourth.

Marybeth could also be endearing, planning affectionate surprises and buying extravagant gifts for Chuck and Janet, as well as for

Joe. Joe struck them as dependable, even-tempered, and a more careful spender than his wife.

"Marybeth could get mad," Chuck commented, "but I never saw Joe mad."

The Tinnings seemed very happy in their new apartment. It was pleasant and quite spacious, and Marybeth enjoyed decorating it. Childless again, she had only her home and job to occupy her. Soon she became a familiar sight on McClellan Street as she hurried to Flavorland in her uniform, a light blue polyester dress with a white trim, worn with low-heeled shoes. In this prescribed outfit she seemed to feel at ease. At other times she would agonize over what to wear and usually end up in the standard outfit of the small-time housewife: polyester slacks or a wraparound skirt with a nylon knit top or cotton blouse. Such clothes as these hung, rack after rack, in the neon-lit chain stores of the Mohawk Mall, where she loved to shop. Despite her earlier extravagances of makeup she seemed too uncertain of herself to be adventurous.

When she felt the need of something special to wear, she asked Carol for advice. Her sister-in-law had style and a self-assurance which Marybeth envied. Carol's taste showed in the imaginative— sometimes daring—way she could put a few inexpensive items of clothing together, and in the decor of her home, where she and Andy had put up hammered wood beams, giving this standard modern house the appearance of a country cottage with charm and individuality. Carol made it look even more welcoming by adding masses of fresh green plants. It was the kind of touch which Marybeth could never quite bring off.

Marybeth's relationship with Carol was tenuous and contradictory. She seemed to envy her, yet she did not like her. But in one important respect Marybeth had the edge on her sister-in-law. She was accepted, even cherished, by her husband's parents. She was also the only one likely to give them the grandchildren they yearned for. Joe and Andy were the sixth generation of Tinnings to live in this part of the country, and the family could be traced directly back to an English ancestor. It was a matter of pride to their parents that the bloodline should be perpetuated. They made a fuss over every baby that Marybeth produced and mourned with her and Joe at every death. Edna Tinning clung to the hope that there was some genetic incompatibility between her son and his wife which might be overcome, and she admired Marybeth for her continued efforts to rear a child.

Carol and Andy decided not to risk parenthood. What with Joel's birth defect on one side and all these suspicions of genetic problems in the Tinning family, they thought it safer to adopt. Amanda, a beautiful fair-haired baby, was only five days old when she came into their family in September 1977, and she was instantly cherished. Amanda's arrival also helped create a bond with the older Tinnings, who had loved and lost five grandchildren. Two years had passed since Nathan died, the longest period of childlessness in Marybeth's twelve-year marriage. She was worried about this and seemed to resent the focus of family attention being upon Amanda. So she made an appointment with her former obstetrician, Dr. August Schwenk, and asked for his help with what she described as an infertility problem. She was in her early thirties, had gone through five healthy pregnancies, and Dr. Schwenk thought he had long since seen the last of her.

'When she came to my office, we were very nice to her, but we told her to consult another doctor,' he recalled.

In her self-made game of one-upmanship with Carol, Marybeth then decided to adopt a baby. By the 1970's this was almost impossible through the established channels of reputable adoption agencies. There would have been exhaustive inquiries into the family history and a long waiting list for an adoptable, healthy, white infant. Legalized abortion and society's changed attitude toward unmarried mothers had almost eliminated the traditional source of supply—the single woman with the unplanned pregnancy.

There was another option, one which established adoption agencies had begun to view with alarm. A few lawyers and doctors were acting as baby brokers, encouraging unmarried pregnant women not to have abortions but instead to sign over their babies at birth to childless couples. Money, a lump sum for the birth mother and a commission for the broker, would exchange hands. In most cases the broker would not reveal the identity of the mother or the couple to each other.

Marybeth and Joe entered into such an agreement. Marybeth told different stories about how this was arranged. In one version the go-between was a woman doctor in Guilderland. In another it was a lawyer from Albany. In both versions this person was so sorry for Marybeth in her bereavements that he or she went to unusual lengths to arrange a quick adoption. Marybeth told a Flavorland colleague that the fee was five thousand dollars.

She and Joe were advised that a baby would be ready for them in the early spring of 1978. As the weeks passed, a complication developed. Marybeth became pregnant.

She reacted very differently to this discovery from the time when she was a foster mother. Although she could have backed out of the adoption agreement, she became all the more anxious for it to go through. She even worried that she might be refused a baby because one of her own was on the way.

Within three months she became a mother twice over. Michael, her adoptive child, was born on August 3, 1978. A neighbor remembers his being brought to the house by two women and Marybeth's delight in showing him off. ("She was on a cloud, tickled pink.") Her own daughter, Mary Frances, was born on October 29. Like her five dead siblings, this baby was blond and pretty. Michael looked very different. Marybeth explained that his olive complexion and black hair were inherited from an Italian father. His mother, she believed, was a young unmarried Schenectady woman of Anglo-Saxon origins. Both babies were healthy and immensely appealing— Michael for his sunny nature and Mary Frances for her delicate features and coloring.

"With two babies you must feel happy," Chuck Ray remarked to Joe.

"Yes, I'm really happy now," Joe replied.

Chuck commented: "He enjoyed babies as much as I did. Janet and I got very close to Mary Frances and Michael. We all went Christmas shopping together in the mall, and I remember Marybeth wheeling Mary Frances. She and Joe seemed so pleased to have a family again."

The babies were taken to Flavorland to be admired by the staff. Years later Sue Normington still remembered holding Mary Frances in her arms while Marybeth chatted with her colleagues. Marybeth was so involved in this conversation that she set her baby down, precariously, on one of the high backless stools by the counter. Sue was appalled at how easily Mary Frances could have fallen on the hard floor. So she picked her up and cuddled her until Marybeth finished talking. The baby was wearing a pink knitted sweater suit, and with her fair hair she looked like an infant version of her mother. Sue thought she was adorable.

On January 20, 1979 tragedy struck again. Marybeth rushed into St. Clare's emergency room with a lifeless Mary Frances in her arms and a familiar story about finding her unconscious in her crib. The emergency room staff was able to revive her with oxygen before there was brain damage. In medical jargon this was a case of "aborted SIDS," an infant in the early stages of Sudden Infant Death Syndrome who responded to resuscitation attempts. Mary Frances was three months old, an age when SIDS often strikes. Her symptoms fitted what was known of the syndrome, which was not a great deal.

As it was imperfectly understood at the time, a SIDS death was precipitated by a dysfunction of the brainstem, resulting in the baby's spontaneous failure to draw the next breath. Only a very small percentage of infants was thought to be at risk, and only in the early months of life. In some of these cases the breathing mechanism might fail only momentarily. Like the motor engine which sputters, seems about to die, then kicks back on, a baby might hover on the brink of unconsciousness, then begin to breathe again and recover unharmed. From all outward appearances, this could have happened to Mary Frances. Although she seemed to recover completely, doctors at St. Clare's insisted on putting her in the pediatric ward for about two weeks so that she could be carefully watched.

Among doctors and nurses who worked on the ward, opinions on the cause of the crisis were divided. Some were suspicious of Marybeth; others argued that there must be a genetic flaw in the family. None of them wanted to believe that she had anything to do with Mary Frances's condition or with the deaths of her five earlier children; indeed, such a heinous act was almost unbelievable. All those on the medical staff who came in contact with Marybeth thought she was strange and were bothered by her disconcerting habit of looking away from the person she was talking to. One doctor used the word "flat" in his attempt to define a personality which struck him as two-dimensional, superficial, even unfeeling. Nevertheless, Marybeth seemed truly to care for her babies. Pediatric nurses get to know by instinct whether an infant feels secure and cherished, or isolated and abandoned, and are sensitive to all the nuances in between. Several of them noted that everything about Mary Frances indicated that she had been loved from the day she was born.

There was other evidence in Marybeth's favor. There was the fact that she had willingly agreed to the records of her children who died at Ellis Hospital being sent to St. Clare's. She could have refused to sign the permission slip. But she did not even argue about it.

There was also her pediatrician's support of her. Dr. Mele, nominally head of pediatrics at St. Clare's, was one of the most respected physicians in Schenectady, and he believed in her innocence. He was one of a dying breed of old-fashioned family doctors who would sit at children's bedsides in the middle of the night for as long as an emergency lasted, who never refused poor patients, for lack of funds, and who made themselves available at all hours. He was probably owed more money and did less about collecting his debts than any other doctor in town. He was a small, nervous, irascible man with a heavy Italian accent and a heart of gold. Over the best part of a lifetime he had cared for thousands of Schenectady babies, and at least two generations of local mothers had their favorite Dr. Mele stories. One of the most touching went back to the pre-sneaker era, when replacing outgrown leather shoes cost more money than some parents could afford. In those depressed days a poor mother would sometimes come into his office with a barefoot child in tow.

"Doesn't that child have shoes?" he would want to know.

Before the mother could stammer a reply, he would snap, "Just you go to the Junior Bootery on Jay Street and tell them that Dr. Mele sent you. And don't let me see that child again without shoes."

He was lovable and admirable, and for a long time he refused to believe that Marybeth Tinning was capable of harming her babies. He saw it as his job to reassure and encourage mothers so that they in turn would be reassuring and encouraging to their children. He would be rough on parents when he thought they were neglectful or abusive, but in his kind of practice child neglect and abuse usually went along with poverty and ignorance.

This was obviously not the case in the Tinning household. Marybeth's children always seemed cared for and content. Frustrated by his inability to diagnose the cause of their deaths, Dominick Mele searched his memory and his reference books for some hint of an obscure disease or genetic aberration. He had been Marybeth's pediatrician since Nathan was born and, with some knowledge of the family history, had hoped to save that child from SIDS by prescribing an apnea monitor. But even if a monitor had been in use when Nathan was stricken, it might not have saved him. Now Mary Frances had come close to the same fate.

When some of the pediatric nurses at St. Clare's timidly suggested to him that perhaps Marybeth was doing something to her children, Mele defensively insisted that she was a good mother. The only conclusion he had been able to reach was that there was "a death gene" in the family. He was determined to find out what it was.

In Marybeth's defense the most striking evidence of all was her own behavior while Mary Frances was in hospital. She hung around the pediatric ward for most of the daytime hours and slept there at night, sometimes on a cot, sometimes dozing fitfully and uncomfortably in a waiting-room chair. Whenever a sympathetic nurse was free to listen, she poured out her troubles. She spoke of her loneliness and isolation, of the friends who had deserted her, of the neighbors who crossed the street to avoid passing her house as if it were stricken by plague, of their whispered suspicions that she was killing her children. She said that even her own mother had rejected her.

She looked so stricken, so desperately in need of love and support that it was hard not to pity her. Or to believe her story. Yet there was this strangeness about her, the avoidance of eye contact, the impression that she was saying the words without feeling the emotions.

"You wanted to put your arms around her and tell her, 'You poor thing,' " said Patricia "Trish" McBreen, who was one of the pediatric staff nurses at that time. "She looked so defenseless and destroyed. And yet the other half of you was ready to make a hot line report to Social Services."

Patricia "Pat" Pilcher, who was the director of pediatric nurses on the day shift, had a similar experience. "Whenever I talked to Marybeth, I felt like I was divided into two people," she said. "I knew of the earlier deaths, and it was my feeling that she could have asphyxiated those babies. But then she acted just like a normal mother, and when she would tell me that people suspected her and that she was innocent, I would be almost convinced. Yet always there was something that pulled me back. She never could look at me while she was talking. Her eyes would be downcast or glancing to the side."

There had been some drastic changes in the system in the seven years since an Ellis Hospital nurse was told by a doctor to keep her suspicions about Marybeth to herself. As the result of an increased awareness of child abuse, the Child Protective Unit had been created in Schenectady's Department of Social Services. Nurses now had the freedom to report suspicious cases without getting a doctor's permission and without risk of reprisal if they were proved wrong. Both their anonymity and their professional reputations were protected. The new unit was not the most skilled or efficient, but its staff was caring and well intentioned. And it was obliged to investigate any suspicion of child abuse as soon as it was reported.

Trish McBreen was one of the most outspoken nurses on St. Clare's pediatric team, and there was no doubt in her mind that the life-threatening trauma of Mary Frances Tinning might be a case of child abuse and that she had a duty to report it. Pat Pilcher felt the same way, and since Pat was the senior nurse, she volunteered to make the report. Pat did Dr. Mele the courtesy of discussing this with him first and was not surprised when he disagreed with her. Where was the evidence, he wanted to know, that Marybeth was abusive? He pointed out that right now she was at her ailing child's bedside, a typical concerned parent.

The nurses had more opportunity to observe her. Like Trish McBreen, Pat Pilcher noted what she described as "this dichotomy between what she said and how I think she acted." She had several discussions about Marybeth with Dr. Mele, whom she respected enormously.

Pat felt comfortable enough to tell him that she thought his death gene theory was wishful thinking. She felt there might be a more sinister explanation for the scourge which devastated the Tinning family. She was not to be deterred from making the hot line report and felt it only fair that Marybeth should be told about it. None of the nurses was anxious to take on this job. In any event, Pat saw it as her responsibility. She braced herself to break the news and was surprised at how calmly it was received. There was no outrage, no fearfulness, no pleading. Just quiet acceptance.

Pat also decided that the interaction between mother and baby should be carefully documented. At her direction the day nurses kept a log of the time Marybeth spent with Mary Frances and of her behavior with the child. As the days passed, this merely became a lengthening catalog of trivia: "Mother cradled baby in her arms for half an hour. . . . Mother talked to baby. . . . Mother fed baby. . . . Mother was concerned that baby might not be taking enough formula. . . ." It was the story of every devoted parent with a sick child in hospital.

As another precaution, a roster of nurses was given the special assignment of keeping a day-and-night watch on Mary Frances. Some nurses told Pat they would rather not take on this job.

"It meant having a lot to do with Marybeth, and some of them suspected she had tried to harm her baby," Pat explained. "This made it difficult for them to face her and talk to her like a normal person. I understood how they felt and tried to honor their requests. I felt the baby deserved the best of care."

In response to Pat Pilcher's hot line report, a Social Services case-worker visited St. Clare's and questioned Marybeth as well as the hospital staff. The nurses had only unsubstantiated suspicions and were not all in agreement. At least one staff pediatrician suspected Marybeth, but Dr. Mele is believed to have told Social Services that he felt she was a good mother. There were simply not enough grounds for action. And by then Mary Frances was doing so well that there was no justification for keeping her in hospital.

Still fretting about the possibility of an inborn genetic error which he might have missed, Dr. Mele decided to have Mary Frances examined by some of the best pediatric specialists in the country. When she was due to be discharged from St. Clare's, he arranged for her to be taken by ambulance to the prestigious Boston Children's Hospital, a journey of almost two hundred miles. She was kept there for several days while chromosomal studies were done, as well as body scans, X rays, cardiac and blood tests. All the findings were normal. As a precaution the Boston doctors recommended that Mary Frances should be put on an apnea monitor. And that is how Marybeth took her home.

TWELVE

We wanted to take the baby from her. She was such a
cute little girl, and we knew something would happen
to her.

—*Flavorland waitress*

On February 20, 1979, a month to the day after Mary Frances was
first admitted to St. Clare's Hospital, Marybeth brought her back
to the same emergency room in full cardiac arrest. She related that
she had fed the baby at about 6:30 A.M., then put her back in her
crib. An hour later she heard the monitor's alarm and found her
unconscious.

This time Mary Frances was past help. The emergency room
staff was able to resuscitate her, but there was irreversible brain
damage. She was put on a respirator and sent to the intensive
care unit. Nurses who had recently looked after Mary Frances so
scrupulously were heartbroken to see her in this condition. They
also had a lot of questions.

It was five minutes' journey from Marybeth's apartment to St.
Clare's Hospital, whether she hurried there on foot with the baby
in her arms, got out her car, or called an ambulance. A baby can
die in five minutes. Why did Marybeth never try to save her own
child? Why did these crises always happen when only she was
there? Yet if she were the cause of them, why would she return to
the very hospital where a hot line report had just been made about
her?

It was, of course, closer to her home. And of the two general
hospitals in Schenectady, Marybeth felt more comfortable at St.
Clare's. At one time she favored Ellis, but after she had taken Joey,
Barbara, and Timothy there on the point of death, three fatal
episodes within two years, an Ellis staff member told her sharply

that she ought to get her tubes tied unless she aimed to fill up the cemetery. In a Catholic hospital she would be unlikely to hear a remark like that.

Most of the St. Clare's emergency room doctors came from cultures with fatalistic attitudes toward infant death; as Indians, Filipinos and Chinese they had grown up accepting it as part of life. Faced with a woman who went on having babies after several had died, they were less likely to ask tough questions. Their American counterparts at Ellis Hospital might be more suspicious. In any event, Marybeth avoided them.

Mary Frances's last hours were painfully remembered by Chuck Ray. It was not true that Marybeth's friends had deserted her, any more than it was true that her mother had withdrawn her support. Eventually these things happened, but not for some time. Right now Chuck Ray was spending most of his off-duty hours at the hospital, running errands for Marybeth, keeping her and Joe company in the waiting room while Marybeth's in-laws took care of Michael, all of them pitching in, just as they had when Mary Frances was last at St. Clare's. Joe would show up at the end of his day's work, looking sad and withdrawn. It was hard to tell what he thought.

In the two days that it took Mary Frances to die, Marybeth behaved like any caring mother about to lose a beloved child. She wept. She asked, many times, if something could be done to save her baby.

At Albany Medical Center, fifteen miles away, there was a pediatric intensive care unit to which Dr. Mele recommended transferring Mary Frances.

"Are they going to be able to do any more for her?" Marybeth asked.

"No," she was told. "It will just be supportive treatment."

"Then I don't want her moved." She seemed to have great faith in St. Clare's.

"She asked me if I thought Mary Frances would survive this," Pat Pilcher recalled. "I told her, 'No, we are just keeping her alive with the machine now.' She seemed griefstricken. When she finally accepted that there was no hope for Mary Frances, she said she wanted her to die at St. Clare's."

Since there was no brain activity, Catholic doctrine permitted the baby's removal from the life support system. The decision was up to the parents. That meant Marybeth. She talked to many of the hospital staff about it, all of whom advised her to have her daughter taken off the respirator. But she could not bring herself to do this.

Chuck Ray tried hard to persuade her. "Mary Frances, as we knew her, has gone," he said. "But Michael needs you."

Marybeth was adamant. "I am going to leave her on this machine until her heart stops."

"And how long do you think that will be?"

"I don't know. But I'll stay here as long as it takes."

It would not have taken long. But Chuck did not know that.

"Michael could be eight years old before this ends," he argued.

After two agonizing days Marybeth agreed. "The priests, the nurses, everybody kept telling her there was no point in keeping Mary Frances alive," Chuck commented. "If I had been in Marybeth's shoes, I would have fought all the way as she did. But that doesn't mean it would have been right. In the end I think I had a big part in persuading her to take Mary Frances off the respirator."

Some of the nurses, meantime, were conjecturing whether Marybeth had precipitated her daughter's fatal crisis—and, if so, how. The more they watched her behavior, the more they were bewildered. She seemed to care tremendously about losing this child, yet the baby's symptoms defied medical explanation. A case of some children's being asphyxiated by having Saran wrap put over their faces had recently been reported in the newspapers, and they wondered if something like this might have happened to Mary Frances. It passed through at least one nurse's mind that this baby might have been electrocuted while in her bath, but that seemed improbable because there were no burn marks. Poisoning was dismissed as a possibility after Mary Frances's stomach contents were aspirated and sent for analysis. Whatever might have happened to her, the clues were likely to be obscured by the trauma of resuscitation attempts in the emergency room.

Dr. Alan Lobovits, chief of pediatrics at St. Clare's, wrote a long summary of the case for Dr. Mele and recommended a very thorough autopsy. He was frank about his suspicions that Mary Frances might not have died from natural causes. While she was alive, Dr. Lobovits consulted other specialists who suggested rare medical conditions which might explain what had happened to this baby. But none of these diseases fitted the symptoms he saw, or her medical history.

"We did a number of tests for poisons and for metabolic diseases without really coming up with anything," he said. "That made me suspicious that something else might be going on. But what held me back was lack of evidence. Even though a doctor is protected under the child protection laws, it's an awesome thought that one might accuse someone of murder unjustifiably. That's why I was so intent on trying to find some shred of evidence which might indicate a traumatic death or an intentional homicide."

The autopsy was done at St. Clare's by Dr. Janet Christman, an experienced staff pathologist. "I remember asking her to look very carefully in light of all that had happened," Dr. Lobovits recalled.

She did so. But as she said later, "In an infant there's virtually no way of detecting smothering. It looks just like crib death."

Dr. Christman was familiar with the Tinning family. Seven years earlier she had done the autopsy on Jennifer, and had found "huge abscesses in the brain." As time went on, she wondered whether the shock of this week-old baby's death may have "tipped her mother's mental balance." This made her very much aware of the possible implications of Mary Frances's death.

At the end of her examination Dr. Christman felt very frustrated. "I went through everything I could think of to find a cause of death," she said. "I looked thoroughly at the heart, took a number of cultures for bacteria, checked for the presence of drugs or poisons, and all these tests were negative. Mary Frances had a touch of pneumonia, but that could have developed after she came into the hospital brain-dead. It was not significant.

"The only room left for doubt was that there might have been some heart defect which we could not find. Things can go wrong with the heart which you cannot always see. And we cannot determine everything at autopsy because of changes which happen after death. In this case we were suspicious, but we could not prove anything."

As the autopsy finding, Dr. Christman wrote: "No anatomic cause of death." She intended to leave the case open. But Dr. Mele signed the death certificate and entered the cause of death as SIDS. Although this did not contradict Dr. Christman's open verdict (since, strictly speaking, SIDS is not a diagnosis), it gave a name to Mary Frances's condition and effectively closed the case. It also precluded investigation by the medical examiner since there was no requirement for SIDS deaths to be reported to his office. According to the official records, therefore, there was nothing suspicious about the protracted passing of Mary Frances Tinning, and, as the district attorney told Police Officers Dan O'Connor and John Zampella, no grounds for a police inquiry.

Three weeks after Mary Frances's death, Marybeth and Joe received a touching letter from Dr. William Berenberg, the specialist who had supervised the metabolic studies on Mary Frances at Boston Children's Hospital. Dr. Berenberg, professor of pediatrics at Harvard Medical School, knew very little about the deaths of the five earlier Tinning children and, as he said later, had "no reason to suspect that anything immoral was going on." On March 15, 1979, he wrote to their parents: "I called Dr. Mele yesterday and was deeply saddened to hear about Mary. I know that both of you did everything possible to prevent her tragic outcome. All of the special studies which were done here have turned out to be negative. I still feel that the primary difficulty is some unusual metabolic error, and probably one which could not be prevented. Please accept my true and considerable sympathy."

Mary Frances was buried alongside her five siblings, on a bitter February day. Despite the icy weather, there was only a slightly smaller crowd than usual for the service at the Daly Funeral Home, and at least fifteen people went on to the cemetery. Unaccustomed to the lack of emotion at Tinning funerals, Chuck Ray felt that "Marybeth held herself together pretty good." He was also surprised to discover Marybeth's religion. He had assumed that like Joe, Janet and himself, she was Protestant. But at the graveside service he was embarrassed by his different knowledge of a familiar ritual.

"When the Lord's Prayer was said, all the others had finished while I kept going. That's how I found out that Marybeth was Catholic. The subject had never come up before."

Marybeth's religion seemed less important to her than it used to be. Her failure to mention it to the Rays in four years of friendship was only one indication. Another was her almost casual attitude toward having Mary Frances baptized. It was left until the baby's life was in danger and was done in the hospital. Eleven years earlier Marybeth had gone to a lot of trouble to arrange the christening of her first child, Barbara, even after she encountered a peculiarly parochial brand of bigotry. At that time the priests and congregation at the Catholic church in her Schenectady neighborhood were predominantly Italian-American, and it was made clear to Marybeth that she and her child, of English and Irish stock, did not belong.

A parishioner related: "There was an elderly priest who would not baptize Barbara because the Tinnings weren't Italian. It was all right for Marybeth to go to his church and put money in his box, but not to receive the sacraments. So she took her baby to St. Thomas's, which was two blocks in the other direction, and had her baptized there."

Marybeth insisted on a Catholic baptism, although her Protestant in-laws were not pleased about it. Her Catholicism was one of the reasons she gave for having so many children. She said it was against her religion to use contraceptives, although Edna Tinning may have been closer to the truth when she said that her daughter-in-law craved love and that having babies helped her feel fulfilled.

Marybeth's mother, who had brought her up in the Catholic faith, had more difficulty understanding her daughter's motives. From time to time she would ask one of Marybeth's Flavorland colleagues, "Why does she keep having babies?"

The answer never varied: "Mrs. Roe, I have no idea."

When Mary Frances was born, Marybeth agreed that this baby would be the last. Since Joe had apparently done nothing about a vasectomy, she finally succumbed to the persuasions of friends, relatives and doctors to have a tubal ligation; at least, so she said. This surgical procedure, sometimes done after childbirth, effectively sterilizes a women by crushing or severing her fallopian tubes. To the relief of all who knew her, Marybeth announced that she "had her tubes tied" after Mary Frances's birth. As a Catholic hospital, St. Clare's did not permit this procedure, so Marybeth said she went to Bellevue Maternity Hospital, where Timothy was born, to have it done. Her report that she had been sterilized made Mary Frances's death, at the age of four months, all the more tragic. Now there could be no more natural children to provide the seventh generation of American Tinnings.

Once again the baby clothes were washed, folded and hurriedly given away. This time there really was no point in keeping them. Chuck and Janet Ray, ever ready to make the bereavement less painful for Marybeth, took Mary Frances's belongings to an unmarried mothers' home in Albany. When the previous baby, Nathan, died, Marybeth had insisted upon giving his clothes to her sister-in-law Sandy Roe, who was pregnant. It did not seem to occur to her that if she did not want these reminders around, her relatives might feel the same way. Sandy's opinion was not asked. She passed the clothes on to a poor mother without telling her where they came from.

"I could not have used them," she said. "Every time I looked at those things I saw dead babies."

Michael, however, showed every sign of flourishing. A lovable, sturdy, contented extrovert, he was six and a half months old when Mary Frances died. Some of the Flavorland waitresses and the McClellan Street neighbors were so taken with him that they said, and clearly meant, they would be happy to rear him as their own. None of these white women showed any prejudice about the fact that Michael's racial origins were increasingly apparent as he developed. His tuft of dark baby hair had grown into a mass of tight black curls. As his features formed more clearly, there was a breadth to his nose and a fullness to his lips which left no doubt of his paternal ancestry. It was not Italian, as Marybeth continued to insist. It was black. She had such difficulty accepting this that the more Michael's racial identity became obvious, the less often she took him to Flavorland.

Nevertheless, she seemed to be deeply attached to him. The adoption had not yet been formalized, and she worried that his natural mother might change her mind and want him back. When Marybeth was not living in the middle of drama, she enjoyed creating it, and one of the stories she told at this time had to do with her sitting in a restaurant and overhearing a conversation between two women in the next booth. They were talking about a baby that one of them had given up for adoption and were wondering if it was possible to discover the adoptive parents' address and demand custody. Marybeth convinced herself that one of these women was Michael's mother.

Chuck Ray adored Michael and became like an uncle to him. He was also trying his best to help Marybeth and Joe recover from the loss of Mary Frances. As soon as spring came, he suggested that the two families go on a camping trip together, to North Lake in the Catskills. While they were there, Michael became very fretful.

That was unusual for him. On their return to Schenectady, Mary-beth took him to Dr. Mele, who diagnosed a hernia.

Michael was admitted to St. Clare's for routine surgery. Although no complications were expected, the hospital staff was more cautious than usual when they saw the name Tinning. They noted areas on Michael's back where the skin had a different pigmentation, a sure sign of black ancestry. The surgeon's reaction was to request a blood test for sickle-cell anemia, a congenital disease which affects blacks only, and he did not want to operate until it was done.

Marybeth refused her consent. Despite all the visual and medical evidence, she continued to insist that Michael was not black. It was explained to her that the sickle-cell test was a vital precaution because if Michael did have the condition, the trauma of surgery could cause his round blood cells to form into a sickle-cell shape and clump together in a clot. This could precipitate a life-threatening crisis. If Michael was at risk, the operating room staff needed to be prepared for an emergency.

Marybeth remained adamant. She got into an argument with the anesthesiologist and became very upset. Eventually he gave up trying to persuade her, and Michael had his operation without the precaution of the sickle-cell test.

"We were all on pins and needles," Pat Pilcher recalled. "I know I was. Marybeth stayed at the hospital through the surgery and helped to care for Michael afterwards. He was fine. Again she acted like a devoted mother, but she did not seem to understand that she had taken a serious risk."

THIRTEEN

I used to wonder how those babies died, but who was I
to point a finger

—*Neighbor*

Larry Daly's funeral home was diagonally across McClellan Street
from Marybeth's apartment. He knew her well by now, and it
struck him that whenever she passed his place, she was either
pregnant or pushing a baby carriage. In the late summer of 1979
she was in both states at the time. Michael was a year old, and
despite her report of having had her tubes tied, Marybeth was
expecting another baby.

She had conceived barely a month after Mary Frances died. The
Rays need not have given away the baby clothes, nor the in-laws
lost hope of grandchildren. Marybeth was surely the most fecund
woman in Schenectady. If she really had been sterilized, hers was
one of those rare tubal ligations which failed. And that was her
story. In one version there was a male obstetrician who was so
dismayed by the poor results of his surgery that he invited her to
"have this one on me," meaning he would waive his fee for delivering her next baby. In another version it was a woman obstetrician
who did the useless operation. According to Marybeth, when she
became pregnant for the seventh time, this woman took her out to
lunch and promised to forgive an outstanding bill if she would have
her fallopian tubes retied after this baby was born. In the version
Marybeth told her mother, who was not at all pleased about this
latest pregnancy, her operation was merely "a partial tubal."

None of these accounts tallied with the recollections of the doctors she named. The male obstetrician who allegedly invited her to
"have this one on me" had not sterilized Marybeth. He tried to

[136]

persuade her, but she refused. Neither had the woman obstetrician done the surgery, although Marybeth did make an appointment with her to discuss a tubal ligation. She arrived at the doctor's office on time but was told there would be a long wait. She became impatient, left, and never returned.

By now the Flavorland waitresses had given up having baby showers for her. They were dismayed to see her pregnant again and began to estimate the months to the next funeral. Some of them were angry with her because they thought she lied about having her tubes tied. She had told them repeatedly that there was a genetic problem, which led them to wonder why on earth she would go on having children. But it was one thing she excelled at: her pregnancies came easily, and her babies were beautiful. She also seemed to take perverse pleasure in being the subject of a medical mystery. After Mary Frances had been sent to Boston Children's Hospital, Marybeth boasted that some of the top specialists in the country were doing a genetic study of her family. "And they have a file on us this thick."

She was usually secretive about her pregnancies until they became obvious. This was easy for her because she carried her babies discreetly; only in the last few weeks would she "suddenly blow up," as a fellow waitress put it. Some of her acquaintances suspected that she concealed her condition until it was too late for anyone to suggest an abortion. She clearly wanted to go on having babies, not necessarily for the sake of producing children but for the sense of importance and fulfillment which pregnancy gave her.

She gave birth to Jonathan, her seventh natural child, at St. Clare's Hospital on November 19, 1979. He was a month premature and weighed less than five pounds. Except for Jennifer, all of Marybeth's earlier children had come into the world in perfect health, but in the homely phrase of one Schenectady doctor Jonathan wasn't made right. None of his physical defects was serious enough to prevent him from living a normal life, and the most troublesome of them could be corrected by surgery. But their very existence led to speculation that there might be other anomalies, as yet unrecognized, which could cause problems later on.

Jonathan was found to have two umbilical blood vessels instead of three, a condition which is often associated with an abnormality of the kidneys. His testicles had not descended. He had hypospadias, a malformation of the penis in which the urinary opening is on the underside instead of at the tip. He was a good-looking baby, fair like his six dead siblings, but an early photograph of him catches an expression which looks blank and strained. This may have been a trick of the camera. Or there may have been good reason to worry about Jonathan.

Because he was premature, and even more because he was a Tinning, the nursery nurses at St. Clare's were unusually attentive to him. One of them was particularly struck by Marybeth's response.

"It was different," she said. "Usually the mothers of preemies are very appreciative of the special care that is given their babies. They realize they could have lost them and are grateful for all the extra effort the nurses make. But Marybeth Tinning had no reactions. Whenever I took the baby to her, she did not smile. She did not even look. Her gaze would be off to the side, looking over my shoulder at the wall. It was rare for her to make eye contact."

Like many of the pediatric nurses, this woman had conflicting emotions. "When Marybeth did not act normally. I was not surprised because I thought that nobody who had lost that many children could be normal. One part of me was sorry for her and wanted to take care of her. Another part of me could not believe that all these babies had died by themselves. She would even say that everyone hated her because they thought she was doing something to them. She was weird. One of my first thoughts was that she was a witch."

Jonathan was kept in hospital for a week or two longer than his mother. By the time he was discharged he was progressing well, and Dr. Mele undertook to watch him carefully. Suspecting that Jonathan's birth defects might provide a clue to his family's problems, he was even more determined to understand the nature of them and, if at all possible, to prevent their recurrence.

In a report to another specialist he wrote: "I have thoroughly explained the whole situation to the mother. Of course, it is still a great puzzle to us all so I cannot say that the mother understands it too clearly either. She is willing to participate and to go along with whatever testing I have asked to be done. She does not want the child taken away from her."

Still looking for clues to an inherited metabolic disorder, he sifted through the medical records of all the earlier Tinning children. One unusual finding stood out. With most of them a high level of blood ammonia was measured when they were close to death. Hyperammonemia, as the condition is known, is usually a complication of liver diseases like hepatitis and cirrhosis. It can cause convulsions and kill a patient. But it is rare in infants unless they have liver defects.

Both Barbara and Joey were reported to have had seizures (seen only by Marybeth). In the emergency room they also had elevated levels of blood ammonia. This combination led to the diagnosis of Reye's syndrome—in Barbara's case at the time of her death; in Joey's case, informally, as an afterthought because nothing else seemed to fit. When Dr. Mele looked back on their records several years later, much more was known about Reye's syndrome. Convulsions and hyperammonemia are part of it, but children with Reye's have other marked symptoms, which were not seen in either Barbara or Joey. Whatever had afflicted them was somehow different.

They did, however, have a condition in common with Timothy, Nathan and Mary Frances. These three also had hyperammonemia shortly before they died. The blood ammonia level of Jennifer, who died very differently from the others, had never been checked.

When the pieces of the puzzle were put together, it could be theorized that since five of the six dead children were know to have had hyperammonemia, all the offspring of Joe and Marybeth might be afflicted by a genetic defect in the urea cycle which caused the elevated ammonia level. This might have poisoned their brains and caused their deaths. Specialists at Boston Children's Hospital who saw Mary Frances seriously considered this possibility. Although both parents were healthy with no family histories of genetic disorders, each of them might carry a recessive gene. But even if they did, it was statistically improbable that all their children would be defective.

There were other problems about the genetic theory. Children who have inborn errors in the urea cycle are sickly from birth. They suffer from frequent diarrhea and vomiting. They are pale and underweight. Marybeth's children were not like that. Until they were suddenly stricken, their health appeared to be excellent. Another strange factor was although Mary Frances's blood ammonia level was an enormously high 339 micrograms percent when she was admitted to hospital for the second time, near death, it dropped to a normal 72 three hours later, while she was being sustained in the intensive care unit. It was baffling.

In his busy pediatric practice Dr. Mele had a devoted nurse. Sandra "Sandy" Ross, who ended up working for him for twenty-one years. She was pink-cheeked and warmhearted, and she looked like every infant's favorite aunt. She loved babies and worried a great deal about what she saw happening in the Tinning family.

"Do you think something in their apartment could be killing these babies?" she asked the doctor whenever the subject came up. "Some chemicals which no one knows are there? Something in the insulation perhaps?"

The reply was always the same. No, he was sure all that had been checked.

Among Dr. Mele's patients were the children of Marybeth's sisters-in-law. Both Carol Tinning and Sandy Roe told him of their distress at losing so many nieces and nephews, and both sensed his frustration. Carol wept in his office after Timothy's death. "Can't you do something to stop these babies dying?" she begged. He told her he was trying, but it was very difficult.

As Chuck Ray remarked, years later, "We were all so close to it we couldn't see what was happening."

Chuck sensed Marybeth and Joe were distancing themselves from him and Janet after Jonathan was born, and he thought they did this out of consideration for him because he was so grieved over the death of Mary Frances.

"They knew I loved that baby. And they knew there was a chance of Jonathan not making it. Marybeth told us that Mary Frances was born without tonsils, which means she was not put together correctly. And if her body wasn't developed perfectly, I figured that maybe her brain wasn't working perfectly and that's why she died. I was very naïve at this point. I accepted that the loss of all these children was genetic. Marybeth told us that Jonathan had only one kidney, so I felt she was protecting us in case anything happened to him. They both knew how I loved Mary Frances and how crushed I was when she died."

Chuck's sense was prophetic. But he did not remain entirely uninvolved. One evening, when Jonathan was eleven weeks old, he had a telephone call from Marybeth.

"Joe is on his way to you with Michael," she said. "We have to take Jonathan to the hospital."

A few minutes later Joe arrived at the Rays' home, clutching Michael and a bag full of toys. Janet and the children had gone out shopping. Alone in the house, Chuck was nonplussed at having to cope with an eighteen-month-old toddler by himself. But before he had time to think about it, Joe was gone, and Michael had made himself comfortable on the living-room floor among his toys. As Chuck remarked, "Joe knew he could count on us."

This first crisis with Jonathan was almost identical to that of Mary Frances. Marybeth took him to St. Clare's emergency room, unconscious. Some of the emergency room nurses cringed when they saw her. They knew why she was there and had difficulty dealing with her yet again. This time there was a slight variation to her story in that Joe was the first to notice that something was wrong with Jonathan. She related that Joe went to check on the baby and saw traces of blood in his mouth. He telephoned Dr. Mele's office, but the staff had left for the day, and it took a while for the answering service to contact one of Dr. Mele's partners. At that point Marybeth said she came in and reportedly found Jonathan at first pale and limp, then blue from lack of oxygen.

Like Mary Frances, Jonathan responded to resuscitation attempts in St. Clare's emergency room. His condition was stabilized, and if he had been anyone else's child, he might have been kept under observation for a while and then sent home. Because he was the seventh and only surviving Tinning baby, a genetic consultant—Dr. Mary Eleanor Toms—was called in, and she made arrangements for him to be admitted immediately to Boston Children's Hospital for intensive studies. She had trained there and felt confident that if Jonathan had a genetic problem, the Boston specialists would find it.

The urgency was thought to be so great that a New York Army National Guard plane was commandeered for this mercy mission. Accompanied by Dr. Toms, Jonathan was rushed to the Albany County Airport, a fifteen-minute journey by ambulance. There a twin-engine plane stood waiting to take off. It landed in Boston at midnight. This dramatic event made headlines in the local daily newspapers.

In Boston Jonathan was subjected to intensive tests. Every enzyme known to geneticists was checked, and all the findings were normal. His birth defects were judged to be unrelated to this crisis and either unimportant or correctable by routine surgery. In one doctor's description, he was "as wiggly and active a child as you can imagine." Like Mary Frances, he was sent directly home with an apnea monitor.

Three days later his mother took him back to St. Clare's emergency room. This time, like Mary Frances in her second crisis, he had suffered brain damage. Like her, he was barely alive and beyond hope. The similarities of the two cases, even to the timing, was uncanny. Doctors and nurses at St. Clare's felt they were reliving the same bad dream, down to the last dreadful detail.

Certainly Trish McBreen did. As a pediatric nurse who had been so involved in the last days of Mary Frances, she was utterly dismayed to be called into the emergency room to help resuscitate yet another Tinning baby.

"It was very cold in the emergency room," she remembered. "We warmed the baby up, wrapped him in blankets, got the IV line in with some difficulty, and were monitoring his vital signs. He was in full cardiac arrest when he was brought in, and essentially he was dead. We were able to resuscitate him a little and put him on a respirator. He was in our intensive care unit for two hours. Then he was sent to the pediatric intensive care unit at Albany Medical Center."

The doctors at St. Clare's strongly recommended this transfer. Although Marybeth had refused to agree to it for Mary Frances, she may have sensed that it would be impolitic to withhold consent for Jonathan. In any event, this time she made no objection.

The St. Clare's doctors did not think that the superior resources in Albany could save her baby. No one could. But the hospital's pediatric intensive care unit was better equipped to keep him on life support systems for as long as necessary. Meantime, there was a slim hope that perhaps the expert at Albany Medical Center could use this time to try to find an explanation which no one at St. Clare's—or even Boston Children's Hospital—had thought of. Every member of St. Clare's medical staff who had ever handled a Tinning baby was deeply troubled about the case. More and more of them were wondering whether Marybeth was doing something lethal to her babies. Some still clung to the genetic theory. But despite all the research and the ever-deepening suspicions, there was still no proof for either of these hypotheses.

The Albany doctors followed two courses. They had Jonathan

checked by almost every expert in the hospital, and as in all suspected cases of neglect or abuse, they made a hot line report to Social Services.

Dr. Richard Cimma, who was a resident in pediatrics at that time, recalled: "Some interviews were arranged with the parents; some investigations were undertaken. There were suspicions, but we saw nothing unusual about the way the parents behaved or responded to questions. They were very upset, and the mother stayed with her baby most of the time, just as we would have expected.

"Her story was that there had been no illness or accident. It had just happened. The baby was brain-damaged and in coma. We gave respiratory and cardiac support, and he lived long enough for all our experts to have a chance to look at him. Among them we had experts in neurology, endocrinology and metabolism. We ran tests for poisons and toxins, far more than we would normally have done. But despite all these evaluations, there was no explanation for what had happened to him.

"At least two of my colleagues said they had been involved in caring for earlier children in the family, that they had been suspicious, and that they had all gone through the routine of making reports to the authorities. There was certainly an awareness in the medical community, and we made continued efforts to try and solve the mystery.

"Despite all the work done on Jonathan, we could not produce enough hard evidence to go to the police. There are channels for pursuing suspicions alone, and those were followed."

In common with the experts who tried to find out why Mary Frances died, staff physicians at Albany Medical Center had another inevitable frustration.

"Before we saw Jonathan, there were intensive efforts to resuscitate him," Dr. Cimma added. "These would cover up any signs of suffocation which might, or might not, exist. When a child comes into an emergency room in the state Jonathan was in, doctors don't stop to look for cause. They concentrate on trying to revive him."

Like the Boston specialists, Dr. Cimma did not think that Jonathan's birth defects had any bearing on his fatal condition. "They indicated some kidney abnormality, but fifteen percent of the population have developmental kidney abnormalities, often without knowing it, and live to a ripe old age."

Comatose and kept alive by machines, Jonathan lingered for four weeks. This time Marybeth was not urged to let him die naturally. As long as a shred of life remained, doctors could continue their investigation. Once he died, there was only the hope of some unexpected finding by the pathologist.

Through this sad and tedious waiting period Marybeth was at Albany Medical Center daily. Her demeanor was the same as it had been when Mary Frances was dying. At first tearful and panicky, she soon became calm and unemotional. Whenever a sympathetic nurse was willing to listen, she would retell the tale of how friends had abandoned her because they suspected her of killing her children. But now she had another strange topic of conversation. She spoke of her ambition to be a funeral director. Earlier, when she had stopped by Daly's to ask what qualifications were necessary she was not taken very seriously, especially in light of her flippant remark that she must have bought a few bricks in the place. But as Jonathan lay dying, she astounded one doctor by confiding that she would love to have a career as a mortician.

Jonathan died on March 24, 1980. He survived ten days longer than Mary Frances. There brief lives were strikingly similar and, in a sense, a continuum. Jonathan was conceived right after Mary Frances died. Both were born in the late fall, flourished over Christmas, sickened early in new year, and failed to survive into spring. Both were taken on two emergency trips to St. Clare's; were referred to Boston Children's Hospital after the first crisis, appeared to recover, but a few days after returning home went into a coma which none of the Boston doctors had foreseen. In both cases this second crisis caused irreversible brain damage. Both infants were the subject of extensive but inconclusive medical studies.

An autopsy was performed on Jonathan by the Albany coroner's pathologist, Dr. Assaad Daoud. He had no access to reports of any of the earlier Tinning autopsies because they were filed in the adjoining county, Schenectady. For the same reason, the Schenectady medical examiner would not see his report, filed in Albany County. Each of them was limited to his own area of jurisdiction, and for all the communication that existed between the two coroners' offices, fifteen miles apart, they might have been at opposite ends of the earth.

Finding no obvious cause of death, Dr. Daoud recorded "etiology undetermined." At one point a high ammonia level was measured in Jonathan, but it was not thought to have contributed to his death. For the purposes of a death certificate, he was listed as having died of cardiopulmonary arrest. This was no news to anyone. Jonathan's heart and lungs had ceased to function a month before he died.

When the news of Jonathan's death reached the pediatric unit at St. Clare's, "a lot of questions were asked back and forth," according to Trish McBreen. "But there were no obvious answers, and nobody was ready to make accusations based on suspicions. We asked some of the doctors what theories they had, but they kept saying they needed to do other investigations, and that if Marybeth had done anything to her children, it would have been discovered. Doctors don't want to be involved in a court situation. If they go to court and can't prove what they think, they lay themselves open to further legal problems.

"Then there was the fact that they had already sent the last two Tinning children to Boston for testing. They had autopsies performed. Everybody was suspicious, and yet everything pointed to these being normal deaths. One of the problems is that when doctors have to put a name to an illness or certify a cause of death, they will not say, 'I don't know.' They have been taught that they are experts, that they have to know everything. It's part of the God complex. So they use phrases like 'cannot rule out' or 'appears to be' or 'similar to.' In that atmosphere it would take a very brave doctor to stick his neck out and accuse a mother of murder.

"Among the nurses we talked about suffocation, but none of the autopsies showed any signs of asphyxia, like broken blood vessels in the lungs. We didn't realize how quietly an infant can die when it is too tiny to put up a struggle."

Sudden Infant Death Syndrome did not seem right either. "It is rare for a SIDS baby to be found when it is on the point of death," Trish explained. "The infant is usually found lying on its abdomen, pressed against the side of the crib, and in most cases some time has elapsed before a parent discovers this. By then morbidity has set in, and there is bruising. There were none of these signs on Marybeth's babies."

With all this conflicting evidence, many of the medical staff continued to give Marybeth the benefit of the doubt. A few of them even went to Jonathan's funeral.

"As a mother myself I wanted to be supportive to this woman, who was, shall we say, sick," one doctor commented. "I had a feeling that there was something wrong from the very beginning because she never showed any degree of emotion. Even the funeral was not a sorrowful event. Jonathan was lying there in his little outfit, but I saw no grief from the parents. The mother could have been in a supermarket checking out the oranges. There was no more emotional involvement than that."

A nurse remembered that although Marybeth's eyes were red, she was chatting amiably to guests. "She acted like she had been there before."

Chuck Ray was not at the funeral. After his single experience of baby-sitting for Michael (who, through the rest of the crisis, was cared for by Joe's parents), he heard very little from the Tinnings, so little that Jonathan's brief life barely impinged upon him. "We were sheltered from Jonathan," he explained. He took this as a kindness. Even for a man of his generous sympathies, there is a limit to the number of nights that can be spent stretched out on a coffee table in a hospital waiting room.

Marybeth knew she would go on needing Chuck and Janet and seemed to have an instinct for how far she could push a friendship. The Rays believed in her, and Chuck was devoted to Michael. This time she did not even ask them to help her dispose of the baby clothes. She did not need to. Jonathan's belongings mysteriously disappeared.

According to Marybeth, they were stolen from her apartment by someone who did not want her to have any more babies. As with the reported robbery of the bowling club funds six years earlier, there were no signs of a break-in. Jonathan's clothes were found scattered on the overpass of an interstate highway half a mile from Marybeth's home. Somehow her father-in-law knew where to look for them. Even in the Tinning family it was acknowledged that she was responsible, that crazed by an emotion they called grief, she behaved in a way which neither she nor they could explain.

FOURTEEN

You knew what was going to happen to the next child,
but you were unable to prevent it because nobody in
authority would listen.

—Clergyman

It was not true that the McClellan Street neighbors shunned Marybeth. In their opinion, she was cool to them. She did not invite
them into her home, and when she spoke to them, it was rarely
about anything personal. Their main contact with her was through
Michael, who had grown into an engaging toddler, so loving and
out going that he would run with his arms outstretched toward
anyone who smiled at him.

"Toss me, toss me," he would call to Dorothy Posluszny, who
lived on the other side of McClellan Street. It was his two-year-old
way of saying, "Cross to me," knowing that she could not resist
the invitation and that when she came, she would bring a cookie.
It was the summer of 1980, several weeks after Jonathan's funeral,
and he was the last child left in the family. There had been three
other children since the Tinning's moved to McClellan Street, and
the Poslusznys who had lived there all along had almost lost track
of them. As Dorothy said, "We got to know Michael the best
because he lasted the longest."

Nathan came and went without her being aware of him, while
Mary Frances and Jonathan made only a slight impression. "I saw
Marybeth out walking a baby in a stroller, and all of a sudden I
didn't see her with the baby anymore and I heard that it died.
Then I saw her pregnant, and she had another. Again she would
be pushing the baby or sitting on the porch, holding him. Then
that one passed away. One day I asked her what happened. She
said they both died of congenital heart defects. I knew nothing

[147]

about the earlier children. She never mentioned them. I told her that if it was me, I couldn't go through the heartbreak of having another; that's why it seemed such a good idea for her to adopt Michael. He was so cute, with his jet black curls."

Michael's racial origins seemed to be his protection from the fate of the earlier Tinning children. Genetically he had nothing in common with them. At two he had already demonstrated his enhanced ability to survive by outliving two Tinning babies who were born after him, and by his uneventful recovery from hernia surgery. If something was poisoning the atmosphere of the McClellan Street apartment, as Dr. Mele's nurse once conjectured, Michael's health would have declined many months ago. Instead, sitting on the porch, smiling to the neighbors, he was a living confirmation of Marybeth's insistence that her own children had a genetic defect. So long as he survived, she was believable. If his life was jeopardized, so was her story.

"We called Michael her insurance card," Trish McBreen remembered, speaking of her fellow nurses at St. Clare's. "We felt that he would be her protection because he lived, which was almost like proving there was something genetically wrong with the others, and that she was a good mother. We thought she would not dare let anything happen to Michael."

He was so robust and high-spirited that it seemed unlikely. sometimes his infant energies were more than Marybeth could manage, and she would ask her in-laws to take him for a few days. In the role that Marybeth's own ailing mother felt unable to fill, Edna Tinning was a most dependable grandmother. She had spent most of her life around little children, having taught for years in the Duanesburg primary school. Ever since she herself left school, she had also taught a Bible class at the Princetown Reformed Church. With her nineteenth-century values centered on God and family, she was firm, loving, patient and steadfast. All through the long time Jonathan was dying she cared for Michael, and whenever Marybeth's energies flagged, she was ready to care for him again. Joe senior, her quiet and kindly husband, told friends that he couldn't wait for Michael to reach an age when he could take him fishing.

As the matriarch of the Tinning family Edna seems to have regarded Marybeth as another kind of child—in need of protection and occasional correction and, above all, understanding. She knew exactly why Marybeth had such an infantile handwriting and such difficulty expressing herself on paper. It was not simply because she was left-handed and a mediocre student but because of the inadequacy of those who taught her. "She did not get the basics in her early years. When she was in primary school, the teaching was in the category of look-and-see. Then it went back to phonetics. Before it did, there was a whole group of children in this country, now around Marybeth's age, who had problems reading. Some still do. With her own peers, Marybeth often had to fake it." To Edna, this explained a lot about her daughter-in-law's insecurities.

As the relationship between the two women deepened, Edna was immensely gratified when Marybeth started questioning her about her religious beliefs. For years she had been uncomfortable about her daughter-in-law's Catholicism, inwardly relieved that it had not rubbed off on her son. But now, as Marybeth's loyalty to the faith of her childhood diminished, Edna was delighted to see a gradual growing of interest in her own fundamentalist religion. At her encouragement Marybeth enrolled Michael in the infant Sunday school at the Princetown Reformed Church. This was close to Edna's house on the outskirts of Duanesburg, and a good twenty minutes' drive from Marybeth's apartment in Schenectady.

Michael also spent a lot of time in the company of Chuck and Janet Ray and of their two daughters, who were now old enough to baby-sit for him. After Jonathan's death the Tinnings' friendship with the Rays was so fully restored that Chuck spent many hours making a doll for Michael in the image of his favorite comic-strip character. Pleasing Michael with this gift was so important to Chuck that years later he could describe it in detail.

"Michael had a thing about Superman," he related. "He had Superman sheets and Superman curtains in his room. So I knit up a Superman doll for him. I knit up red for his socks, blue for his legs, red for his briefs, blue for his chest. I put on a yellow shield; pink for the head and black for the hair. I knit stocking stitch for the body, and for his hair I knit plain so it would look wavy. I make the points of his boots, and then I made a red triangle with a blue shield for his cape. I stuffed him with Polyfill, and I stitched it for his legs and arms so he could stand up with his hands on his hips. Then I showed him to all the ladies on my route. I loved Michael, and I really wanted him to have this doll."

When he was two and a half, Michael had an accident. As

Marybeth described it, he fell the length of the steep back stairs in their apartment. She said he had heard the mailman and was eager to greet him. Did she mean Chuck? This was never explained. Michael's head was bruised and cut, enough to warrant a trip to St. Clare's emergency room, diagonally across the street.

It seemed to be one of those mild emergencies that every mother has to deal with, almost routine considering Michael's exubrance, but Marybeth panicked. Perhaps she sensed what the staff at St. Clare's might think. In any event, she was too scared to handle the crisis alone. She called for an ambulance, and as the paramedics were carrying Michael into it, she spotted Dorothy Posluszny and her mother on the other side of the road.

"I'm so nervous and upset, I can't go to the hospital alone," she told them. "Will one of you ride with me?"

Dorothy's mother, Judy Lionarons, volunteered. It was difficult for either of the women to leave their house because they both were caring for Judy's seriously ill mother. Marybeth's crisis was mild compared with theirs, but she was shaking and talking so rapidly that she barely made sense.

Michael needed only a small dressing on his forehead and may also have had a mild concussion, but Marybeth was still panicky after she brought him home from the hospital. That evening he asked to visit Dorothy and Judy's house for cookies, and while he was quietly eating them, still scared from his experience. Marybeth recounted how someone in the hospital had warned her that the accident would be investigated. Recognizing the name Tinning, a nurse had placed a hot line call to the Child Protective Unit of Social Services. Judy told her not to worry. "I knew it was normal for a hospital to make a report when a child has an accident," she said, "so I didn't think anything of it."

A caseworker is believed to have called on Marybeth. In the Tinnings' pleasantly furnished apartment there were no indications of child abuse—just an anxious mother and a well-nourished child who was active enough to be accident-prone. The case did not appear to need following up, so once again Social Services put it aside. But as the days passed, Michael was obviously not recovering well. Marybeth's brother and sister-in-law, Alton and Sandy Roe, became very concerned about him when his adoptive parents took him to their home in Duanesburg a week after his fall.

"He still had symptoms of a head injury," said Sandy. "All that week he had been throwing up. At our house he kept screaming, holding his head, and losing his balance. Marybeth said that when he fell, he hit the hot-air duct at the foot of the stairs. After this happened, she said she took him shopping one day and could not control him. I told her there was something very wrong and she should get him to the hospital. But she did not want to go back to St. Clare's.

Over the next few days Michael seemed to be less dizzy, but developed a heavy cold. The following Sunday, March 1, 1981, Edna and her husband visited Joe and Marybeth. This was a special time for the four of them. As the result of her mother-in-law's prayerful encouragement Marybeth was ready to join the Princetown Reformed Church, the same church which nurtured Joe and his brother, Andy, to which their parents had devoted most of their lives. The older Tinnings were among its most valued members.

During the past three years Edna and her husband had given much time and energy to an ambitious rebuilding program, made necessary because the church building had been almost totally destroyed by a mysterious fire in March 1978. The blaze originated in the bride's room at the front of the church and was thought to have been caused by a defective heater. Hampered by the lack of a nearby water supply, the local volunteer fire brigade was not able to salvage much. The older Tinnings were devastated by the loss of their church and, along with others, worked diligently to ensure that a finer building would rise from the ashes. At this time their daughter-in-law's eagerness to join their dedicated band of worshipers made them particularly happy.

Marybeth's application for membership was to have been considered by the consistory of church members on the evening of Saturday, February 28, 1981. After this formality of being interviewed by the elders, she was to be officially accepted into the congregation the following morning. At the last minute she asked if her meeting with the consistory might be deferred because of Michael's illness. Edna fully understood that Marybeth's first duty was to her adopted son and that this was merely a brief postponement.

During the Sunday visit from his grandparents Michael was much more cheerful and lively. It was a favorite game of his to pick up Edna's handbag, dump its contents on the floor, and sort among the treasures while she watched fondly. Today he did it again, and she remarked that he must be feeling better.

At seven-thirty the next morning, right after Joe had left for work, Marybeth called her sister-in-law Sandy Roe. She sounded panicky. "I can't wake Michael. What shall I do?"

It was a strange question for the mother of eight to be asking a younger mother of two. Sandy repeated her advice of a week earlier, this time more firmly: "Get him over to the emergency room at St. Clare's."

Rather than do this, Marybeth called Dr. Mele's office. The doctors in his group practice made a point of being available at 10:00 A.M. every weekday to see children who had developed medical problems overnight, and Marybeth was told to bring in Michael during this scheduled "sick hour." If she had said that this was an emergency, which she didn't, she would have been instructed to take him to hospital. Instead she waited more than two hours for the doctor's appointment, then drove Michael to Dr. Mele's office on the other side of town. She didn't do this because she wanted to see Dr. Mele personally; as she must have known, he was on vacation in Florida. It can only be assumed that she wanted to avoid St. Clare's. Almost five years later, when she was asked about this episode by the police, this was her halting description of it: "During the night his [Michael's] temperature went up and so I just, I just sat with him. Then I went back to sleep, and back and forth. And when I went in in the morning to get him up so we could go to the doctor's, he was not, I mean he was responsive to a point but he was very limp, and so on and so forth. And so instead of calling the ambulance I went from our house on McClellan Street, put him in the car, literally threw him in the car, and went to St. Clare's—or, I mean, I went to Dr. Mele's office, and went in there, and the paramedics from Broadway there came and they took him."

The pediatricians' office was a good ten-minute drive from McClellan Street, while St. Clare's was so close she could have carried Michael there. Only two weeks earlier she needed an ambulance and a neighbor to make the short trip to St. Clare's emergency room; now in a more serious crisis she took a longer route alone.

In Dr. Mele's office there was also less likelihood of her getting immediate attention. Monday morning was the busiest time, with a crowd of mothers bringing children who had sickened over the weekend. Marybeth was the first of this group to arrive, even before the pediatrician who was on duty that day. Sandy Ross, Dr. Mele's faithful nurse, was alone in the office, preparing for the influx of patients. She would never forget what happened in the next few minutes.

"It was about nine forty-five A.M., and I was alone in the little back room where I had all the allergy shots. I heard the front door of the house open, and I went around and saw Marybeth standing there with her child wrapped in a blanket. She was yelling, 'We need help.'

"Until this moment I had never suspected her of having anything to do with her babies' deaths. But when I saw who it was, I wanted to run out of the back door. It was the only time in my entire nursing career I have wanted to run. If it had been any other patient, I would not have felt that way, but I knew something was terribly wrong. I laid Michael on a little wooden bench where the children usually sit, and as soon as I did this, Marybeth started running all over the office, wringing her hands and yelling hysterically.

"I knew what I would find even before I unwrapped the blanket. Michael was dead. I reached up to the wall phone, and as the phone hit the floor, I dialed 0. I told the operator I had an unresponsive child, and she said, 'Help is on the way.' The fire department was at the end of the street, and within minutes the fireman and paramedics arrived. In the meantime, I did CPR.

"By now the other patients were coming in. I called out to them to please go back to their cars and wait outside. One of our doctors arrived, injected a stimulant into Michael's heart, and did everything possible. Then the ambulance took him to St. Clare's.

"We knew that Marybeth lived across the street from the hospital, and we asked her why she didn't go there instead of driving five miles to our office. She said she had talked to the doctor earlier that morning and he told her to bring Michael at ten A.M. On the way to our office she said she heard Michael make a gurgling noise. Instead of pulling over to see what was wrong, she felt she should get to the doctor's as fast as possible."

Afterward, when she had time to think about it, Sandy Ross realized that the reason she wanted to run away was not just her fear that Michael was dead, but her instinct that his death was unnecessary. She was an experienced middle-aged nurse who had seen death many times, but never quite like this. "His skin was gray—very, very gray. There was a lot of bubbling mucus rolling out of his mouth, and he looked as though he had been dead some time. I found it hard to believe that he died on the road. He was still warm, but he was wrapped in a lot of big, thick blankets, which would have retained his body temperature."

Michael's death was all the more heartbreaking to Sandy because she had known him so well. For two and a half years Marybeth had taken him to Dr. Mele's office for regular checkups and shots. "He would walk in the doorway with his arms outstretched. He was such a lovable little child. He was gorgeous."

Following the ambulance, Sandy drove Marybeth to St. Clare's emergency room. Marybeth had calmed down by the time they arrived, much as she dreaded going there in the first place. Someone had telephoned Joe at work, and he met the two women at the hospital. In all the years that Dr. Mele had been caring for Tinning children, Sandy had never seen Marybeth's husband before. She was struck by the lack of emotion on his face and between the two of them. There was no embrace, no gesture of comfort, not even a kiss. This was their eighth bereavement, and they were either totally numbed by it or so overwhelmed by the repetition of death upon death that they had no feelings left.

Chuck Ray heard the news on his way home from work. He stopped at Knapp Service Ltd. on Steuben Street, the automobile station where he always had his Volkswagen serviced. Doug Knapp and his wife lived in Duanesburg and belonged to the same church as Joe's parents.

"Mrs. Knapp was there, and she had such a look in her eyes that you wanted to take her in your arms and comfort her," Chuck remembered.

"What's the matter?" I asked.

"She said to me, 'Did you hear about Michael?'

"What do you mean?" I said. "I knew he fell downstairs, but he's all right now."

"Then she said, 'I just heard from the minister at church that Michael is dead.'

"I couldn't believe it. I picked up the phone and called Joe and Marybeth. No answer. Then I called Rick and Laurie. Rick is a mailman who works with me. He and I always eat lunch together, and at that time his son lived downstairs from Joe and Marybeth.

Laurie answered, and she said, 'Michael is in the hospital, and I think he's dead.'

"I turned to Mrs. Knapp, and I said, 'You're right,' and I put my arms round her.

"I didn't know how I would be able to tell Janet, but when I got home I found her crying, so I knew she knew."

Marybeth had called her during the afternoon. "I have something to tell you," she said to Janet. "I thought it better you should hear it from me than from anyone else. Michael died." Almost word for word, it was the way she broke the news to other friends about other babies.

"She was very calm," Janet related. "She told me that she had taken him to the doctor's and that he died there."

Later Marybeth told the Rays that the cause of death was viral pneumonia. Chuck checked this with his colleague Rick, who checked it with his daughter, who was a nurse in Albany. The word came back from her that viral pneumonia could quickly be fatal. Chuck promptly accepted this as the explanation of Michael's death. "Once I knew that viral pneumonia was very fast-acting, I did not ask any more questions."

Michael was buried in a Protestant ceremony conducted by the Reverent Harold Irish, minister of the Princetown Reformed Church. Some of the mourners were surprised when he did not invite Marybeth to say her usual prayer at the graveside. When the service was over, Harold Irish left abruptly, although the ladies of his church were ready to take away the edge of everyone's sadness with their customary offerings of food. Their minister may have been in a hurry to keep another appointment, although it was unlike him not to stay awhile and offer condolences. Afterward, some of his church members wondered whether he was more uneasy about Michael's death than he cared to discuss.

Chuck Ray had to steel himself to go to the funeral service at Daly's. "I was in a state," he said. "Marybeth came up to me, and I just hugged her and cried. I hugged Joe and cried. I told them I could not go on to the cemetery. They were calmer than I was. I left, and I found Rick on his route. I asked if he had time for coffee. He knew I needed to be with someone and that I couldn't burden Janet because she was already very upset. We went to a little restaurant at the end of Albany Street, and I cried while he just sat there."

He was able to draw comfort from a touching gesture which must have been Marybeth's. When Michael died, Chuck remembered the Superman doll and all the loving care which he had put into it. He thought of its being given away with the rest of Michael's toys, and because it symbolized a very special relationship between the two of them, he couldn't bear to think of its going to a stranger. He was tempted to ask for it back, but Janet persuaded him against this. She said that it would be too painful a reminder of Michael and that it would be best to let it go.

At the Daly Funeral Home he went to say his last good-bye to the little boy who had meant so much to him. There he noticed something which brought fresh tears to his eyes. "I saw the Superman doll in his casket. I had wanted so badly for Michael to have it, and seeing it there did a lot of beautiful things for me."

FIFTEEN

After Michael died, I did not even want to be in the same room as her. I could not handle it.
                                        —*Former friend*

"At this autopsy the illness showed acute pneumonia. The family history is bizarre."

With these comments Schenectady's medical examiner, Dr. Robert Sullivan, closed his inquiry into the death of Michael Raymond Tinning. Among the police, the medical staff at St. Clare's, some of the Social Services caseworkers, the waitresses at Flavorland, the neighbors and former neighbors in different parts of Schenectady, many hoped for a different resolution. Essentially they all said the same thing: that with the death of baby after baby they became more and more suspicious. "But when Michael died, we knew."

Some of them telephoned the child abuse hot line and demanded an investigation. George Barker, husband of Sara Barker, the Flavorland cook, was so incensed that he made several telephone calls.

"I called the hot line, the welfare department, Barney Waldron the sheriff, the Schenectady police and Daly's funeral home. Barney said that if there was anything wrong, the medical examiner would have found it. Mr. Daly said there was not a mark on the child. I told them, 'There has to be some reason why these kids are dying.' I was very rude. I can be rude when I'm upset, and I was upset because I love kids. The only person I got results from was a lady on the child abuse hot line. At least she listened to what I had to say. And I raised hell."

Some of the waitresses also placed hot line calls. So did Dr. Kevin Karpowicz. After watching Jonathan die at Albany Medical

Center, he had resolved to follow the progress of any subsequent Tinning children. He was limited in what he could do because he was not Marybeth's pediatrician. But as a consultant at St. Clare's he reacted immediately to the news of Michael's death by urging Social Services to investigate.

Like her close friends the Rays, most of Marybeth's relatives were troubled but accepting. Edna Tinning was terribly shocked by Michael's death but unwavering in support of her daughter-in-law. So was her husband. Sandy Roe convinced herself that a blood clot on the brain killed Michael and was critical of Marybeth for neglecting his head injury. Only one member of the family called the hot line: Carol Tinning.

Marybeth had been afraid of this sister-in-law ever since she had been confronted about stealing from Carol's purse, seven years earlier. She told several people that Carol was the perpetrator of the anonymous calls which plagued her whenever one of her children died, and that Carol did this because she hated her. Marybeth certainly did receive some abusive calls, and she seems to have imagined a great many more. But none of them came from Carol, nor (as Marybeth also alleged) did Carol call anyone else to make accusations about Marybeth. That was not her style. If Carol felt the need to criticize, she did it bluntly and directly to a person's face. Her relationship with the Tinning family might have been much easier if she had been less forthright.

She did not suspect Marybeth of harming her children until Michael died, and then she was open about her suspicions. For many months she refused to have any contact with her sister-in-law.

For every one of Marybeth's acquaintances who called the hot line, there were many who simply gossiped to one another. "I called my sister and told her, 'You'll never believe this. Now the adopted one has died.' "

Or, "If I said it to my neighbor once, I said it a hundred times, 'There has to be something very strange going on in that household.' "

Such remarks went on over the coffee cups, over the telephone wires, on supermarket checkout lines all around Schenectady. On McClellan Street Marybeth tried to forestall the gossip by making an early call on the Poslusznys the morning after it happened.

"Have you read the newspaper yet?" she asked almost casually.

Dorothy always read the *Schenectady Gazette's* obituaries and advertisements before she started on the news, while her husband, John, went for the sports and comic strips. She shook her head.

Marybeth was tense but calm, a lot calmer than she had been when Michael hurt his head. "Well, I'd just like to tell you people before you read it in the paper that Michael died."

"What happened?" Dorothy gasped.

"He had viral pneumonia."

After she left, Dorothy turned to her husband. "I can't believe it," she said. "This is the third death that we know of. There has to be something wrong here."

She could not understand how Marybeth could be in such good control of herself. "If it was me, I'd be a basket case."

The diagnosis of pneumonia was made with a mixture of reluctance and relief by Dr. Thomas Oram, chief of pathology at Ellis Hospital. As the senior pathologist in Schenectady he was called in by the St. Clare's pathologist, Dr. Young Sim, a former student of his, just as she called him in almost five years later for the autopsy of Tami Lynne.

When Dr. Oram began the autopsy on Michael, the forensic scientist in him was excited at the prospect of solving a mystery. But his longer experience, that of a conventional hospital pathologist, was more accustomed to deaths from natural causes. He found it difficult to imagine that a woman would do away with her own children, one after another, in cold blood and for no apparent reason, and at this very human level of his consciousness he did not want to find evidence of murder.

Investigating Michael's death was doubly nerve-racking because so much depended upon it. After the deluge of hot line calls, the police, the medical examiner's office, and the Child Protective Unit at Social Services were all anxious for the results of this autopsy.

One of the first possibilities which Oram ruled out was brain damage. There was still a bruise on Michael's face from his fall downstairs, and Oram thought he had probably suffered a concussion; but there was no longer any evidence of this and certainly no brain damage. The only unusual finding at the autopsy was a small patch of bronchial pneumonia in one lung.

It was discovered only on microscopic examination and seemed too mild a condition, by far, to have killed a sturdy toddler. "We were stumped," Dr. Oram admitted. "We both thought that this child could have been smothered, but because of the pneumonia, we knew this wasn't a case to take to court. The defense would argue that the pneumonia caused Michael's death, and we could not find enough evidence to prove it didn't. And that's why this case came to an end. As soon as we found pneumonia, we knew we could not go any further."

This must have been an immense relief to Marybeth. She must have known that Social Services doubted her story of Michael's fall downstairs and suspected her of mistreating him. She must have had a good idea of what some of the St. Clare's nurses and doctors were thinking. After her years of faith in St. Clare's, she had begun to feel that she had to avoid this hospital as much as she avoided Ellis. Now, unexpectedly, she was vindicated. The most respected pathologist in town had ruled that Michael died of pneumonia, and the medical examiner's office accepted his judgment. She was free . . . yet her actions continued to show that she felt the net closing in on her.

A week or so after Michael's death she went to Dr. Mele's office and insisted upon speaking to the doctor on duty in the presence of Nurse Sandy Ross. She told the two of them that some people had criticized her for not taking Michael directly to St. Clare's emergency room, and she wanted to explain why she had gone to their office instead. It was because one of the pediatricians in the partnership had told her to do so. For the record she wanted that clearly understood. She made no mention of the fact that when she telephoned, she had failed to describe the seriousness of Michael's condition. She behaved like a person who had been unjustly accused and was determined to set the record straight.

Michael's death had left her vulnerable. The story of a death gene in the family was no longer convincing, and his final adoption papers remained unsigned. Somewhere in the Schenectady area Michael had a mother, still his legal parent, who might raise some very awkward questions. She did not come forward, although there was a report that on the day of his burial a white woman and a black man slipped into the funeral parlor before most of the mourners arrived, gazed at the open casket, and left without identifying themselves.

Shortly after the funeral all of Michael's toys and infant furniture were loaded into a small trailer and taken to the Princetown Reformed Church, to be donated to the nursery. A few weeks later the

Tinnings themselves moved out, without saying good-bye to the Poslusznys. By that time Dorothy had heard from other neighbors that it was not three Tinning babies who had died but eight. She was incredulous. "I couldn't believe that fate could strike that many times in the same household." Many neighbors on McClellan Street wondered aloud why Joe had not 'done something' to prevent the succession of tragedies. None of them felt it to be their responsibility although several of them had known all along how many babies Marybeth had lost. One neighbor argued defensively, "People think that one of us should have spoken up, but why didn't he? We didn't live with her twenty-four hours a day, and he did."

Marybeth had impressed them as moody, Joe as uncommunicative. In warm weather, when the windows were open, the occasional sounds of their marital arguments had filtered down to McClellan Street. It was also noted that in their six years of living there the Tinnings had very few visitors except for his parents and her mother. What with their aloofness and the horror of all that happened in their upstairs apartment, none of the neighbors was sorry to see them leave.

Chuck and Janet Ray understood their need to get away from the home where there had been so much unhappiness, and sensed that they would hear very little from the Tinnings after they moved. "There were a lot of bad memories, and we were part of them," Chuck acknowledged. Emotionally he felt drained by the demands of this friendship and was glad of the respite.

In their fifteen years of marriage Joe and Marybeth had rented four Schenectady apartments, but they were still not ready to buy their own home. As a white-collar worker in a blue-collar setting Joe had a steady skilled job at General Electric which some of his neighbors envied. Many of them were paid by the hour; he was on salary. This put him in a higher social category although his take-home pay may not have been much better than theirs. Overall he was probably worse off, burdened by medical bills, funeral expenses, and a wife who liked to shop.

Understanding their son's need to save money and their daughter-in-law's anxiety to get away from McClellan Street, Joe's parents made a generous offer. They invited the younger couple to share their house on the outskirts of Duanesburg for several months, so they could build up their savings and plan for a home of their own.

This was a household, like the younger Joe's, in which the husband deferred to his wife's wishes, and Edna had strong feelings about how best to help Marybeth and, by extension, their son.

She explained: "I thought it better for her to get away from the apartment where she had lost so many children. I could not see how she could stand to live there."

Duanesburg, the village where Marybeth grew up, was only a dozen miles from Schenectady, but it was another way of life. It was reached by driving past some of the shabbier sections of town, through one of the older suburbs (ROTTERDAM—A NICE PLACE TO LIVE said a road sign not far from the Shoporama Flavorland), across a bridge over the interstate highway, and then between the broad fields and undulating hills of the Mohawk River Valley, where the next frame houses were built farther apart and a homemade road sign read: DUANESBURG—THE LAST FRONTIER.

It wasn't, of course. It was a village with a character and momentum of its own, and it was also exurbia for commuters to Schenectady and Albany. These were roughly divided between blue-collar workers at the General Electric plant who were picked up at the village crossroads by the company bus and white-collar employees who drove their own cars to the vast complex of government offices in the state capital. The rest of the populace had jobs in the village.

It was an old village, inbred and insular, which still looked upon those who had been there for only one generation as newcomers. Although it had long ceased to be a last frontier, some of the old families continued to behave as though it were, and people who had lived in Duanesburg for twenty years continued to feel as though they had to keep proving themselves in order to be accepted. There were intense loyalties which defied reason and old rivalries which died hard. There were neighbors who could always be depended upon in times of trouble and cliques that went to the same church but did not speak to one another. It was a place where people never locked their doors at night; where when terrible things happened, as they did from time to time over the years—murder and suspicions of murder, cases of incest, a clergyman sent packing for unacceptable behavior—the villagers always closed ranks and refused to discuss the scandal in public. The longer a person lived in Duanesburg, the more he knew and the less he said about it.

Much of this was based on the conviction that when this was a frontier society, the survival of its inhabitants depended upon their being neighborly to one another. But as in the Bible story of the good Samaritan, neighborliness did not have to involve friendship. Up to the 1950's this was dairy farming country, and the tale was told of two neighboring Duanesburg farmers who were vehement enemies. Neither they nor their children had spoken for years. One day one of the farmers was taken to hospital with a serious illness, whereupon, without a word, his enemy took on the daily chores of cleaning his barn, feeding his cattle and milking his cows. The neighbor went on doing this faithfully until the first farmer was well enough to return to work. Then he withdrew to his own farm and continued the feud. Such a tale did not need explaining to old Duanesburg families. Its motives and its mores were well understood.

When Marybeth Tinning returned to Duanesburg, it was to a very different circle from that in which Marybeth Roe had grown up. Her lonely childhood had centered on the grade school and the high school to the west of the village and on Our Lady of Fatima Church in the same small area—a hamlet known as Delanson. Back then she had few friends and made very little impact, except to be remembered as a withdrawn and rather pesky child who was seen sitting beside her mother at Sunday morning mass. The Roes did not involve themselves in community activities and were barely known in the village.

The Tinnings, whose lives touched on many others, lived in the hamlet of Princetown on the eastern side of Duanesburg, close to the church in which they were so deeply involved. Run in the direct tradition of the area's early Dutch settlers, this church was a second home to Edna and her husband, and they took pains to ensure that Marybeth was made welcome. Edna introduced her to the women's guild, and Marybeth soon became one of its officers, to the chagrin of some of the long-established members. Although they were too well bred to raise this issue in public, it was their belief that a woman should serve the church in some lowly capacity for several years before she earned the right to do an important job. As secretary of service Marybeth was responsible for organizing food for the guild's monthly meetings, for arranging funeral receptions, and for a variety of chores like making sure the church flowers were in place. She did this work conscientously and well.

Marybeth's father-in-law found her yet another outlet for community service, one which soon dominated all her other interests. In his retirement from a factory job at General Electric, the senior Joe Tinning was as busy as he had ever been, working part-time as a van driver, helping his church, and serving on the Duanesburg Volunteer Ambulance Corps. The ambulance work was particularly important to him; without fail he gave up one day a week to active duty, served a term as president of the corps, and used his carpentry skills to improve the facilities at the ambulance station. A supply room which he built at the back of the garage was named the Tinning Room in appreciation of his efforts.

The corps maintained a well-equipped ambulance which served a rural area of seventy-two square miles and was staffed by a force of between thirty and fifty trained volunteers. Marybeth's father-in-law was one of its most reliable members, and remembering how as a young woman she had been a nurse's aide, he thought that she would find it rewarding to work with him and that the work would take her mind off her own troubles.

She readily agreed. A new phase of her life was opening up. It was not ideal in the sense that living with in-laws is never ideal, but she was exchanging the knowing stares of the McClellan Street neighbors for a home in which she was encouraged and nurtured as she may never have been before. She was also safe. In the Tinning household family loyalties were so fierce and unshakable that no matter how suspicious others might be, however strange her own behavior, however persuasive the evidence of the guilt, so long as she protested her innocence, she would be believed.

During her years away from Duanesburg a well-known local family had been tragically afflicted in a way which made the deaths of her own children less remarkable. A much-loved physician and his wife, Dr. and Mrs. James K. Cooley, had lost three of their five children without warning, one after another, when apparently in robust health. Later a fourth child was to die.

After the second death Dr. Cooley insisted upon an intensive medical examination of his family. It revealed that all his children had inherited a rare abnormality of the heart which was likely to cause sudden death after strenuous activity. The mystery had barely been solved when his third child was stricken.

People of Duanesburg were overwhelmed by the Cooley's loss. They felt such profound sympathy for the doctor and his wife that when Marybeth returned to the village similarly bereaved, they tactfully avoided asking painful questions. They accepted, more readily than the Schenectady neighbors, that the death of all one's children can happen naturally. Some of them even talked about the hand of God reaching down, time and again, into the same family, as if the repeated tragedies were part of some inscrutable divine plan.

With her return to Duanesburg, Marybeth put most of her Schenectady life behind her. Once in a while she showed up at Flavorland, but only as a customer. Occasionally she went bowling with Joe. She did several odd jobs in the Duanesburg area—as a companion to an elderly lady, as a waitress in a motel restaurant, and as a packer in the egg room in Jewett's Poultry Farm—but none of them lasted long. The Jewetts, who were influential members of the Tinnings' church, were amazed at how tense she was. Whenever eggs fell off the conveyor belt and smashed on the floor, which from time to time was inevitable, then like a child caught doing some damage, she would burst into tears.

As the weeks went by, most of her energies were concentrated on the ambulance corps and upon her search for a house in the Duanesburg area. In her fortieth year she was not expected to have any more children, and her in-laws were encouraged to see her building another life for herself.

The danger of an investigation into Michael's death had passed, and her new acquaintances at church and in the ambulance corps avoided mentioning it. In Schenectady, however, Dr. Mele's nurse, Sandy Ross, could not forget. For years she was to be haunted by the memory of that winter morning when she laid Michael on the little blue bench in the waiting room and turned back his blanket. Every time she saw that bench, the horror came back to her. In the middle of the night she tortured herself with thoughts of what she might have done to save this little boy who had so enchanted her.

"I would wake up and think, if only I had a suction machine. If only I had oxygen. Day after day I would cry about it. If only. If only. Yet I knew the minute I took the blanket away that the child was dead and could not be saved. I also felt that this was a death which shouldn't have happened. It was a most terrible feeling of frustration."

Reminded that there was nothing she could have done to revive Michael, she replied sadly, "My head tells me that, but not my heart." She made this comment more than six years after the event, but the memory was still so painful to her that she suddenly burst out, "I can't sleep at night. How can she?"

SIXTEEN

She was so nervous and jittery that when she talked to
you—and it's something you couldn't put a finger on—
a little red flag went up.

—*Ambulance volunteer*

Ever since her first job as a nurse's aide Marybeth was attracted to
work which involved caring for others and which brought immediate recognition of her services. On the pediatric ward of Ellis
Hospital she had the satisfaction of seeing sick children get better; at
Flavorland there were the tips and the smiles; in the churchwomen's
guild and the volunteer ambulance corps there was the glory of
making an important contribution to a worthy cause.

Most people do jobs for which there are few thanks but which
may offer other kinds of rewards; Marybeth needed instant gratification. Always uncertain of herself, she was constantly seeking
reassurance, and no matter how hard she tried or how well she did,
she seemed unable to appease her own sense of inadequacy.

Even when a baby whimpered, she blamed herself. "I mean,
whatever I did just did not turn out right." She said this so often
and for such a variety of reasons that it became a self-fulfilling
prophecy. Back in her childhood someone must have told her, not
just once but many times, if not in words, then by behavior, that
she was no good; since then her conviction of failure had become
part of her personality. Through one bereavement after another she
insisted that she was a bad mother because her children died, as
though the very fact of her giving them life had doomed them. And
in a way, it had.

It was ironic that her in-laws' well-intentioned efforts to help her
make a fresh start should bring her back to Duanesburg, the place
where all her feelings of inadequacy had developed. Her return to

this village was a turning point in her life, but not in the direction her in-laws planned for her. Although she was escaping from the painful memories of McClellan Street, she was returning to the place where she had grown up, with half a lifetime of failure behind her. Many of her school classmates still lived there, successful in their jobs, their mortgages almost paid off, their children grown, even, in some cases, ready to make them grandparents. She could not possibly compete.

Some of them were active members of the ambulance corps, and even there she was at a serious disadvantage. Although she attended all the required classes and read the necessary books, she was unable to qualify for the New York state license as an emergency medical technician, held by most of the volunteers. The examination had to be taken in two parts: first a practical test, which she passed, followed by a more difficult written test which required about a hundred hours of classroom work. A passing grade was seventy; Marybeth scored in the low sixties. Ashamed of her failure, she avoided telling other members of the corps for as long as possible. At first she said the results had not come in; then she claimed they were lost; finally she tearfully admitted that she had failed. Subsequently she made another two attempts at the written test, but even after a refresher course she was unable to improve on her original score.

Her father-in-law, who was beloved and respected by all the other ambulance volunteers, had a kindly explanation. "In the ambulance corps she was always a little bit too fast for her own good, and maybe that's why she flunked the course. If there was a shortcut, she would take it." Or, as his wife, Edna, maintained, "She was able to do it physically right but not able to put it on paper."

Another requirement for the state license was proficiency in life-saving techniques, and this, too, was beyond Marybeth's capability. Classes were held in the swimming pool at Schenectady's YWCA, where she did well until she was required to put her head under water. The she went into a panic. Refusing even to try, she kept screaming. "I can't! I'll suffocate!" Her reaction was so extreme and her choice of phrase so unexpected that the incident stayed in the mind of a fellow member of the corps who was there with her. Not drown, but suffocate. Why, in a moment of terror, would that word occur to her? And why, in the presence of people who were experienced lifesavers, would she be so frightened about the possibility?

She managed to pass the basic Red Cross first-aid test, which meant that she could work on an ambulance crew, but only under qualified technicians. She was also allowed to drive the ambulance, a job she greatly enjoyed. It gave her a childlike thrill to speed along a highway with a finger on the button that set the siren screaming, and on at least one occasion she prolonged the pleasure by taking a long route to the hospital.

In small towns the volunteer fire brigade and ambulance corps attract a surprising number of public-spirited people who undertake to keep these essential services going. The Duanesburg ambulance corps volunteers were a particularly convivial group who gave a lot of their free time to work which was often disagreeable and draining. They went out on emergency calls in teams of three, and most volunteers made themselves available for stints of twelve hours a week, during which time they would be at the end of a telephone line ready to respond to an emergency. Some members with full-time jobs gave up their days off to this, but even for housewives it could be a hardship to be stuck indoors all day, unable to start on a chore which could not be instantly dropped if they had to rush out at a moment's notice. Marybeth made these small sacrifices willingly, was always available when she was needed, and cheerfully volunteered for some of the menial work.

At one time she took on the responsibility of setting up the roster. "It is a lousy job," one of the ambulance workers explained. "It is picked by allocation because nobody ever wants to do it. You have to set up the schedule for a whole month in advance covering twenty-four hours a day, seven days a week, all with volunteers, some of whom can spare only a few hours. And there was Marybeth pleading to do it. Looking back, I think this was because she was so anxious to be in the limelight.

"She soon had problems with the roster. There were gaps which needed filling, and although she spent a lot of time on the telephone persuading people to fill in, some of the gaps remained. It was a disaster. She was willing to go on doing it, but we had to maneuver it so she did not continue the job for a second year."

Marybeth was one of three members of the Monday crew, on call from 6:00 A.M. to 6:00 P.M. The others—both qualified emergency medical technicians—were the Reverend Burnham H. Waldo, min-

ister of the United Methodist Church at Delanson, and Barbara
Munson, and Englishwoman who was a recently retired schoolteacher. Both of them were genial and easygoing, more tolerant of
Marybeth's oddities and more sympathetic to her problems than
some of the other volunteers who tried to avoid working with her.

For a long time Barbara Munson assumed that Marybeth had
never been a mother since she never mentioned children. Then one
day, as they were driving home together, Marybeth remarked that
she had had eight and they all were dead.

"I didn't know what to say except that I was terribly sorry,"
Barbara remarked. "I found it hard to cope with that piece of news.
It was almost too incredible to comprehend. But it was said in a
matter-of-fact way, as though it was not unusual."

Burnham Waldo had the same reaction. At that time he knew of
only two of the eight deaths. Almost disbelieving, he checked the
statement with Marybeth's father-in-law. "When he said it was
true, I suggested taking air samples from the house on McClellan
Street, to see if it was contaminated by radon or a virus." Joe senior
said he thought that had been done.

Sensitive to the trauma she must have suffered, Marybeth's fellow
crew members tried to be especially gentle and understanding with
her, but their patience was severely tried.

"When we had to meet at the ambulance garage for an emergency
call, I never knew which Marybeth would show up," Waldo related.
"Either she would be totally cool, calm, collected, efficient and
dependable, or else she would be a basket case, cowering inside the
ambulance or running around in circles, unable to function. Her
behaviour would have nothing to do with the type of emergency
we were dealing with. It was completely unpredictable. When she
was at her best, she would be helpful and would not back away.
At other times she was so unreliable that I was afraid to have her
there in case she jeopardized the life of a patient."

Barbara Munson's first encounter with Marybeth's terrified reactions was not easily forgotten. "There was this man on the floor
having a heart attack," she said. "I was on my knees beside him,
and I asked Marybeth to hand me the oxygen tank. When she didn't
respond, I looked up and saw her clutching her arms, shaking. She
was immobilized by panic, and I had to yell at her to get her to
move."

On the way home from a hospital run Marybeth always asked

her companions if they thought she had done well. If they praised her work, she was instantly relieved and happy. But when the conversation turned to other matters, she became sulky and withdrawn. Waldo was constantly reminded of an unhappy, unwanted child, forever seeking approval, never at peace with herself. He felt very sorry for her.

In time to come, when discussing her work on the ambulance corps, Marybeth claimed that she actually enjoyed helping at accidents "and the bloodier, the better." This was far from the truth as her fellow volunteers saw it.

It was her contention, however, that many of the accidents at which she assisted did not happen when her co-workers were around. She would show up at ambulance meetings with detailed descriptions of how her minimal experience had been put to the test, frequently, dramatically, and always to her credit.

There was her tale about being at a bowling club banquet with Joe when a man at another table started vomiting blood. While an ambulance was being called, Marybeth diagnosed an aneurysm, gave first aid, and was enterprising enough to look in her patient's wallet for the notation of his blood type, which he happened to be carrying. The ambulance workers brought a supply of blood and, thanks to Marybeth's prompt action, were able to give a lifesaving transfusion, right there in the restaurant.

Another time she was shopping in Schenectady's Mohawk Mall when a pregnant woman who was walking a few steps ahead of her fell on the floor in premature labor. Marybeth delivered the baby single-handedly because no one else was around (in a large shopping mall?) and protected the newborn from losing body heat by wrapping it in some aluminum foil, which was among the groceries she was carrying.

Every tale had what one of the women ambulance volunteers described as a "Marybeth touch," the addition of some telling and explicit detail which gave it realism. The search through the afflicted man's wallet was a Marybeth touch. So was the aluminum foil. Several years later, when some of her former colleagues on the ambulance corps read her confession to the murder of Tami Lynne, there was a passage they instantly recognized: her description of how she took a pillow from the bed in which Joe was sleeping, placed it on the sofa, and rumpled it up to look as though she had been lying there. This was a Marybeth touch again.

"Many of these stories, minute in detail and totally believable, could not be checked," commented the Reverend Burnham Waldo. "However, when she was confronted with the truth, she would admit to having lied, and she would go into this little-child mode— not just her voice, like a frightened whisper, but her total body language. She would kind of shrink down.

"She led us to believe that while she was on the Duanesburg corps, she was also an observer for one of the city ambulances and that sometimes she would help with emergencies. When she would relate these fictional runs with the commercial ambulance corps, a lot of the emergencies she described involved babies or children."

In one of these alleged episodes Marybeth helped rescue a pregnant woman who jumped from the window of a burning building. The woman aborted on the spot, and Marybeth tried hard to save her baby, but it was too premature to survive. Another time she reported accompanying a sick child on a 170-mile commercial ambulance ride to New York City, a tale which did not ring true because New York was well outside the radius of this particular ambulance company.

Some of her listeners expressed incredulity that she found herself in the midst of so many medical crises, whereupon she shrugged her shoulders and gave a helpless little smile. "I just don't know why these things always happen to me," she might say.

When she told these tales at meetings of the ambulance corps, she would be bright, talkative and enthusiastic. At other times, particularly if she showed up late, she would hang her head and, with hands clasped in her lap, timidly roll up her eyes and whisper, "I'm so sorry."This exaggerated apology reminded her listeners of a child caught in an act of naughtiness, scared of being spanked.

There was also a very appealing side to her. "She was a very caring, affectionate person," said Pat Wall, who served as president of the ambulance corps during the time that Marybeth was a member. "Seldom would she greet you by just saying hi. She would put her arms around you. She was also very conscientious about showing up. And often, after she had taken a patient to hospital, she would follow up by visiting the person, either at home or in hospital, to see how he or she was doing."

Pat, the wife of a General Electric executive, had a lovely home on the outskirts of Duanesburg. She sometimes invited Marybeth there during the daytime because she sensed that the woman needed to relax, away from her in-laws' household. During their many conversations Marybeth mentioned only one of her dead children, Michael, and her account of his death was somewhat different from the reality.

"She said that first he had a bump on the head, and then he had a cold, so she took him to the doctor's office. She left him outside in the car while she waited her turn. When the doctor was ready to see him, he went out to the car with her and found the child dead."

Marybeth told several people in the ambulance corps that after Michael's death she received some anonymous phone calls accusing her of killing him. One mysterious caller was said to have told her that her children's deaths were a judgement upon her for changing her religion. These alleged calls came to her in-laws' house, and the caller always seemed to know when she was there alone or when her mother-in-law was out of earshot. The timing was extraordinary. Sometimes there would be calls to remind her that this was one of her children's birthdays, and she would relate this to selected members of the ambulance corps to explain her sad expression that day. But of all her stories about anonymous telephone calls, the strangest had to do with her preparation of a lenten luncheon at a church in Schenectady. The lunch was one of a series held at churches in the neighborhood of the General Electric plant, the meal and accompanying program being timed to fit in with the workers' lunch break. As a volunteer from a participating Duanesburg church Marybeth did much of the cooking.

Afterward, when she was complimented on the meal by Burnham Waldo, who was among the clergy present, she told him of a strange incident. She said that as she began to cook lunch, she realized that there was not enough hamburger meat to go around, so she hurried out to a neighborhood store to buy more. While she was waiting for the beef to be wrapped, one of the clerks told her that she was wanted on the store's telephone. As she picked up the receiver, a male voice said, "We know you killed your children." And hung up.

As an experienced counselor Waldo was accustomed to the delusions of troubled people, but he did not know what to make of this story. It sounded improbable, but Marybeth half convinced him that someone had been watching her every move, had followed her to the store, and had called her from a nearby pay phone. It was her theory, which seems to have had no foundation whatsoever, that Carol and Andy Tinning were somehow responsible.

This incident left Waldo even more distressed than she appeared to be. As he thought about it, there were three possible explanations. First, the story was true, and some mischief-maker was doggedly following Marybeth in order to persecute her. Second, she had invented the incident, either out of paranoia or to get attention and sympathy. The other possibility was one he did not even want to contemplate. Suppose she had indeed killed her children. Was this her oblique way of unloading a troubled conscience? She must have known she could trust him with a confidence and that he would try to help her. As he pondered this possibility, he realized the depth of the dilemma in which this would place him. If she were to confess to him that she was guilty, where would be his greater duty? To the law or to his own religious principle of confidentiality, which he held inviolate?

In his role as a chaplain to the ambulance corps, where he was affectionately known as Rev, he had many sessions with her, trying to help this clearly troubled woman as well as to arrive at the truth. As the weeks went by, he felt he was making no headway. "I tried to discover from her what she thought to be the cause of the babies' deaths, but the more she talked about them, the more involved the story became. She would add and embellish."

For years she had rejected all suggestions that she seek professional help; now, suddenly, she was ready to take up as much of Burnham Waldo's time as he was prepared to offer. He was not entirely comfortable about this; the demands of his own congregation and of the ambulance corps allowed him very little free time, and having recently survived a life-threatening medical crisis of his own, he had to conserve his energies. But he had never yet refused an appeal for help, and his devotion to the well-being of others was extraordinary: at the same time as he was working with Marybeth, he, with the help of his wife, Ann, was able to save the lives of two women, one on the verge of suicide and the other a desperate alcoholic. In years to come he tried to comfort himself with the wry comment, "I suppose two out of three isn't bad." But he continued to agonize over the fact that despite all his efforts, he seemed unable to make any impact on Marybeth.

One reason why Marybeth felt so comfortable with Waldo was that at their first meeting she had been in the role of the care giver—or, at least, perceived herself to be. It was early in 1980, some time before she joined the ambulance corps, when Waldo was in the early stages of recovery from surgery for an aorta aneurysm which had almost killed him. As captain of the corps at that time Joe senior visited him in Ellis Hospital and took his daughter-in-law with him. Waldo had only a groggy recollection of the visit. "It was my first day out of intensive care, and so many people came to see me that it was as though the doors had opened for a Macy's giveaway." During their later conversations Marybeth claimed that she had been sitting at his bedside immediately after he came out of surgery. He thought this unlikely but made no comment.

As he and others noted over the years, all of Marybeth's stories—even the least believeable—had an element of truth. She had indeed visited the hospital, but probably not when she said. Her subsequent tale of the man in the restaurant whose life she saved when he suffered an aneurysm may have come out of her memory of Burnham Waldo's brush with death. It seemed to be in the same vein as her comment to another ambulance volunteer that her husband had gone to Chicago for the day on company business, and that she would have gone with him but for the fact that she was on ambulance duty. This remark, casually made, not only made her seem noble and self-sacrificing but gave her the importance of being married to a General Electric executive. In fact, it was Pat Wall, president of the corps, who fitted this description. Pat's husband got sent to places like Chicago, while Joe Tinning stayed at the GE plant in Schenectady, working shifts.

Similarly, there was the time when Marybeth told how she had to hurry home from duty because she had a roast in the oven, a story which would have been accepted at face value if only she had not been seen having a modest meal with Joe that evening at a diner in Schenectady. It was other, wealthier women in the ambulance corps who cooked roasts for their husbands.

Burnham Waldo's second meeting with Marybeth was unplanned. In the early stages of convalescence his wife took him to his doctor to have his stitches removed. On the drive home they stopped at the Shoporama Flavorland for coffee. Marybeth was there, also as a customer, showing off her newest baby, Jonathan. The three of them chatted for a while. It was January 1980; Jonathan, who was two months old, had another two months to live, and Michael was barely eighteen months old. Waldo went to both funerals, mainly in support of the children's grandparents, whom he knew through the ambulance corps, and, in thus showing his concern, became painfully, almost inextricably involved in the complex life of Marybeth Tinning.

SEVENTEEN

My sense of her—not that I believe in witches—is that she is almost like a woman who is possessed. Sometimes she would have such a look in her eyes that I would become very frightened. I can only describe it as a look of the devil.

—Social worker

As chaplain of the ambulance corps "the Rev" seemed the obvious person to help Marybeth cope with her personal problems. When she moved into her in-laws' house and became an active member of the corps, he thought he was dealing with a woman who needed to work her way through the normal stages of grief but who was basically stable. Grief therapy was one of his fields of expertise, but he soon realized that with Marybeth he was perilously out of his depth.

She barely mentioned her children, and when she did, there were no outward signs of sorrow. She recited their names and dates as though she were reading off a list, citing a cause of death in each case but having nothing more to say about them. There were no affectionate little anecdotes, no spoken memories to give them substance, no sense of tragedy at their loss. They seemed to have slipped in and out of her life like wraiths, leaving no palpable impression. It was other things, more personal to herself, which threw her into paroxysms of misery.

One day she showed up at the ambulance station so distraught, her eyes red and swollen that some of the volunteers called Waldo to come and talk to her. In other circumstances they might have called her husband, but even in the small world of Duanesburg, where everyone knew everyone else, the younger Joe Tinning barely seemed to exist. He went to work, and he went bowling. That much was known about him, and little else. He was rarely seen socially or spoken of by his wife.

[177]

Marybeth's bitter tears had to do with one of the few occasions when she and Joe would be seen together. The time was approaching for the annual installation dinner of the corps, one of the social events of Duanesburg, at which Marybeth was eager to make an impression. She had told some of the women volunteers about "*the* most gorgeous dress" that she had bought for the occasion and gave them a detailed description of it. She said that it was rather daring, low-cut, with spaghetti straps and that her in-laws did not approve of it.

"If you like it, then wear it," they all told her.

The next time the dress was mentioned was when she showed up in tears. She related that while it was hanging in a closet at her in-laws' house, some indelible ink had inexplicably been spilled on it. The implication was clear, but no one who knew Edna and Joe Tinning could believe that they had anything to do with this alleged incident. The tale of the risqué dress seemed as unlikely as the tale of the anonymous telephone calls, all of them recounted as a way of drawing attention to Marybeth and, perhaps, of communicating something she could not put into words. Was she trying to say that she could have been the belle of the ball if only something beyond her control had not spoiled it in advance? If the sensational dress she had bragged about did not exist, she had to find a way of explaining its nonexistence. The tale of the spilled ink sounded suspiciously like another Marybeth touch, one of those telling little details which gave her account realism at the same time as it made her seem either a heroine or a martyr—in this case both. The Rev, summoned to calm her down, was not sure what to make of it.

As he talked to her, session after session, he felt increasingly overwhelmed by the complexity of this woman's problems as well as by her demands upon his time. The more he tried to help her, the more she clamored for his attention. She would telephone him from the ambulance station saying that there was an emergency and he should come at once. When he got there, often at the cost of some other call of duty, the emergency was merely Marybeth needing to talk to him. She rarely had anything vital to say, her accounts of her own problems did not hang together, and the details kept changing. Nevertheless, she behaved as though this human contact were a lifeline to her. Waldo was probably the first man in her experience who had the sensitivity to try to understand what was going on in her confused, unhappy mind and to show that he genuinely cared about her welfare.

Her husband, painfully shy and inarticulate, seemed so out of touch with his own feelings that he could never have been much emotional support to her. His own childhood home was a place where love was taken for granted rather than demonstrated, and anger never got out of control. Equally, Joe's religious unbringing—fundamentalist, authoritarian and scriptural—gave him no insights into the emotional tempests which could tear at the soul of a Marybeth. Theirs was a marriage of unrecognized emotional longings, in which both partners were barely cognizant of the existence of their own needs, let alone each other's; a partnership held together by habit, duty and fear of the alternative.

Burnham Waldo must have seemed like a savior to Marybeth. She could talk to him as she had never talked to Joe. He, of course, was looking for a different outcome from their relationship—her emotional health—and after weeks of trying to counsel her he felt dispirited.

"I found that I could not get anywhere," he said. "I was out of my expertise. I told her she needed a psychiatrist or a psychologist and suggested a name to her, but she rejected the idea."

It occurred to him that perhaps he could get her some expert help by the back-door method of introducing her to a counseling organization with which he was associated, Haven of Schenectady. This group provided support services for the recently bereaved and for those whose relatives were terminally ill. He arranged for Marybeth to do some volunteer clerical work at its office, in the hope that if he said a discreet word in the right person's ear, she might be introduced to a clinical psychologist who was a consultant at the center. He visualized this psychologist (forewarned of the situation, of course) casually putting a hand on Marybeth's shoulder, winning her confidence and using his professional skills to get to the root of her problems.

To his lasting frustration, his message did not get passed on. The person to whom he gave it, Marybeth's superior, did not judge her to be in need of therapy. And far from helping her, Marybeth's association with Haven allowed her to create yet another grandiose image of herself. Back in Duanesburg she told stories, which appear to have been believed by her in-laws, of how her experience and skills were in demand at Haven as a counselor to bereaved parents.

She said that the administrators of Haven quickly recognized her ability to empathize with those who had lost a child, that because of the way she had dealt with her own losses, they were grateful to have her to call upon when newly bereaved parents needed to be helped through a crisis. She described in considerable detail some of the cases she had been asked to handle. The most memorable concerned the parents of a little girl who was killed when she ran in front of a car. This accident had actually happened; the rest of the story was Marybeth's.

"Do you know those parents can't bear to change a thing since she died?" Marybeth recounted. "All the dishes with her food in them are still on the table." She said she had visited the house, persuaded them to clean up the room and to get on with their lives.

As these stories began to circulate around the ambulance corps, some volunteers began to ask Waldo if he thought it was all right for Marybeth to be doing this kind of counseling. "She was such an unhappy person," one woman member recalled. "Most of the time she seemed tense, nervous, unbalanced, and on the verge of emotional collapse."

Waldo was appalled to learn that Marybeth had been representing herself as a counselor and insisted that her volunteer work with Haven of Schenectady must cease. What he did not know was that she had often left the Tinnings' home on late-night missions, purportedly at the request of Haven to assist a family in crisis, when in fact she had gone on less altruistic errands of her own.

It is hard to lead a double life in a place like Duanesburg, not only because it is small and inbred enough for gossip to spread fast but also because most villagers have acutely photographic memories of one another's cars. Newcomers to the area are struck by the frequency with which they will be told by neighbors, "I saw your car outside the post office the other day." Or outside Charlie's Restaurant or the Duanesburg Pharmacy. Thus the prosaic details of one another's daily lives are observed and reported. The times when no comment is made to a car owner are the times when a car is seen in a place it shouldn't be; then the word goes around to everyone else.

Thus it was that one member of the ambulance corps, driving home from working a late shift in Schenectady, saw Marybeth's car on more than one occasion parked three or four miles east of the village, not far from the interstate highway and close to Kathy's Motel, a somewhat seedy establishment which had a bar and restaurant. Rumor had it that Marybeth was making friends with truckers. One of her briefly held Duanesburg jobs, lasting only a few days, had been in Kathy's restaurant, where she seemed to have made a memorable impression. A permanent resident of the motel—a lonely widow named Connie who looked like an elderly version of a Raggedy Ann Doll, with orange hair, carmine cheeks, and thickly arched black eyebrows—became friendly with Marybeth and gave this description of her activities: "She would hang around at different bars in the neighborhood—Kathy's, Giovanni's, and the one at the airport. She wasn't a drinker, she would just have a glass of Blue Nun wine, and I would introduce her to these men. I couldn't blame her after what she told me about her husband bringing home his girlfriend. A pretty girl, Marybeth said she was, Spanish-looking. She was very generous about it; she even praised her." Connie believed this story, but there was no evidence that any of it was true.

"She was supposed to be getting a divorce," Connie continued, "and whenever I would ask her about her court case, she would say it was coming up any day now. When I first met her, she told me she had three children that were dead. She said they died of blood poisoning.

"I liked Marybeth. She would go shopping for me and bring me presents." Privately Connie referred to her new friend as Back Seat Mary.

Marybeth's car was also seen, sometimes late at night, outside Giovanni's Hilltop Tavern, which stood on a lonely stretch of road on the other side of the village. In its quieter moments Giovanni's was patronized by some members of the ambulance corps on their way home from duty, but at weekends it could degenerate into a rowdy bar from which loud music blasted until, in the small hours of the morning, patrons who appeared to be feeling no pain would stumble out to their cars and trucks.

Among the assorted membership of the ambulance corps, a few volunteers were gossiped about as being the kind of people who "ran around." To women of this description, Marybeth is said to have confided explicit details of her sexual encounters. Others who would have been shocked by such behavior got no hint of it from her demeanor but saw only that side of her which was socially correct, even prim.

When the gossip reached Marybeth's brother, Alton, as was inevitable since he lived in the village, he decided to have a word with his brother-in-law. He already had grievances of his own against his sister. When her compulsive spending got her into the kind of debt she did not want to admit to Joe, she sometimes borrowed from her brother, a few hundred dollars at a time, and took months to pay back with ten-dollar bills squeezed out of the housekeeping money. Since she moved back to Duanesburg, he had become tired of her increasing demands upon him, of her childish tears when she could not get her way, and of what he was now hearing about her cheating on her husband. One day, when he and Joe were splitting logs together at a woodlot near his house, Alton broached the subject.

"Joe," he said, "I want to talk to you, not as a brother-in-law but as a friend. People are talking about Marybeth running around with another man. I've seen her with him myself a few times, and I thought you ought to know about it."

Joe indicated that he had already been told about this by some of his colleagues at work and that he was past caring. Marybeth's interest in other men was not mentioned again. It was Alton's impression that "there hadn't been anything in that marriage for years . . . It was like Joe was numb."

In the meantime, it was becoming embarrassingly apparent to the Rev that Marybeth was infatuated with him. Although this is an occupational hazard for clergy who counsel lonely women, it can be intensely difficult to deal with. Where another professional might feel free to walk away from an awkward situation, a concerned minister still wants to do the best he can for the person he is trying to help, and by now there was no doubt in Burnham Waldo's mind that he was dealing with a very sick woman who was unlikely to get help anywhere else. In self-protection he stopped seeing Marybeth in his study at the Methodist church and invited her to the parsonage at times when his wife would be at home. One day the two women came face-to-face, and Ann Waldo would never forget the look Marybeth gave her. It was venomous.

At other times he felt it safest to meet her for coffee at Gibby's, which was near his church. It was the only restaurant in that part of the countryside, about four miles from the village center of Duanesburg and near the school which Marybeth had attended as a teenager. It looked exactly as it had in her bobby-sox days, a vintage diner from the 1950's, all burnished steel and pale green plastic—the hard, shiny kind which isn't made anymore. It was warm and welcoming with good home cooking, a place where customers were always asked how they were today as they gave their orders. There Marybeth and her counselor would linger over coffee, she talking compulsively yet telling him nothing, he feeling frustrated, sympathetic . . . and trapped.

It was Waldo's impression that she had been criticized and put down throughout her childhood; otherwise how could she have developed into such an insecure woman, so filled with self-hatred, so desperate to be accepted and acceptable that she felt a frequent need to lie? From the little she told of her early years, it was evident that she had not felt happy or secure. She was an only child until she was five, and during much of that time her father was out of the country, serving in World War II. While her mother worked to make ends meet, Marybeth was shunted between various baby-sitters—or, at least, perceived herself to be.

One of her sitters, an aunt, was tactless enough to tell her that she was an unplanned baby, that her parents had hoped to wait a little longer before having their first baby. She never forgot this. From the time he was old enough to understand she hurled at her brother, the accusation that "you were the one they wanted, not me."

Their father was the dominant parent, the one she feared yet wanted to emulate. Alton later recalled his punishing Marybeth for "her crying spells," which were like tantrums, chasing her with a flyswatter or a ruler, sending her up to her room and telling her to stay there until she could act right, then citing her crime and his punishment to her younger brother so that he could profit from Marybeth's mistakes.

Although Waldo heard none of these details from Marybeth, who was always defensive about her father, he sensed that she had very ambivalent feelings toward him; that all these years after his death she still yearned for his approbation; that whatever had gone wrong in her relationship with him was still unresolved because it had been buried so deeply in her subconscious. He could only speculate on the origins of her ambivalence. On the rare occasions when she

hinted of some early trauma it was in an oblique way which could
have had a variety of interpretations.

*When Marybeth eventually confessed to the police that she had murdered
three of her children, she was asked if she had been punished harshly
when she was growing up. It is a widely accepted premise that abusing
parents are the adult versions of abused children. Such children are often
strangely protective of the abusers, having been conditioned to believe
that their own wickedness, rather than parental cruelty, brought on the
punishment. This perverse thinking makes it possible, even excusable in
their own minds, for them to abuse their own children later on.*

*Marybeth's responses to her police interrogators convinced them she
fitted this classic pattern, but she refused to use it as a defense. At a
pretrial hearing after the death of her ninth child, Tami Lynne, William
W. Barnes, senior investigator for the New York State Police, described
a conversation with her after she admitted to murder.*

"I asked her why she did it, and what had happened," he said.

"And what did she say?" he was asked.

*His reply may have been the most significant statement that was ever
made about her. "She said that when she was a child her father misused
her, that he locked her in a closet, that he hit her with a flyswatter, that
she did not feel she was important or any good, that she never really
felt she was anything in her life, that she had a child and that her first
child died, and that she was an unfit mother, that she wasn't a good
mother. Other mothers' children would not cry like hers, that she wasn't
a good mother. She couldn't stop her children from crying and that she
suffocated, she specifically stated three children, and that the other ones
she didn't know what happened to them, but that she suffocated three
with a pillow."*

*When, in the same pretrial hearing, she was given the opportunity to
corroborate this tale of an abused childhood, Marybeth became defensive
about her father.*

*"Investigator Barnes brought up the fact that my father, he thought
my father was rough and maybe mean, although he was a nice man,"
she related.*

*Her response to Barnes's suggestion was revealing, not only of the
abuse itself but of her readiness to excuse it. "He hit me with a flyswatter
because he had arthritis and his hands were not of much use, and when
he locked me in my room, I guess he thought I deserved it."*

Of the various police who eventually questioned her, Barnes was the

only one to ask about her childhood. He did so because he already knew
something about it. And she let her defenses down enough to admit to
her father's strictness because she knew he knew. As a young teenager,
more than thirty years earlier, Barnes had been the monitor on the school
bus which came lumbering down from the high ridge north of Duanesburg
on which his family lived, pausing halfway down the crooked hill outside
a lonely frame house to pick up little Marybeth Roe. Ever since then
he had held the memory of her father watching from the open porch,
stern and unsmiling, as his daughter plodded across the front yard to the
bus stop. Other parents led their small children by the hand and gave
them hugs of farewell. Alton Roe, Sr., just stood there.

This memory remained so vivid that even after Bill Barnes had
become a senior police investigator with grown children of his own, he
never passed the Roe house (as he did every day on his drive to work)
without thinking about it. After Marybeth's father had died and her
mother had moved to an apartment in Schenectady, the welcome touch
of the younger Roes changed the appearance of the house enormously.
With baskets of flowers hanging across the porch, it looked lighter and
brighter. But Barnes, who had a police officer's photographic memory,
always saw superimposed upon it, like a monochrome snapshot from
another era, an image of the house as it used to be, dark, sullen and
forbidding, with a slightly built man standing on the porch, watching.

It was to this house that Joe Tinning came as a youth to pick up
Marybeth for a blind date. A friend had arranged the meeting, and
Marybeth confessed years later that when she opened the door, she
expected to find a tall, dark, handsome Prince Charming. Instead, she
was dismayed to see an underweight and painfully shy young man,
almost two years younger than she was, who had never taken a girl out
before and did not know what was expected of him.

"I almost ran back into the house and told my father I couldn't go,"
she related.

It may be significant that it was her father rather than her mother to
whom she was tempted to turn, that she did not in fact follow this
instinct, and that before long she and Joe were married.

After her father had died, Marybeth rarely spoke of him. But when
she returned to Duanesburg as a middle-aged woman, her mother-in-
law noticed that whenever she, Edna, picked up a flyswatter, Marybeth
cringed.

One day, when they were driving home together from an ambulance call, one of the women officers of the corps summoned the courage to tell Burnham Waldo what was on her mind. "I had been thinking about telling him, for a long time," she said, "but it was hard to find the right opportunity. Then we got talking about Marybeth's lies, and that made it easy. I told him that people were gossiping because she claimed to be having an affair with him. He just listened, but he was obviously very upset. Afterward I had a feeling of great sadness, knowing what the gossip might do to his reputation."

A few years later, after he had moved on to another church, he acknowledged that Marybeth's stories about this imaginary affair, embellished with Marybeth touches, came close to ruining his career. Some people believed them, citing as evidence the number of times that the two of them were seen together in Gibby's. It was a nightmarish situation for a happily married clergyman with grown children. He asked Marybeth to meet him one more time at the ambulance corps headquarters.

He was angry, but not as angry as she was after she heard what he had to say.

"I told her that she had done enough damage to me, that she needed a psychiatrist, and that she was not to call me for counseling anymore. She saw this as rejection and became enraged. She was like a child in a tantrum, but it was much deeper, and her eyes were so black. There was a look of hatred on her face such as I have never seen on anyone before or since. I thought she was going to assault me physically. Then she said, 'I don't forgive and forget. I get even.' It was meant as a threat, and I took it seriously."

Although he never again saw her alone, he did not stop agonizing about the fact that her emotional disintegration, which he felt he was watching, seemed likely to continue unchecked. "The worst thing you can do in medicine," he remarked several years later, "is to pretend that if you do something about a disease, it will go away. That's how cancer metastasizes. And here was a patient with cancer of the human spirit.

"The most frustrating thing for me was to have wanted so badly to help this woman, who was so sick, and not to have been able to. I still feel angry about the way she almost ruined my reputation, but I also feel very, very badly about the fact that in all those years nothing was done about her. There were social workers, police, doctors, nurses, clergy—all these professionals doing their darnedest to get her some help—and all of us failed. All of us failed."

EIGHTEEN

What Marybeth didn't like she got rid of.
—*Former friend*

Early in 1982 Chuck Ray was delivering mail in Schenectady's business district when a car pulled up alongside him and Marybeth jumped out. To the amusement of some men in a passing pickup truck she gave Chuck a big bear hug, right there on the sidewalk of State Street. "Congratulate me!" she announced. "I've become a property owner!"

She was her old bubbly, affectionate self, the Marybeth he liked to remember, elated as a child at a party. It warmed Chuck's generous spirits to see her so happy. She told him that she and Joe had bought a trailer in the Duanesburg area, about half a mile from her in-laws' house, and would soon be moving in. Her demeanor gave no hint of the emotional conflicts which had distressed the Reverand Burnham Waldo only a few months earlier. On the contrary, Chuck marveled at her cheerful ability to overcome tragedy and get on with her life.

She did not admit to him that the trailer was not her dream home. There was a small house for sale in Duanesburg which she would have preferred, but Joe complained that its lawn was larger than he wanted to mow. The price may also have been too high for him. Although in local terms he was making good money, a secondhand trailer may have been the best he could afford. His parents's generosity in saving him several months' rent had helped him pay off some of his debts, but it could not possibly solve all his problems. It was ironic that Joe, who started his working life with such good prospects, should still be struggling as he approached forty and that his retired parents should be helping him out.

The trailer was pleasantly situated near a cluster of houses and other trailers, with broad views of the open countryside. Joe was working on renovating it at weekends with the help of his brother and brother-in-law. As the time to move in drew near, Marybeth's enthusiasm waned. She did not like the idea of living in this lonely spot, and if she had to settle for a trailer, she wanted a new one. Or at least a new bathroom in this one. Alton's wife, Sandy, told her there was nothing wrong with the trailer that a little elbow grease wouldn't put right, but it was not what Marybeth wanted to hear.

Early one afternoon she was there alone, measuring the windows for curtains. A workman had stopped by that morning to repair the furnace, which had been giving some trouble. He was said to have left it in good working order. It was a bitterly cold day, and at about 2:00 P.M. Marybeth returned to her in-laws' house, where Edna Tinning was entertaining some of the ladies from her church. A few minutes after Marybeth had left the trailer, a woman whose house was close by noticed smoke coming from it, called the nearest volunteer fire brigade at Pine Grove, then called Edna Tinning. Marybeth flung on her coat and rushed back to the trailer. It had burned rapidly, sending up a cloud of choking fumes from the melting polyurethane of its fixtures. While firemen were vainly trying to get the blaze under control, a neighbor invited Marybeth into her house. The neighbor noticed that she seemed appropriately upset. She had not stopped to put on a hat or gloves and was glad to warm her hands around a cup of coffee.

The trailer was totally destroyed, and nothing could be saved from the wreck. The most valuable item to be lost was Joe's 35 mm camera. Officially, it was assumed that the fire was caused by an electrical fault, but some volunteers from the Pine Grove Fire Department suspected arson. Although the fire started on the wall where the electrical box was fitted, an experienced fire fighter noted that the first flames seemed to emanate from the floor immediately beneath the box, rather than from the box itself, which was about three feet from floor level. When fire breaks out, the first flames usually travel upward. In the Tinnings' trailer he noticed that the floor burned before the upper wall. "I wouldn't have been able to swear in court that it was arson," he said. "But I had a strong gut feeling." The furnace by the opposite wall of the trailer remained intact.

Arson is almost impossible to prove after a property has burned to the ground, as this trailer did. There were careful inquiries by the Schenectady fire investigator and by the company with which Joe had only just insured the trailer, but their findings were inconclusive. After a delay of several months the insurance claim was paid, but in Duanesburg the doubts remained. It was gossiped around the village that when Marybeth walked into her mother-in-law's house after leaving the trailer, she smelled of smoke. Or was it gasoline? The stories gathered new details in the telling.

Edna denied that there was anything strange about Marybeth's behavior or smell that day. In her account of events Marybeth knew about the fire before she left the trailer. "I think it broke out while she was cleaning," Edna said. She said that Marybeth hurried to her house and called the fire brigade from there. But why drive half a mile to her in-laws' telephone when closer to the trailer there were occupied houses with phones in them (including the house of the neighbor who also called the fire brigade)? It did not make sense.

Serious fires, the kind which destroy entire homes, are rare in rural communities. Of the forty to fifty calls received by the Pine Grove Fire Department every year, only one or two involved major damage. These were such outstanding episodes in the lives of the local firemen that they were talked about for long afterward. The biggest local fire in recent memory was the demolition of the Princetown Reformed Church in March 1978, almost four years before the loss of the Tinning trailer. This was followed, within two months, by a fire which gutted a large chicken barn at Jewett's Poultry Farm, close to the church site.

Both the church and the chicken barn fires were assumed to have been caused by faulty wiring, but they were linked by coincidence which gave rise to speculation. The Jewetts were generous supporters of the Princetown Reformed Church. After the church fire they donated land for the rebuilding project and offered one of their barns as a temporary place of worship until the new building was complete. Neither the church elders nor the Jewetts made any public allegations of arson, but the proximity in time and place of the two fires caused some of the fire fighters to speculate that there might be an arsonist who wanted to eliminate the church and everything connected to it.

After the trailer fire another speculation was added. If an arsonist had set fire to the church and barn four years earlier, could it have been Marybeth? There were similarities in the ways that all these fires started. But if Marybeth had a grudge against the church, what was it? Later, she confided to Cynthia Walter that some members of the congregation had accused her of killing her babies. Perhaps she also sensed some disapproval from the minister, the Reverend Harold Irish, whose behavior was to seem so cool toward her at Michael's funeral.

Another speculation had to do with Marybeth's troubled attitude about her own religious beliefs. She told some women in the ambulance corps that the death of her children was God's judgment upon her for changing her religion; if so, God had started punishing her several years before she strayed from the Catholic faith.

To add to the coincidence there was also a fire at Kathy's restaurant, where Marybeth had worked and flirted, and as time went on, that, too, was linked to her. It was indeed curious that she had some acquaintance with all these places which burned so mysteriously. But only with the trailer fire was there the slightest evidence of her involvement.

In New York State there is a three-year statute of limitations relating to crimes of arson, and not until Tami Lynne's death at the end of 1985 did the Schenectady police begin to take a hard look at the activities of Marybeth Tinning. They concluded that she had probably set her own trailer on fire, but it was too late to prosecute. From that suspicion grew a widespread belief that she had something to do with the other fires—at the church, at Jewett's farm and at Kathy's—but there was no evidence that she was even in those neighborhoods when the fires broke out. When the church burned, she was living in Schenectady with two small babies, Michael and Mary Frances, making only occasional family visits to Duanesburg. Nevertheless, after her trailer burned, her name became linked with these earlier fires, at first tenuously, but eventually, as the tale was told and retold, as positively as if she had been caught with the matches in her hand.

On the face of it, she was a victim of mischievous gossip. But the gossip was easily believed because something about Marybeth engendered real fear in people who crossed her. Out of this fear the stories of her potential for evil were born and flourished. The firemen who suspected arson at the trailer agreed to be interviewed for this book only if his name were kept out of it. So did several Flavorland waitresses, former neighbors, hospital nurses, dozens of people who knew her in various contexts over the years—all of them fearful, even after she had been sentenced to twenty years in jail, that if they spoke out against her, she would eventually seek them out and claim revenge. And the form of revenge which most of them feared was arson.

"Don't get me wrong, I'm not afraid of her," one waitress explained. "But I am afraid she might do something to my kids, now they are grown and have homes of their own. I'm talking fires. And who knows what else she might do?"

Another waitress, a former friend of Marybeth, was frank about her fears. "I would not as much as write her a note. I don't want her even to think of me. If she is capable of killing her children, she is capable of anything. She is not the kind who would shoot people in cold blood. But in their own way they will pay, and she will see to it that they pay."

Even Burnham Waldo was afraid that day she threatened him in the ambulance garage. Despite his innate belief in the human capacity for goodness, he felt himself to be in the presence of an evil so forceful that for a moment it seemed to have taken possession of Marybeth. It was something about the look in her eyes, a passing look, briefly noted but never forgotten, so smoldering with rage as to be almost inhuman. He was not the only one to be affected by it. A woman social worker and a hospital nurse had the same experience with her, and the look remained so strongly in their memories that they, too, were afraid to be quoted by name; afraid, perhaps, of the look coming back to haunt them. It was a look which in earlier times made strong men cross themselves, a look which could as quickly be replaced by the generous smiles and personal warmth which made the other Marybeth so endearing.

Many strange stories, some of them entirely fictional, circulated about Marybeth while she lived in Duanesburg. Their value lies less in their questionable truth than in the fact that she was the kind of person about whom such tales were told. At one time she was rumored to belong to a witches' coven which existed in the area of Central Bridge, a village six miles to the southwest of

Marybeth with her first child, Barbara

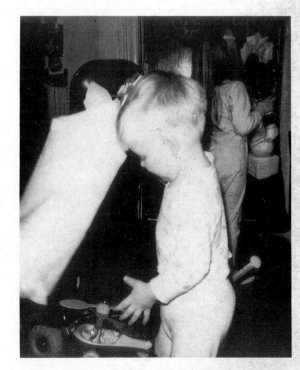

The second child, Joseph, with Barbara in the background, taken shortly before they died

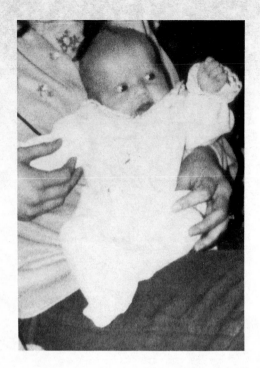

Mary Frances

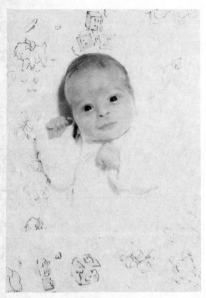

ABOVE: Jonathan, aged fifteen days

RIGHT: Michael at one year old, on a vacation trip to Maine

Tami Lynne

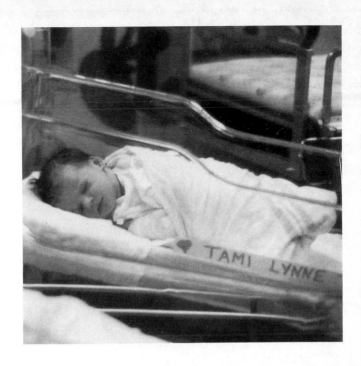

Marybeth and Joe with Tami Lynne

The house on McClellan Street where Marybeth and Joe were living when Nathan, Mary Frances, Jonathan, and Michael died (Stephen Longmire)

The house on Michigan Avenue where Tami Lynne died. The bay-windowed section above the porch is the living-room alcove where she slept. (Sid Brown, *Schenectady Gazette*)

LEFT: Cynthia Walter, the neighbor who tried to save Tami Lynne's life

BELOW: The Reverend Burnham H. Waldo

ABOVE: District Attorney John Poersch (Garry Brown, *Schenectady Gazette*)

RIGHT: Paul Callahan, defense attorney (Sid Brown, *Schenectady Gazette*)

Dr. Thomas F. D. Oram (National Photo)

Investigator William W. Barnes

Investigator Joseph V. Karas

Marybeth and Joe outside the courthouse cafeteria, waiting for the jury's verdict (Garry Brown, *Schenectady Gazette*)

Sheriff Bernard Waldron leading Marybeth to jail immediately after the jury found her guilty (Garry Brown, *Schenectady Gazette*)

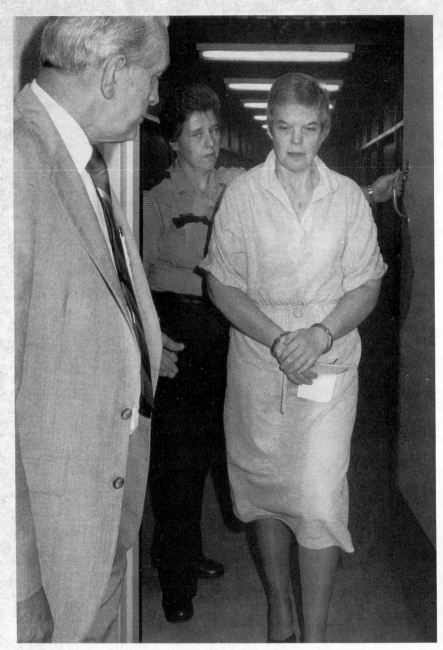

Marybeth being brought into court from jail to be sentenced. She is holding a piece of paper with her written statement, protesting her innocence. County Sheriff Bernard Waldron is at the far left. (Garry Brown, *Schenectady Gazette*)

Duanesburg, where the landscape loomed large and forbidding. There is not a shred of evidence that she participated, or even knew of the coven's existence, but in the late 1970's before Marybeth came back to the area, its presence was real enough. There was a woman in Central Bridge who wore a talisman for jewelry and openly talked about her membership, and there was a nearby farmer who curiously followed a group of black-robed women into the woods and saw them dance naked in a clearing. There were the thirty-foot circles mysteriously burned in the grass at the change of seasons. And there was the tenacious illness of a Duanesburg woman who angered a witch without knowing it; inexplicably she felt as though all her energies were being drained out of her until a fundamentalist preacher tried to lay hands on her and recognized the prior touch of an evil spirit. Fortunately he was able to pray the spell back onto the witch. In a rural community where such strange things happen, it took only a small stretch of the imagination to associate Marybeth, with her dark moods and the curse upon her babies, with the witches who cast spells on their enemies and danced naked under the moon.

This Marybeth of legend seemed to have no connection with the Schenectady housewife in polyester pantsuits who appeared to be so down-to-earth and dependable. People who saw her in this role felt guilty for ever thinking ill of her. Thus, when she moved back to Duanesburg, she had no difficulty persuading two male acquaintances, unknown to each other, that she needed to own a gun. It seemed such a rational request, the way she put it—the importance of having a weapon in the car for self-protection on these lonely country roads—that they found it impossible to refuse her. Only after signing her application for a pistol permit did both men remember that there was another side to this woman, a side which one of them described as "kind of flaky" and the other as profoundly troubled.

They were so appalled by what they had done that one of them contacted a state police investigator, the other the office of Schenectady County Sheriff Barney Waldron, where the gun permits were issued. Independently of each other both men said that on consideration, they thought Marybeth was too emotionally unstable to own a gun, and recommended that if the permit had already been issued it should be revoked.

Despite their attempted intervention, Marybeth's pistol permit was issued by the sheriff's office. Occasionally she was seen at target practice on the open land behind her in-laws' house. There is no record of her firing the gun for any other purpose, but one day she did threaten to shoot her sister-in-law Sandy Roe.

Sandy had caught her in a lie to Marybeth's mother, one which had caused trouble for Sandy. So she set the record straight, at some embarrassment to Marybeth.

"If you do that again, I'll come up to your house with my gun," Marybeth told Sandy on the telephone. "I won't kill you, but I'll hit you damn good."

Sandy took the threat seriously. "Marybeth had never liked me because I could see through her," she acknowledged. Another cause of friction was the fact that Marybeth's mother would sometimes cite Alton's wife as a model for her daughter. "Why can't you be more like Sandy in your ways?" she would ask plaintively, meaning, "Why can't you be more thoughtful and industrious?" Marybeth already felt uncomfortable with Edna Tinning's loving but firm attempts to guide and improve her. Her own mother's criticisms made her want to explode, and she was ready to take out her anger on Sandy. She never did, and it was Alton's feeling that Marybeth was more likely to use the gun on herself than on someone else.

During the eleven months that she lived with her in-laws, Marybeth's behavior became increasingly self-destructive. "I think she liked riding on the edge of being discovered in a variety of things," one of the women officers in the ambulance corps observed. "For a long time she fooled most of us because she could lie so convincingly and appear to be so sincere and misunderstood. But after a while her lies were beginning to catch up with her."

The most bizarre episode during her service in the ambulance corps was one which she claimed to know nothing about. It involved the theft of a piece of equipment known as a Resusci baby, a life-size model of a newborn infant used for practicing cardiopulmonary resuscitation. Made of vinyl, the doll had a head which could be moved back and forth, a mouth slightly open so that it could be breathed into, and a resilient chest wall which responded to the compressions of artificial respiration. For some time the ambulance corps had owned an adult-size mannequin known as Annie; the Resusci baby had been recently acquired as a companion teaching aid.

The two mannequins were kept in a downstairs closet at the ambulance corps headquarters, but in the early spring of 1982 they were borrowed for a demonstration at the local high school. Subsequently they were returned to a downstairs room at the garage but were not locked in the usual closet. When they were needed for a class a week later, Annie was there, but the Resusci baby had gone. The back door of the garage was found slightly ajar, indicating a burglary, but there were no footprints on the snow-covered path outside. Two things were obvious to senior members of the corps who tried to solve the mystery: the burglary attempt had been staged, and the theft was an inside job.

The baby doll was expensive, worth three or four hundred dollars, but seemed unlikely to attract the kind of thief who was looking for a quick way to raise cash. There was other equipment in the garage, more valuable and more marketable. Further, no one in the corps would have any reason to perpetrate such a bizarre theft. No one, that is, except Marybeth—and most of the ambulance volunteers believed she was capable.

"The thought was on everybody's mind, but none of us confronted her with it," said a senior officer of the corps. "We knew about her losing all those babies, and we had seen enough of her strange behavior. There was no other explanation."

Another official of the corps was more positive. "We didn't just think she stole the baby mannequin," he said. "We were sure she did. But we could not prove it."

The mystery was why. If, indeed, she had stolen the Resusci baby, was it as a poor replacement for the real babies she had lost, a doll to hold in her arms and imagine alive? One could try to breathe life between those parted plastic lips, not with the emotional detachment of volunteers practicing on a mannequin but with the passionate caring of a mother trying to bring her own child back from death. Could she be remembering all those times when she had failed to save her own babies? Was she thinking of a baby yet unborn, an infant to whom she might be tempted to allow something to happen, then want to rescue before it was too late? Or did the mannequin represent the only kind of baby who was never any trouble, who was more the way other people's babies seemed to be, the kind who did not cry? One could speculate forever and still not understand the appeal of an imitation baby to the mind of a Marybeth.

Other equipment had begun to disappear from the ambulance corps headquarters, and again she fell under suspicion. Her latest job in the corps was as supply officer. This involved keeping a constant check on medical supplies and reordering as necessary. This equipment was kept in a cupboard to which the supply officer had the key. After a while volunteers began to notice that items were not being replenished as they should be. When asked about them, she would report that they were on order and had not yet arrived or that they were temporarily out of stock. "We ordered glucose, airways, dressings, and none of them ever seemed to come," one board member grumbled.

All of Marybeth's explanations were feasible. Orders can get muddled. Mail can be delayed. Equipment may be stolen. These things can happen, just as tiny babies can suddenly die or an old trailer can suddenly ignite. What made all these episodes difficult to accept was that too many of them were happening around the same person.

"At first we all felt terribly sorry for Marybeth," a woman volunteer commented. "She seemed to have such hellish bad luck. But after we had worked with her for a while, we began to wonder if she wasn't making all these things happen."

There was a sense of relief in the ambulance corps when Marybeth announced that she and Joe planned to return to Schenectady. With their insurance claim from the trailer fire still pending, they did not yet have the money to buy another home, but the time had come to move out of the in-laws, house. Edna and her husband had shared their home for eleven months, and now they wanted to move to a smaller place on the other side of the village. So the younger Tinnings answered an advertisement in the *Schenectady Gazette* and settled for a rental apartment similar to the one they had left after Michael's death: the upper floor of a turn-of-the-century frame house on a straight street where all the houses were similar. It was a gesture of defeat, but they had little choice.

Michigan Avenue, their new home, was less attractive than McClellan Street. All day long trucks rumbled by on their way to the interstate highway, and the road's asphalt surface was cracked and pockmarked by the weight of them. Marybeth told her new landlord, Steven McGiffin, that she and Joe had no children and did not plan to have any. The apartment was taken on the understanding that there would be just the two of them.

After her return to Schenectady she continued to put in twelve hours a week as a Duanesburg ambulance volunteer. At her father-in-laws' request the ambulance corps waived its seven-mile residency requirement on the understanding that whenever she was on call, she would spend the day at his home in the village. If the truth were told, and it wasn't, many members of the corps hoped for her resignation when she left Duanesburg, but none of them wanted to upset her father-in-law. A long-standing member of the corps described him as "a dear, good man . . . you couldn't find a better." And although her emotional reactions were not dependable, Marybeth herself was. One day a week she left Schenectady at 5:30 A.M. to be at her in-laws' house by 6:00, when her twelve-hour stint began. At the end of the day she was sometimes seen visiting her old haunts, Giovanni's Hilltop Tavern and Kathy's Motel.

Her weekly trips to Duanesburg for ambulance service continued for two years after she had moved back to Schenectady and ended abruptly in the summer of 1984. A chance incident precipitated her resignation from the ambulance corps: the discovery of a first-aid kit on a sports field near her new home on Michigan Avenue. The kit was in a large wooden box such as the ambulance volunteers used, and this box was Marybeth's personal property. The contents, however, had the identifying labels of the Duanesburg Volunteer Ambulance Corps. The man who found the kit returned it to the corps headquarters, and that set off an inquiry into how so much equipment, including items which should never have been in the possession of an unlicensed volunteer, had found its way into Marybeth's possession.

Among other things, her box contained at least ten infant-size plastic airways. An airway is a curved tube with a mouthpiece at one end, used in mouth-to-mouth resuscitation when the patient's throat is blocked. It holds the tongue down while the rescuer breathes air into the tube, but it is very rarely required to revive an infant. An experienced ambulance worker might carry one or two infant-size airways in his kit as a precaution, and go for years without using them. Marybeth was not qualified to use airways, yet there were as many of them in her box as the entire ambulance corps would need to keep in stock,—all in the smallest baby size.

Asked to account for them, she insisted that they all belonged to her. She said that every time one of her babies was taken ill or died she had been given an airway at the hospital. This was not believed. All the airways in her first-aid box were in their original plastic wrappers, unopened and identical. She offered no explanation for any of the other unauthorized equipment in her box.

Board members of the ambulance corps agreed that there had to be a showdown. They told Marybeth that they knew she had stolen the equipment and that if she did not resign from the corps, they would prosecute. Further, she was requested to appear at a board meeting to give an accounting for all the missing equipment.

It was a painful and tense situation for the officers. They felt very sorry for "big Joe" Tinning, who had always been a staunch defender of his daughter-in-law. This time he looked distressed and had even less to say than usual. Marybeth did not attend the board meeting. A few hours before it was scheduled she stopped by the ambulance garage and left a note of resignation on the table. In it she expressed the hope that the board would accept her first-aid box and its contents as her donation to the corps.

The Resusci baby was never found.

NINETEEN

I do not believe she is guilty. She is a very nice person.
I like Marybeth a lot.

—Her last employer

Schenectady had changed very little in the year that the Tinnings
were away from it. It is a tired town designed for a different era,
trying without much visible success to undergo corrective surgery.
In the late nineteenth century, when the locomotive and electrical
industries flourished, it was built up in the sturdy, prosperous
manner of the Victorians, but it has not aged graciously. Various
architectural styles have been added over the years so that the
downtown section of State Street, the hub of the city, is a juxtapo-
sition of Victorian Gothic, Renaissance revival, Greek Revival,
modern plate glass and rectangular concrete, all these designs sufficiently diluted from their original pure forms as to have been
homogenized into small-town functionalism. This is overlaid with
the trappings of an industrial city: the power cables draped above
the downtown streets like Tuesday washing lines; the rumble of
railroad trains passing over the top of State Street on their way
between New York City and Montreal; the drabness of shopwin-
dows where goods are dumped rather than displayed, as if to make
them look stylish would be to deny the utilitarian nature of Schenectady.

It was not always so. The name of the city was Indian and meant
"pathway through the pines." At first it was a trading post. Then
the Dutch settled through, followed by the British—Joe Tinning's
ancestors among them—and there are still some lovely remnants of
prerevolutionary architecture. Early in the nineteenth century the
city's growth was spurred by the opening of railroads and the

[199]

excavation of the Erie canal. But it was Thomas Edison who put Schenectady on the map when he arrived on August 20, 1886, and like Brigham Young looking down on the valley of the Great Salt Lake, decided that this was the place where he would create his kingdom. A plaque by the railroad parking lot marked the spot.

Edison's machine works soon grew into the vast General Electric Company, which has dominated Schenectady since 1892. In its early years the plant attracted poor immigrants—Irish, Italians, Germans, Poles and Jews fresh off the boats from Europe—and around the turn of the century the population swelled rapidly. As housing was hurriedly built for this new labor force, Schenectady developed into a city in which most people lived pleasantly enough, but on the wrong side of the tracks. In this essentially working-class community one neighborhood—known as the GE Plot—was landscaped into leafy, winding avenues and set apart for the company's senior scientists and executives. The rest of the city was built up into straight streets of identical houses, where for several generations people like Joe and Marybeth had lived in rental apartments.

Their situation was typical of thousands in town: the daughter of a GE worker married to a GE worker who was the son of a GE worker. Young Joe Tinning had lifted himself out of the blue-collar rut by spending three and a half years in the GE apprenticeship program, learning engineering skills. Before that he had tried to do even better for himself by working for a college degree, but flunked out of Southern Methodist University after two years. He was now a methods specialist. As he described this job, "I develop cooling and fixtures for making specific products, also the operation sequence to make a product." In lay terms, it meant he translated engineering designs into technical reality, figuring out step by step how the machinists would create a tool or a piece of machinery from a draftsman's drawing. It was skilled work, requiring a background in engineering and a precise knowledge of the company's equipment, but it was also limiting. He was unlikely to move on to an executive job or to progress beyond a defined salary structure. Although this is true of most industrial employees, what was striking about the GE workers in Schenectady was the extent to which their jobs determined the neighborhoods in which they lived and the social circles in which they moved.

These constraints applied to all levels of staff. The wife of a GE executive gave this graphic description of her prescribed social world. "When we arrived in Schenectady," she said, "I soon learned that if I did not play bridge, belong to the GE Wives Club, and worship at St. George's, I didn't stand a chance of success." (She was referring to a historic Episcopalian church with a wealthy, conservative membership.) Marybeth and Joe were locked into a larger and less distinguished social group, several rungs down the company ladder.

By 1983, when the Tinnings moved back to Schenectady, this benignly feudal system was beginning to crumble. For decades the General Electric Company had dominated not only the city but, in its own field, the international market. The Schenectady plant produced turbines and generators which ran power stations around the world, and while the demand for electricity continued to increase, GE's market was secure and immensely profitable. Against this background the unwritten rule had developed that "What's good for GE is good for Schenectady", translated, it meant being powerful enough to keep competition out, the company could guarantee jobs for most of its citizens. It also did its best to ensure that the city's social and cultural institutions were well endowed and that local government was as solid and progressive as their influences could make it. For blue-collar workers Schenectady was a good place to live, and GE an excellent employer.

In the wake of the 1974 oil crisis GE's international sales fell heavily. By the time prices stabilized, measures for energy conservation had been introduced and worldwide demand for electrical power had decreased. For the first time in its history General Electric was also faced with stiff competition from Japan and Western Europe. GE struggled along for a few years before it became clear that some sections of the Schenectady plant would have to be closed down. In 1983 the layoffs began, wave after unsettling wave of them. Along with all his colleagues, Joe Tinning worried about the future which previously had seemed so secure. At the peak of its production the Schenectady plant had about 29,000 people on its payroll; by the end of 1988 it expected to reduce the work force to only 11,700.

Joe worked in the large turbine section, which was particularly vulnerable. Although he had less reason to worry than most because he was on salary, he could never again count on a GE income for life with a pension at the end of it. It must have seemed to him that whenever he tried to stabilize his finances, he was hit from another direction. After settling for a trailer home, then losing it, he was now worrying about whether he could hang on at GE.

In the early summer of 1984 an unexpected call from a stranger gave him the chance to sell the trailer site and at the same time brought Marybeth the offer of a new job. Madeline Harding, a Schenectady businesswoman, was driving around the Duanesburg area looking for a place to put a trailer of her own when she saw the spot where the fire had happened more than two years earlier. She liked the site, found out who owned it, met with the Tinnings, and made a deal with them.

Madeline talked about her job as the office manager of a privately owned school bus company. Marybeth responded by describing her work in the ambulance corps. The rest followed naturally. Since Marybeth was experienced at driving an ambulance, how would she like to drive a school bus?

Marybeth jumped at the suggestion. It was the kind of work which had always appealed to her, a service job which involved dealing with people, and being in charge of a busload of children gave her the same feeling of importance as ambulance driving. She started work with Dubb Transportation in September 1984, three and a half years after Michael's death. At this point in her life she seemed destined to remain childless. She did not tell her bus company colleagues about her eight bereavements, only, when she felt in a confiding mood, about one or two of them.

One of her assignments was to drive a busload of small children to a Schenectady nursery school. She may not have noticed a young-ish man with a light brown beard and shoulder-length hair who looked very hard at her when she delivered some children to the school one day, after she had been with the company a few months. Kevin Karpowicz did not have the conventional appearance of a doctor, but of all the pediatricians in Schenectady, he was the most outspoken in the crusade against child abuse. He remembered Marybeth Tinning very well indeed, from the time of Jonathan's death at Albany Medical Center.

Seeing her at the nursery school where he worked as a consultant was a shock to him, not so much because it brought back memories but because of the way she looked. She was obviously pregnant. It seemed incredible, and it was also horryifying—because when this baby was born, neither he nor anybody else would have the authority to do anything to protect the child.

Marybeth herself seemed to have mixed feelings about becoming pregnant at the age of forty-two. Although she flaunted her condition at the christening party for Carol and Andy's adopted daughter, she waited until the fifth month before tearfully phoning her obstetrician's office for her first medical appointment. He was a Catholic doctor attached to a Catholic hospital, St. Clare's, and among the reading matter in his waiting room there was usually some right-to-life literature. If abortion was on her mind, she would have gone elsewhere and seen a doctor sooner. From then on she was faithful about keeping medical appointments, but she often arrived at the obstetrician's office in a nervous and weepy state. On one visit Marybeth clung to a nurse, sobbing, and confided that she was very, very scared. The nurse assumed this was because of her age and the fact that her previous babies had died. So far as Marybeth's own health was concerned, there were one or two minor problems during her pregnancy, but essentially she was strong and well.

She wept again when she broke the news to her landlord, Steven McGiffin.

"Steve, I'm pregnant," she sobbed. "You're not going to kick me out, are you?"

"Of course not," he told her.

"But when Joe and I took the apartment, we told you it was just for the two of us," she reminded him, her voice still quavering.

"It's all right, Marybeth," he told her. "Of course, you can stay."

She showed the same tearful timidity with her sister-in-law Carol, as though she anticipated Carol's warning: "Don't you dare let anything happen to this one." She also claimed that she was afraid to tell her Michigan Avenue neighbor Sue Lencewicz, despite the fact that Sue had never criticized her. Once again she was giving double messages, acting as though she were scared of having a baby when, in fact, she was scared of what people would think of her. Beneath her diffidence she seemed to want to have another child. In her mind a baby was an extension of herself, and when the infant was admired, it was she who received the compliments. With every birth (as at every death) she was briefly surrounded by affection, and this filled a great gap in her life. In all her experiences of motherhood she never seemed to understand that babies do not give love, they make demands, and so the gap would open up again as soon as the novelty wore off and her latest baby became fretful and no one was around to reassure her. After every death she would compulsively put herself through the process again, always hoping that this time would be different.

Her baby was due in August 1985. She continued to work for the bus company until the school year ended at the beginning of June. It was her habit to leave home very early in the morning and return briefly during the day, parking one of the small school buses outside her house while she took a break. On one occasion a neighbor noticed that a male colleague accompanied her to her apartment. The neighbor thought this was odd, but Marybeth gave a plausible explanation. She said that her clothes had been soiled when one of the child passengers vomited on the bus, and that this colleague had driven her home to clean up.

Sometimes, sharing a cookout in the backyard with Sue Lence-wicz, she would recount some of her more dramatic bus-driving experiences. These were similar to her ambulance stories. One day, she said, a schoolboy got on her bus and threatened her with a knife, but with great presence of mind she stopped the bus and refused to move on until he handed over his weapon.

It was after her bus company job ended that she struck up a friendship with Cynthia Walter, having noticed that they were both at the same stage of pregnancy. She seemed to be as happy about having a baby as Cynthia was. In all their months of knowing her, neither of these neighbors caught a hint of any other aspect of Marybeth—either of the frightened child or of the angry, half-demented woman—which had been so troubling to other people.

One hot August evening, a few days before Tami Lynne was born, one of the former Flavorland waitresses had a chance meeting with Marybeth in a restaurant and was more shocked than Dr. Karpow-icz had been when he saw her at the nursery school. It was the same waitress to whom Marybeth had confided, with a faraway look in her eyes during an earlier pregnancy, that "God told me to kill this one, too."

This woman would never forget that moment of horror and helplessness, with just the two of them together in Flavorland's back room. Seeing Marybeth pregnant again brought it all back.

She was a widow having a pleasant dinner out with a man friend, and the brief encounter ruined her evening.

"Marybeth was sitting at a table in the restaurant, engrossed in conversation with her husband and another man," she recalled. "My friend and I came in later and sat in a booth nearby. Suddenly Marybeth got up to go to the ladies' room, and as she did so, I saw that she was very pregnant, ready to pop. I turned white. My friend said to me, 'What's the matter?' I said, 'Marybeth is pregnant again, and she is going to kill another baby.'

"As she passed by me, I said her name. She was trying to avoid me, but I wouldn't let her. She stopped to say hello, but I could tell she didn't want to talk to me. I said, 'Marybeth, you're pregnant again!' 'Yes,' she said, 'and I could have it right here.' She had a great big smile on her face when she said it. Then she walked on. I was going to follow her to the ladies' room, but I thought that if I did, I would lose my temper.

"I could not eat my dinner. I had the waitress put it in a carton. I kept telling my friend that Marybeth was going to kill this next baby, and he kept looking at me like I was crazy. 'They had better take you to E-wing,' he said." E-wing was the psychiatric ward at Ellis Hospital.

"I just couldn't make him understand."

A few days later Joe Tinning, Sr., shyly told a fellow ambulance worker that he had a new grandchild. More than a year had passed since Marybeth resigned from the ambulance corps, and none of the volunteers had any idea that she was pregnant. Now that the baby was born, her father-in-law seemed to sense that his announcement would not be greeted with the usual enthusiasm.

The news spread around Duanesburg very quickly. It was told to Connie, the elderly resident of Kathy's Motel, by a younger woman who used to frequent the motel restaurant with Marybeth.

"Marybeth has a beautiful new baby," she announced. Anticipating Connie's question, she added, "I don't know who the father is."

Chuck and Janet Ray missed the announcement in the *Schenectady Gazette*, so it was an enormous surprise to Chuck to see Marybeth pushing a baby carriage near Michigan Avenue.

"This is Tami Lynne," Marybeth told him.

"Whose is she?" he asked as he peeped inside. He assumed that Marybeth was baby-sitting.

"She's ours," Marybeth smiled. Chuck could hardly wait to hurry home and tell Janet.

It felt like old times to have the Tinnings back in town, proud parents again. Michigan Avenue was only a block from the post office where Chuck worked, so one day toward the end of 1985 he decided to take his sandwiches and visit with them during his lunch break. "We had been friends for a lot of years, and I had no qualms about ringing their bell and sitting down at their kitchen table," he said.

Marybeth and Joe were both home. After peeping at Tami Lynne, Chuck sat down with them and chatted. They told him that they had just contracted to buy a small house in Ballston Spa, about twenty miles north of Schenectady. It was somewhat remote, but property prices were lower there than in the Schenectady suburbs or in the Duanesburg area. Joe cheered himself with the thought that it was closer to the Adirondacks, where he loved to go fishing. Both he and Marybeth seemed excited about the house purchase and planned to move early in the new year. They had already started packing.

On Christmas Eve Chuck was again delivering mail on Michigan Avenue. When he reached number 367, he rang the doorbell. Joe answered.

"Merry Christmas to you and the family," said Chuck, smiling broadly. "And how is Tami Lynne?" He was pleased with himself for remembering her name.

Joe did not smile back. "She died last Thursday night," he said. "We buried her yesterday."

There was a long silence while Chuck tried to pull himself together. "I'm so sorry, Joe," he mumbled. "I had no idea."

He walked back to the post office, where he started to share the news with a friend, but became too choked up to continue. He couldn't believe that this ninth baby had died, he couldn't deal with it, and he couldn't concentrate on his job. After a while he punched the time clock and went home.

Part Three

MARYBETH

TWENTY

All these years and nobody did anything. It took this
last baby before the authorities acted, and then they had
to because there were just too many people who knew.
—Former colleague

Dr. Thomas Oram, chief pathologist at Ellis Hospital, had never
done a more careful autopsy than the one he performed on Tami
Lynne Tinning. But when all his detailed tests came back from the
laboratories, every one of them was negative. He considered the
possibility of an inherited tendency to hyperammonemia—the high
ammonia level in the blood which had been noted in some of the
earlier Tinning children—but ruled it out. If Tami Lynne or any
of her siblings had suffered from hyperammonemia from birth,
they would have been sickly and underweight. Instead, they all
flourished until suddenly stricken. Noting that "if you are at death's
door, you will get hyperammonemia anyway, under certain circumstances," Oram theorized that there may have been other life-
threatening incidents in the lives of some of the earlier Tinning
children, unknown to medical authorities, which could have caused
a surge in the blood ammonia level. But in Tami Lynne's case it
was too late to tell whether this happened before she died.

"We searched for everything and came up with nothing," Oram
related. Nothing, except for the congestion of brain and lungs
which denoted asphyxia, and asphyxia is the outstanding finding in
Sudden Infant Death Syndrome. It can also be caused by
smothering.

When he performed the autopsy on Michael, almost five years
earlier, Oram had not known about the subtle and microscopic
differences between the two forms of death from asphyxia, differences which SIDS researchers had barely begun to appreciate at

that time. Even if he had been able to show that Michael had been suffocated, the presence of that small patch of pneumonia at the base of one lung would have discouraged any prosecuting attorney from pursuing a charge against Marybeth.

Tami Lynne's death was less complicated, and for the first time in this family it was not considered in isolation. The medical histories of all the Tinning children were reviewed as an entirety. Looking at the various causes of death as they were certified—Reye's syndrome, cardiopulmonary arrest, acute pulmonary oedema, Sudden Infant Death Syndrome, even Michael's pneumonia—one could hypothesize that all the Tinning children, except Jennifer, could have been suffocated. Seven of the eight earlier diagnoses were either inadequate or questionable. The label of Reye's syndrome was attached to Barbara and, in retrospect, to Joseph largely on the basis of Marybeth's report that they suffered convulsions. Looking back over the records, Dr. Oram noted that no one but Marybeth saw these convulions. If, indeed, they had happened, they could have been in reaction to an incomplete suffocation attempt. While it might be fairly simple to smother an infant, he knew it would be "a very nasty business" to suffocate a child of almost five years old.

The seven other Tinning children—Joseph, Timothy, Nathan, Mary Frances, Jonathan, Michael, and Tami Lynne—might also have been suffocated. All their diagnoses left room for doubt, and some of their bodies had not even been autopsied. Jennifer was the only Tinning child who had obviously died from natural causes. Her multiple brain abscesses were of such severity that there was no mistaking them. Her death, the first of the nine, seemed to be the catalyst for all the questionable deaths which followed.

The theory, developed during Oram's discussions with other members of the Tinning Task Force fitted the known facts. Proving it was going to be difficult. If Marybeth Tinning were to be charged with murder, the prosecution would have to show beyond reasonable doubt that she had deliberately killed Tami Lynne. Her defense attorney would have an easier job—simply to cast enough doubt on the prosecution's case so that at least one person on the jury would lack the certainty to convict. There were no witnesses to Tami Lynne's last moments other than her mother, and no apparent motive for her murder. Any case against Marybeth would have to depend heavily upon medical evidence. That meant Oram would have to be very, very sure that this was a homicide.

There was a lot of circumstantial evidence surrounding the death of Tami Lynne, but this was not good enough. Nevertheless, it was intriguing. After he had heard some of the details of Marybeth's lifestyle from police and social workers, Oram wondered why a woman who had lost eight previous children would put her baby's crib at one end of the long apartment while she and her husband slept at the other. He would have expected her to have been so overprotective of her latest baby that she would never have left the infant alone. Yet there was no suggestion that Marybeth was a harsh or an uncaring mother. It was Oram's assessment that "in a funny kind of way she probably liked having children around."

He was also concerned that when every one of the last eight children was taken fatally ill or died, only Marybeth was present. She gave believable descriptions of the symptoms she saw, but there was never any explanation of what led up to them. Also, her estimate of the times of death was questionable. When he performed the autopsies on Michael and Tami Lynne, Oram suspected that both these children may have died an hour or two before their mother said they did.

He remembered that Michael was very cold when he did the autopsy, only an hour or two after the child had been rushed to Ellis Hospital from Dr. Mele's office. This surprised him. If, as Marybeth reported, Michael had been alive when she put him in the car to take him to Dr. Mele's, then he would not have expected his body to be quite so cold when he began his examination.

With Tami Lynne he used a standard test to determine the time of death by checking the clear fluid in the eyeballs, known as vitreous humor. Normally the vitreous humor is locked away behind the lens of the eye, but after death potassium from the cells lining the eyeball seeps into it. The longer a person is dead, the more potassium has entered the vitreuous humor, and in Tami Lynne's case the potassium level indicated that she had died two hours earlier than Marybeth reported.

"The trouble is that this is not a precise test," Oram admitted. "But I think Tami Lynne died about 10:00 P.M., not near midnight, when her mother sounded the alarm."

Although his suspicions were aroused, he was still reluctant to reach a diagnosis. He was not an expert in Sudden Infant Death

Syndrome, and some of Tami Lynne's autopsy findings puzzled him, so he telephoned a former colleague, Dr. J. Bruce Beckwith, Chairman of the Department of Pathology at the Children's Hospital in Denver and Professor of Pathology at the University of Colorado School of Medicine.

"It was one of the longest telephone conversations I have ever had," Oram related. "I told him the whole story from beginning to end. I had known him since 1964, when he and I did our boards together in pathology. At the time SIDS was new, and he was interested. Over the next twenty years he became one of the country's leading experts in it.

"When I called him about Tami Lynne Tinning, I was still a little hung up on the ammonia level and whether this might mean some abnormalities in the urea cycle. I described to him all the autopsy findings and also told him about the things I didn't find. In SIDS you usually get tiny hemorrhages in the face and eyes, but these were not present in Tami Lynne. I talked about hemorrhages of the stomach, and he explained that these probably happened during the resuscitation attempts. Other than that, he said very little until I had finished. Then he remarked, 'There's only one explanation for all this, and it has to be smothering.' "

Later Dr. Beckwith commented: "The logic is pretty straightforward. I believe very firmly that SIDS is rarely, if ever, a familial problem. There have been some reported instances of several cases in a family, but most of them can be explained by genetic diseases which may resemble SIDS but which in fact are quite different. Two out of every thousand babies die of SIDS, which means that the random statistical odds of there being two cases in a family are very small indeed.

"Of the twelve hundred SIDS cases I have dealt with, only seven were the second instances in a family. Five of those were later explained as inherited diseases which we failed to indentify at first. That leads to the conclusion that SIDS is nonfamilial. It also has distinct features. It is very rare in the first month of life and uncommon after six months. Most cases happen between the ages of two and three months; none after a year. Dr. Oram was describing with an age distribution curve which did not fit the known facts of SIDS.

"If it was not SIDS he was dealing with, the other possibility was a hereditary disease. There are two kinds of genetic disease:

dominant, the kind which can carry a fifty percent risk, and recessive. If it is dominant, you will see the same abnormalities in a parent. Both Tinning parents were healthy, so it would have to be recessive, in which case the highest risk of a child inheriting the disease is not one in two but one in four. But in the Tinning family all the babies died, including an adopted child. The statistical possibility of this happening to every child in a family of this size is so small that one can exclude it.

"Therefore, this was most unlikely to be a genetic disease. It was also totally inconsistant with SIDS. The circumstances of the deaths were so varied and covered such as age range that they simply could not be SIDS. Also, a SIDS death is hardly ever observed. It happens during sleep and is discovered later. For a parent to see a baby die of SIDS is very unusual. To see two babies die of it is unthinkable.

"That left only one possibility: that these children were murdered. And as I said to Dr. Oram, the question was not whether the mother did it, but how she did it.

"He asked me whether you could tell the difference between suffocation and SIDS. My response was that if you put a pillow over an infant's face, you can imitate SIDS. It is, however, an imperfect imitation. There is characteristic finding in SIDS of small pinpoint hemorrhages in the face and chest which can only be produced by obstructing the airway at the end of a breath. In eighty-five percent of all SIDS deaths that happens. But if you suffocate a child with a pillow, you will obstruct the airway at random points of the respiratory cycle, which means that very few babies who die of suffocation will show these hemorrhages. This baby whom Dr. Oram described did not. Nor did any of the others in the family whose records he had. And that strengthened the case for suffocation."

Oram had not seen a suffocated baby before, and at first the absence of visible hemorrhages puzzled him. He was familiar with them in victims of strangulation, and he thought that if Tami Lynne had been suffocated, he would find these same tiny broken blood vessels in her eyes and face. That would only be true, Beckwith explained, if someone had manually held her nostrils and mouth closed or if a constriction had been put around her neck. Then there would be visible lesions. There would probably be lesions of a different kind with SIDS. But if the baby was suffocated with a pillow, the pressure on the face would be equalized with the pressure from within, and there would be no surface hemorrhages. Hence it was the absence of facial marks on Tami Lynne which should arouse suspicions.

After that conversation Oram talked with Dr. Michael M. Baden, director of the New York State Police's forensic sciences unit. Baden, former chief medical examiner for New York City, reviewed all the medical records of the nine Tinning children and came to the same conclusion as Beckwith.

"I felt they all died of suffocation, except the first, and that the causes of death as attributed were incorrect," he commented. "It didn't make sense for all those deaths to be natural. Except for rare occasions, natural deaths don't occur suddenly and unexpectedly, and if there is more than one in a family, you have to be very suspicious.

"The records showed some indication of genetic factors. In two cases there was a high ammonia level in the blood, but I was not persuaded that this was of any significance. It would certainly not be a cause of sudden death. As I went over each case, the only one which made sense was Jennifer's because there was a legitimate diagnosis of meningitis and brain abscesses. These would have been very obvious at autospy. But it is odd for a baby to develop meningitis in utero unless there is an injection of bacteria. Usually we see these deaths in the babies of women drug addicts, which Marybeth was not. There had to be some other source for the bacteria. One likelihood could have been an attempted abortion, but there was no indication of this in the records. So that first death has to remain a mystery.

"Whatever happened to that baby, there was a great outpouring of sympathy for Marybeth Tinning. As we talked about it among the members of the forensic unit, the thought came up that she may have become a sympathy junkie. This would have given her an identity, made her feel important."

Beckwith had another theory about the effect of Jennifer's death. He was reminded of two other mothers he had known, both of whom reacted to the natural death of an infant by attempting to suffocate subsequent babies. "In some cases the mind can be so shell-shocked by that first loss that it becomes totally focused on it, and there seems to be a need to work through the grief by re-creating the experience. It is as though the mother is trying to punish herself, over and over, for her first baby's death."

Oram went through the world medical literature by computer and came up with a case which was uncannily like the one he was dealing with. It related to Martha Woods, a U.S. Army wife who between 1946 and 1969 had seven children die while they were in her care. Three were her own, one was a nephew, one a niece, one a neighbor's child, and one was adopted. Two others survived, but they also suffered several life-threatening episodes, always when Mrs. Woods was alone with them. These medical crises were striking in their similarity. Mrs. Woods would rush to a hospital emergency room with an unconscious child, stating that she had found the infant blue and lifeless. The baby would be revived and sent home; then a few hours or days later the incident would be repeated. And repeated. Eventually the child would be brought into hospital in a fatal coma. As with the Tinning children, unsuspecting doctors performed a variety of tests in a futile search for some rare disorder. None of these doctors was aware of the whole story because the Woods family moved around the country from one military base to another. Nor did it strike any of them that this concerned and caring mother could be harming her children. Only after the seventh death—of an adopted baby named Paul—was Martha Woods charged with murder.

After a five-month trial in Baltimore she was convicted of the first-degree murder of Paul and sentenced to life imprisonment. She was subjected to intensive psychiatric tests and found to be sane.

Oram found a detailed description of the Woods case in a 1974 issue of the *Journal of Forensic Sciences*. The account was fascinatingly familiar—not only in the way the children died but also in the mother's behavior. Like Marybeth, Martha Woods told tall stories. After adopting a child named Judy, she claimed to have received threatening demands from the little girl's parents, just as Marybeth claimed to have overheard a conversation about Michael's mother's wanting him back. Martha Woods alleged that a couple (presumably Judy's parents) came to the door and threatened her; that a man in a car kept circling the house; that someone was planning to burn the house down. The Criminal Investigation Division of the Army found no substance to any of these complaints. At the time Judy's parents were many miles away in another state. But, in what might have been a Marybeth touch, the investigators found flammable fluid splashed over the side of the Woodses' house.

The implication was that Martha Woods had made up the tale and fabricated the evidence. It was surprisingly like the story of Marybeth's untraceable burglars and of the mysterious fire which destroyed her trailer.

The article about the Woods case was written by Dr. Vincent J. M. DiMaio, who at the time of the trial was a young forensic pathologist in Baltimore, and by Charles G. Bernstein, who as an assistant U.S. attorney was in charge of the prosecution. DiMaio had since moved on to become chief medical examiner for San Antonio, Texas, and Bernstein was now well established in private practice. The Woods trial, which lasted five months and filled sixteen thousand pages of transcript, left such an impression on them both that more than a decade later Bernstein was still promising himself he would write a book about it, if only he could find time, and DiMaio had become an expert in infanticide as well as in a rare psychological condition known as Munchausen syndrome by proxy, which, he felt sure, fitted the behavior of Martha Woods.

The Munchausen syndrome by proxy to which DiMaio referred was first described by a British pediatrician, Professor Roy Meadow, in 1977. Twenty-six years earlier another British doctor, Richard Asher, gave the name Munchausen syndrome to those cases in which people either invent or manufacture symptoms of disease in order to be nurtured and gain sympathy. Although these cravers of attention have been known to medical practice for centuries—some of them fabricating diseases so successfully that they have been able to fool leading medical specialists— Dr. Asher was the first to put a name to the syndrome. He borrowed it from the eighteenth-century German baron, Karl Friedrich Freiherr von Münchausen (originally spelled Münchhausen), who was known as a teller of fanciful and improbable tales.

In his work at a large hospital in Leeds, England, Dr. Meadows subsequently came upon cases in which the fabricators of the symptoms were not the patients but the care givers, which in his kind of practice meant the patients' mothers. These women would repeatedly and deliberately make their children ill, or appear to be ill, by such strategies as administering poisonous substances, attempting suffocation, or tampering with blood or urine samples. They would then rush the children to the hospital and gain vicarious satisfaction from the nurturing which followed and from their own role as heroines in this medical drama. In the course of this drama even more harm might be done to a child by unnecessary medical treatment.

It was a complex, almost unbelievable form of child abuse in which a woman who craved attention would use her child as a pawn in a bizarre battle of wits with the medical authorities. Such women seemed to enjoy sitting around hospitals, consorting with nurses and doctors, feeling important. Many of them, like Marybeth, had worked in and around hospitals and gained a basic knowledge of medical procedures. Among these mothers Meadow noted many ex-nurses who had failed in their profession, now enjoying a game of one-upmanship with doctors. It was typical for them to boast, as Marybeth did, that some of the best specialists in the country had assembled a file on their families "this thick."

After repeated episodes some of their children would inevitably die. A striking factor about these Munchausen by proxy cases was that when the mothers were confronted by doctors, they stopped abusing their children.

Oram's next move was to telephone Dr. DiMaio, in San Antonio.

"There's a strong similarity to these cases of repeated infanticide," DiMaio commented. "Over the years I've handled three of them. One was Martha Woods. The other two mothers were never prosecuted. District attorneys are reluctant to take these women to court because the evidence is circumstantial, and there are never any witnesses. The only way you can prove murder is to show a pattern of behavior."

This was not encouraging news for the prosecution. According to their death certificates, the first eight Tinning children died of natural causes. That was also true of the first six Woods children, but Martha Woods's trial had created a legal precedent, one which could make an enormous difference to the outcome of the Tinning case. Although Martha Woods was charged only with the murder of seven-month-old Paul, a federal judge in Baltimore permitted the introduction of evidence that all nine children suffered a total of twenty life-threatening respiratory attacks while they were in her care. Seven of these attacks were fatal; all of them, when reconsidered, could have been caused by smothering even though they were attributed to natural causes at the time. As with Marybeth, there did not seem to be sufficient evidence to convict Martha Woods on any one particular incident. Only when the stories of the nine children were considered collectively did the pattern become clear. Then it seemed evident that despite the variety of causes listed on the seven death certificates, all these children probably died in the same way.

Martha Woods's appeal was denied by a federal court of appeals; subsequently the U.S. Supreme Court refused to review the case. Hence the legal precedent that evidence of similar prior acts by the defendent may be introduced by the prosecution in cases of child abuse or infanticide, was upheld right through the federal court system to the highest level. The rationale for this was that in the inevitable absence of witnesses, evidence of repeated incidents may be the only means of showing that a crime was committed. It was an important ruling which, if Marybeth were to be charged with murder, could make the prosecution's case very much easier.

DiMaio had reached his own conclusions about why certain women repeatedly kill their babies and how they are able to avoid suspicion.

"It's a classical pattern," he said. "A mother will come to an emergency room and say that her child turned blue and stopped breathing. A doctor resuscitates the child and sends it home, but she is back in a day or two with the same story. This time the hospital staff gets really worried and does a work-up on the child but can find nothing. Before long the mother is back again, and a whole lot of specialists get called in. All these doctors keep looking for some mysterious disease, but they do not get suspicious.

"With these repetitive suffocations, the mothers don't mean to do away with the child. They are not psychopaths. They just want attention. Some of them make multiple trips to the hospital, and if only pediatricians could recognize what is going on, they might prevent a few babies from dying.

"Some of these deaths get described as SIDS, but that's a wastepaper basket diagnosis. All it means is that you have a dead child and no obvious cause of death. Forensically we know that some babies are murdered, but their deaths go unnoticed.

"A lot of doctors, especially pediatricians, are very naïve about these cases. Most physicians come from middle-or-upper-class backgrounds and have never been exposed to violence or crime. They have been so insulated from the seamy side of life that it's even hard to get some of them to believe in the battered baby syndrome. Part of the problem is mind-set. Most of them go to good colleges and medical schools and live in nice suburbs. They think that everyone else leads the kind of sheltered lives that they do.

"They think that all mothers care about their children and find it very difficult to accept that some mothers don't. A forensic scientist has a different approach. In my job I see a murder a day, and I can pick up on a case like this in thirty seconds. I would be able to recognize when a mother had been killing her children while the standard physician would be shaking his head and saying that this could not be.

"These cases are not common, but they are out there. And in my experience, most of these women will confess if you face them with it. But very few of them get prosecuted because this is the kind of case which the prosecution can easily lose, and DAs don't like to lose cases. So the legal profession isn't doing much about pursuing mothers who kill babies, and some of them are getting away with it."

In January 1986, within a month of Tami Lynne's death, everyone who had been involved in the Tinning case met at the New York State Police headquarters in Albany. At this conference they shared information and discussed strategy. There, too, Oram went over all his findings with the medical experts of the state forensic unit.

Later he recalled: "After going through all the studies and lab results together, we all solemnly—and I was the last to agree with this, but in the end I was the most convinced—came to the conclusion that suffocation was the only explanation. At this combined conference we also made up our minds that the only method of approach was to confront the mother."

TWENTY-ONE

I want to see her punished for what she has done. I want
to see her put away for a long time.
                                        —*Flavorland waitress*

Marybeth was counting the days to the move to Ballston Spa. She
was anxious to leave Schenectady, to get away from the hushed
gossip and the strange glances, from the questions neighbors asked
her as well as the ones they didn't ask, from the subtle ways in
which the loss of her ninth child had begun to change her relationship with everyone around her.

Her two sisters-in-law were ignoring her. An unsuspecting
neighbor wanted to know whether there had been a medical investigation into the cause of Tami Lynne's death, and if not, why not,
hinting that she thought Marybeth was lacking in concern because
she wasn't spending her days sitting on the medical examiner's
doorstep. Another neighbor, her good friend Cynthia Walter, had
become withdrawn. On the surface she was just as warm and caring
as she had ever been, but a tension had developed between the two
women, a shrinking back on Cynthia's part whenever Marybeth
asked, as she had often asked when Tami Lynne was alive, whether
she might hold Cynthia's infant son. Cynthia told herself that she
was being irrational and unkind. How could she deprive this mother
who had been deprived of so much? Nevertheless, it troubled her
that Marybeth seemed more anxious to hold Aaron than she used
to be, as though she wanted him for her own. Cynthia would hand
over her baby reluctantly and feel miserably uncomfortable until
he was back in her arms.

She could not say why. It had not yet crossed her mind that
Marybeth might have had anything to do with the death of Tami

Lynne, But on that night of December 20, when they were at St. Clare's Hospital together, Cynthia had cornered Dr. Bradley Ford, who was her pediatrician as well as Marybeth's, and asked him, "Should I let Marybeth near my child after this?"

It was an odd question from an experienced nurse. Crib deaths aren't contagious, as Cynthia well knew. But the words were out of her mouth before she had time to think about them, as though a sixth sense were warning her that her friend should not be around babies. Dr. Ford tried to reassure her, but he, too, knew very little about Marybeth's history. Cynthia had recommended him to Marybeth without knowing that the reason why her neighbor was looking for a pediatrician was that the doctor who had cared for most of her earlier children, Dominick Mele, had ended his association with Marybeth after Michael had been brought dead to his office.

One day, still struggling with her conscience, Cynthia left Aaron with Marybeth while she went to get a haircut. It was late January, about a month after Tami Lynne's death, and Cynthia was preparing for a ten-day trip to Florida to visit relatives. She wore her dark brown hair in a neat bob which did not take long to shape, but the beautician had barely begun when Cynthia suddenly panicked.

"Please hurry and finish," she pleaded. "I have to leave. The woman I left my baby with has just lost hers, and I have a funny feeling about leaving her alone with him."

She hurried home. Everything was normal. Aaron looked content, and so did Marybeth. Cynthia felt immensely relieved but was still uneasy. "Something in my subconscious told me that I had to get back to my baby,' she explained, long afterward.

On January 30 Marybeth drove her to the airport and warmly wished her a happy vacation. "Call me when you get there. Call me collect," she insisted.

In this typically generous gesture Marybeth dispelled the awkwardness between them. Cynthia hugged her and went to catch her plane. Neither of them could have guessed it, but this was the last time they would see each other as friends.

On Tuesday February 4, 1986, five days after Cynthia's departure, Marybeth was packing up her belongings. In her own description, the living room of her Michigan Avenue apartment was a disaster area with piles of linens on the chairs and sofa and packing cartons scattered around. She was tired and a bit disheveled, and she had paused to watch her favorite television soap opera, *Days of Our Lives*. She hated to miss an episode. At about 1:35 P.M., shortly after the mid-program station identification break, there was a knock on the front door.

As she went down the flight of stairs to answer it, she saw two pairs of men's legs through the door's glass panel. One pair belonged to Bob Imfeld, the Schenectady police investigator who, along with Betsy Mannix, the Social Services caseworker, had called on her and Joe right after Tami Lynne died. Her other visitor, also heavyset and middle-aged, was Investigator Joseph Karas of the New York State Police's Bureau of Criminal Investigation. They were in plain clothes, and Karas's unmarked gray Chevrolet was parked outside the house.

Marybeth had to clear things from the sofa and chairs to give them places to sit. They told her that they would like to discuss Tami Lynne's death but would prefer to do this at the station, where they had their files. Would she come with them?

She did not realize this, but she was not obliged to agree. They had no warrant for her arrest, and she need not have let them in. Or she could have answered their questions in her chaotic living room. It was not because of their files that they wanted to take her on to their territory; it was for the psychological reason that she would be less able to walk away from unwelcome questions and for the practical one that a polygraph (lie detector) machine would be on hand. Marybeth said later that she went with Imfeld and Karas because she felt she had no choice. Many people react to a police presence in that way, and the state police captain who formulated the strategy in this case counted on it.

Timidly she asked if she might first telephone Joe. They readily agreed, but Imfeld followed her through the dining room and into the kitchen, where she picked up the phone. She had to try twice to get Joe's number at General Electric, and her nervousness was showing. Imfeld was edgy, too, knowing that she had a permit for a .22 caliber pistol which was probably in the apartment. He heard her tell Joe that "the police are here and they want me to go down to their office about Tami" and ask him if she should do so. He must have said yes because her next question was: "Should I call Paul?"

Paul Callahan was the Duanesburg lawyer who had acted for the

Tinnings in their recent purchase of the Ballston Spa House. He was five years younger than Marybeth, a high school classmate of her brother, Alton, and the only lawyer she knew.

Joe's response to his wife's question of whether she needed legal advice astounded Imfeld, Karas, Paul Callahan himself, and, eventually, the jury that determined Marybeth's guilt.

"Have they read you your rights?" he asked her. Although this was hardly a time for levity, Joe said later that his reply was half made in jest. ("You have to know my husband," Marybeth explained.)

"No," she replied.

"Then there's no need to call Paul." Joe urged her to calm down and relax.

Listening to her end of the telephone conversation, Imfeld noted that "the more she talked, the more excited she became. She started shaking. She started trembling. And her voice—I thought she was going to break down and cry—her voice started to get crackly like she was upset. Then she handed me the phone. Joe wanted to talk to me, to know what was going on."

Imfeld repeated to Joe that he was investigating Tami Lynne's death and wanted Marybeth to go "to the office" to answer some questions. Joe said he did not see any problems about that, but he would like to be there, too. He was told that this would be arranged.

In fact, it had been arranged already. Picking up Joe from work and taking him to the same police headquarters were part of the strategy. Police had carefully chosen a time when he would be in his office and Marybeth at home. The two of them were to be questioned separately to make sure there was no collusion over the story Marybeth told. Joe was not a serious suspect, and it does not seem to have occurred to him that his wife was. Even so, it is extraordinary that having heard her near tears on the phone, having seen her jittery reaction when Imfeld called at the house because she (Marybeth) thought he had come to arrest her, having surely wondered how and why all his babies died in his absence, and having just learned that the police wanted to interrogate her again, he did not think she needed legal advice.

Imfeld and Karas asked Marybeth if she was ready to leave. She wanted to know how long she would be gone, and they told her an hour or so. She said she would like to change her clothes and went into her bedroom, leaving the door slightly ajar. They waited uneasily outside, pacing the creaking floor. A few minutes later she rejoined them, wearing a different blouse, the same slacks, and with her short blond hair freshly brushed. She picked up her handbag and a coat from the hall and followed them down the stairs.

It was a bitter day with a forecast of snow. Karas got into the driver's seat of his Chevrolet, and just as she would have done on an outing with Joe, Marybeth settled beside him. Somewhat surprised, Imfeld took a back seat. Marybeth had expected a short drive to the Schenectady police headquarters on Liberty Street, but instead of heading downtown, Karas turned the car in the opposite direction, onto the New York State Thruway.

"Where are we going?" Marybeth asked. Only then did Karas tell her that she was being taken to a state police barracks at Loudonville, an Albany suburb, almost half an hour's drive away. She was not given the reason: that Loudonville was where the polygraph equipment was kept and where other investigators would be on hand.

The barracks, a low, modern building in a parklike setting, was unfamiliar to her. Karas led the way to the second floor, and as they were climbing the staircase, he turned to Marybeth and asked if she had her pistol with her.

"Of course not," she remembered answering. "I'm not allowed to carry a concealed weapon. Only special people."

Was she carrying her pistol permit? he asked.

"Yes," she told him.

"May I have it?"

She delved into her handbag and handed him the permit from her wallet. As a state police investigator Karas was on his home territory, and taking charge, he led her and Imfeld into a small upstairs office and sat behind the desk. There were two other chairs, a hard upright one to the right of the desk, where Marybeth sat, and a badly worn overstuffed green chair for Imfeld directly opposite Karas. The only other furniture was a wall clock and some file cabinets.

Karas ordered coffee for the three of them, and for about an hour he and Imfeld led Marybeth in conversation about herself, her family, her education, and her various jobs. They were not wasting time. This was all part of the strategy. Over the past several days they had gone over it in detail with Dr. Oram at Ellis Hospital and with Dr. Virgil January at the State Police Academy. Dr. January was the behavioral scientist on the state forensic unit; his job, in this case, was to reach a psychological understanding of Marybeth from the available evidence, and to advise law enforcement officers about the most effective ways of dealing with her.

From what he had already learned of her, January was struck by the way in which her personality could shift from fearful and passive to strong and manipulative, depending upon the situation in which she found herself. He saw Marybeth as a woman who liked to be around children but who could not handle the stresses which go with a nurturing relationship, and he wondered whether she might have been abused in childhood—mentally, physically, or sexually. Duanesburg was the kind of community in which such things were more likely to happen than in most. A recent survey by the New York State Police had shown that there were more reported cases of incest in that general area of the countryside than in any other part of the state. It was an unexpected finding, considering the proximity of Albany and Schenectady, both sizable towns. But until recently this had been farm country, its people self-sufficient and a law unto themselves.

Although some of the emerging profile of Marybeth was conjecture, the Tinning Task Force—and by extension the state forensic unit—had recently received a great deal of unexpected information about her. In the belief that Tami Lynne had not died naturally, Andy and Carol Tinning had gone to the Schenectady police. Alton and Sandy Roe had followed them a few days later. Both couples had spent several hours telling investigators what they knew about Marybeth.

This bold move created a deep rift between their generation of the family and their parents, one which might never be mended. Joe's parents and Marybeth's mother disapproved strongly of their actions. Carol was the first to suggest talking to the police, and she acted out of conscience. "I thought I was doing my best to prevent anything from happening to Tami Lynne," she said, "but it wasn't enough. After she died, I said to Andy, 'Something has to end here. I can't take it anymore, this business of standing by and saying nothing.' It was important to me to see some justice done. And that made us the bad guys in the family."

Sandy shared her feelings. "I had felt guilty about keeping quiet ever since Michael died," she admitted. "That morning when

Marybeth called me to say she couldn't wake him. I knew something was very wrong, not just with Michael but with the tale she was telling me."

Consequently, when Marybeth was taken to the state police barracks at Loudonville, her interrogators knew more about her than she thought they knew. They had learned about her attempt to poison Joe with the pills she had picked up from the drugstore for Carol's son, about her emotional detachment from her babies right after they died, about the stagy funerals which she seemed to enjoy, about petty thefts of money from Carol and other members of the family.

With this knowledge of her in mind, Marybeth's interrogators had been advised by Dr. January to encourage her to talk about herself before they broached the subject of Tami Lynne, throwing in a few leading questions such as, How did she feel about death? Why, if her babies kept dying, did she continue to have more?

After more than an hour of this conversation Karas determined that Marybeth was sufficiently relaxed for some serious talking. He then took the action that Joe Tinning had joked about: he advised Marybeth of her rights, the constitutional safeguards against self-incrimination.

Karas handed Marybeth a card on which the rights were printed. At the same time he went over the wording with her:

> You have been advised of the following: You have the right to remain silent, and you do not have to make any statement if you do not want to. If you give up that right, anything you say can and will be used against you in a court of law. You have a right to have a lawyer present before making any statement or at any time during this statement. If you should decide you want a lawyer and cannot afford to hire one, a lawyer will be appointed for you free of charge and you may have that lawyer present before making any statement. You have the right to stop at any time during that statement and to remain silent and have a lawyer present.

Karas later testified that he asked Marybeth if she understood these rights and that she said she did. She maintained that she was never read them. Although the words on the printed card were plain enough, she does not seem to have understood their full intent. She told Karas that she would not give a written statement but was willing to talk about Tami Lynne and that she did not want a lawyer. To his correct interpretation of the law, in agreeing to talk, she was waiving her rights. She seems to have believed that so long as she did not sign anything, what she said to Karas and Imfeld was somehow privileged.

"Read rights to Marybeth Tinning," Karas wrote in his notebook. "Waived at 4:30 P.M." Then he and Imfeld began to ask her about the night of December 19–20.

Although they went over it with her several times, she stuck to her original story. She had gone to bed but was unable to sleep. She got up, leaving Joe asleep, went into the living room, and watched television for a while. Then she checked on Tami Lynne and found that she was not breathing. As she lifted the baby out of her crib, she noticed a spot of blood on the sheet. She tried to resuscitate her, woke Joe, called for Cynthia, and summoned an ambulance. This account differed in one important detail from her original story. At that time she said Tami Lynne had turned blue. Now she described has as "gray-looking."

Karas asked Marybeth about her resuscitation attempts. She told him she had learned the technique as a volunteer ambulance worker in Duanesburg. As Karas related the conversation, "she explained to me . . . that she was qualified because she had passed the test on Annie, the resuscitating dummy, that she had passed a written test on the same subject, and that she was qualified to treat babies as well as adults."

That was untrue. She wasn't qualified. But the strange thing about her statement was that when she recalled learning the technique of reviving babies, she talked about working on the adult-size mannequin Annie, not on the logical learning tool, the Resusci baby which had so mysteriously disappeared from the Duanesburg ambulance headquarters.

Karas tried to draw her out about her other children. She said they all cried a lot, making her nervous, making her feel that she was not a good mother. She recalled that Tami Lynne had been crying and fretful on the evening of her death. Barbara, who was almost five when she died, needed to be disciplined shortly before she was taken fatally ill, and Marybeth did this by making her stay in her room. Nathan she remembered as a very quiet child . . .

and then her conversation turned back to herself and the things she liked, horror stories and romantic novels.

Primed by Carol and Andy Tinning's revelations to the Schenectady police, Karas asked her about the time when Joe almost died from an overdose of phenobarbital.

Karas recalled her response: "She said she had a problem with her husband. They had been fighting over money for a long time. She spent the money faster than he would make it, and they would fight over that. She had a prescription at her house for a relative, I believe it was a nephew, and it was phenobarbital . . . She said there were fifty to seventy small pills in the bottle, and she put them in some juice, grape juice or iced tea—she wasn't quite certain at this time—and gave them to her husband.

"I said, 'Well, what happened after that?' She said he went in and lay down on the couch in the living room—this is at their home on Cleveland Avenue—and I said, 'What did you do then?' She just looked at me and said, 'Well, I let him sleep.' "

She became excited after she described poisoning Joe, talking faster and louder and waving her hands, but she didn't finish the story. It made her think of her husband, and suddenly she wanted to stop talking and be taken to see him. She had been told that the police had called for him at the General Electric plant and that he was in a room across the corridor, waiting until she had finished with the investigators. It was 6:30 P.M., and in the two hours of questioning since Marybeth was read her rights Karas and Imfeld had learned very little. Her only admission was about her attempt to poison Joe, but that was almost twelve years earlier, and since New York State had a five-year statute of limitations for such cases she could not be charged with the crime. She continued to insist that she had not harmed her children.

They decided to take a break. Karas remained at his desk. Imfeld went to get something to eat. Marybeth refused the offer of a sandwich but asked for more coffee. It was understood that after a while the questioning would resume.

During the afternoon there had been some conversation between Joe and the two policemen who had picked him up. Answering their questions mostly in monosyllables, Joe said that no, he had not been suspicious about the children's deaths, that he had accepted his wife's description of their last moments, that he assumed what happened was "just one of those things."

"I was with him for five hours," one of the police officers commented later, "and do you know what I found out about him? Nothing."

There might never have been a break in the case but for the fact that late in the afternoon Investigator William Barnes arrived at the Loudonville barracks. He had been kept on standby duty by Captain Looney of the State Bureau of Criminal Investigation, and Looney, who had orchestrated Marybeth's interrogation, knew that this was precisely the moment to bring him in. If anyone could get the truth out of Marybeth it would be Bill Barnes, one of the bureau's most skilled investigators.

Looney formulated his plan for Marybeth's interrogation after receiving a memorandum from Dr. Baden, head of the forensic unit. It read: "It is clearly my opinion beyond a reasonable medical certainty that the Tinning children died as the result of homicidal asphyxia."

That broadened the focus of the investigation. Now it was not just Tami Lynne's death which was a possible homicide. Marybeth was also a prime suspect in the deaths of seven of her other eight children.

TWENTY-TWO

Marybeth would do things out of desperation without thinking of the consequences. If a baby was crying, I could see her putting a pillow over its face, just so she could hush it and get some sleep.

—*Former friend*

Bill Barnes was not part of the Tinning case until the afternoon of February 4, and when he left the Loudonville state police barracks that night, his involvement ended. But the six hours he spent on the job were crucial.

His presence had been requested by Alan Gebell, a senior assistant district attorney for Schenectady County. John Poersch, the district attorney, had assigned Gebell to the job of putting together the prosecution's case against Marybeth Tinning, and having already done much of the research, Gebell knew that what was needed now was a meeting Barnes and Marybeth. He had enormous respect for the talents of this man.

"Bill is a master of his trade," Gebell explained. "He's a street psychologist. When he talks to you, it isn't just a conversation. He is taking in everything you say, and at the same time he's observing your reactions. He's a very unassuming kind of guy, but there's no one more skillful at interrogating. Once I watched him take a statement through a one-way mirror. The man was a murderer, and Bill soon had him on his knees, begging him to listen to his confession. Another time we had been questioning a guy for three hours on a sex crime. We could not wring an admission out of him, and we all knew he was guilty. Bill Barnes came in and got a confession in seventeen minutes. He's just marvelous. He has cracked more homicides than anyone in the history of the state police. I consider myself a skilled investigator, but I can't hold a candle to Bill Barnes."

Working his way up through the ranks of the state police, Barnes had become a polygraph expert. In the process he had acquired such an extraordinary skill in assessing the mental processes of criminals that he was able, ever so gently, to find the chink in their armor which opened the way to their consciences. Then, without realizing what was being done to them, they would begin to talk . . . and talk. He was so adept at this that he hardly ever used the polygraph equipment. He felt it got in his way, creating a barrier between himself and the person he was talking to, just as a tape recorder can get in the way of a good investigative reporter.

Barnes had a natural asset in his appearance. Of average height and build, with prematurely gray hair and mild blue eyes, he had a facial expression which was so open as to be almost ingenuous. He was genial and kindly even in his approach to criminals. "If you did something illegal," he would say to friends, "I wouldn't hesitate to turn you in. But I would try to help you as much as possible."

This summarized his feeling toward Marybeth. He had known her since childhood, had grown up in the same village, had gone to the same school and was on friendly terms with her brother, Alton, who lived less than a mile down the road from him. He had a clear recollection of her mother, frail and diminutive, as "a sweet lady." He remembered her father as a formidable presence on the front porch of his Duanesburg house, watching little Marybeth walk out to the school bus. He also remembered Marybeth's behavior on that bus, the way she antagonized other children as she clamored for attention. He could guess the kind of home life she had.

Over the years he had kept track of her children's brief lives and mysterious deaths. He knew about her attempt to poison Joe and the suspected arson of their trailer. He believed the time had come for a reckoning, but this did not prevent him from feeling sorry for Marybeth.

He already knew the chink in her armor. She was a very dependent person, and if she were to be accused of murder, most of her friends and relatives would desert her, as her brother and Joe's brother and their wives had done already. In the last analysis the only person who could be depended upon to stand by Marybeth was Joe. During twenty years of marriage she had often been contemptuous and inconsiderate of him, and she had even tried to kill him; but now she desperately needed his support. Barnes judged that she would lie and go on lying about her children's deaths rather than forfeit that. He also had some idea of Joe's amazing capacity for loyalty to his marriage vows. Barnes's method of approach was therefore very clear to him.

He arrived at the Loudonville police barracks at about 4:30 P.M., found Joe sitting in an upstairs room, and suggested that the two of them go to the basement cafeteria for coffee. Marybeth's questioning by Investigators Karas and Imfeld had just begun. It meant that Joe had a long wait ahead. He seemed glad of the chance to while away some time.

As soon as they had settled at a quiet table in the cafeteria. Barnes came to the point. "Joe, you don't have to talk to me. You have the right to remain silent . . ." and he ran through the list of constitutional rights. Joe said he was aware of them but was willing to talk.

"Then I think you should know that the police now believe Tami Lynne's death was a homicide. And that this wasn't the only homicide in the family. The state police now have a forensic unit which has been working on the case. Some of the experts on it are internationally famous for solving difficult crimes, and they have been looking back over your children's records. What they've come up with is not that most of those children died of Reye's syndrome or SIDS but that they were murdered. They're able to tell more about these things than they could a few years ago, and in their opinion the evidence is conclusive."

Bill Barnes leaned across the table. He spoke very quietly, looking straight at Joe. "Now if that's true, there are two possibilities. Marybeth was always there with the children when they were taken fatally ill or died, and that leads to the conclusion that she was solely responsible for their deaths or else she had someone to help her.

"You know, Joe, you don't have to actually commit a crime to be an accomplice. It's like in a bank robbery. The guy who drives the getaway car is just as guilty as the one who forces his way into the bank and steals the money. If a child is forcibly suffocated, the person who holds the pillow or holds the child down while someone else puts a pillow over its face is just as much of a murderer."

He paused, waiting for Joe's careful and deliberate mind to process this information. He did not think that Joe was involved in his children's deaths, but he wanted to be certain. And as he watched Joe's reaction and listened to his response, he was certain. Essentially Joe told him that he had never been present when the children were stricken, and that although he had accepted Marybeth's word for what happened to them, he had sometimes had his doubts. Being the withdrawn, uninvolved kind of person that he was, Joe had done nothing about those doubts. Now the truth was being brought out, Barnes judged that Joe must surely feel guilty about his silence.

"If Marybeth did do anything to the children, she needs help," Barnes pointed out. "But before she can get help, we have to know the truth about what happened to Tami Lynne. Otherwise this thing could go on and on. And I'm sure you don't want to see anything happen to little Bucky or little Linda." Bucky and Linda were Sandy and Alton's children. They were well known to Bill Barnes because his wife had often baby-sat for them.

He continued: "If it turns out that Marybeth did do something to Tami Lynne, for whatever reason, would you stand by her? It would be very important to her to know that."

Without hesitation. Joe said he would. Having carefully laid his groundwork, Bill Barnes could have predicted that response. No matter that this woman might have killed his children, as well as tried to kill him, Joe Tinning would not desert her. Even if his loyalty should waver, his guilt at standing by and doing nothing for all these years would hold him to her. Given his strict religious upbringing, his innate honesty, and his introverted personality, he would not let her face a murder charge alone.

Almost an hour later the two men walked upstairs together. Barnes was over his first hurdle. One of his jobs was to teach criminal investigation at the State Police Academy, and he made a point of telling his students that they should take a long, hard look at a case before taking action. "You look at all the pieces of the puzzle, and you try to fit them together. You are dealing with human beings, and you need to try to understand them. You also need to feel convinced in your own mind that you have a case. Then you begin to lay your foundation for questioning the key witnesses."

He had just done that, over coffee with Joe. Later he made the comment that "in twenty-four years I never had a case in which the pieces of the puzzle fit together as perfectly as this one." He was thinking not only of Joe's passive acceptance of repeated infant death as a fact of life but also of the factors which shaped Marybeth's personality. She had grown up thinking that she was unwanted and no good, and all the rest of her life had been a striving for attention and acceptance. Barnes was saddened that she had not received professional help years ago.

He saw Joe back to the upstairs office. In a nearby room Karas and Imfeld were finishing their questioning and were about to take a break. Barnes learned that throughout two hours of conversation Marybeth had continued to insist that she had not harmed her children. During the break he spoke to her.

"Hello, Marybeth," he said. "I'm Bill Barnes. Remember me?"

Of course, she remembered. Billy Barnes, the monitor on the school bus. Billy Barnes, outgoing and clean-cut; one of the most popular students at Duanesburg Central High School. More than thirty years ago, when he was a teenager and she was in grade school, she had a crush on him. Although she must have known why he was at the state police barracks, she saw him as her rescuer. Later, when she recounted meeting him in the hallway, she described embracing him warmly "because I was glad to see a friend." Barnes had no recollection of the embrace; he felt it must have happened in Marybeth's imagination. Gently he led her into the polygraph room where Joe was sitting.

"You don't have to talk to me," he said to Marybeth. "You have the right to remain silent, and you do not have to make any statement if you do not want to . . ." He was so familiar with the phraseology that he recited the words without referring to the printed card which he always carried in his breast pocket.

When he came to the end, he asked Marybeth if she would like to call an attorney, and—in his recollection—she said no. Later she alleged that Bill Barnes neither read her her rights nor asked the question.

The polygraph machine, a piece of equipment about the size of a suitcase, was on a desk behind a partition. Barnes did not anticipate using it and settled down at the table with Marybeth a few feet away and Joe to her right. He opened the conversation the same way he had done with Joe, by telling her that the forensic team had ruled Tami Lynne's death a homicide and that there were strong suspicions about the deaths of the other children.

Her reaction was exactly the same as when Carol and Andy found Joe comatose from the effects of phenobarbital.

"I didn't do it, I didn't do it, I didn't do it," she told Barnes.

He pointed out that she was often the last person alone with her children before they died. Then he played his trump card. Addressing Joe, he repeated the question he asked in the cafeteria. "If for some reason that maybe she can't understand, Marybeth did something to Tami Lynne and the other children, what would you do, Joe?"

"I'd stand by her," Joe replied.

"I wanted you to hear that, Marybeth," Barnes told her. "I know it's important to you. And now I want you to tell Joe the truth about what happened to Tami Lynne."

"I didn't do it," she repeated.

"Come on, Marybeth," Barnes pursued. "You can go on and on with this, but enough's enough. How many more children are going to have to die?"

Joe remained silent.

Marybeth gulped. There were tears in her eyes.

Very quietly she said, "I killed them. I killed my children."

She began to sob. Joe did not move from the chair. He seemed unable to take in what he had just heard, let alone react to it. Barnes had to suggest to him that he should embrace his wife.

Turning to Marybeth, he went through the names of her nine children, asking her to explain how each of them died. As he read the names of Jennifer, Joseph and Barbara, Marybeth responded that they died naturally. When he got to Timothy and Nathan, she admitted to suffocating them both with pillows but had difficulty remembering which of the two babies was which. She denied doing anything to Mary Frances, Jonathan and Michael. She said that Tami Lynne had been crying, so she put a pillow over her face until the crying stopped.

"Why did you do that?' Barnes asked.

It was then that she told him about her father; how, when she was a child, he had hit her with a flyswatter and locked her in a closet. Nodding sympathetically, Barnes remarked that he remembered her father as a stern man, and she responded by confiding that she had grown up feeling that she could never do anything right. Consequently, when she had children of her own and they became ill or cried a lot, she assumed that this was because she was a bad mother. When some of them died, it had to be her fault.

And because she was a bad mother, she put a pillow over Tami Lynne's face.

It was so simple and so illogical. She was relieved to have unburdened herself and, in a childlike way, seemed to think that now she had told the truth, she would be forgiven and sent home. She explained that she and Joe were about to move to Ballston Spa, and she didn't want those plans upset. She was worried about what people would think of her and what might eventually happen to her. Cautiously Barnes responded that she would have to go to court and be examined by lawyers; then the court would decide.

After they had talked for about half an hour, Barnes led Marybeth across the corridor to the office where Karas was sitting.

"Marybeth has something to tell you," he announced.

As she walked into the room, Marybeth stated, 'I did Tami." She was tearful, flushed, and slightly trembling.

"What do you mean, you did Tami?" Karas asked.

"I killed her," Marybeth told him.

"How did you do that?"

"I smothered her with a pillow."

"What about the other children?"

"I didn't do anything to any of them, except Timothy and Nathan."

It was the breakthrough Karas had been hoping for. "I'd like to write that down exactly in your own words," he said. Then, with Investigators Barnes and Imfeld as witnesses, he took a piece of lined office paper and wrote in longhand: "I did not do anything to Jennifer, Joseph, Barbara, Michael, Mary Frances, Jonathan. Just these three, Timothy, Nathan and Tami. I smothered them each with a pillow because I'm not a good mother. I'm not a good mother because of the other children."

She signed it in her awkward left-handed scrawl which looked even more childish than usual because her hand was shaking: "Marybeth Tinning, 2-4-86, 8 P.M." As she put down the pen, she took a deep breath to compose herself.

Left to himself in another room, Joe asked one of the policemen who had brought him to Loudonville how long he thought "all this" would take, meaning the interrogation of Marybeth for a more detailed statement. Joe was looking intently through a window, watching a new fall of sleety snow.

"I've got to get home to shovel the driveway," he explained. He also worried aloud about the fact that it was the fourth of the month and he hadn't yet made the February payment on the Isuzu pickup truck which Marybeth had recently persuaded him to buy. He seemed to be concentrating his energies on everyday domestic problems to avoid dealing with the fact that his wife had just confessed to murder.

He did, however, remark to the same police officer that he felt both Marybeth and he needed help.

"Do you mean psychiatric help?" he was asked.

"Yes," Joe replied.

TWENTY-THREE

People do confess to crimes they don't commit. But these
are not the detailed kind of confessions such as Marybeth
made.

—State police official

"Please don't make me tell it again."

It was 9:00 P.M. before the police were ready to take Marybeth's
detailed statement, and she was back in the second-floor office
where Joe Karas and Bob Imfeld had begun their questioning six
hours earlier. Bill Barnes's job was done; but she begged him to
stay with her, and he readily agreed. He felt very sad, knowing
what her arrest would do to her family. When this long day was
over, he would drive home past her brother's house, the house
where Marybeth had grown up, with all kinds of mixed emotions.
In the meantime, he wanted to be sure that this last vital interrogation was handled as sensitively as possible. Not that he mistrusted
his colleague—he had known Joe Karas for many years and had a
lot of professional respect for him—but his personal involvement
in the case made him anxious to stay with it.

Marybeth did not want to tell the story again, but it was essential
that she do so, with as much detail as she could be persuaded to
add. There were still many unanswered questions.

The four of them, Karas, Imfeld, Barnes and Marybeth, had to
wait almost an hour while Margot Bernhardt, an official court
reporter, was summoned from her home in Albany. As she set up
her equipment, she noted that Marybeth was crying a little but was
in control of herself. For the third time that day Marybeth's rights
were read to her—again by Karas—and she nodded her head when
asked if she understood them.

"Do you want to talk to these gentlemen? It is up to you to do," Barnes emphasized.

"Okay," she replied.

"You do understand these rights, and you are willing to give them up?" Karas interjected.

Again she nodded.

This exchange, written into the record by Margot Bernhardt, was to take on an unexpected importance. Later Marybeth argued that she was never read her rights and that the investigators bullied her and put words into her mouth. As an impartial observer Margot Bernhardt had a very different impression. She said that the officers spoke to Marybeth quietly and that she seemed willing to answer their questions. The dialogue between her, Karas and Barnes lasted more than an hour and filled thirty-six pages of transcript. It began with her amended description of the night of Tami Lynne's death.

"I came home from shopping about 8:30 P.M.," she related. "I had gone to Toys for Joy in Rotterdam with my friend Cynthia Walter who lives I think at 371 Michigan Avenue. It is next door anyways to me. When I got home Joe's mother and father were there. They had babysat for me. Cynthia stayed and visited a while and everyone was finally gone at 9:30 P.M.

"After everyone left I played with Tami Lynne for about an hour and I sat in a brown recliner chair and had Tami on my lap. After we played I put Tami to bed. I tried to give her a bottle but she didn't want it. She fussed and cried for about half an hour. She finally went to sleep. I then went to bed. I lay in my bed and watched TV and dozed. Finally Joe came home around 11:00 P.M. Joe and I talked for about ten minutes. He finally got in bed and went to sleep. We were in bed talking. . . .

"I was about to doze off when Tami woke up and started to cry. I got up and went to her crib and tried to do something with her and get her to stop crying. I finally used the pillow from my bed and put it over her head. I held it until she stopped crying. I didn't mean to hurt her. I just wanted her to stop crying. I had gotten the pillow from my bed. Joe was still sound asleep and didn't know I came in and got the pillow. When I finally lifted the pillow off Tami she wasn't moving. I put the pillow on the couch and made it look like I had been sleeping on the couch, and then screamed for Joe and he woke up and I told Joe Tami wasn't breathing."

"Tell us what happened after that," said Karas.

"I did do CPR, stupid as it sounds, but I knew, I knew that she wasn't alive anymore. They called the ambulance and, I don't know why, things got all screwed up—or they just told me that to confuse me—with the name and the wrong address. But I told them my name and my address, that I needed an ambulance immediately. And they asked me what the problem was and I told them that my baby wasn't breathing. And when I called Cynthia, she was working on the CPR, and paramedics came in, never said a word, just grabbed her and took her off, and I took off after them. . . ."

She was asked why she put a pillow over her baby's face.

"Because she was always crying and I couldn't do anything right."

"You couldn't do anything right?" Barnes asked.

Marybeth shook her head.

"Is that what you mean?" he continued.

"She was always crying," she said.

"And you as a mother could not make her stop? Is that what you are telling me?"

"Uh-huh." She nodded.

"Did that happen all of a sudden, that you felt you couldn't do anything with her?" Barnes asked. "Did it just come over you all of a sudden?"

"It came over me all of a sudden."

"Was this a feeling that built up in you over a period of time?"

"No."

"Joe, your husband, was sleeping?"

"Yes."

"And at that point, because of the baby crying, this feeling came over you to do this. Correct?"

She nodded.

"And to get it perfectly straight in my mind and your mind and the other people that are here, you are saying you felt inadequate as a mother?"

"Yes."

"Could you explain to me what you mean by that? What do you feel about that? What do you mean by that? How did it happen? How did you begin to feel inadequate?"

"Nobody else, Cynthia's kid and the little boy hardly ever cried. Tami was always crying and I just thought it was something I was doing wrong."

By the "little boy" she was probably referring to Sue Lencewicz's son Brian for whom she baby-sat. In pursuing this sympathetic line of questioning, Bill Barnes was doing his best to elicit a confession which would give some psychological understanding of this deeply troubled woman, and which might be the basis of a plea of temporary insanity.

Picking up on her feelings of inadequacy, he commented: "All of us feel like that maybe at times, okay. But what made you do what you did at that time in reaction to her not doing what you wanted her to do—by that I mean not stopping crying?"

There was no response.

"Do you follow what I am asking you?" Barnes continued.

She nodded.

"I would ask you to explain to me why you took Tami's life. What made you do that?"

"I just felt I wasn't a good mother."

The questioning turned to her fourth and fifth babies, Timothy and Nathan, whom she had already confessed to killing. She had difficulty remembering anything about them, when they were born or even which child was which. In her original accounts she had found Timothy dead in his crib when he was only three weeks old, while Nathan (who was five months) went into a fatal coma when he was sitting beside her in her car. Now she confused them and, in answer to Karas's question about how they died, responded: "They were all the same."

Then when he asked her to "tell us about Nathan as best you remember," she began to describe what seemed to be the last moments of Timothy.

"When was he born?" Karas asked, referring to Nathan.

"I can't remember."

"You don't remember?"

"I can't remember."

"Do you remember when he died?"

"No, please."

"I have to ask you. Try to get a hold of yourself."

"No."

"Do you remember how he died?"

"The same way as Tami."

"And where did that happen?"

"At home."

"Who was there?"

"I don't—Joe, I guess—I don't know."

"And you?"

"Yes."

"Anyone else?"

"I don't think so. I can't remember."

"Did you put a pillow over his face?"

"Yes."

"When you were alone?"

"I can't remember."

"Would you remember if anyone else was with you?"

"I don't think so. I don't know. I don't know."

She was becoming so vague that Karas decided to refresh her memory by summarizing her earlier statement to Barnes.

Repeating her words, he said, ' "I had two children. Nathan and Timothy, who both died because I put a pillow over their faces, as I did with Tami.' "

"Yes," Marybeth agreed.

Karas continued. ' "I did this because I felt I was not a good mother.' "

"Right," said Marybeth.

' "I felt I was not a good mother because I lost the other children.' "

"That is right."

"You were alone when you did it?"

"Uh-huh. Well, Joe was there but sleeping."

"But Joe was sleeping. He was in the house but asleep?"

She nodded. Having already confused Nathan's death with Timothy's, she now seemed to be confusing them both with Tami's.

"Did you tell anybody about it?" Karas continued.

"That I did it?"

"Yes."

"No."

"Never told anybody about it?"

Marybeth shook her head.

"Were the children crying when you did it?"

"Yes."

"They were irritating you or crying or annoying you?"

"They were crying."

"You could not make them stop crying?"

"No."

"Did you use the pillow from your own bed each time?"

"Yes."

"And you put it back?"

"Yes."

"And you called the ambulance right away?"

"Yes."

"Or you had somebody else call, do you remember?"

"Joe might have. I don't know."

Karas reminded her that Nathan did not die at home, as she had just described.

"Think about Nathan for a minute, and think about driving the car up Balltown Road. Did that happen in the car?"

"Yes," she agreed, contrary to her earlier response. She then told her improbable tale of putting a sofa cushion, which she kept in the car, over Nathan's face "while he was asleep but crying" as she was driving along. She said she held it over his face "until he stopped crying." Karas asked her when this happened, and she couldn't remember. Nor did she remember Nathan's age beyond the fact that he was "just a few months."

"Timothy," Karas pursued. "Do you remember Timothy?"

"Uh-huh."

"He was at home?"

"Timothy," Marybeth repeated. She seemed to be mentally searching for his whereabouts.

"It happened at home?"

"Yes."

"He was in the crib?"

"Yes."

"Was he making funny sounds?"

No answer.

"Or was he crying?" Karas suggested.

"He was making funny sounds."

"What sort of sounds?"

"Gurgling sounds. . . . He had a cold."

"And that, did that upset you?"

"That he had a cold?"

"That he was making these sounds."

"Yes."

"And how did it make you feel?"

"I mean, whatever I did just didn't turn out right."

"You mean whatever you did to help him?"

She nodded.

"And were you alone there with him or was Joe in the house at the time? Do you remember?"

"I don't remember but I think Joe was in the house."

"And what did you do this time?"

"Same thing."

"When you say 'the same thing' you have to say what it is."

"I put a pillow over his face."

"Do you remember where you got the pillow?"

"It was my bed pillow."

"You held it over his face?"

"Yes."

"Until he was quiet?"

"Yes."

"And then what did you do?"

"Called for help."

"Do you remember what exactly you did for help?"

"Called an ambulance." She could not remember whether it took him to St. Clare's or Ellis Hospital.

Karas went on to ask her about the other children.

"Some died at home and some died in the hospital," she replied.

"Was it because of you putting a pillow over their head?"

"No."

"You had nothing to do with it?"

Her denial was firm and strenuous. "No, sir."

She went on to describe what happened to them. One night when she was almost five years old, Barbara had a convulsion. Marybeth took her to Ellis Hospital's emergency room, where "they gave me a choice, I could either leave her there—nothing would be done until morning—or I could take her home and watch her and bring her to the doctor's the next day, which I decided to do. Then we went home and I kept going back and forth, back and forth, and she went into another convulsion, and we took her—the ambulance took her—and she died at about 4:20 or so the following day."

"Did you cause the death of Barbara?" Barnes interjected.

"No, I did not cause the death of Barbara."

"Did you do anything that might have contributed to her death?"

"Other than contributing by putting a spoon handle in her mouth to prevent her from swallowing her tongue, no."

"Have you had nurse's training?" Barnes continued.

"Yes . . . I had been a nurse's aide."

The next child to be discussed was Jennifer, the first baby to die. She had no difficulty remembering Jennifer, unlike some of the children who were born later and lived longer. Fourteen years after her death this baby still seemed special to Marybeth.

"Jennifer was born, I believe, the twenty-sixth of December, the day after Christmas, 'seventy-one." It was the only birthday she quoted, and she had it right. "And she died seven days later. She was fine at the beginning and then I knew there was something wrong, but no one would do anything. So she finally developed meningitis and died of a brain abscess, so they say."

"This is what you were told?" Barnes asked.

"Yes, sir."

"Did you do anything to directly or indirectly cause her death?"

"No, I had nothing to do, directly or indirectly, to cause Jennifer's death. No, I did not."

She had no difficulty remembering that the next death was that of two-year-old Joseph. It was as time went on that her memory became hazy.

"What happened to Joseph?" Barnes wanted to know.

"I have no idea."

"Can you tell me the circumstances around his death?"

"He was taking a nap. It was close to his birthday and he had slept unusually long. Unfortunately I did not go in to check on him and when I did he appeared to be having respiratory problems which I did not cause."

She said she took him to the hospital, where he died. "All the death certificate said was respiratory and cardiac arrest, I believe. I may be wrong. Maybe it was only one that they put on, or maybe both, I don't know. . . . But I had nothing to do with his death." She did not mention that she took Joseph to Ellis Hospital twice, for the same reason.

Barnes then asked her about Mary Frances and Jonathan.

"There is really nothing to say," she commented of Mary Frances. "I found her in her crib unresponsive."

"Did you administer first aid prior to that?" Barnes wanted to know.

"I tried, yes."

"What did you do?"

"CPR."

"Tried CPR on the child?"

"Uh-huh." She nodded.

"Was anybody at the house when Mary Frances . . . ?"

"I believe Joe was there. I can't remember. . . ."

"Did you call an ambulance?"

"One of us did."

"And the baby was taken to the hospital?"

"Yes, St. Clare's, I think."

"Were you told the cause of Mary Frances's death?"

"I don't believe so. I think it was just the same."

"The same? What do you mean?"

"Cardiac arrest and respiratory arrest, and I didn't have anything to do with her death."

"Did anyone else in the household?"

"No, they did not."

"To your knowledge?"

"Not to my knowledge."

"Jonathan Tinning was the seventh child to die."

"Uh-huh."

"Could you tell me the circumstances surrounding his death?"

"It was the same as the previous two and I had nothing to do with it. . . . Jonathan died the same way as Mary Frances to my knowledge."

"But not the same way as Nathan or Timothy died?"

"No."

"Could you tell me—you said that Jonathan died the same way as Mary Frances."

"Yes."

"And how would that be?"

"He had been to bed, and when you go in to check or however, he was not responsive."

"Was that at night time or day time?"

"I believe that it was at night. . . ."

"What happened at that point with Jonathan? Did you or your husband try to administer first aid, if he was home?"

"I did. Joe did."

"Who called an ambulance?"

"Probably Joe."

"Were you ever told the cause of Jonathan's death?"

"No."

"What were you told concerning Jonathan's death?"

"Not too much. I just believe the same as the others. Respiratory, cardiac arrest. Sometimes they put them both down, sometimes one or the other, but it really doesn't matter."

She made these last two deaths sound so uncomplicated. There was no mention of the fact that both Mary Frances and Jonathan suffered two major crises, that in both cases the first episode was considered so serious that these babies were sent from St. Clare's to Boston Children's Hospital and seen by several specialists, that in each case the second episode left them permanently comatose, and that they died slowly in an intensive care unit. Her response to Barnes's questions gave the impression that these were sudden, painless deaths.

Last of all, Marybeth was questioned about Michael, her adopted child.

"He had been sick with a cold," she explained. "I was going to—well, I had called the doctor and he said to bring him in on Monday which I was going to."

During Sunday night Michael became feverish, "so I just sat with him then. Then I went back to sleep, and back and forth. And when I went in, in the morning, to get him up so we could go to the doctor's, he was not, I mean he was responsive to a point but he was very limp, and so on and so forth. And so instead of calling the ambulance I went from our house on McClellan Street, put him in the car, literally threw him in the car and went to St. Clare's—or I mean I went to Dr. Mele's office and went in there, and the paramedics from Broadway there came and they took him. But by the time one of the doctors, Dr. Lee, I guess, took me they said that he died if viral pneumonia."

Her slip of the tongue about St. Clare's Hospital may have been Freudian. Sandy Roe had urged Marybeth to rush Michael to St. Clare's; instead, she had made the longer journey to Dr. Mele's office.

Barnes asked her if she or anyone in her household caused Michael's death.

"Myself or no one else that I know of," Marybeth replied.

"And by that I mean did you put a pillow—"

"No, I did not, or no one else to my knowledge."

Barnes returned to the case of Tami Lynne, and for the third time Marybeth admitted to suffocating her.

"You stated that you put a—"he began.

She finished his sentence. "Yes, I did. A pillow over her face."

The interrogation had taken almost an hour and a half. Barnes had two last questions. Had anyone helped Marybeth kill Timothy, Nathan, and Tami Lynne? And had she ever caused the deaths of any other children?

"No, no," she said firmly.

The ordeal was almost over. She was asked to swear to the truth of her statement, and without hesitation she did so.

"Now that you have had time to think back on what you have said in your statement, is there anything that you would like to change?" Karas asked.

"No," Marybeth told him.

"Is there anything that you would like to add?"

"No."

"You mean it is all the truth?"

"Yes."

It was as much as she was ever likely to tell them. For months afterward members of the Tinning Task Force wondered why Marybeth admitted to suffocating Timothy and Nathan while she denied harming her other children. She knew that the evidence in Tami Lynne's case was damning. But of her nine children, why did she pick these other two for her confession? What was different about the deaths of Timothy and Nathan? There is one persuasive theory. Confronted with the information that police believed all her children but Jennifer were murdered, she probably realized that justice would take its course. But she needed Joe's support, and there were some admissions which might have strained his loyalty to breaking point, despite his promise to stand by her. Joe loved children, and three of them had lived long enough for him to become deeply attached to them: Barbara, Joseph and Michael. Of the other babies, Mary Frances and Jonathan suffered so much and were in the hospital for so long that he would remember the agony of their protracted deaths with considerable distress. If any of those five deaths were unnecessary, Joe might find them very hard to forgive.

That left Timothy and Nathan. They lived briefly and died

swiftly, so were less easily remembered. Marybeth had difficulty recalling which of the two was which, and according to a social worker who once questioned him, so did Joe. On the evening of February 4, 1986, he had already faced the fact that his wife murdered Tami Lynne. If she was responsible for any of the other deaths, Timothy's and Nathan's were probably the easiest for him to deal with.

When her confession was over, Marybeth looked tired but calm. In almost nine hours at the Loudonville barracks she had drunk four cups of coffee but refused offers of food. Physically and emotionally she was drained. Now there was another wait while Margot Bernhardt prepared her statement for signature.

"Stay with me," Marybeth asked Bill Barnes for a second time.

When the statement was handed to her, she seemed flustered because she had left her reading glasses at home, so Barnes offered to lend his. She tried them on, found they suited her, and wore them to read through her confession. It was to be their last friendly contact.

After she had signed this second statement, Marybeth Tinning was formally charged with the murder of her daughter Tami Lynne, fingerprinted, and driven through the snowstorm to the Schenectady County Jail.

Joe went home alone to shovel his driveway.

TWENTY-FOUR

Accused child killer Marybeth Tinning seems to have "two personalities" and has displayed markedly alternating attitudes about her nine children, officials involved in the murder probe said Friday.
—*From the Albany* Times-Union, *four days after the arrest*

It was the first item on the early-morning radio news. The announcer at WGY didn't say her name at first, just stated the fact that a Michigan Avenue woman had been charged with murdering her baby, but all over town people knew immediately whom he meant. Neighbors from Michigan Avenue, McClellan Street, Cleveland Avenue, Second Avenue and Duanesburg, former colleagues at Flavorland and at the school bus company, members of the Princetown Reformed Church and of the Duanesburg Volunteer Ambulance Corps, nurses at St. Clare's Hospital, Joe's colleagues at General Electric and in the bowling club—all of them instantly recognized, before the local radio announcer got as far as naming her, that the mother who had been arrested was Marybeth Tinning. For a woman who complained that she had no friends, Marybeth had made an impact on a great many people.

"So they finally caught her!" one of Marybeth's former waitress colleagues thought as she prepared her children's breakfast. Fourteen years earlier, when Marybeth was still just a customer at Flavorland, this woman had expressed her condolences over the loss of the first three children and then berated herself because just saying sorry didn't seem good enough.

Another of Marybeth's Flavorland colleagues heard the news shortly before she checked into St. Clare's Hospital with a case of pneumonia. "I was really sick and had a hundred-and-four-degree fever, and all I could talk about was Marybeth Tinning," she recalled. "I was blathering away about her in the emergency room.

One of the nurses asked if I knew her. 'I worked with her for fourteen years,' I said. Then the nurse told me that she had caught Marybeth trying to smother this latest baby right after she was born. She said she reported it."

Shocked by the radio announcement, Mark Walter wondered how he would break the news to his wife, Cynthia. He decided to delay telling her until she returned from her Florida vacation. The other neighbor with whom Marybeth was friendly, Sue Lencewicz, was wakened by the first WGY bulletin of the day when her clock radio went on at 6:00 A.M. She was incredulous.

Later, as she was about to leave for work, Joe walked over to her car.

In her forthright manner Sue asked, "Joe, what is going on?"

"Marybeth admitted that she killed Tami and a couple of the other babies," he replied. He was not visibly upset. He seemed quietly accepting. But that evening he asked if he might come and sit with the Lencewiczes.

Expecting to administer sympathy, Sue was baffled by his silence. "He just sat and said nothing. I was uncomfortable with his presence, and finally I said, 'Joe, what happened? Did you know that Marybeth had a problem?'

"He said, 'Well, Tami did keep us up a lot. We didn't sleep much.' And that was all."

To Sue, who described herself as "an up-front kind of person," his reaction was incomprehensible. Men who worked with Joe Tinning had a better understanding of him.

"You have to know Joe," one of them said. "He is entirely capable of ignoring a bad situation. He knows the facts, but he files them away so deeply that he can continue as though they do not exist."

"Same as at work," another man added. "He does a job, and then it's history. He never mentions it again."

So on the week of Marybeth's arrest Joe went bowling as usual, just as he was to do throughout her trial. His prowess in local bowling leagues won him frequent mentions in the *Schenectady Gazette*, at the same time as the background to his wife's murder charges was being reported in another section of the paper.

It was widely assumed in the town that Marybeth was guilty. She was described in upstate New York newspapers and on local television news as "accused baby killer Marybeth Tinning," and those who couldn't remember her name referred to her as "that woman who murdered all her babies." For days reporters and cameramen hung around her last two homes on Michigan Avenue and McClellan Street, seeking the opinion of neighbors. (A devoted mother, most of them said, although there was something odd about her.) To Sue Lencewicz's dismay, even her small son Brian was interviewed. Afterward he sat in front of the TV set for hours, hoping to see himself in a star role. Instead, he learned that the woman who once baby-sat for him had tried to poison her husband, and that led to his having nightmares about the peanut butter and crackers she had once fed him. "Mommy, should I have eaten them?" he kept asking. Overnight Marybeth had become a monster.

Sue still couldn't think of her that way. She had felt honored when Marybeth used the name she picked out for the daughter she never had, and that made her feel especially close to Tami Lynne. "Marybeth would ask me to hold her and kiss her. And she was so attentive to the baby herself, jumping up at every whimper. If she did anything to hurt her, her mind must have snapped."

She agonized about this for months. "If I had ever had the least suspicion that she had the ability to do what they accused her of doing, I would have taken the baby from her and got her help. But she never came across as that kind of person." Then she remembered Marybeth's oblique warning to her: "My sister-in-law called. . . . She knows I've been baby-sitting for you, and she wants to warn you about me because she thinks I might do some harm to Brian." Of course, Carol Tinning hadn't made that telephone call. If she'd wanted to warn Sue, she would have done so herself. Was it Marybeth's way of saying that she was afraid of what she might do when she was left alone with Brian? After the arrest Sue talked to Joe about her son's concern over the peanut butter and crackers. "Why does it worry you?" Joe asked. "You know Marybeth would never have harmed him."

Sue was no longer sure. When Marybeth began packing to move, she had given Sue a large box of Popsicles and a can of Nestlé's Quik chocolate powder, which she had bought when she was baby-sitting for Brian. She had also given her some gold curtains for Sue's identical-size living-room windows. When she read that Marybeth had once attempted to poison Joe, Sue threw the food items away. Then she had second thoughts, recovered the Quik from the garbage and sent it to the state police laboratory for analysis. "The report was negative, which made me relax," Sue recounted. But she continued to vacillate in her feelings about her neighbor. At first she had been delighted with the gift of the curtains. "They were expensive drapes, but after her arrest I didn't want them anymore. Then, when I hung them, I felt better."

Some of Marybeth's other recent acquaintances shared Sue's uncertainty about her guilt. They thought of Joe as the strange one. But those who had known her through the deaths of earlier children were quicker to condemn her. The general opinion in Schenectady, and there was scarcely a citizen who didn't have something to say about the case, was that Marybeth had committed a heinous crime and deserved severe punishment. Police Chief Richard Nelson, normally a genial and warmhearted man, had no doubt about where he stood. "I would like to see her get the maximum, and I'd like to carry out the sentence myself. With a pillow. When you think of those babies gasping for their lives . . ." He shook his head. "It's an emotional response, but that's the way I feel about this woman." (By this time New York State's death penalty had, in fact, been declared unconstitutional.)

Many mothers were just as angry with Marybeth. Some of them confessed to one another that at times they themselves had felt so bone weary exasperated with the rearing of children that they had been tempted to do something dreadful to a whining baby. A few acknowledged that only the grace of God separated them from Marybeth. Others, secure in the knowledge that they had resisted the temptation and had grown-up children to prove it, felt she had so violated a sacred trust that there was little room left for forgiveness. One way or another the case of Marybeth Tinning excited tremendous passions, long before it came into court.

Having been charged with the murder of Tami Lynne, Marybeth was sent to the Oneida County Jail, near Utica. While she was there, she wrote a letter to Cynthia Walter, protesting her innocence. She said this would probably be her last communication, although she hoped they might remain friends. Cynthia, who was in a state of shock, did not respond. Marybeth also sent this letter to her brother, Alton Roe, and his wife, Sandra:

Dear Bud and Sandy,
   Before I start this letter I want you to know that I know
that you have both disowned me as a sister and sister-in-law.
My brother's words have reached all the way up here. There
is nothing I can do now but be at the mercy of the court and
hope that some day you will be able to forgive me a little. I
know that some day God will.

                                                    Marybeth.

   She spent almost six weeks in the Oneida County Jail before
being released on a hundred-thousand-dollar bail. Joe and his
parents went to extraordinary lengths to raise the money, he calling
every acquaintance he could think of, and they telephoning around
Duanesburg to members of their church and the volunteer ambulance corps. This must have been painfully embarrassing for such
very private people, but all three of them had committed themselves
to supporting Marybeth, who by now was protesting her innocence.
Joe, who rarely asked a favor of anyone, even begged one former
associate to take out a loan on a piece of property he owned. With
some embarrassment the man refused. Joe's father's calls were more
oblique. "He didn't come straight to the point," said one recipient.
"He talked about how difficult it was to raise bail money and how
it didn't have to be cash, that other people could put up securities
and these needn't pass out of their hands. He was giving me this
information in the hope that I would volunteer, but I avoided the
issue by asking how Marybeth's case was going. Later young Joe
called and asked straight out if I could help."
   More than a hundred people were telephoned. Most of them
refused. Joe also took a lot of teasing at work from colleagues who
had their own crude suggestions about why he was so anxious to
have his wife at home. He and his parents seemed unable to understand how most Schenectady citizens felt about Marybeth's widely
publicized arrest and confession, despite the fact that their own
family had been bitterly divided on the issue ever since Andy and
Carol decided to collaborate with the police. Eventually, with the
help of his parents and a few friends, Joe was able to scrape the
bail money together. He also retained Paul Callahan to defend
Marybeth.
   Marybeth's mother, Ruth Roe, remained silent. She declined to
talk to the police, to investigators from the district attorney's office,

or to the press and was rarely seen outside her small apartment in Schenectady. Her only response to inquiries was: "I am not talking to nobody." In contrast, Edna Tinning made it very clear where she stood:

"Unless Marybeth comes to me and tells me she did it, I shall go on believing in her innocence. I think she is a victim of the medical profession. Instead of helping her to have healthy children, they condemned her."

While Marybeth was in the Oneida County Jail, the story circulated that she was pregnant again. At first the report was taken to be somebody's sick joke until it emerged that the information came from Marybeth herself. She had been required to fill out a form on which the question was asked, "Are you pregnant?" and she had put a check mark against the word "yes." It was an honest error, her husband explained; she misunderstood the question and marked the wrong box. Others who knew her had a different opinion. If there was an error, they felt it must have been Freudian.

At Marybeth's bail hearing a psychiatrist's report was presented. Submitted by Dr. James F. Cunningham of Schenectady, it stated:

The patient presents as a somewhat youthful, alert, tearful and tense woman who is concerned about being out of jail. She wants to be out of jail. She is a passive, dependent woman who would not intentionally flee to avoid prosecution. There is the chance that she would panic and attempt to flee but she is incapable of maintaining herself once she reached her destination. She would then realize her situation and return home or call for assistance. Mrs Tinning neither shows nor demonstrates any feelings of hostility or impulse to commit any crime if she were released from custody.

This brief statement was the only psychiatric report on Marybeth which was ever presented to a court. Bail was set on March 1, 1986, and she was released on March 15.

By that time Joe had accomplished the move to Ballston Spa. Friends and neighbors who helped him were as surprised as he was at the large quantity of household goods which Marybeth had stashed away, boxes of china and linens which had never been used. "She's got too much junk," Joe muttered as he carried boxes out to his pickup truck. "Some of this will have to go."

Meantime, the work of the Tinning Task Force continued. District Attorney Poersch told reporters that the deaths of all Marybeth's other children were being investigated and that there might be further charges against her. Poersch, a bluff and expansive man, liked to give the impression that he was in command, but it was his assistants Alan Gebell, Gary McCarthy and a few hardworking public servants in Schenectady—like Dan O'Connor and Bob Imfeld of the city police, Joe Karas and Bill Sprague of the state police and Betsy Mannix of Social Services—who were knocking on doors, interviewing witnesses, and putting the prosecution's case together. It was also the medical experts on the state police's forensic unit, but they were still a long way from investigating the deaths of all nine Tinning children. They were concentrating on the three Marybeth had confessed to killing and were having difficulty agreeing on how to set about those.

Dr. Michael Baden, head of the forensic unit, wanted to exhume the bodies of Timothy and Nathan. A charge of murder cannot be based on a confession alone. It must also be backed by medical evidence, and Baden hoped to find clues to suffocation in the remains of these two children. He thought there was a risk in trying to convict Marybeth for the single murder of Tami Lynne and that the prosecution should secure its case by assembling as much medical evidence about the other babies as possible.

John Poersch was reluctant to agree to any exhumations. He argued that no fresh medical information could be gained by digging up dead babies and that the defense would capitalize on the horror of it. This would give his office, which had to issue the exhumation orders, a dreadful image in the eyes of the general public. Despite Poersch's public statement about investigating all nine deaths, it was becoming clear that he would prefer to limit his prosecution to the case of Tami Lynne. There would be fewer witnesses, a shorter trial, and less of a drain on county funds. And if the judge accepted the legal precedent of the Martha Woods case, he could still introduce evidence of the other suspicious deaths.

Poersch explained his thinking: "I did not want to let this city get involved in a Scopes trial." It was a strange analogy. He was referring to the 1925 trial of John Thomas Scopes, a young biology teacher who was found guilty of violating a Tennessee state law by teaching the theory of evolution to his high school students. The issue—whether progressive education could prevail over old-time fundamentalist religion—became a cause célèbre and brought a great deal of unwelcome publicity to the little town of Dayton, Tennessee. To the embarrassment of its residents, several books were written about the case, and the "monkey trial" became the subject of a popular play and movie. John Poersch did not want his hometown of Schenectady to become another Dayton. He envisaged the case against Marybeth Tinning becoming the focus of a larger argument over Sudden Infant Death Syndrome. Was it a medical condition or was it a euphemism for infanticide? He imagined cameramen trampling all over the courthouse lawn while "experts in the field, people who write books about these things, would volunteer their services to explain in great depth and at great length what SIDS really means." Poersch didn't want to get embroiled in all that.

"All we have to do," he explained, "is prove that she killed Tami Lynne Tinning, and she should get twenty-five years to life, which is the maximum anyway. Having a circus here will confuse the issue. It might even confuse the jurors, and then she could get away."

All this was bitterly argued at a meeting with the state police experts in Albany. Dr. Michael Baden continued to press for the exhumations. Poersch was opposed to them on grounds that all this extra research would be an unfair burden on the Schenectady taxpayers. State Police Colonel Hank Williams, who had recently put together the forensic unit, was so anxious to see his team succeed on this, its first major case, that he dragged himself to the meeting from bed. He had been on sick leave for several weeks and was in such agony with terminal cancer that he had to be helped down the corridor to the conference room; nevertheless, he insisted on being there to ensure that nothing in this investigation would be left to chance. The resources of his unit were far superior to those of the Schenectady police or of the D.A.'s office, and it infuriated him that local considerations should get in the way of thorough research. John Poersch caught all of his pent-up pain and frustration.

"Son of a bitch," Williams said. "If you don't want to pay for the exhumations, I'll do so out my own pocket!"

At that Poersch backed down.

So, early one morning, three pathologists gathered at Most Holy Redeemer Cemetery on the outskirts of Schenectady. Drs. Baden

and Oram were joined by Dr. Jack N. P. Davies of Albany, who
had been retained by the defense. When Marybeth's lawyer, Paul
Callahan, had recently approached him, Davies's first reaction was
to refuse. Infanticide was repugnant to him, and at first sight,
Marybeth appeared to be guilty. But as he perused the medical
reports of the eight children she had borne, it struck him that there
was a case to be made for some genetic aberration in all of them.
According to the records, the one adopted child died differently,
from a straightforward case of pneumonia. Davies was intrigued by
the high blood ammonia levels in several of Marybeth's own children, just as Oram had been. Paul Callahan had outlined his client's
case to him: how she was so intimidated by the questions of three
police investigators that she finally said she killed her baby because
she thought that was what they wanted to hear, and that when they
had heard it, they would let her go home.

Davies could accept that. He knew very little about Marybeth,
but he could see how a woman of limited education and experience
might feel so threatened at being interrogated for several hours that
she would confess to anything. Her confession made this a tough
case for the defense, but Davies thrived on challenges. It would be
a great achievement if he could demonstrate to an admiring jury
that she was falsely accused and that all these children suffered
from some metabolic defect missed by every other doctor, his old
colleague Tom Oram included.

They greeted each other warmly at the Tinning family grave site.
Davies and Oram were the best-known pathologists in the area and
had much in common. Both were English and had their early
medical experience in former British colonies. While Oram ran a
hospital in Malaysia, Davies was a medical officer and professor of
pathology in Uganda, where he did pioneer work in tropical pathology, writing texts to teach Ugandan medical students. Like Oram,
he had returned to England in the 1950's and emigrated to the
United States in the early sixties. Their parallel careers converged
in New York State's capital district, where for the last twenty years
they had lived and worked—Oram in Schenectady and Davies in
Albany.

After many years as coroner's pathologist for Albany County,
Davies had set up his own practice as a forensic pathologist and
consultant. He and Oram frequently testified in court cases, sometimes as adversaries, sometimes on the same side. A friendly rivalry

existed between them, to the amusement of students at Albany
Medical College, where they both taught pathology. "None of us
would ever want to miss their lectures," a former student recalled.
"They were such good shows. Both of them were very impressive,
and to some extent they would dispute one another's theories. This
was always lighthearted. They knew each other's position, so it was
more a battle of wits than a battle for truth."

Now in his early seventies, Davies was the elder of the two and
the more flamboyant. While Oram impressed juries with an almost
military correctness, Davies overwhelmed them with his theatrical
manner. He would bow low to the judge on his way to the witness
stand, take the oath in a loud, clear voice, open his briefcase, and
shuffle importantly among his papers for just the right amount of
time to get a jury's full attention. His appearance, too, was impressive: he was very portly, and wore a neatly clipped gray beard. Like
the Albany medical students, juries instinctively knew that they
were about to enjoy a fine performance. In another incarnation Jack
Neville Phillips Davies would have made a wonderful character
actor. As an expert witness he was a convincing and eloquent
representative of his own profession.

When he realized that they would be on opposite sides of the
Tinning case, Oram worried about the effect that Davies might
have upon a Schenectady jury. A cross section of people from this
unsophisticated small town might be enormously impressed by
whatever he chose to say, and Davies had a way of presenting
controversial medical data as though they were established fact.
Having reached his own painstaking conclusion that Tami Lynne
had been murdered, Oram was disturbed by the realization that
Jack Davies must be working on some plausible theory that she
had died naturally. But in one respect they were equals on the
witness stand. Oram, who had a nice sense of humor about these
things, remarked that "if you speak in the kind of la-di-da English
accent that Jack and I do, people believe you are telling the truth.
Jurors say to themselves, 'There's a chap who knows what he's
talking about.' "

Neither of them enjoyed watching the men from the Daly Funeral
Home dig up the caskets of Timothy and Nathan Tinning. They
had agreed to early-morning exhumations to avoid press coverage,
and as an extra precaution police were posted at the cemetery gates.
The task was completed in secrecy, and the two concrete caskets

were taken to Ellis Hospital, where they were opened by Drs. Oram and Baden. As a defense witness Davies was not invited. In the Ellis laboratory it was discovered that one of the caskets had become waterlogged, and that after twelve years Nathan's body had deteriorated too much for a meaningful examination.

The contents of Timothy's grave were even more disappointing. The skeletal remains were clearly not his. The body was the size of a three-week-old baby, but it had been autopsied—and Timothy had not. From the way in which the autopsy had focused on the area of the brain, the body in the casket had to be Jennifer's. It could not have been that of any other baby because the other Tinning children were larger when they died. Evidently markers were not put on the graves of Jennifer and Timothy until some time after they were buried, and then these two markers must have been placed incorrectly.

Baden wanted to have another exhumation, but Oram thought it would be pointless. Undertakers find it extremely difficult to embalm babies because their veins are so tiny; hence, even if Timothy's body were exhumed, it might be in the same decomposed state as Nathan's. Oram explained this to the district attorney, who was easily persuaded. John Poersch had not been happy about issuing orders for these two exhumations, and didn't want to authorize another. Baden was insistent that the search be continued.

"We must have Timothy," he argued.

But Poersch prevailed, and the mortal remains of Timothy Tinning were left to rest in peace beneath the metal marker with Jennifer's name on it.

TWENTY-FIVE

The only thing we could boil it down to was that she
was so enamored of the affection she received when a
baby died that she liked to see it repeated.

—*District attorney*

There was a dead body, a confession and only one suspect, and in
the conventional wisdom of police officials that should add up to a
quick conviction. Instead, almost fifteen months elapsed between
Marybeth's release from the Oneida County Jail and the opening
of her trial. There was only one county court judge in Schenectady
County, and his calendar was booked for months ahead. If Marybeth had remained in prison, Judge Clifford T. Harrigan would
have been obliged by law to hear her case as soon as possible, but
even then she might have waited a year. There was room for much
reform in New York State's judicial system, but in this instance the
antiquated machinery of the criminal courts worked to Marybeth's
advantage. For fifteen months she was free to lead the life of a
housewife in her new home at Ballston Spa.

It was not an enviable existence. The notoriety of her case ruled
out any hope of her getting work. She and Joe tried to join a church
in their new community but did not feel welcome. When they went
to a restaurant, she worried about people recognizing her from her
photographs in the newspaper, and although she reacted as though
she were mortified, in a negative way she still seemed to enjoy being
the center of attention.

Before her arrest, moving house always gave her the opportunity
to make new friends, replacing those who had begun to feel uneasy
about her. This time there were no new friends to be made, and
Ballston Spa itself had little to offer. "Out in the sticks" was how
many Schenectady citizens thought of it.

Few of Marybeth's former acquaintances visited her. After a long, tearful conversation with one of them she was politely told that it would be appreciated if she did not call again. One day, shopping in a supermarket near her new home, she was spotted by a former pediatric nurse from St. Clare's, a woman who had comforted her when Mary Frances was dying. Before Marybeth's arrest, the nurse would have gone out of her way to talk to her; instead, she became preoccupied with a display of groceries.

On another occasion Marybeth was visiting her mother in Ellis Hospital when she encountered the Reverend Roger Day, who was also making a sick call. He was the Methodist minister who had conducted Tami Lynne's funeral service and, at Joe's request, had subsequently visited Marybeth in jail. During the jail visit Day had felt a lot of sympathy for Marybeth. He asked her bluntly why she made the confession and accepted her story that it was because she felt guilty about the fact that her children died—not because she killed them.

"I am innocent," she told him. "I was just worn out by all that questioning."

He could understand that. What he couldn't understand was her demeanor when he spoke with her at Ellis Hospital a few months later. Her mother was very ill with a gangrenous infection on her leg, a complication of the diabetes she had suffered for years, and Marybeth herself was due for a pretrial hearing.

"She was laughing and smiling," Day recalled. "After talking with her, I wondered how she could be so happy in the face of all that was happening. If I lost my child and my mother was seriously ill and I was about to be tried for murder, I would hope my faith would sustain me. But I would be crushed. I would find it very difficult to smile."

He could think of only two explanations for Marybeth's light-hearted behavior. Either she was innocent and had made peace with herself, or she was guilty and out of touch with reality. The second possibility had only just crossed his mind, but the more he thought about it, the more he wondered.

When her mother came out of the hospital, Marybeth offered to nurse her. It was not a pleasant task. During the winter Ruth Roe moved in with her daughter so that Marybeth could keep changing her dressings. Their relationship had never been a close one, but for the first time Marybeth was in control of it and in the role of the care giver. It was like being a mother again, but with her mother dependent on her. By the time she was well enough to return to her own home, Ruth Roe was convinced of her daughter's innocence.

Edna Tinning had nothing but praise for Marybeth. "She saved her mother's life," she stated admiringly. "Where the gangrene had set in she had to scrape the wound until it bled, every time she changed the dressings. She would come out of the room white and shaky, and you could hear her mother's screams down the street."

Marybeth could certainly count on the continued support of the elder Tinnings. While she was in the Oneida County Jail, her father-in-law bought a plastic lapel pin from the Duanesburg Pharmacy, fashioned in the shape of the word "love," and wore it every day thereafter as a symbol of his faith in the ultimate triumph of her innocence. He and his wife seemed to find it impossible to understand why their younger son, Andy, and his wife, Carol, had gone to the police. Ruth Roe developed the same difficulties with her son, Alton. Marybeth became a name which could not be mentioned between the generations, and the rifts on both sides of the family became deep enough to last a lifetime.

In his modest office by the Duanesburg crossroads Paul Callahan worked hard on his defense strategy. A Schenectady grand jury had handed down an indictment for second-degree murder in the case of Tami Lynne Tinning. There were no charges against Marybeth relating to any of her other children. Callahan was frequently asked if he was going to plead insanity, but it was never a serious possibility. If he had been able to find a psychiatrist to swear that his client was not responsible for her actions, she would then have to submit to a psychiatric examination from the prosecution before her plea could be accepted. And Marybeth gave every appearance of being sane. Another possibility was to plea-bargain with the district attorney's office. It was intimated to Callahan that if Marybeth would plead guilty to causing the deaths of the three children she had confessed to killing, Poersch might reduce the murder charge to manslaughter and recommend concurrent sentences.

Either of these options would mean spending a few years in confinement. Marybeth's only chance of acquittal was to plead not guilty to the murder of Tami Lynne. However, if a jury were to convict her, she could spend the rest of her life in prison. Callahan decided to take the risk and enter a plea of not guilty. In any event, his client insisted to him that she was innocent.

This was Paul Callahan's first murder case. His one-man practice in Duanesburg was normally concerned with real estate transactions, petty larcenies, burglaries and what are known in the business as DWIs (driving while intoxicated). A manslaughter charge resulting from a street accident had once come his way when he was an assistant district attorney under John Poersch. "There are not many murders in Schenectady County," Callahan explained.

Soon he would be pitting his legal experience against that of his former boss in the most notorious Schenectady trial for more than a decade. "The biggest since Lemuel Smith" was how the Tinning case was being described in local legal circles. Lemuel Smith—who in his own description was "big, black and ugly"—was a vicious rapist who eventually confessed to murdering five women from the Schenectady area. He was attracted to a certain type of white woman whom he would abduct and mutilate. District Attorney Poersch was proud of his part in helping put Smith behind bars, and had a fund of stories which began, "When I tried Lemuel Smith . . ." That had been back in 1976, and Poersch still saw it as his finest hour.

The interrelationship of people who were to be involved in the Tinning case was even more complex than one might expect in a small town. The police officer who persuaded Marybeth to confess had been her high school hero. The district attorney and Judge Harrigan had gone to school together and had remained friends, despite the fact that they campaigned against each other for the county court judgeship, which Harrigan narrowly won in 1984. The defense attorney, Paul Callahan, had attended the same high school as his client and her brother and had worked for the prosecuting attorney. Three years after he was graduated from Western New England Law School, Callahan was offered a job by Poersch. "He was the first assistant I hired after I was elected," Poersch recalled. "He was running for supervisor in Duanesburg when I was running for D. A. in Schenectady. I heard him speak at a political meeting and was impressed with him. He took my literature and distributed it. Then I was elected, and he was not."

Even now that they were on opposite sides of a major murder trial Poersch could not resist offering Callahan fatherly advice.

"Look, Paul," he said, "you have to make a motion for a change of venue to protect your back. Of all the cases where there's an argument to be made that you can't get an impartial jury, I never heard of a better one than the case of Marybeth Tinning. You'll probably be refused—they haven't granted a change of venue from Schenectady County since that family court judge's son was had up for murder—but as a tactical matter you should go for it. If your client can't afford it, the state will pick up the tab."

He meant this kindly. Poersch was counting on winning the case. He reasoned that after the verdict Marybeth would be certain to appeal. If she thought the jury was unfairly prejudiced by local publicity, she might conceivably claim incompetency of counsel. The district attorney didn't want to see his former assistant put in that position. Callahan, on the other hand, may well have thought of the financial effects of shutting down his law practice for several weeks while he put all his energies into an out-of-town trial. He might lose other clients and never recoup the loss. It was a real problem for a man running his own business. The district attorney's job would be unaffected by his absence, and his expenses were paid out of county funds. Also, if a change of venue motion were successful, the Tinning trial could end up in one of those sparsely populated Adirondack counties where juries can be a lot more conservative. Callahan decided to leave the arrangements as they were.

The district attorney also wondered why his former assistant did not give more consideration to an insanity plea. "I asked Joe and her brother if Marybeth had ever been seen by a psychiatrist, and they said no," Poersch remarked. "If I had been Callahan, I would have snuck her off somewhere and had her looked at."

Paul Callahan's biggest liability was Marybeth's confession. If only Joe had said yes when she asked his advice about calling Paul, instead of making that feeble joke about whether she had been read her rights, there might never have been a murder charge. Callahan would have advised Marybeth to say nothing at the Loudonville state police barracks, and without her confession the prosecution wouldn't have had a case. Now his best hope was to try to get that confession thrown out of court by arguing that she had been intimidated into making it. Then, if he lost that round, he would argue that since Marybeth had been accused only of murdering Tami Lynne, her admission to killing Timothy and Nathan should not be shown to the jury. Drawing from his everyday experience,

Callahan observed: "That's how it works with DWI cases. If you are on trial for one, the prosecution can't mention any prior DWI charges against you. Hence they shouldn't be allowed to bring up what she said about killing the other two children."

At Callahan's instigation, there was a pretrial hearing on the admissibility of Marybeth's confession in December 1986, a year after Tami Lynne's death. Judge Harrigan presided; there was no jury. Over seven days, detailed testimony was taken from Investigators Karas, Imfeld and Barnes about their interrogation of Marybeth at the Loudonville barracks. Imfeld bore out Karas's statement that he had gone over Marybeth's constitutional rights with her twice, and Barnes testified that he did so once. Legally just one of those three warnings would have been adequate.

The Miranda warning, as it has become known, has been crucial to every criminal investigation since 1966. In that year the U.S. Supreme Court reversed an Arizona court's conviction of Ernesto Miranda, who had been found guilty of kidnapping and rape, on the ground that he had made a written confession without being told of his right to a lawyer. Since then the Miranda warning has become so essential to the interviewing of suspects, so much part of every investigator's vocabulary that men who have been in the business as long as Karas, Imfeld and Barnes can be counted upon to recite it automatically. It was Marybeth's contention that they did not.

This was her first appearance in court. She wore the kind of clothes which would become familiar to Marybeth watchers throughout her forthcoming trial: a patterned blouse, polyester pants which fitted a little too snugly, and high-heeled shoes. She was accompanied by Joe—a meek figure in a navy blue suit, his thinning brown hair trained over his bald patch—who was there to substantiate her story, which was a strange one. She maintained that after arriving at Loudonville, she asked to see a lawyer but was told by Karas "that I would get a goddamn lawyer when he was goddamn good and ready." She said that when she explained to him how she had found Tami Lynne unconscious, he told her she was lying; then, when she described how her other children died from Reye's syndrome and from SIDS, Imfeld insisted that the doctors were liars and there were no such diseases.

In Marybeth's version, her interrogation by these two officers got so rough that at one point Karas "said if I didn't tell them the truth that they would take my kids out of their graves and rip them limb from limb."

She added, "I was frightened that they were going to do that, not that they were going to find anything, but just that they were going to hurt my kids."

During this initial questioning by Karas and Imfeld, Marybeth revealed that she was asked about several other alleged crimes, "about money, about the Duanesburg Ambulance Corps and about the pill incident."

Judge Harrigan seemed bewildered. "About what?" he asked.

"Pill," Marybeth repeated. It was all she was going to say about Joe's overdose of phenobarbital. "About the trailer fire," she continued. "About the fire at Kathy's restaurant, about Princetown Reformed Church fire. There might have been more."

"And did they tell you what the purpose was of asking you all these questions about fires?" Callahan asked her.

"Well, they said that they knew that I had set them."

"All of them?"

"Every single one, and there were more. There were at least two or three more."

"And what was your response to these statements?"

"I told them I didn't and Karas said, 'Well, we know different.' "

In his attempt to show that her rights had been violated, Callahan was pursuing a line of questioning which seemed to incriminate Marybeth more deeply. Not that she was being charged with arson, but these revelations didn't help her image. In some ways she gave the impression of being a good witness, clear and precise in her responses, with her nervousness only slightly showing. It was what she said that was so extraordinary.

After the initial questioning by Karas and Imfeld at Loudonville, she said she told Bill Barnes "that they had been screaming and hollering and hadn't read me my rights." She also stated, "I told Joe that I had asked for a lawyer and they would not give me one. They had not read me my rights and they kept telling me that you, meaning Joe, saw me kill Tami."

By the time she gave her confession she realized that Barnes was not the friend she had imagined, that he wasn't going to deliver her from the probing questions of his colleagues. She testified that she was intimidated into making a confession in words which were not hers, but ones which Barnes dictated to her. She claimed that as her statement was being taken down, she tried to catch the eye of Margot Bernhardt, the stenographer, and silently mouthed a message to her. "I just made my mouth go that I wanted her to help me, to get me help, but when I did, she would turn away."

She conceded that Margot Bernhardt "took down what I said, but it wasn't the truth. . . . Karas and Barnes were telling me what to say."

At this pretrial hearing Alan Gebell was in charge of the prosecution. While the district attorney's technique was often to dispense with detail, his assistant went after it like a ferret. In a faintly sarcastic tone he asked Marybeth if she was moving her lips while someone else's voice was being projected through her.

"No," Marybeth replied. "My mouth said it and she put, Mrs. Bernhardt put it down, but Barnes was telling me what to say. He was telling a story. Then he would say a comment and I would repeat it."

She testified that it was Barnes, not she, who gave the detailed description of how she suffocated Tami Lynne.

Gebell ask her, "When you said that you were repeating those answers that Mr. Barnes was whispering to you in your ear, no one was threatening you to repeat those responses, were they?"

"I felt I was being threatened, yes," she said.

"You felt that?"

"Uh-huh."

"No one was physically threatening you?"

"Only psychologically. They didn't physically hurt me, no."

"You were hurt by having to tell that story, weren't you?" Gebell pursued.

Here Marybeth scored a point. "Yes," she replied. "Because it wasn't the truth."

She added that having been "more or less prompted as to what to say," she was told to sign the confession and that she was "shaking like a leaf" when she did so.

Gebell had a calculated reason for taking her through her remarkable account in such detail. "I wasn't just playing around," he explained later. "I went through her statement with her inch by inch, having her commit herself to unbelievable testimony. My vision was down the road at the trial. If Paul Callahan were to put her on the stand in front of a jury, I would use what she said at this hearing and go through it with her all over again."

Margot Bernhardt testified, as she was to testify at the trial, that Marybeth's rights were read to her, that she appeared to be listening, and that while her statement was being taken, the police officers did not prompt or threaten her. They were calm and considerate, to the point of taking a break during the confession to get her another cup of coffee.

Paul Callahan had only one witness who was likely to support Marybeth's story, and that was her husband. Joe Tinning confirmed that when his wife telephoned him at work, he told her there was no need to call a lawyer. Later in the afternoon, when he was taken to the Loudonville barracks, he was questioned by police. "The questions pointed to my wife being a bad person," Joe said.

"Did you agree with them?" Callahan asked.

Joe's answer must have surprised him. "I was listening to them. I hadn't really formed an opinion at the time."

Did he mean he hadn't decided whether his wife was guilty? If so, this was not the place to admit it.

He confirmed that in the few minutes he was alone with Marybeth, after she had been questioned by Karas and Imfeld and before she made her confession, "she said that they wouldn't let her call Paul, that they didn't read her her rights, and they kept yelling and screaming at her." She was very tense, sobbing and wringing her hands. "She said that they had told her she could get a lawyer when they damn well pleased to get her one."

Callahan asked him how he reacted to this.

Joe replied: "I think I was quite shaken and just quiet and trying to figure out what was going on."

In his cross-examination Gebell took advantage of Joe's disarming honesty. Referring to the police investigators at Loudonville, he asked: "Did you tell them you wanted a lawyer for your wife?"

"No," Joe admitted.

"Did you tell them you didn't want the police or anyone else to question your wife?"

"No."

"Did you tell them she was being questioned and you wanted it to stop?"

"No."

"Did you tell them you wanted to talk on the phone to get help for your wife?"

"No."

"Did you tell them you wanted to call Paul or any other person in the world?"

"No."

"Did anyone threaten you?"

"No."

"Did you ever feel that you were in fear, or your safety was in fear?"

"No."

"Or danger?"

"Not danger, no."

"I have no further questions, your honor." Gebell sat down, looking well pleased.

Joe's testimony had done nothing to help his wife. Callahan tried to rescue the situation. "Mr. Tinning," he asked, "you said 'not danger' to that last question. Was there something else you felt that particular evening?"

Joe seemed to be dredging his memory for an emotional reaction "Just uncertainty," he finally admitted. "I didn't know what to do."

On re-cross-examination, Gebell reminded Joe that he had said he heard Marybeth tell the police she killed her children. Was that correct? Joe thought about this for a moment, then responded that those weren't quite the words his wife used. What he remembered her saying, he told the court, was: "I killed Tami."

As he walked down from the witness stand to join his wife, Marybeth gave him a look of undisguised contempt. Joe's expression was of acute bewilderment, as though he weren't sure what he had done wrong.

Two months after the hearing Judge Harrigan ruled against Callahan's motion to have Marybeth's statement suppressed. In a written opinion he stated that he found the testimony of the police investigators to be "candid, straightforward and worthy of belief," that Marybeth had been fully informed of her rights, and that neither she nor her husband had been "tricked or deluded."

Callahan had lost round one, but in a separate pretrial ruling the prosecution also suffered a defeat. Judge Harrigan refused to let the district attorney's office introduce evidence relating to the deaths of any of Marybeth's other children. He ruled that testimony at the trial must be limited to the case of Tami Lynne, and that none of the other Tinning deaths could be mentioned.

In vain Gebell cited the precedent of the Martha Woods case—how the federal court judge in Baltimore allowed the prosecution to introduce evidence of other suspicious child deaths in the Woods family, in order to demonstrate a pattern. As a state court judge Harrigan had no obligation to follow this decision; instead he was bound by a much older, precedent-setting New York case, People versus Molineux (1901), which held that when a person is charged with a crime, evidence that he or she has committed other crimes may not be introduced in court.

There are allowable exceptions to the Molineux rule and the prosecution felt that Marybeth's case qualified as one of them, arguing that her admission to suffocating two earlier children was legitimate evidence that she had a criminal disposition and was likely to repeat the crime. In ruling against this, Harrigan gave a considerable advantage to Marybeth, and presented the jurors with a peculiar challenge: to behave as though they didn't know certain facts which they couldn't help knowing if they read the local news-papers, listened to the local radio stations, or watched television news.

Part Four

JUDGMENT

TWENTY-SIX

I kept wishing I didn't know what I know so they could
put me on the jury and I could find her guilty.
—*Flavorland waitress*

For an average trial in Schenectady County, 150 voters are summoned for jury duty. For Marybeth's trial the figure was increased
to 700, and the process of jury selection dragged on through seven
working days. As every new batch of prospective jurors was brought
into court, Judge Harrigan repeated his warning that the trial could
last at least a month. By now it was June 1987, the beginning of
vacation time, so those who were unwilling to serve were allowed
to leave without giving an excuse. Day after day they left in droves.

Many had to be excused because they had already made up their
minds about the case, on the basis of what they had learned from
the media. Others were rejected because they remembered Marybeth from Flavorland. Many more worked at General Electric and
knew her husband. What they remembered most about him, some
of them said, was the number of times they were asked to contribute
to collections as his various children died.

A big issue in the questioning of prospective jurors was the extent
to which they might have been influenced by what they already
knew about the case. It was impractical to suppose that any adult
in Schenectady County could be ignorant of the story of Marybeth
Tinning. Nevertheless, a few people were so eager to serve that
they claimed to have missed all those page one news stories. "I may
have read about it, but I have completely forgotten it," one woman
said of the most sensational story in town. Another woman claimed
that "I only read the headlines," implying that no matter what they
said she was always able to resist reading on. (Could she really

bypass HOTLINE CALL PROMPTED BABY DEATH PROBE AFTER 9TH CHILD DIES, SCH'DY MOM FACES MURDER CHARGE?) Several prospective jurors indulged in what became known on the press benches as media bashing: "I don't pay any attention to the newspapers. They always get everything wrong" and "The thing that bothered me was the way the press picked on her." One man had an interesting interpretation of television reporting: "My first reaction was she must have been guilty for it to make the evening news." None of these individuals was selected.

Both the prosecution and defense attorneys favored jurors who admitted to some knowledge of the case but thought they could be impartial. Those who said they knew nothing about it were assumed to be either lying or out of touch with events. Two scientists were rejected by Paul Callahan, apparently because he was looking for jurors who might be more influenced by their emotions. After seven days of questioning and eliminating, a jury of seven men and five women was sworn in. Four of the male jurors were General Electric employees who did not know Joe Tinning, one was a recently retired General Electric engineer, one was a supervisor for the New York Telephone Company, and one was a personal worker. One woman had been a schoolteacher, another had recently retired from the telephone company, one was a real estate developer, one a department store sales-clerk, and one a housewife. Their ages ranged from early twenties to mid-sixties. Two of the men were black, and one was Jewish.

"It was a jury which could have been painted by Norman Rockwell," a prosecution witness observed. "A real cross section of small-town America."

When the jurors were being questioned by attorneys, the most eloquent statement was made by the real estate developer, Susan Bokan, who said that after travelling in Communist countries, she had come to realize "that the criminal justice system we have here is the best around." She was feeling distressed that so many prospective jurors were excusing themselves from the Tinning trial when her own jury summons arrived in the mail. She showed up at the courthouse, determined not to say that she couldn't afford to put her own business aside for a juror's fee of five dollars a day. Both Poersch and Callahan accepted her promptly.

In addressing the jurors, Callahan stressed that they should not be influenced by his client's appearance or behavior in court. This

led people on the public benches to wonder why he hadn't persuaded her to dress more like a mother. Alan Gebell, who watched
much of the trial from the back of the courtroom, remarked, "If I
were Paul, I'd soften her up a bit. Have her wear a dress. Tell her
to do something more feminine with her hair."

In this summer weather Marybeth had taken to wearing sleeveless, scoop-necked tops with her pants, displaying more tanned
flesh than anyone else in court. The courthouse air-conditioning
system was so frigid that other women drew sweaters around their
shoulders, yet she seemed able to tolerate it with bare arms. As the
trial proceeded the style of her clothing hardly varied; only the
color was different. There were the black polyester pants with the
black and white blouse, the burgendy pants with the sleeveless pink
top, the royal blue pants with the sleeveless white top which had
a multicolored design in front. And always the high-heeled shoes,
clicking to the slight sway of her hips as she crossed the courtroom
floor. She was very concerned about her appearance, frequently
stopping to ask a woman court officer, "How do I look today?"

"Fine" was the unvarying reply.

"Oh, no, I don't. I'm too fat." Or, "I can't wait for the weekend
to get my hair fixed."

Avoiding the press, she would arrive at the second-floor courtroom by a back elevator, usually with Joe at her heels, and settle
herself at the defense attorney's bench to the left of Paul Callahan.
There she would unzip a new leather briefcase, take out some
papers, and shuffle them around importantly. As the testimony
proceeded, she made copious notes, occasionally passing one of
them to Callahan as though presenting him with vital information.
The half glasses which hung from a silver chain around her neck
were taken on and off as she glanced from the papers on her desk
to the witness box. Something about her was familiar—not the
clothes but the behavior, something about her efficient attentiveness
to her lawyer, her eagernes to help and please him, the way she
cocked her head to one side to hear him better. From the first day
of her trial Marybeth had cast herself in a new role, Della Street
to Callahan's Perry Mason. She no longer bore any resemblance to
the dowdy little housewife whom St. Clare's nurses remembered,
or to the vamp of Duanesburg who hung around Kathy's Motel.
She was playacting again in the part of a lifetime. Joe, sitting on

the other side of her, might not have been there for all the attention she paid him.

In the court of her six-week trial Marybeth filled many pages of a spiral-bound notebook with her left-handed scrawl. Callahan told curious reporters that he did not know what she was writing down at the same furious speed as they wrote, but that he encouraged her to do it as therapy. She did not, however, give an impression of a nervous woman who needed to have her attention distracted. She appeared to be in complete command of herself, an interested observer rather than a hapless victim. She showed no emotion, except an occasional smile in response to a whispered remark from her attorney. Watching her day after day, one had a powerful impression of a woman who was sitting in on somebody else's trial, as interested in the unfolding tale as the jurors, and with no more personal involvement.

Chatting with reporters in the courtroom corridor, Callahan had an unusual approach to his client's misfortunes. When asked whether nine infant deaths in the same family didn't seem suspicious to him, he responded in the metaphor of one of his favorite sports: "There's no doubt that nine is a high number, but if some baseball player hits nine home runs in a row, you don't cry fraud." The weekend before jury selection began, he admitted to having "more butterflies in my stomach before the Celtics game" than over how he would handle his case for the defense. "But that doesn't mean I don't care about Marybeth Tinning," he added quickly. It was merely his way of saying that he was confident of proving her innocence. He was a Celtics fan and had driven all the way to Boston to root for his team in the National Basketball Association's championship series. The trip was worthwhile. That day the Boston Celtics beat the Los Angeles Lakers, putting him in an exuberent mood for the start of the trial.

Callahan was an ambitious man, approaching his fortieth birthday. He had established his Duanesburg law practice before leaving the D.A.'s office and had made all the right connections for a small-town attorney. He was a member of the Elks Club, a past president of the Kiwanis Club, and the current president of the Kiwanis Foundation. A practicing Catholic, he belonged to the Schenectady Knights of St. John and taught Sunday school at Our Lady of Fatima near Duanesburg, the church which Marybeth had attended as a child and where she and Joe had been married.

After he began to represent her, Callahan had to take some good-natured teasing from his many associates. With his wife and three children he was about to move into a handsome new house by Duane Lake, and as a commentary on the large fee which his neighbors felt he must be getting, this became known locally as the Marybeth Tinning House. And when he passed up an invitation to take his wife to an out-of-town baseball game because they couldn't get a baby-sitter, a Kiwanis colleague remarked: "Why don't you ask Marybeth to sit for you? That would really show confidence in your client." Callahan was not amused.

He was a serious-looking man, eminently suited in appearance to be a teacher at the kind of Jesuit college from which he had graduated. Perhaps it was his Roman nose and the bald patch which was developing like a tonsure, plus the fact that he always raised his head and held his small mouth slightly ajar after addressing witnesses, as though looking for an answer somewhere in the back row. At the beginning of the trial he seemed suspicious of the press but soon learned to use the media to his advantage by granting impromptu television interviews on the courthouse steps. Poersch had no public comments to make until the trial was over. Then he admitted that he hadn't wanted to risk saying something intemperate which could be used against him in an appeal. "I am sometimes aggressive in my comments," he acknowledged.

John Poersch was almost fifty-eight, stocky and florid with a short neck and heavy jaw. He was fond of good living, and it showed. He had spent almost all his life in Schenectady, and in addition to being district attorney, he had inherited the law practice of Poersch & Poersch which had been established by his father, Mathias P. Poersch. "An awesome personality, everybody loved him," the D.A. remembered. "He was eighty-nine when he died and still practicing law. A Phi Beta Kappa, died with his boots on. He had been practicing for sixty-five years. He'd call me at seven o'clock in the morning when he was already at the office and I'd be still in bed. He was bright as a dollar. Just awesome. The day he died he had gone to the hospital to write a will for a woman. Then he had clients in, had his lunch, went to his desk, and collapsed. His secretary is still running the office. She's eighty-two and been there for sixty-four years."

Some Schenectady citizens confused the D.A. with his father, who had served as a traffic court judge. Sometimes they referred to the son as Judge Poersch as though he had hereditary right to the title, and it seemed to please him. One way or another he had come very close to occupying the space of his old friend Clifford Harrigan.

Instead, as the Tinning trial opened, he was pacing the courtroom below Harrigan's bench, treading heavily but warily like a man with marbles in his shoes, telling the jurors that when they heard all the evidence, he was sure they would go to the "delivery room" and agree that Marybeth was guilty of murder in the second degree. It was a macabre slip of the tongue in this trial about a dead baby. He meant deliberation room, of course.

Callahan, also pacing the room uneasily, presented his argument that Marybeth had been coerced into making her confession. He gave a plaintive description of a woman exhausted by hours of questioning, without food. Knowing that the jury would eventually see the confession, he was trying to provide annotations in advance. "Several times she did not answer. She just shrugged her shoulders and said 'uh-huh.' Wasn't that the reaction of someone who was tired, who had not eaten? In the report they just used the words she said, not the facial expressions, not the emotions. You can't see any of that. I don't know whether I can convey to you what happened that night . . .''

He was not doing very well at it. How could he convince a jury that the intimidating atmosphere of the police barracks, Marybeth's tiredness, her refusal of the offer of a hero sandwich, had forced her to make a detailed confession of three murders she did not commit? And that, it seemed, would be the crux of his case.

The court adjourned for lunch. As people streamed down the broad courtroom steps into the sunshine, it seemed appropriate, in this town where everyone knew everyone else, that on this first day of the Tinning trial the undertaker who buried all nine babies should just happen to be standing on the sidewalk. He was waiting for the end of a requiem mass at St. Joseph's Church, a few yards down the block from the courthouse. It was a busy week for funerals, and Larry Daly was in his working clothes, dark striped pants and a well-tailored black jacket which appeared to have been molded onto him. His facial expression had settled into one of kindly concern for the bereaved as the moment approached for the casket to be carried out to his hearse. Suddenly he sighted a familiar reporter coming down the street from the courthouse. His eyes brightened.

"How did she seem?" he asked. "Did she say anything?"

A few minutes later he was on his way to the cemetery.

TWENTY-SEVEN

Even when you have to testify, you can't help feeling
that something like this never happens. Or, if it does, it
happens to someone else. Then you realize it's happening
to you, and you feel like you are in a twilight zone.
                                              —*Prosecution witness*

Cynthia Walter had not seen Marybeth since they kissed goodbye
at the airport eighteen months earlier, and it was agony to face her
now across the courtroom. Cynthia had hoped to be spared that.
Instead, she was one of the first witnesses for the prosecution.

More times than she cared to remember, she had mentally relived
the night of Tami Lynne's death. Having at first accepted her
friend's story about finding the baby unconscious, she was shocked
by Marybeth's arrest and even appalled to realize that Tami Lynne
might have been murdered, and she herself used. Standing to the
left of Judge Harrigan with Marybeth and Paul Callahan sitting
almost directly in front of her, Cynthia avoided Marybeth's eyes
by focusing on the back wall. As she testified, Marybeth occasionally looked up, twiddling her pen. After she had finished, Cynthia
walked stiffly out of the courtroom, her head held high, not even
glancing at her former friend. It was a wretched ordeal for her.

It did not, however, last as long as she had feared. Poersch's
questions about the night of Tami Lynne's death were brief and
direct. Within a few minutes he had elicited an account of how the
two women had gone on an evening shopping expedition and how
at one-fifteen the next morning Marybeth had telephoned for help.
"She sounded very quavery and very panicky." Cynthia described
her own attempts to give the baby artificial respiration. "I grabbed
her and put her on the living room floor. I sat on the floor and gave
her CPR until the paramedics got there . . . She was purple and
she wasn't breathing."

"Were your attempts successful?" Poersch asked her.

"No," Cynthia looked immeasurably sad. Watching her, Marybeth shook her head ever so slightly. Was it over the loss of a friendship or in disagreement over details? Recently she herself had changed her story, stating that Tami Lynne's appearance was gray, the color of a SIDS baby, not the cyanosed purple Cynthia had just described.

After spending part of the night with Marybeth at St. Clare's Hospital, Cynthia said she called on her at 7:30 A.M. and found her to be "calm and not emotional." When she saw her again in the afternoon, Marybeth was in a different mood.

"She said that I probably thought she wasn't a good mother because she didn't continue doing CPR until I got over there, and I didn't know what to sat to that."

At the funeral Marybeth was nervous and fidgety and told her friend, "Cynthia, I cannot do this."

"And I said, 'Yes, you can do it. You can be strong.' "

But immediately after the burial her mood changed again, and she was happily welcoming people to her apartment, where she served brunch. "She was eating, conversing with everybody there, and didn't appear to be upset," Cynthia added.

"Object to 'didn't appear to be upset,' " Callahan interjected.

"Sustained," said Judge Harrigan. But the point had registered with the jury.

On cross-examination Callahan asked, "You and Marybeth were very good friends?"

Cynthia nodded. "I would say very good friends, yes."

A few minutes later Callahan put the question: "Prior to Tami's death, would you and Marybeth ever have disagreements?"

"We had an—I don't know if you'd call it a disagreement. We both felt different ways about abortion."

It was more of an answer than Callahan wanted. Cynthia had introduced a sensitive subject, and if it had been pursued, she would have gone on to tell how Marybeth once admitted to her that she had an abortion. Seeing that this shocked her friend, who was strongly opposed to abortion, Marybeth had not gone into details. If that had come out in court, some jurors might have been influenced by the knowledge that at some point in her life, Marybeth had deliberately ended a pregnancy. Callahan had expected a yes or no answer to his question, and he could have asked to have

Cynthia's remark about abortion stricken; but that would have drawn more attention to it. So he let it pass, leaving the jury wondering where Marybeth stood in the abortion argument.

Cynthia was one of several witnesses who were to feel frustrated about the questions they weren't asked, but John Poersch pared his prosecution down to essentials. His almost cursory examination of his first few witnesses caused one news agency reporter to mutter to a colleague on the press bench, "The D.A. is prosecuting this case like he's double-parked."

When Betsy Mannix testified, she was limited to testimony about her two visits to the Tinning home on behalf of Social Services. She described Marybeth's frightened reaction to her first call with Bob Imfeld of the Schenectady police: "Her eyes became tearful and her hands became very shaky . . . and she repeatedly asked us if we were going to take her to jail, and if we thought she had hurt her child."

Betsy Mannix wished it were possible to give the jury a better sense of the woman they were called upon to judge, how her swiftly changing moods seemed to denote a disturbed personality; and how Betsy herself had been so burned out by this case that she had resigned from Schenectady's Department of Social Services. In the course of her research she had learned a great deal about Marybeth which she would like to have talked about, but within the narrow constraints of court procedure none of it was acceptable. The jury was there to hear the details of Tami Lynne's death, not the story of Marybeth's life. Eventually some of the jurors would feel as ambivalent as these early witnesses, wishing they had been told more about her, yet glad to be spared personal information which might influence the single decision they had to make: Did she or didn't she murder her baby? In his brisk manner John Poersch gave them no time for sympathy. He was also limited, by the judge's prior ruling, to testimony which had a direct bearing upon the charge.

When Dr. Bradley Ford, Marybeth's last pediatrician, testified, Poersch tried to bring in an oblique mention of the earlier Tinning deaths. After Ford had described Tami Lynne as a healthy baby with normal development, Poersch asked: "And did there come a time when you recommended a monitor?"

Callahan stood up. "Objection, your honor," he broke in. "This is getting to be highly prejudicial. I would instruct the district attorney to stop this line of questioning." Mention of an apnea monitor carried the suggestion of earlier infant deaths in the family.

"Sustained," said Judge Harrigan. "The jury will disregard that. Go on to another question, please."

There the matter might have rested. But when Callahan's turn came to cross-examination Dr. Ford, he developed a line of questions which created a trap for himself, then fell into it. Was Joe Tinning ever present when Tami Lynne was taken to the pediatrician's office? he wanted to know. Dr. Ford indicated that he was not.

"You more or less left it to her to decide about the monitor?" Callahan asked.

"A monitor . . . is only as good as the people using it," Ford replied. "It requires the parents' cooperation. Our recommendation was to use it but we could not guarantee it would prevent anything, nor could we point to proof positive that it was mandatory. It was just a recommendation that was declined."

The amazement on the press benches was audible. Now that the defense had mentioned the monitor, so could the prosecution. Poersch jumped in.

"You recommended it and she refused?" he asked.

Ford gave the response that Callahan had managed to prevent a few minutes earlier. "Yes, the monitor was recommended and it was elected by the parents not to use one."

As it stood on the record, Bradley Ford's testimony seemed bizarre. Here was a pediatrician recommending an extreme precaution to protect the life of a thriving, healthy baby. It didn't make sense unless he could explain why, but he wasn't allowed to. The jurors knew why, of course, but they were supposed to put that knowledge out of their minds. And it was in this Alice in Wonderland atmosphere that much of Marybeth's trial was conducted.

There were two unexpected prosecution witnesses: Marybeth's brother and his wife, Alton and Sandy Roe. Poersch subpoenaed them so he could introduce as evidence the letter Marybeth wrote them from the Oneida County Jail which they had passed on to the police. Its statement, "I . . . hope that some day you will be able to forgive me a little. I know that some day God will," could be taken as an admission of guilt.

He also wanted to have Sandy Roe tell the court that Marybeth had once threatened to use her gun on her, but after conferring with both attorneys in his chambers, Judge Harrigan refused to allow this testimony.

Poersch's handling of female witnesses like Sandy Roe, Cynthia Walters and Betsy Mannix was very different from his approach to male police investigators and doctors. The men were addressed formally, by title. Characteristically his questioning of Marybeth's sister-in-law began, "Sandy, would you please state in a nice loud and clear voice so everyone can hear you your name and address? . . . D'you mind if I call you Sandy?" It was his way of trying to put women at ease, but Sandy Roe didn't need that. She was not intimidated by the courtroom atmosphere and determined to get a few statements of her own on the record. She said she had visited her sister-in-law's home four or five times during the four months of Tami Lynne's life.

"The baby was well taken care of," she related, "but she was always crying, very nervous. You know, the mother was very nervous."

"Do you have any firsthand knowledge as to why the child was crying?" Poersch asked.

"For one thing, the baby's bottles were always left on the counter. They were never refrigerated. A lot of times there was sour milk in these bottles . . . There was a time I was there and Joe was feeding the baby, and Joe said, 'Give me another bottle. This one is a little thick.' " These unrefrigerated bottles of formula were also a concern of Cynthia's, but she had not been asked about them.

Poersch asked Sandy if she had disowned Marybeth. Here she made her last damning point. "No, but my husband had made that statement when she was having the affair with Giovanni, John Giovanni." She was using a local nickname for the owner of Giovanni's Hilltop Tavern.

"Objection," Callahan interjected. "This is totally irrelevant."

Sandy didn't think so. She had her suspicions about this man's relationship to Tami Lynne.

"Sustained. The jury will disregard it," Judge Harrigan ruled.

Alton Roe had less to say. Crossing the courtroom to the witness stand, he passed within four feet of his sister with no sign of recognition. For three days Marybeth had sat next to Paul Callahan watching significant people from her life pass by as though they had never known her. Cynthia . . . Sandy . . . now her brother. Perhaps without realizing the irony of it, her lawyer began cross-examining Alton, whom he had known from high school, as though addressing an old friend.

"Good afternoon, Al."

"Hello, Paul."

"Would you describe your sister as being nervous at times?"

"Yes,"

"Is it easy to upset her?"

"Oh, yes."

"Are there many times when she might be termed as having a guilt complex?"

"Yes."

"Is she always worried about what people think about her?"

"Yes."

"Could she be considered paranoid?"

"At times, yes."

Poersch asked: "Has your sister ever been under the care of a psychologist or psychiatrist, or anybody like that?"

"Not that I know of."

"Have you ever seen her angry?"

"Oh, yes. We used to get angry at each other, yes."

"Could she be violent when angry?"

"Maybe if she was pushed to that point, maybe yes."

One other family member was often in court during Marybeth's trial, but not to testify. Sitting in the front row of the public section, Carol Tinning attended as many sessions as family responsibilities and her job in a women's clothing store allowed. On the first day of the trial she and Marybeth stared at each other for a moment without acknowledging a relationship. From then on only Carol stared. She wanted Marybeth to see her there, taking in every detail of the case for the prosecution. Day after day in the courtroom Carol tried to look nonchalant but was visibly nervous. Her entrances were memorable for the fact that in order to pass the metal detector, she had to remove a collection of jangling bracelets and a heavy chain belt which hitched her straight skirt to unusual heights, showing off the longest, straightest legs in town. During recesses she was often seen stalking the corridor on stiletto heels, tossing back her mass of red-brown hair, blowing smoke rings. One day a reporter asked her name. "Lois Lane," she snapped. Beneath the lighthearted pretense she was feeling terrible.

Testimony about Marybeth's interrogation and arrest was given by Investigator Robert Imfeld of the Schenectady police and Investigators William Barnes and Joseph Karas of the state police. As at the pretrial hearing, they emphasized that although Marybeth was questioned at the Loudonville police barracks for almost seven hours, she was not coerced or bullied, she was given coffee and offered food, and she was free to call a lawyer. Up to the moment that she confessed to smothering Tami Lynne she was also free to leave the barracks. Once again the evidence was offered that the Miranda warning was read to her three times and that Marybeth waived her constitutional right to remain silent.

The officers were, of course, in no position to know whether she understood the implications of what she was giving up. Only Marybeth could testify to that, and at this stage of the trial Paul Callahan wasn't telling whether she would go on the witness stand. What emerged from the police officers' testimony was that although these three men conscientiously stuck to the rules, none of them spelled out to her—other than in the prescribed phrases of the Miranda warning—that she could have refused to cooperate. From their standpoint, why should they? If they had made a point of telling her that she could have stayed at home watching her soap opera, she might never have admitted to smothering Tami Lynne. But did they so intimidate her that even understanding her rights, she was too scared to exercise them? Did they encourage her to think that if she confessed to murder, she would be allowed to go home? Did they browbeat her into saying what they suspected but couldn't prove? If so, her confession could be invalid.

These questions more than any others were to be debated among jury members. What clearly emerged from the testimony of the three investigators was the picture of a lone and frightened woman who spent the best part of seven hours sitting on a hard chair in a small, cheerless office being interrogated. That in itself must have been intimidating. Even when she needed to go to the ladies' room, a woman employee went with her. Technically she was not a prisoner until she confessed, but she must have felt like one. In court, when Imfeld testified that none of the investigators raised a voice to her, she shook her head strenuously. Evidently this was not how she remembered it.

Karas explained the thinking of the police in taking Marybeth to Loudonville and in picking up her husband from work. At that point in the investigation it was felt that "perhaps one of them was not involved and might be a witness against the other. Or they might give us a lead which we did not realize existed." As for Marybeth: "We discussed whether or not we would have enough to arrest her, and we agreed that we wouldn't, so if she refused to go we couldn't have been able to get her to come in any other way . . . We were going to try and convince her to leave her house. If we couldn't do that we would interview her there."

"Why didn't you want to interview her there?" Callahan asked.

Karas replied: "As I say, there were two reasons. One, the material we intended to use in the interview was being taken to Loudonville so it would be available to both teams [referring to the state police and the district attorney's office] and secondly, that should we need the polygraph it would be available at Loudonville. In my mind it was equally possibly a witness interview or a suspect interview. It could have been either at that point."

"There were things you wanted to talk about other than Tami Lynne, is that correct?" Callahan asked.

"Yes."

"But you told her only that you wanted to talk about Tami Lynne."

"Yes."

The things to which Paul Callahan referred could not be mentioned. At the beginning of the police evidence Judge Harrigan explained to jurors that their copies of Marybeth's confession would be heavily edited. "I have made a decision that certain portions be redacted, stricken out . . . because they do not relate to this case," he explained.

Judge Harrigan's ruling had the effect of narrowing the verbal testimony of the three police investigators, leaving the jury to assume that Tami Lynne's death was all they discussed with Marybeth in hours of questioning. Inevitably, however, mention of other Tinning babies crept into the police testimony. Sometimes Paul Callahan objected to this; sometimes he let it pass; once he inadvertantly introduced it himself. Referring to Marybeth's interrogation at Loudonville, he asked Karas: "Did you ever tell her, between three and seven o'clock, that 'your husband has told us that you killed the babies' "—he corrected himself—' "that you killed Tami Lynne?' "

The answer was no.

When Karas started to say that he and Marybeth "went on in the discussion about the other children," Callahan raised an objection, and the judge sustained it. But Barnes was able to tell the jury that Marybeth "did not want to hear what she had done . . . she was visibly shaken after she told us that she killed her children," and his statement went unchallenged.

The prosecution's most important witness, Dr. Thomas Oram, also showed some uneasiness about Judge Harrigan's constraints, but once again there was the irony of the defense attorney's slipping in mention of a topic which he had striven successfully to keep out. In his cross-examination of Dr. Oram, Paul Callahan asked whether a high blood ammonia level had been noted at Tami Lynne's autopsy. Oram responded that he did his examination several hours after the baby's death when a test for blood ammonia levels would have been very unreliable.

"I did not consider it at the time and I do not think it would have been any use, even in retrospect . . . You would have to have it done while the child was alive to be of any value . . . I would not trust the results even if I had them."

"But the test was done with a number of the other children, is that correct?" Callahan observed.

"I thought we were not talking about the other children," Oram responded. "I could say a lot more about them."

Callahan couldn't have it both ways. Having won the argument that this case should be judged as though it were the only infant death in the family, he could not bring on the other deaths to support an argument for genetic disease—not without risking a demand from Poersch that Marybeth's confession be given to the jury in its original form. Throughout the early stages of the trial the fate of this thirty-six-page document hung in the balance. Jurors would not be given copies until they began their deliberations. Would all references to Marybeth's admission to suffocating Timothy and Nathan be excised, as the judge had ordered? This ruling held good only so long as Callahan refrained from mentioning the other Tinning children, and at times the words seemed to slip out inadvertently.

As Dr. Oram was beginning his testimony, Callahan whispered to his client, "Can you take this?" He warned her there would be a detailed clinical description of Tami Lynne's autopsy. She assured him she would be all right.

It baffled some people in the courtroom how she could seem so unmoved. Pathologists have a way of describing dead people in terms that laymen would rather not think about. After giving his credentials—Chief of Pathology at Ellis Hospital, Professor of Clinical Pathology at Albany Medical College ("where I teach pathology from page one to the end of the book")—and a list of other appointments. Oram identified the autopsy photographs. "This is the body of Tami Lynne Tinning clothed in night clothes, lying on her back with her head to the side—This is a photograph of the heart and lungs of this child, having been taken out . . . This is a representation of the inside of the stomach of this child . . . This represents the brain . . ." Then the autopsy itself. "We used a Y-shaped incision, which is the usual one, which opens the body, then we examined the chest cavity, the neck, the abdomen, the viscera . . . Then we opened the skull and examined the brain . . . We took blood for a toxicological examination . . ." And on through all the grisly details.

As he proceeded, various members of the jury, press and public glanced across at Marybeth to watch her reactions. She seemed interested. All the time that Oram was on the witness stand she was either watching him intently or taking notes. He might have been talking about a total stranger for all the emotion she showed, she who in other circumstances wept so readily. "Stoic" was the word Callahan used of his client. But this seemed more like detachment, as though Tami Lynne's death had nothing to do with her.

Oram's testimony was clear and precise. Like his opponent in this case, Dr. Jack Davies, he fitted into a long tradition of British forensic scientists who take professional pride in being good trial witnesses. Their American counterparts, trained in a more litigious society, are often reluctant to appear in court; indeed, several medical experts who were approached by the district attorney's office to give opinions on the Tinning case found reasons not to testify.

Oram seemed fully at ease. He went into detail about the toxicological, viral, bacterial, and chromosomal studies which had been done on Tami Lynne, all of them negative.

Poersch asked if he then determined the cause of her death.

"Yes, I did," Oram responded. But he wasn't ready to make known his decision until he had gone into some detail on how he arrived at it. The suspense in the courtroom could almost be felt. He explained that he found no obvious anatomical cause of death but that there was marked congestion of the lungs, liver, and brain. The lung congestion was not accompanied by the kind of inflamation which would denote bronchial pneumonia. The stomach was a little red, probably from the resuscitation attempts. There was "a rather nasty" diaper rash, but it was certainly not life-threatening.

"There is—and I have to talk about this—a diagnosis recognized from the fifties called Sudden Infant Death Syndrome. This occurs sometimes in a child of this age . . . The differential diagnosis here is of extreme importance. There are now many studies done of this peculiar syndrome." Oram anticipated that his colleagues Jack Davies would argue that Tami Lynne died from SIDS, and knowing how persuasive Davies could be, he wanted the jury to understand why he thought differently.

"These children," he said, referring to SIDS victims, "are usually pale and have some blueness of the finger tips, and they seem to be found dead. Classically there are little hemorrhages on the heart and in the thymus. These were not found in this child. It has been suggested that these children die of chronic oxygen deprivation. We believe that they do not spontaneously take another breath. They do not answer to the usual alarm signals to breathe. This is a congenital abnormality, and these children are normally underweight. They show symptomatology of anoxia, that is, lack of oxygen. This child did not show any of these. This child had no marks on the external body. None. We did total body X rays, by the way, and showed no evidence of fractures."

Oram added that he found no inborn error of metabolism in Tami Lynne. Having eliminated all other possibilities, he concluded: "This child obviously died of asphyxia. What else could have done this? One of the tragedies is that it is so easy to stop a child breathing, and the way to do this would be to smother the child."

Callahan tried to object, but Oram continued: "I am saying, sir, in essence that I came to the definite, positive conclusion that this child had been smothered because it would be the only thing that would answer the features I have described."

During his cross-examination Callahan tried to suggest other possibilities. One by one, Oram eliminated them. Could there have been a heating problem in the room where Tami Lynne slept? No, the air had been tested for carbon monoxide content. Also, there was no sign of the characteristic cherry pink lung tissue. Could the room temperature have fallen dangerously low? No, Tami Lynne had no symptoms of hypothermia—or of hyperthermia from being too hot. Could she have fallen from her crib? No, there were no bruises and no evidence of trauma. Could a baby of Tami Lynne's age suffocate itself?

"It used to be thought that a child could do so," Oram replied, "but in point of fact it is extremely rare unless a child is quite ill. We now know that the power of movement in a child, the life force to survive, is very powerful. Otherwise many more children would die. It has been generally concluded that the ability of a child to move its head, to clear its airway, is remarkably good."

Callahan tried another approach. "One of the grand jurors asked you," he recalled, "that if you came into the case blind to the family history but you still did a thorough analysis, would there be a question in your mind as to whether or not it was smothering? And was it your answer at that time, 'From now onward I am always going to have a question in my mind'?"

Oram responded: "What I meant by that was—"

"Was that your answer?" Callahan insisted.

"That was my answer." Oram looked dismayed at this interpretation of his earlier statement.

It was a classic legal maneuver but John Poersch wouldn't let his former assistant get away with it. As Callahan sat down, he leaped to his feet. "Would you clarify your answer to that particular question?" he asked.

"My answer is this: If I ever have a case where there is any suspicion of sudden death in infancy I would now consider the possibility of smothering."

His testimony could not have ended on a more satisfactory note. As Oram left the courtroom, Poersch made an unexpected announcement. "I have decided not to put Mr. Tinning on the stand. I therefore rest my case."

TWENTY-EIGHT

What came across to us was that she loved her husband,
and they seemed well suited to one another. They were
both strange.

—Flavorland waitress

It was another classic legal maneuver, and in the privacy of his
office above the courtroom John Poersch explained it. Although he
had subpoenaed Joe Tinning as a witness for the prosecution, he
decided to let Paul Callahan put him on the stand. Poersch's
intuition told him that subconsciously Joe Tinning had wanted
Marybeth to make that confession without a lawyer present. Joe
might never be able to admit this to himself, but Poersch was
convinced of it. When the police came to interrogate her, why else
would he have made a joke about it and told her not to call Paul?

Poersch reasoned that Joe already knew his wife was under suspicion. For years he must have wondered why she was always alone
with the children when they became fatally ill. He may also have
ben afraid to confront her, especially since his overdose of phenobarbital. But when the police finally started asking questions, he
stood back and let events take their course. "That's why I thought
it would be better if I let Callahan put him on the stand," Poersch
explained. "He would be a better witness for me on cross-examination than on direct. On direct I am limited in what I can ask him,
but on cross I can get away with a lot more. I also felt Joe Tinning
wouldn't lie. And if he wouldn't lie and wanted subconsciously to
turn her in, he would be a hell of a witness. And he was. I think
he had had enough."

The trial was in its fourth week when Joe was called upon to
testify by Paul Callahan. He walked slowly, almost painfully, into
the courtroom—neatly dressed and undistinguished in a beige

sports jacket, a cream shirt, a brown tie and brown trousers. He blended into the brownness of his surroundings: the brown tiled floor; the rust-brown upholstered benches for the jury, yellow-brown for the press; the brown walnut desks, the brown wood paneling; the extraordinary mural with its pious precepts in a variety of earth tones (JUSTICE IS TRUTH IN ACTION, THOU SHALT LOVE THY NEIGHBOR AS THYSELF, ALL MEN STAND EQUAL BEFORE THE BAR OF JUSTICE AND THAT NONE SHALL BE ABOVE THE LAW, THERE IS NO RIGHT WAY TO DO A WRONG THING, WE HOLD THESE TRUTHS TO BE SELF-EVIDENT THAT ALL MEN ARE CREATED EQUAL). Overshadowed by this lettering on the long wall behind the jurors, Joe looked small and uneasy on the witness stand. If he was wishing that the courtroom would swallow him up, visually it had already done so.

Although he had been attending court frequently since jury selection began, sometimes after working a twelve-hour shift at General Electric, he still looked as though he were unsure of his whereabouts and too embarrassed to ask directions. The only conversation he was seen to initiate was during a break in the police testimony when he went up to a free-lance court artist and asked if any of her drawings would be for sale after the trial. "My wife really likes them," he told Eileen Allen-Bruni, whose sketches of Marybeth had been shown on local television news programmes. She was astounded. Of the many court witnesses she had sketched over the years, Marybeth was the first to want a visual reminder of being on trial for murder.

Callahan had two good reasons for putting Joe Tinning on his witness list. He wanted some testimony about the police's treatment of Marybeth on the day of her arrest, and he wanted Joe's opinion of Tami Lynne's physical condition. These continued to be his defense tactics: that Marybeth's confession was invalid because her constitutional rights were violated and that Tami Lynne had died of natural causes. If he couldn't cast enough doubt in the jury's mind on one issue, he hoped to succeed on the other.

Joe was not much help to him. As he began to describe Tami Lynne, she seemed like any other baby. Sometimes she was good; sometimes she would cry. Sometimes it was a normal cry; sometimes it was "real loud and just very irritating." She would begin to take her food quickly and then very slowly. Occasionally she had diarrhea. He noted only one unusual symptom: "It was almost like she would be startled when she woke up, and she would cry real loud." Her body movements were all right, but two or three times she woke up in a cool sweat. It didn't sound life-threatening.

Marybeth was very upset over Tami Lynne's death, Joe related. "She would sit down and cry and be depressed at times. At other times she would seem all right." He acknowledged that before she was taken to Loudonville for questioning, "I jokingly asked her if she had been read her rights, and she said no, so I said, 'Then there's no need to call Paul.' . . . I told her she should go with them and answer their questions."

After he, too, had been taken to Loudonville, Joe recalled being asked some "very personal" questions by two police officers, Bill Sprague and Dan O'Conner. He did not elucidate to the court, except to say that the interrogation lasted two hours and he was not happy about it.

What was his mental state at the time? Callahan asked.

"I was just confused as to what was going on. I wasn't sure, you know, what to do or how to handle it, so my natural instinct is to kind of retreat into myself and kind of stay there."

Callahan tried to elicit more. Any other feelings he had?

"Just confused. I really couldn't comprehend what they were trying to get at."

That evening, before Marybeth made her confession, Joe had a few minutes alone with her. After being interrogated by Karas and Imfeld, she came into the room where he was waiting. "She was sobbing at the time and wringing her hands, very nervous, shaking." He had not seen her so nervous in their twenty-two years of marriage.

"What were your thoughts and concerns when you first saw her like that?" Callahan asked.

"It was just a blank. At that time I had withdrawn into myself. I just wasn't reacting to many things at that time."

"Did you have any feelings of anger?"

"No, not with her or with the police at that time, no."

"What did your wife do when she came into the room?"

"She sat down for a little while, about half a minute. Then she started to talk to me."

Poersch objected to testimony about the conversation on the legal ground that discussions between husbands and wives are privileged. But from a question Paul Callahan had asked Investigator Karas, the jury already knew what Marybeth had sobbingly recounted to

Joe: that Karas had allegedly said to her that "your husband told us that you killed your babies." Now Joe described his reaction: "It bothered me." Just that.

When Investigator Barnes came into the room and spoke to the two of them, Joe recalled that his wife was "getting more fidgety, wringing her hands, still sobbing . . . She asked him to stop, please stop, at least once."

"What was her tone of voice?" Callahan asked.

"It was sobbing and pleading."

"What did Officer Barnes do after she made that request?"

"He continued with statements that to get her the help she needed she had to tell the truth."

"Did Mr. Barnes in talking to your wife mention any other relatives?"

"Yes, one of the statements he made was that he didn't want this thing to happen to little Bucky and little Linda . . . They are my niece and nephew . . ."

"And what happened after that?"

"After that, I'd say about maybe five or ten minutes, Marybeth said that she killed Tami, very low, and she had to repeat it twice for Mr. Barnes."

"Tell the jury exactly what she said."

"She said, 'I killed Tami.' "

"Are you positive she said that?"

"Yes."

"Is that something you will always remember?"

"Yes, it is . . . Officer Barnes asked her why she had done it. She mentioned something about her father hitting her with a fly-swatter and being locked in her room while they went shopping."

"Did she say anything to you about 'I killed the children' or 'I killed them' or anything to that effect?"

"No, she did not.

"What happened then?"

"I was escorted from the room. I went to another room where two assistant D.A.s were sitting. They were waiting."

"Did you ever ask Officer Barnes to stop questioning your wife?"

Joe's response showed great naïveté about Bill Barnes's role in this unfolding drama: "No, I did not. Officer Barnes is a personal friend of the family. He is a police officer. He knew basic procedure and how to get out of this better than I did. I had never been in this situation before. I was waiting for him to make the first move."

"Why did you wait for him instead of taking affirmative action yourself?"

"Well, like I said, I had withdrawn into myself for one thing."

"You had what?" asked Judge Harrigan.

"I had withdrawn into myself emotionally, kind of protective type shell."

"And why did you do that?" Callahan asked.

"Just, I don't know. Just a psychological thing, I guess. I'm not sure. Just trying to get away from the questions and stuff like that. I was hearing but I was not reacting."

"And what was the total overall effect of all this questioning, and being in the police station, upon you?"

"I really didn't know at the time. It was just, you know. I just didn't really know."

"Were you like mentally paralyzed?"

"I could have been, yes."

"Did you try to think about what you should do?"

"I just wasn't thinking at all. I was hearing but I was not reacting."

"So just what anybody told you to do, you would do it?"

"Pretty much so, yes."

Callahan asked him: "What was your general attitude at that time about Marybeth?"

"They asked me if I thought she was guilty. I told them no."

At about 8:00 P.M. Joe's statement had been typed, and he had signed it. Its contents were not revealed in court. He had waited about two more hours until Marybeth had finished making her confession. Then Bill Barnes came in and advised him to get a lawyer, "someone that wouldn't bust me or bankrupt me." Joe related that he then heard Karas say to O'Connor, "Congratulations. We didn't have anything on her until we got her statement."

Before Marybeth was taken away, Joe was allowed to see her for a few minutes. "She wouldn't even look at me," he said. "She turned her back, was crying, sobbing, just a wreck."

In his cross-examination Poersch reminded Joe that he had promised to stand by his wife "no matter what."

"Is that your general attitude?" Poersch asked.

"Yes."

"And you are standing by her right now?"

"Yes, I am."

"And you would do it no matter what?"

"I would do it no matter what, yes."

Later Callahan asked him:: 'Would you lie for your wife?"

"No."

"Would you under oath perjure yourself for your wife?"

"No, I would not."

Joe's reactions may have been lacking, but his integrity was incredible. That night in the police cafeteria he had given his word to Bill Barnes, and he would never go back on it, even though he felt that later on Barnes failed his wife as a friend. Barnes had judged Joe's enormous capacity for loyalty correctly. And Poersch was right about his truthfulness. He could have predicted the answer he would get when he asked Joe whether he heard his wife say: "I killed Tami Lynne."

Another man in Joe's situation might have said he didn't remember. Instead, Joe seemed to be giving much thought to the question. Then, carefully correcting Poersch, he replied: "She said, 'I killed Tami.' " It seemed important to him to have her exact words on record, even though this meant emphasizing her admission of guilt.

"And she said it twice?" Poersch was making sure the jury hadn't missed this.

"Yes, she did."

As John Poersch had predicted, Joe Tinning would never lie, no matter what. He would stand by Marybeth, and he would tell the truth as he saw it. Through an entire morning on the witness stand he held to these apparently conflicting principles so rigorously that by the time he had finished it was hard to tell whose witness he had been. What was evident from his testimony was that on the night of her arrest he had given absolutely no emotional support to his wife.

This was Thursday, July 2, and after Joe's questioning was over, the court went into recess for the long Fourth of July weekend. Paul Callahan planned to present his medical evidence the following Monday morning, his chief witness being Dr. Jack Davies, the pathologist. Since Davies would have to base his case on the results of Dr. Oram's autopsy, and since Oram had been so sure that Tami Lynne was smothered, the trial of Marybeth Tinning seemed to be as good as over. Chatting among themselves, court officials and reporters predicted a conviction within a week.

Davies, as anyone who knew him might have guessed, had other intentions.

TWENTY-NINE

If this woman is convicted of murder, it will be for
emotional reasons, not on a scientific basis.
                                                 —*Dr. John L. Emery*

John Poersch had already warned jurors about the impression Dr.
Jack Davies was likely to give, and he was obviously worried about
it. "You will hear from two doctors," explained before the trial
began. "One is a great guy"—stretching his hands around his own
stocky waistline to indicate considerable girth—"and the other is a
much smaller man. Understand that you must not allow yourselves
to be influenced by appearances, only by testimony."

The prosecution's expert medical witness, Dr. Thomas Oram,
was the much smaller man. The defense was expected to open its
case with Dr. Davies, who, predictably, would enter court with his
customary flourish and a deep bow to Judge Harrigan. Instead,
Paul Callahan surprised the court by announcing: "My first witness
will be Dr. Arnulf Koeppen, who is not on the witness list."
Callahan was playing his trump card first.

Koeppen, chief of neurology services at the Veterans Adminstr-
ation Medical Center in Albany, had been consulted by Davies on
the Tinning case only eighteen days earlier, shortly after Davies
first saw the slides from Tami Lynne's autopsy. (The standard
autopsy practice is to take thin slices of tissue from various sections
of the body and set them by a fixative on glass slides so that they
can be examined microscopically.) Callahan complained bitterly
that Davies was denied access to Tami Lynne's slides until a few
days before the trial began. Oram had been willing to lend them
when Davies called on him six months earlier but was constrained
from doing so by the district attorney's office. In the absence of

this important material, Davies began to build his case on the evidence he had: the medical histories of all nine Tinning children, some of them detailed, others more sketchy. When jury selection began, he was preparing to go to court with the theory which had fascinated Dr. Dominick Mele over the years: that many, if not all, of the Tinnings' natural children had a congenital defect which led to their death. The clue to this was the high level of blood ammonia which, in some of the children, Dr. Mele had noted in the emergency room before they died. Davies theorized that the blight on the Tinning family was not SIDS but hyperammonemia caused by a genetic error in the metabolism of unknown origin, resulting in fatty changes in the liver, convulsions and a poisoning of the brain.

(There is an adage that doctors differ so that the art of medicine may prosper. Noting the same phenomena, Dr. Oram had come up with a very different theory. In his view, these symptoms were not a cause of death but happened as the direct result of a suffocation attempt. Many doctors believe that when a person is being smothered, chemical changes take place in the body during the last desperate fight for life, such as increases in the white blood cell count and in the level of blood ammonia. Obviously no one has ever actually observed this.)

Davies was able to borrow Tami Lynne's autopsy slides only four days before jury selection began. When he looked at the tissue samples of Tami Lynne's brain, he noted some cells which did not appear normal to him and showed these slides to a fellow professor at Albany Medical College. This man did not want to get involved in the Tinning case because he was leaving for Florida the next day; however, he agreed with Davies that Tami Lynne's was "a sick brain," lending credence to Davies's theory that it could have been poisoned by a high level of blood ammonia.

Davies then consulted Dr. Arnulf Koeppen, who was also a professor at Albany Medical College and whose specialty was neuropathology, a science which deals with tissue changes in the brain, spinal cord, nerves and muscle. Davies supposed that Koeppen's findings would coincide with those of the colleague who had just seen Tami Lynne's slides. This man had pointed out certain cellular changes in Tami Lynne's brain which, in his opinion, indicated liver damage. Since no one had measured Tami Lynne's blood ammonia level while she was alive, this seemed to be the missing link in the puzzle. If Koeppen agreed, a case could be made for an entire family devastated by a congenital liver disease.

At about this time Davies had come upon a piece of evidence which the district attorney's office had overlooked: the detailed autopsy report on Jonathan, the only Tinning child who did not die in Schenectady County. Jonathan, it will be remembered, spent the last few weeks of his life being studied by specialists at Albany Medical Center after Marybeth had taken him to St. Clare's Hospital in an irreversible coma. He had also undergone intensive tests at Boston Children's Hospital, following an earlier episode. Medically more must have been known about Jonathan than any of the other Tinning children, yet the results of his detailed autopsy were not part of his file in Schenectady. They remained in the Bender Laboratory at Albany, where Davies found them.

By the time he was able to consult Koeppen, Davies had already been obliged to return Tami Lynne's autopsy slides. So, until he could borrow them back, he asked Koeppen to look at the slides of Jonathan's autopsy. Davies was hoping for further confirmation of the liver disease theory, but what Koeppen observed in his examination of tissue from Jonathan's spinal cord told a more dramatic story.

Subsequently Koeppen had a conversation with Oram, one which gave Davies considerable satisfaction when he heard about it. Assuming that the defense's tactic would be to claim that Tami Lynne died from SIDS, Oram felt it would be useful to have a neuropathologist—very few of whom were in the area—to back up his testimony for the prosecution. Certain changes in the upper cervical cord and brainstem are believed to take place in SIDS cases. Unaware that Koeppen had already been approached by Davies. Oram telephoned Koeppen to ask if he would look at these particular slides of Tami Lynne and give an opinion, in the expectation that this would agree with his own and rule out SIDS. As he remembered Koeppen's response, it was brief and final. "I am sorry, Dr. Oram, you are too late. I have already promised to say a few words for the defense. But I would very much like to have a look at those sections."

Still thinking in terms of a SIDS defense, Oram sent slides of the upper cervical cord and medulla—essentially the upper neck area. He assumed this was the material Koeppen wanted, and it was only after Koeppen had testified that Oram realized he would have liked a great deal more. Subsequently Oram commented: "I think he didn't want to be more specific because I would have known the line of research he was following."

The few words that Koeppen promised to say in court made headlines in all the local newspapers, sent many people in search of medical dictionaries, and changed the direction of Marybeth's trial.

On that Monday morning, as the defense opened its case, Koeppen began by stating that he had examined slides of tissues of Tami Lynne, Jonathan, Nathan, Mary Frances and Jennifer for neuropathological changes and specifically for the presence of ammonia in the blood.

"What did those slides tell you?" Callahan asked him.

In his German-accented English, Koeppen began, "In the case of Jonathan the spinal cord is—" He got no further. Poersch jumped up.

"I object to any testimony about any of the other Tinning children," he said. "As your honor has limited the testimony of the prosecution, I would presume you would also limit the defense's testimony to the case of Tami Lynne Tinning."

Callahan argued that it was essential for him to introduce some testimony about family medical history in order to show that Tami Lynne had a serious genetic problem. Poersch argued back that if this were permitted, he should be allowed to recall the prosecution witnesses and ask them about the other children's deaths. After a heated exchange Judge Harrigan ruled that he would permit Koeppen's testimony about Jonathan "so that the defendant has every opportunity to defend herself . . . but it has unquestionably opened the door for the People to recall witnesses for a wide range of rebuttal, and that, of course, I will allow them to do. I shall also change my ruling about the redactions of the statement which had been held in abeyance until this time."

Callahan was taking a calculated risk. He must have known, when he put this witness on the stand to introduce evidence about Jonathan, that he might lose his hard-won advantage of keeping all mention of the other Tinning children out of the case. Now the jury would get Marybeth's confession to killing Nathan and Timothy as well as Tami Lynne, all thirty-six pages. It was a strange turn of events.

Koeppen went on to describe what he had seen in Jonathan's

autopsy slides. The spinal cord was seriously diseased, he said, and he felt certain that Jonathan was afflicted by Werdnig-Hoffmann disease—the infantile counterpart of amyotrophic lateral sclerosis or Lou Gehrig's disease (named after the baseball player who died from this rare form of muscular atrophy). Koeppen added that while Lou Gehrig's disease was rarely hereditary, Werdnig-Hoffmann disease was always passed down from the parents in a recessive manner, meaning that while neither of them would be afflicted, both would carry a recessive gene. Werdnig-Hoffmann disease was always fatal, and few of its victims were likely to live beyond the age of eighteen months.

"Can death by this disease be sudden?" Callahan asked.

"Indeed," Koeppen replied.

"Is there any doubt in your mind after your examination of the slides of Jonathan that he did in fact have Werdnig-Hoffmann disease?"

"No doubt. I went back and examined the slides again and again."

It was a wholly unexpected piece of testimony. During the month that Jonathan lay dying at Albany Medical Center, subject to all kinds of medical tests and under constant observation in the hospital's pediatric intensive care unit, there was no suggestion of Werdnig-Hoffmann disease. Not does it seem to have been considered by the specialists at Boston Children's Hospital who examined him several weeks earlier.

After this surprising analysis of Jonathan's last illness, Koeppen went on to describe what he saw in the autopsy slides of Tami Lynne. He explained that the main characteristic of Werdnig-Hoffmann disease was a loss of nerve cells which supply the skeletal muscles—that is, the muscles which move the extremities. In examining the brainstem, he noted that the nerve cells which give rise to the nerve that moves the tongue were abnormally small. Hence the tongue would be small and move poorly.

"Are there any other slides that it would be helpful to you to examine of Tami Lynne to determine Werdnig-Hoffmann disease?" Callahan asked.

"Yes, the spinal cord."

"And were you able to examine those slides?"

"No."

"Do you know why you weren't able to?"

"Yes."

"And the reason?"

"Looking at the autopsy protocol, the spinal cord had apparently not been taken . . . It is a prolonged procedure and requires delicate hands."

"Time-consuming?"

"Very."

An autopsy protocol is a list of the procedures completed by a pathologist. Oram later agreed that in Tami Lynne's case not every item may have been listed in detail. However, he was not attempting to hide anything. If Koeppen had asked whether there were any slides of the spinal cord, he would have handed them over; instead, the defense assumed that because these slides were not listed they did not exist. Koeppen saw only twenty-one slides out of about three hundred.

"If you had a slide showing the spinal cord of Tami Lynne Tinning, would you have been able to make a conclusive opinion as to whether she had Werdnig-Hoffmann disease?"

"Yes."

"And is it your appraisal that . . . it appears she had the disease?"

"So it is."

Later Callahan asked him: "What are the chances of a second child having the disease?"

"The risk ratio is one in four, twenty-five per cent . . . The risk is viewed as unacceptably high for a subsequent pregnancy."

Callahan asked what would have been his advice to the Tinnings about having more children.

Koeppen repeated: "The risk is one in four which is high, considering an infant mortality rate of one per cent in the country."

Callahan persisted: "So your advice would be not to have more children?"

"That is correct."

Poersch asked Koeppen if he had done any tests on Mr. and Mrs. Tinning.

"The problem with this disorder," he replied, "is that there is no test available for the carriers. The carriers are identified through the occurrence of a defective child, I'm afraid."

"But from your examination of some slides you cannot tell us what Tami Lynne died from, isn't that true?"

"That is correct."

"And you cannot tell us what Jonathan Tinning died from?"

"That is also correct."

Referring to the five children whose slides Koeppen had seen, Poersch asked, "Could they have died of smothering?"

After a pause Koeppen responded: "Yes."

Was this unexpected testimony strong enough to cast reasonable doubt in the minds of jurors? Callahan seemed pleased by its startling effect, which had been almost as much of a surprise to Marybeth and Joe as to others in the courtroom. "I told them all along there would be some medical evidence of a genetic defect," Callahan told reporters. "But I didn't go into details." During the lunch break the two of them were seen poring over medical journals in which relevant passages had been underlined. Marybeth was smiling and pointing them out to Joe. She looked immensely relieved.

Also during the lunch break, Jack Davies gave an impromptu press conference. He was much more positive than Arnulf Keoppen had been about the cause of Tami Lynne's death. She had Werdnig-Hoffmann disease, he stated unequivocally. This condition was evident from the nerve cells at the top of the spine. Regretting the absence of the spinal cord, he remarked of the autopsy. "They took the brain from the top of the spine."

"Which is what a pathologist would normally do?" a reporter asked.

"Which is not what I would have done if I had suspected some unusual disease of childhood," he responded firmly.

Standing on the courthouse steps, his bright red tie fluttering in the breeze like a banner, Paul Callahan looked elated. Someone asked him why he had been denied the autopsy slides for so many months. "I suppose the other side had something to hide," he remarked. "Maybe they knew they didn't do a very thorough job."

Davies's testimony followed Koeppen's and took up much of the afternoon. His presence seemed to fill the courtroom. He bowed, sat down heavily, cleared his throat and launched into the customary list of his credentials from his medical degrees earned at the Universities of Bristol and Edinburgh, through his years of service in Uganda, his appointments in the United States and "at least fifteen thousand autopsies."

In Tami Lynne's case he said he consulted Dr. Koeppen because some of the slides from Tami Lynne's autopsy showed changes in the central nervous system which felt indicated neurological disease and should be examined by a neuropathologist. Koeppen pointed out other findings which indicated Werdnig-Hoffmann disease.

This was borne out, Davies said, by Joe Tinning's testimony: that Tami Lynne was a slow feeder, was irritable and had a clammy feeling. "These babies may take ninety minutes or more to finish a feed. They are liable to inhale food during feeding because they don't control the tongue very well. They are cold and clammy because they often cannot and do not want to move their limbs. They are irritable for reasons I do not know, but I think because they cannot move their limbs satisfactorily. Finally, they show no signs of mental retardation in any respect."

Davies was asked if he found any evidence that Tami Lynne was smothered.

"None whatever," he replied firmly. He added that "as to the question of whether she had Werdnig-Hoffmann disease or not there was no disagreement at all" between himself and Koeppen.

This showed some poetic license on his part. Koeppen had not said that he was certain Tami Lynne had Werdnig-Hoffmann disease, only that he was certain about Jonathan.

After he finished testifying, Davies held another impromptu press conference in the courtroom corridor, and this time he was ready to talk about all the Tinning children. Two of the deaths, he said, were easily explained. Jennifer died from meningitis and brain abscesses, and Michael from severe pneumonia.

"You can eliminate those two deaths. Then, in addition to Tami Lynne, we have six children all of whom died the same way. They had vomiting, diarrhea, were irritable, and screamed a lot. Two of them, Joseph and Timothy, had no autopsies but thanks to Dr. Mele's foresight, the blood ammonia level was measured in the emergency room. We know they all had high blood ammonia except for Tami Lynne, and she was not cared for by Dr. Mele, so her level wasn't measured. Now if you have a damaged liver, the ammonia gets through the bloodstream and poisons the brain."

How was that connected with Werdnig-Hoffmann disease? he was asked.

"I don't know of a connection. But if there is, we may have uncovered a previously unknown disease of childhood."

Why was it that in all these years none of the doctors who examined the Tinning children had suspected Werdnig-Hoffmann disease? Davies had a ready answer for that, too. "I think they were all fixing on high blood ammonia, and therefore they were looking for a metabolic error rather than a nervous, genetic error. The doctor who examined Mary Frances in Boston was sure she had a metabolic disease."

Surrounded by reporters and cameramen, Davies looked well pleased: an expert on the brink of a great discovery. There was only one flaw to it. "You have to take skeletal muscle and the spinal cord to make an absolute diagnosis of Werdnig-Hoffmann disease. That was done at Jonathan's autopsy in Albany, which is why there is no question about him. But no one took Tami Lynne's spinal cord." He stroked his beard as though wondering how his old colleague Tom Oram could have slipped up so badly.

"Did you ever ask Dr. Oram why he didn't take the spinal cord?" a reporter wondered.

"No. We did not appreciate the importance of it until Dr. Koeppen discovered what had killed Jonathan."

But didn't it defy the odds to suggest that six out of eight children had Werdnig-Hoffman disease?

"The odds aren't fixed at one in four. They are at least one in four. We are talking about a recessive gene, and I think both Mr. and Mrs. Tinning carry it."

But what about the fact that she confessed to killing three of her children?

Davies looked amiably at his questioner, a young, huskily built television news reporter. He ventured: "If you have a not too bright female—perhaps you had better not put that—but a not too bright female with some hulk sitting opposite her larger than you, m'boy, she might be scared into confessing to anything."

That evening the testimony of Koeppen and Davies was a leading item on the local television news, with Davies's press conferences largely featured. It was also prominent in the next morning's newspapers. In a banner headline the Albany *Times Union* announced: DOCTORS: TINNING BABY HAD GENETIC DISEASE. And in the *Schenectady Gazette*:RARE GENETIC DISEASE KILLED TINNING INFANT, PATHOLOGIST TESTIFIES. Hurriedly assembled sidebar stories explained Werdnig-Hoffmann disease. Quoting a researcher for the Muscular Dystrophy Association, the *Times Union* informed its readers that only one in eighty people is a carrier of the defective gene and that the disease affects only one in fifteen thousand to twenty-five thousand of live births. Another of the Association's experts expressed surprise at Marybeth's contention that Tami Lynne cried a lot. When the disease is severe, the expert told the *Times Union,*- babies are unable to cry at all because their muscles atrophy.

Marybeth's trial had taken an unexpected turn, and when she came into court on the morning of the big headlines, she looked flushed by success. For the first time she wore a skirt—khaki twill, neatly tailored—with a short-sleeve shirt blouse in a soft shade of pink, and a fine gold chain at her throat. The color scheme was in pleasant contrast with her tanned complexion and blond hair, and she walked firmly on high heels with the poise of a woman who knows she is dressed well. Overnight she was transformed from a Mohawk Mall housewife to a smart secretary. As she unzipped her briefcase and smiled across at Paul Callahan, she looked more like Della Street than ever. The word went around the press bench that "with Marybeth all gussied up like that, Callahan must be ready to put her on the stand."

There was only one thing to disturb her equanimity: the presence of her sister-in-law Carol Tinning. Carol had not been in court for several days on account of a medical emergency with her son, a strapping young man made helpless by the tragic complications of cerebral palsy, but now, irritated and incredulous at the previous day's testimony, she was back in the front row of the public section. She stared hard at Marybeth, who avoided looking at her. "She doesn't like it when I'm here," Carol commented with some satisfaction.

Marybeth did not testify. Callahan explained to reporters: "The case is going very well. Why change things?"

The next and last witness for the defense was Dr. John L. Emery, Emeritus Professor of Pediatric pathology at the University of Sheffield, England. Half a century ago he and Jack Davies had been in college together, and although their medical careers had gone in separate directions, they had kept in touch. Emery had become recognized as Britain's leading expert in SIDS and other forms of unexplained infant death as well as an international authority on genetic diseases. Not that he regarded SIDS as a disease; outside the courtroom he bluntly described it as "a dustbin into which doctors put all the cases of sudden infant death which they don't have the time or the knowledge or the understanding to investigate with the kind of painstaking skill which may be necessary."

Emery was known for his painstaking skill and for his consuming interest in why some children fail to survive, an interest which began, he told the court, when the first of his own seven children died in early infancy. Jack Davies had urged Paul Callahan to bring John Emery over from England as a defense witness long before Arnulf Koeppen came into the case. At that time Davies felt Emery could help solve the mystery of the high blood ammonia level noted in several Tinning children, before they died. Callahan hesitated, thinking of the cost, until Emery let it be known that the Tinning case was so fascinating to him that he would come for a nominal fee and expenses. At the time of Marybeth's trial he happened to be in the United States already, researching some infant deaths in Madison, Wisconsin.

He was a small, slightly stooped, professional-looking man, somewhat bald, with a neat gray beard and twinkling blue-gray eyes behind gold-rimmed spectacles. There was a kindly, old-fashioned fussiness about his manner, particularly when he spoke about rearing babies, a fussiness which must have inspired confidence in many uncertain British mothers but which annoyed the district attorney intensely. John Poersch seemed to mistrust outside experts. He had resisted calling Dr. Michael Baden, head of the state forensic team, as a prosecution witness despite Baden's certainty that Tami Lynne was smothered. Poersch made no secret of his dislike of Dr. Davies and was impatient when Dr. Emery launched into a brief history of SIDS, which Judge Harrigan allowed over the district attorney's protests.

"If you go back into the literature of sudden infant deaths," Emery explained, "it was claimed that most of the mothers were drunk, and a lot of parents were being harassed by the police and other people and blamed for these deaths, when in fact was no evidence that they had done any harm to their babies at all. There was a group in Seattle in the state of Washington in this country who felt very strongly about this, and they had some meetings and said, let us, as it were, invent a term to describe babies that are found unexpectedly dead, and we will say that this is a natural cause of death so that these parents shall not be harassed. They called it Sudden Infant Death Syndrome and this had a very calming effect and made it possible to help these people."

Callahan asked him about Werdnig-Hoffmann disease. Emery replied: "It is a condition in which the nerve cells of the spinal cord do not grow, and the muscles controlled by these nerves do not grow, and the children become progressively weak and frequently die . . . We do not know the cause. It is quite definitely genetically determined; that is, if there has been one child affected there is a very high likelihood of the next child being affected. Whether it's one disease or many diseases we do not know yet."

Did these children die suddenly? Not necessarily, Emery replied, but it could happen.

What about bereaved parents? How did they react? Having interviewed about two thousand parents whose babies had died from SIDS, Emery was eloquent on the subject. The first reaction was usually one of disbelief, he said. In mothers this was followed by a loss of confidence in their own mothering skills and by a great deal of guilt.

Had any of these parents told him that they killed their children?

Emery seemed to find the question of great clinical interest. "Oh, yes," he replied calmly. "I have had many people tell me that they killed their children when in fact I know they have not, but at the time they felt they killed the child . . . Many women behave in a completely irrational way under stress and they will make statements to the police and to others for a whole number of reasons, and if you talk to them two or three months later they will tell you that they hardly knew what they were saying at the time."

Poersch asked him, on cross-examination, whether any of the women had confessed to him in detail how they killed their children

"Oh, yes," Emery replied.

Poersch seemed incredulous. "Time and again?" he asked.

"Oh, not stopping at one, sir."

Emery did not think this unusual; it was all part of the grieving process. "I am not a psychiatrist, sir," he said in response to a question from Callahan, "but I have had more experience of dealing with bereaved parents than almost anyone."

There was another aspect of John Emery's reputation which was not mentioned at the trial. Two years earlier, in 1985, he had published a controversial paper in the British medical journal *Archives of Disease in Childhood* in which he expressed the opinion that one in ten of all SIDS deaths might happen as the result of smothering by a parent. He still held to that view, so he was not blind to the mental aberrations of motherhood. What troubled him about Marybeth's trial was the isolation of Tami Lynne's death from the other eight and the absence of a correlated study of the Tinning children to determine whether or not there was a genetic factor in their deaths. He also believed that one in ten of crib deaths was due to an error in metabolism, and there were hints of such an error in the Tinning family. Determining the nature of the error, if needed it existed, would be a delicate and time-consuming task for which techniques were only just being developed. He was intrigued by the possibility of working on it but estimated this would take him at least two weeks, and there was no likelihood of the trial's being held up for that long.

What he had already seen from Tami Lynne's autopsy suggested "a possible diminution in the motor cells of the spinal cord" and that "there were probably a whole number of features present which came together" at the time of her death.

He was shocked by the legal aspects of the case: that in New York State a woman suspected of killing her baby should be charged with second-degree murder, the same category of crime as a brutal, premeditated slaying.

"We do not use the word murder in England for cases like this," he told the court. "We call it infanticide . . . In England they believe that for the first year after delivery a mother is—I will not say that she is absolutely *non compos mentis*, if you understand me— but is not completely rational in her relationship to a child; so if she kills a child it is never considered murder. It's called infanticide. And therefore the crime is of a lower order."

As Emery left the courtroom, reporters and photographers gathered around him. "What did kill Tami Lynne Tinning?" he was asked.

"The answer is I don't know and I think it's appalling for anyone to come to a definite conclusion on the basis of the evidence," he replied. "There is no positive evidence to support the charge of asphyxia, no bruising of the mouth, nothing to suggest that anything was done physically to this child. She may have had some partial asphyxia but that may have been only a minor part of the cause of death."

But was it likely that so many of the Tinning children would inherit Werdnig-Koffmann disease?

"I don't know of any family in which there were six Werdnig-

Hoffmann children. But in most families after two deaths the parents do not have another child. What you have here is a very curious constellation of deaths associated with this woman, and that needs investigating. But to say she murdered them is an emotional reaction which is not based on evidence. This family needs a major research project."

Emery's curiosity led him to seek out Marybeth at the end of the day's session. Afterwards he related: "I talked to her for twenty minutes. She said I was one of the first doctors who made sense to her. I asked her about Tami Lynne. She said, 'I was never quite certain whether Tami was normal or not because when I would pick her up she would seem to slip through my hands.' Now I didn't put those words to her. But what she described is typical of a number of conditions of muscular hypotonia, which means that the muscles have reduced tone. I asked her, did she tell anybody about this. 'Oh, no,' she said."

In his office at Ellis Hospital, Dr. Thomas Oram was saddened to hear about the day's testimony. He had thought that the autopsy slides of Tami Lynne's spinal cord were among those which were picked up by Paul Callahan from St. Clare's Hospital and delivered to Dr. Jack Davies, but since he was not part of that transaction, he couldn't be sure. Whether they were temporarily missing or whether Davies had overlooked them during the short time he was allowed to borrow the slides might never be known. In the meantime he, Oram, had been publicly criticized for failing to carry out a complex autopsy procedure which he had in fact done. He could live with the criticism; what bothered him was that Davies and Koeppen had reached medical conclusions which might have been different if only they had asked him for the evidence.

From their point of view, if they had asked him for slides of the spinal cord, he would have guessed what kind of disease they were looking for and had time to prepare some contradictory evidence. "It has become a game," Oram commented sadly, "and it shouldn't be."

THIRTY

My biggest fear is that they will convict her and she will get no help.

—Former friend, during the trial

Dr. Marie Valdes-Dapena, president of the National Sudden Infant Death Syndrome Foundation and head of the pediatric pathology section at the University of Miami School of Medicine, had impressive qualifications. She had actively researched sudden death in infancy for more than twenty years and was currently working on a book on this subject, to be published by the federal government. She had written two previous medical books, many articles and a text describing how an infant autopsy should be performed. She started investigating the causes of crib death before the term "Sudden Infant Death Syndrome" was invented, and had done about three thousand child autopsies since 1945. During this intensive professional career she had given birth to eleven children. It boggled the minds of the jurors, among whom she became known, since her name was difficult to remember, as the woman who never had time to sleep.

She was visiting a daughter in Bermuda when she was summoned to Schenectady as the prosecution's first rebuttal witness: John Poersch's answer to Dr. Emery. On the witness stand she was trim, businesslike and precise. She stated that she had seen the results of Tami Lynne's autopsy and discussed them with Dr. Oram. "I think this was a good autopsy. It was well done, and included in there was virtually everything that I would recommend be done." Anticipating questions about blood ammonia levels, she added. "I would not recommend blood chemistry. After death the sugar goes completely out of control. The Ph level drops. We do not

[315]

recommend those tests which are not productive . . . but some extra things were done in this case. The spinal cord was removed and sectioned." That last comment was clearly for the benefit of the defense.

Upon examining the slides, she saw no evidence of Werdnig-Hoffmann disease. She said she had never heard of its being diagnosed for the first time at autopsy. The symptoms were evident, sometimes even before birth. "These are very quiet babies in utero, and when born they are as limp as a rag doll . . . The cause of death is failure to be able to breathe because the muscles in the chest wall are not strong enough."

"And most of them die in hospital?" Poersch asked.

"They do."

"Because this disease is easy to discover?"

"Yes." She added that she had reviewed Tami Lynne's birth record at St. Clare's Hospital, and her Apgar score (the standard system for assessing the health of a newborn) was "as good as it gets."

Had she done any research on the suffocation of children?

"Yes, a good deal . . . The infant who dies that way has a negative autopsy, if the suffocation is caused by a soft object. The only thing you find is tiny hemorrhages in various parts of the body, particularly in the thymus and in the lungs." These are present in about 50 percent of crib deaths, "so there is no way to distinguish between the two." She defined crib death, or SIDS, as "the sudden unexpected death of an infant who has seemed well."

"Have you made any determination in the death of Tami Lynne?" Poersch asked.

She replied: "I think there is a strong possibility of suffocation with a soft object in light of the family history which we have in this case."

"Is your feeling that this child was smothered strong?"

"Very strong."

"Is it based on the fact that you knew Mrs. Tinning confessed to smothering?"

"It is based in part on that and in part on the fact that there were a considerable number of cases, far more than I have ever seen or heard of with SIDS."

Outside the courtroom Dr. Valdes-Dapena was asked by reporters if like Dr. Emery, she had known of mothers who said they killed their babies when in fact they were innocent. She replied that it was in the nature of mothers to blame themselves when a child died, even if they had no reason to do so. "But I never heard of a mother saying that she smothered a child when she did not. Ever."

Two prosecution witnesses were recalled by John Poersch to answer questions about whether Tami Lynne showed signs of Werdnig-Hoffmann disease. Marybeth's last pediatrician, Dr. Bradley Ford, said he had done three complete head-to-toe examinations of the baby during the first two months of her life and found no symptoms of the disease. He was familiar with the condition because he was currently treating a Werdnig-Hoffmann baby whose muscle tone was so poor that she was unable to lift her head. In contrast, Tami Lynne was developing normally.

Cynthia Walter, still calm and controlled but again avoiding looking at Marybeth, told how she held Tami Lynne in her arms and gave her a bottle between 8:30 and 9:00 A.M. on the day of her death. "Her arms and legs were going all the time." She was able to hold her head up by herself and would wiggle until she was in a comfortable position."

Cynthia saw Tami Lynne at 4:00 P.M. that day ("She was fine. She was awake") and yet again when she and Marybeth returned from shopping between 8:30 and 9:00 P.M.

"How did she appear then?" Poersch asked.

"She was very normal. I held her. I played with her. She was cooing and kicking."

"So you saw nothing to indicate the baby was sick that day?"

"No."

"She appeared as normal as your own child?"

"Yes."

A more detailed description of Werdnig-Hoffmann disease was given by Dr. Sidney Gospé, Jr., assistant professor of pharmacology at Albany Medical College. In a typical case, he said, a baby's cry was weak, the arm and leg movements were feeble and the body would be limp. As the disease progressed, the muscle strength would diminish and swallowing and sucking would become difficult.

"This is a recessive genetic disease," he explained. "For the couple who carry the genes there is a one in four chance of each child having the disease. As the children go on you must multiply

that, so the odds of having two successive children with the disease
are one out of sixteen. It does happen but it is uncommon."

Dr. Gospé said he was willing to accept Dr. Keoppen's diagnosis
of Werdnig-Hoffmann disease in Jonathan, but Cynthia Walter's
description of Tami Lynne's behaviour on the day of her death
"would indicate that this child did not have any symptoms of the
disease."

Recalled to the witness stand by Paul Callahan, Dr. John Emery
argued that diagnosis was not always so clear-cut. A syndrome like
Werdnig-Hoffmann disease had many manifestations, and every
case was different. Sometimes death happened slowly, sometimes
unexpectedly. It was also important to know the family history.

Callahan seized on this point. Would it be fair to say, he asked,
that it was necessary to understand how Jonathan Tinning died in
order to determine the cause of Tami Lynne's death?

"I would think so, yes." Emery replied. "For me it is."

What about the fact that Cynthia Walter said that Tami Lynne
was a wiggler? There were two ways of interpreting that, Emery
responded. It could mean that she was a very active baby or that
she was difficult to pick up because of poor muscle tone. "It also
indicates the difficulty of diagnosing children of this age."

Poersch was unable to conceal his irritation at seeing Emery on
the witness stand again. With some defense witnesses the district
attorney used the technique of a bulldozer, but it simply did not
work with this benign, imperturbable man. The harder Poersch
tried to fluster him, the calmer Emery became, peering at his
interrogator through his spectacles with a mild and patient curiosity, as though observing a troublesome child with an interesting
ailment.

"Let's begin, doctor, with your association with Dr. Davies,"
said Poersch, opening the attack. "He's a good old buddy, isn't
he?"

"He was a medical student with me at Bristol."

"How long have you known him?"

"Since that time."

"How long ago was that?"

"Oh dear, it was before the war. We qualified about the year
before the war. I'm not good at this sort of arithmetic. It must be
sort of forty-five years."

"You are a good friend. You correspond with one another?"

"Occasionally. We have not been close friends. I have not written or done any research with him, but we have been aware of each other's activities."

"You are not staying in his home now?"

"I am now, yes."

"Oh," said Poersch meaningfully, 'you *are* staying in his home?'

"I am now, yes."

"And it was he who contacted you and asked you to come all the way over from England to give your testimony in this case, isn't that right?"

"That is quite right, sir."

"You don't think in any way that the association or friendship between yourself and Dr. Davies would sway your testimony in this particular case, would you?"

If Emery was feeling nettled, he gave no hint of it. Still in the same quiet, patient tone he replied: "It would mean I could be more frank with him than I should be with some people, and probably I have disagreed more than I might have with a person I knew less. So maybe it would make me disagree rather than agree, sir."

"Well, you agree on this Werdnig-Hoffmann disease, don't you?" Poersch asked gruffly.

Emery smiled back. "No, we do not completely agree on it, sir. No."

For a moment the district attorney seemed nonplussed. "What portion of that theory of old Dr. Davies there, what portion of that do you disagree with?"

"He feels that his observations on the spinal cord at the top end show a diminution of nerve cells. I agree with that, that they do show this. I think he is more happy to accept his observation of one section. I am a man who has done research on the spinal cord, and I would want to see a lot more sections."

Still, Poersch seemed determined to get the better of these two Englishmen. "Is it perhaps that he accepts that because he is more inventive in his diagnosis?" he asked. "He has a flair for inventiveness in diagnosis."

It was an improper remark, but Callahan did not object. Emery responded: "I look upon Dr. Davies as a very intelligent man, sir, and his skills are not all exactly the same as mine. I do not know whether you mean he is more inventive than I am. I would have thought that we would have equal powers of invention, but maybe in different directions."

There was more in this vein, all of it taking this trial farther and farther from the question it was supposed to resolve: Did Marybeth Tinning kill her baby daughter? For several days now it had strayed off course into a game of one-upmanship among professionals, with doctors arguing over interpretations of a disease which may or may not have been significant in this case and—at this moment—with a smalltown lawyer trying to make a medical specialist of international renown look foolish. Meantime, the central figure in the trial was almost forgotten: Marybeth, back in her royal blue pants and sleeveless white top, still writing notes in that spiral-bound exercise book as though every word of this quibbling were of vital importance to her. As indeed, it might be.

When Dr. Davies was recalled, essentially to repeat his earlier testimony, a shouting match developed between Poersch and Callahan. It was brought to order by Judge Harrigan telling them both to behave like attorney's. Even so, Poersch couldn't resist needling Davies about how much he was being paid to give evidence. ("And you get $2,000 a day for that?" "I wish I did," Davies chuckled. "I wish I did get $2,000 a day. I'd love that.") The trial was drawing to a close with tensions and tempers visibly mounting. On the last day of testimony, July 13, an unexpected defense witness— the baby's grandmother Edna Tinning—was a salutary reminder of what this case was supposed to be about.

She walked heavily across the courtroom on a cane, a sturdy gray-haired woman in a lilac cotton dress with a white cardigan draped across her shoulders. Callahan had called her to counteract Cynthia Walter's observations about Tami Lynne's condition on the last day of her life.

When she baby-sat that evening, Edna Tinning said, the baby did not seem well. "She was slow in eating very slow . . . When I picked her up there were no body movements. No kicking. There was no waving of the hands."

The baby cried when being fed, although the grandmother conceded that Tami Lynne was teething and her mouth was sore. But "it was more of a whine, not a loud boisterous cry." When Marybeth and Cynthia returned from shopping, Cynthia played with the baby, and she smiled in response. "But she did not feel well," Edna Tinning asserted.

Referring to Cynthia, Poersch remarked: "If I told you that she was there every single morning and many evenings and had taken care of the child, and had testified here that this was a normal child who reacted in a normal way, what would you say to that?"

"Well, for the first couple of months she was normal, but that night she was sick."

"Did you tell your son and daughter-in-law that they should do something about this terrible situation?" Poersch's tone was sarcastic.

"I took it that she was going to."

"That is all, your honor."

As the time for a verdict drew near, the small crowd in the public section had grown larger, overflowing into the press benches. Most of the spectators were women. There were two former Flavorland waitresses, plump and aging, who frequently whispered to each other like dowagers at a matinee. "What did he say? I missed that." But they had no words of encouragement for Marybeth. In the corridor outside the courtroom one of them met her head-on. "I said hi to her," she reported. "I didn't know what else to say. I couldn't wish her well because I think she is guilty."

There was also a large gray-haired woman wearing sunglasses: "My husband told me to come to the trial. It really interests me. But I have to confess my mind was made up before I came."

And there was the old lady who never missed a session, bundled in brown woollens despite the July heat, toothlessly chewing on her gums as she dozed off. She seemed to have slept through the entire proceedings, but from a remark made as she hobbled out of the courtroom she had grasped the essentials. "I think it's a terrible thing for a woman to kill her children." she said to no one in particular, as though that settled the case.

Many more Marybeth watchers followed the trial on the local radio, on television, and in the newspapers. This coverage was considerable.

"I was so angry at her that I was afraid to go to the trial," one of Marybeth's Flavorland colleagues explained. "I did not want to look at her and was afraid I would blurt out something. But I did follow the story, and every single thing that was written about her I have read ten times over." Several times during the trial she picked up her telephone to call D.A.'s office and tell of that conversation in the back room of Flavorland, more than twelve years earlier, when she heard Marybeth say of another baby, "And God told me to kill this one, too." But something always constrained her from making the call, a fear of consequences which she couldn't articulate, a fear of Marybeth.

She was not alone in this. Another former waitress who also stayed away from court commented: "Everyone who testified would have been in danger if Marybeth had been let free. One way or another she would have gotten them."

Compared with the drama surrounded the courtroom, the summation speeches of John Poersch and Paul Callahan were unremarkable. Neither of these men was an orator, although oratory seems called for at times like this. Both had the habit of pacing the floor while addressing the jury. Callahan with his head down, treading the silences between sentences while he thought of what to say next, Poersch with the wary and slightly rolling gait of a heavier man, picking his way carefully as though he were on board ship.

Once again Callahan insisted that his client was tricked into making a confession. The police officers could have talked to her at her own kitchen table, he said, "but they wanted to get her in their environment in a restricted place, in a small room behind a closed door, out of the county . . . They will say she had the opportunity to leave, to make a call to go home. But did anyone ever say to her, 'Marybeth, do you want to go home?' Would they let her out of that police station twenty miles from home? She did not have a pocketbook with her, and it was snowing outside . . . You have heard Joe Tinning say how he reacted that evening after two or three hours of questioning. He was paralyzed, he drew himself into his shell, he was intimidated, he just let everyone steamroll over him.

"Next we have the medical evidence. You have heard doctors testify that yes, it is possible that Marybeth smothered the child. But you have also heard them say it is possible she did not . . . Can you as jurors convict this woman of murder based on the evidence you have heard here?"

John Poersch had a blunter view of this case. He began his summation by stating: "This defense, in my view, was contrived by Dr. Davies. He is a professional testimony giver and defense creator. He testified on the stand the other day that that is what he does for a living."

There was a lot of poetic license here. What Davies had said was that he was an independent pathologist who currently had thirty-six homicides on his hands.

"If you have a problem you go to Dr. Davies," Poersch continued. "He is a problem solver. He looked around and looked around and saw if he could create a defense that would be the slightest bit feasible in a case where a woman killed several of her children by smothering. And he brought over his buddy from England and they sat down together and they created a defense."

In a single sentence Poersch dismissed Dr. Koeppen's opinion that Jonathan had Werdnig-Hoffmann disease. Koeppen "did not see what he thought he saw" when he looked at Jonathan's autopsy slides, Poersch argued. Dr. Oram, on the other hand, was "the hands-on man. He was there when the autopsy was done. He took apart all the parts."

The district attorney made his pathologist sound like an automobile mechanic.

As for Marybeth's questioning at Loudonville: "Nobody put chains on her, nobody grabbed her by the arm, nobody hollered at her . . . She was read her rights three times, and at the end of a 36-page statement she acknowledged that this was her statement." He pointed out that she confessed to killing only two other children. "If the police were going to have her confess and she was under such terrible duress, the logical thing would be to have her admit to all eight of them."

The final speech was Judge Harrigan's charge to the jury. He had just finished summarizing the evidence and was about to explain the nature of the charges when Callahan stood up and asked for a recess. It was such an inappropriate interruption that something had to be very wrong. All eyes switched from the judge to Marybeth. She looked tense and shaken. Throughout this trial she had been in such command of herself that it was a shock to see her emotionally affected.

"Does your client want to take a break?" the judge asked, surprised.

With a protective hand on her shoulder, Callahan led Marybeth from the courtroom. They were gone for several minutes. She looked a little more composed when they returned. With a glance at her to reassure himself, the judge resumed his address to the jury.

Only the district attorney and his staff knew what this interruption was all about. Marybeth's discomfiture was not on account of the speeches she was hearing or because the jury would soon be considering its verdict. It was related to her feelings about a man she had just noticed in the courtroom for the second time in the past few days, a man she had not expected to see in this place or perhaps ever again. He was youngish, casually dressed with a strong, muscular body, a healthily tanned complexion, and a lock of heavy black hair falling seductively across his forehead—handsome in an entirely macho way and obviously aware of it. When Marybeth became conscious of him, he was staring hard at her. The stare followed her as Callahan led her out of the courtroom.

Only when she was out of sight did he look in another direction, toward John Poersch and his assistant, Alan Gebell. This time it was a look of recognition and satisfaction. As clearly as if the words were spoken, it said, "I told you so."

THIRTY-ONE

The defense's idea was to confuse the jury and make the case go on as long as possible, whereas I asked a few questions and sat down. That's the big secret about lawsuits—knowing when to sit down.

—*District Attorney John Poersch*

His name was Harley Spooner, and he was a school bus driver for the transportation company where Marybeth last worked. Normally he didn't pay much attention to newspapers, but he had been following the Tinning trial in detail and, as he put it, "got tired of hearing all this bullshit about how the baby died of a genetic disease." So he telephoned the district attorney's office and offered to testify.

"I had to call several times," he related. "It was hard to get a hold of anybody there."

Eventually his call was returned by Gary McCarthy, one of the assistant district attorneys. Crank calls are common in a trial like this, and at first Harley Spooner's message—that he had some important information about Marybeth—seemed no different from the rest of them. But as McCarthy talked with him, he realized that this man's information was devastating. Harley Spooner claimed to be the father of Tami Lynne, and he wanted to go on the witness stand and say so.

"How can I be sure you are telling the truth?" McCarthy asked.

"That's simple," the caller replied. "All you have to do is put me in the courtroom and watch her face when she sees me." Which is exactly what McCarthy did.

In the months before the trial the police had interviewed many people who knew Marybeth at various stages of her life, but Harley Spooner's name was never mentioned. None of her relatives or acquaintances seemed to be aware of his existence. Joe Tinning had

met him briefly in 1985, when, through Marybeth, it was arranged
that Spooner would buy the 1976 Dodge Charger which Joe was
replacing with a new Isuzu pickup truck. It was Marybeth who
wanted the truck, and that puzzled Spooner. "She didn't use it to
haul nothing around in," Spooner observed. But he was glad to
buy the old Dodge from Joe, who apparently knew nothing about
this man's relationship with his wife.

"All he ever said was hello," Spooner recalled. "The car was
made out in his name, but I gave her the cash. I was going to give
her three hundred dollars. I had given her two hundred and thirty
of it when Tami Lynne died. After that I didn't want to give her
no more money."

There was no doubt in Harley Spooner's mind that Tami Lynne
was his daughter. He had four other children that he knew of, all
by different mothers, and the resemblance between Tami Lynne
and the rest of his progeny was uncanny. But there was more to it
than the black hair, dark eyes and winsome smile, and Spooner
willingly talked about it to the district attorney's staff, the police,
and anyone else interested enough to ask. He told his story as he
relaxed in the living room of his sister Kathy's house on a sweltering
July evening, the television set soundlessly on, curls of flypapers
hanging from the ceiling, a smell of fried food coming from the
kitchen. It was a small house in an unfashionable section of Schenectady, its front yard fully occupied by a rusting trailer which
blocked the view from the living-room window. Its owners, Kathy
and her husband, Al, seemed just as anxious as Harley Spooner
was for his story to be told. In their minds a great injustice had
been done to a blood relative, and Harley had a right to seek
revenge.

"When I first met Marybeth, she was driving a school bus, and
I was doing the same," he recalled. "That was in September of
1984, and she worked for one school year after that. We worked
at the same school and would go for coffee together. One day in
October she asked what I was doing that evening. I said I was going
bowling, then I was going out. She said she would like to go out,
and that was when everything started.

"Before that I really didn't talk to her. She seemed like two
different people. She would be in a good mood; then all of a sudden
she would give a look that could kill. She came into the garage one

night all bent out of shape because her car had a flat tire, but when everything was going her way, she was fine.

"That first time we went out we was sitting at a bar, and she was talking for about three hours. The way she put it was that we could have a relationship, but she didn't want it to be like my driving. I said, 'What do you mean? Good?' She said, 'No, fast.' I said, 'If you go on like this, you will end up getting something.' But I didn't mean pregnant.

"That night we did it in the car right in front of her house. Afterwards she apologized. She said she didn't mean for it to happen. I said, 'No problem. We can do it more often.' That was a Saturday, and on the Sunday she came looking for me."

Kathy, Al and their two teenage children were listening intently, Kathy occasionally adding a comment. She said she remembered the day Marybeth came looking, and there was something about her she didn't like. Her brother paused to take a cigarette from the breast pocket of his denim jacket.

"After that we got together every night," he continued. "We used to go up to the garage. We used to do it in the car, in the bus. It didn't matter to me where so long as it got done. Sometimes we would park her school bus in front of her house, go upstairs, have a piece of ass, and drive off. Then I would do my kindergarten run. After that she would meet me at the garage, and we'd have coffee at McDonald's or Burger King."

Kathy frowned at her brother, not on account of the story he was telling but because of his unseemly language in front of her children. Harley ignored the look and continued his narrative.

"She told me that she was not sleeping with Joe because he used to beat her up all the time. She also told me that they had two children who died when their trailer caught fire. She never told me about the others. I didn't find out until after she was arrested that there had been eight kids and none of them ever lived in the trailer. Joe and she were supposed to split up after they sold the lot where the trailer was, but they never did split. When I think about it, what she told me may have been nothing but lies. I never saw a bruise on her, so maybe she was the one that beat him up.

"She said that after she sold the land, she was going to get an apartment and I was going to move in with her. I said, 'I am?' and she said, 'Yes.' Now I'm not sure whether she never did it because we stopped seeing each other or whether she never did it because she never planned it.

"One time she said she would like another child. It was when she told me about her two kids that died in the fire. She was forty-two, and I told her that at her age she should be a grandmother. I laughed at her because I thought she was too old to get pregnant. I never took any precautions, and nor did she."

Five months after their first date they had a falling-out. "I told her I didn't want to be bothered that day. It was nothing to do with her, just the mood I was in, but she wouldn't talk to me for two months. So I thought to hell with her. That was in March of '85. When we did start talking, I noticed she was getting fat, but I didn't think nothing of it until Al mentioned that they were taking up a collection at the garage for a baby shower. She never said anything about being pregnant to me."

Al, a fellow bus driver, made his only contribution to the conversation. He had summoned one of his children to help him ease his boots off, and as he gratefully wiggled his toes, he remarked, "I knew because everyone was telling me at the garage."

"Yes," said Harley. "She told Madeline, and Madeline told Peggy, and Peggy told Al, and Al told me. But I don't think I was supposed to know about it. It was all hush-hush from me. She worked until June and had the baby in August, and by then we had been split up three or four months.

"The baby was about three weeks old when Marybeth brought her up to the garage. The first time, supposedly, was to show Madeline. She was the terminal manager, the one who bought the land the trailer was on. Marybeth had Madeline call me into the office, and then she asked me if I would walk her out to her truck. She wanted me to carry the baby, and I told her no. I told her I don't hold babies because all they do is puke on me. She said, 'Don't you want to carry your daughter?' But I still said no. And she said, 'If you hadn't pulled that stunt on me, we could have had this together.' She had made all these plans about us living together, and she must have just assumed that I was going along with them. But I didn't love her. She was just convenient." She was also twelve years older than he was.

"The second time she brought the baby she again asked me to walk her to the truck, and she said right out, 'You're her father.' I kind of knew it right along, so hearing her say it didn't make no difference. From what I understand she put Joe's name on the birth certificate, so I didn't say nothing because I didn't want to break them up if they wanted to stay together. And I didn't want her back because she was so flaky."

After Marybeth left that day, he was proud enough of Tami Lynne to go to his car and get out the baby pictures of two of his older children for comparison. A colleague agreed that Tami Lynne looked just like them, and this gave Harley immense satisfaction. "You dirty dog," the colleague remarked, and Harley took it as a compliment. While he didn't care to acknowledge this baby or feel any responsibility toward her mother, he saw her as a remote but reassuring extension of himself, living proof of his virility.

There he would have been happy to leave the situation but for some news he heard on December 23, 1985. "The schools were closed for Christmas, so I wasn't working at the garage. I was in Albany, helping to clear out a place that used to be a motel. At eleven o'clock at night Al told me he had just heard that Tami Lynne was dead and had been buried that day. I didn't know what to do. Babies don't just up and die for no reason. My mother had thirteen, and none of those has up and died.

"I didn't get in touch with Marybeth because I really thought she had done something to that baby and I was mad. She come out to the garage one day after the baby died, and I was sitting in the drivers' room playing pinochle. I wouldn't even look at her. I was with Ann, the girl I was going with at the time, and I said to her, 'This woman killed my baby.' Then I didn't hear nothing more about it until she was arrested.

"When she got out on bail, she tried to talk to me. I was going to the Latham Circle Mall, where I was supposed to meet Ann, and I saw Marybeth there. I had to bite my tongue and restrain myself from hitting her, so I hit the wall instead. Ann came over and said, 'What's the matter?' I said, 'I just seen her.' She said, 'Who?' and I said, 'The baby killer.'

"That first time I saw her after Tami Lynne died I didn't have nothing to go by, so I just wouldn't talk to her. But now she had been arrested and made that statement, I wanted to kill her."

Harley Spooner did indeed seriously consider murder. He attended the preliminary hearing at the Schenectady County Courthouse, and Ann went with him. His deer hunting rifle was in the trunk of his car, and he intended to use it on Marybeth. "I was

serious, and Ann knew it, so she grabbed the car keys. Then we
went right into the courtroom. When Marybeth saw me, she went
back through the doorway. Every time she sees me now she gets
shook up. And I started shaking and grabbed Ann's hand so hard
I almost broke it.

"When it came to the trial, I just couldn't stand listening to those
doctors saying that this baby died of a disease and that Joe was the
father. So I called the D.A.'s office and told them who the real
father was."

The D.A.'s legal staff and the Schenectady police believed his
story. But how would it stand up in court? Harley Spooner had a
police record—not a serious one, but enough for the defense to cast
doubt on his credibility as a witness. He had spent three weeks in
jail after getting in a fight with the Albany police and didn't mind
talking about it. "It's no place for somebody human," he said,
"but I'd be glad to see Marybeth there."

As a rule, last-minute mystery witnesses show up only in detective
novels, but here was a live one straight out of the pages of pulp
fiction: the ex-lover seeking retribution for the death of a child he
barely knew, and in the same gesture negating the complex
testimony of medical experts. If Jonathan had Werdnig-Hoffmann
disease, it could have come only from a recessive gene carried by
both Marybeth and Joe; if Joe wasn't Tami Lynne's father, the
chances of her inheriting the same rare condition could be
discounted.

A baby's blood type is the same as one or other of its parents,
and if Tami Lynne's matched Harley Spooner's, not Marybeth's or
Joe's, that would be persuasive evidence of his claim to paternity.
John Poersch was unwilling to put him on the witness stand without
being sure of it. His assistants were more eager to take advantage
of this man's offer to testify. Even without proof of paternity, they
felt his impact upon the jury could be enormous. The trial was
almost over, Judge Harrigan had privately warned both attorneys
not to drag it out much longer, and there was very little time
in which to make a decision. Dr. Thomas Oram was hurriedly
consulted.

Normally it would be a matter of straightforward checking. The
blood types of Tami Lynne, Marybeth and Joe should be in their
medical records, and there was no problem about getting Harley

Spooner to submit to a blood test. He was ready and eager. Theoretically the answer could be found in minutes, but the reality was more frustrating. When he looked through Tami Lynne's records, Oram discovered that sometime previously, as an economy measure, St. Clare's Hospital had discontinued its practice of typing the blood of healthy newborns. Her blood group had never been recorded, and so far as he knew, the test had to be done while the patient was alive.

In all his years as a pathologist this question had never faced him before. He searched through his reference books to see if there was a way of discovering a blood group eighteen months after a body had been autopsied, but none of the standard texts addressed the problem. Eventually he came upon an outdated manual, at least thirty years old, which stated that it was possible to get an accurate reading of the red blood cells from autopsied material. But it did not explain how.

Oram had assumed that the Formalin, used in the pathology laboratory as preservative, would coat the red cells and mask the blood type. By now it was Friday afternoon, July 10, and across town at the Schenectady County Courthouse Dr. Emery had been recalled to testify for the second time. He was one of the last of the defense's rebuttal witnesses, so if the district attorney was going to put Harley Spooner on the witness stand, Oram had to get the blood typing done fast. From his office at Ellis Hospital Oram telephoned the New York state police laboratory, which had very sophisticated testing equipment, but most of the staff had already left for the weekend.

"I finally found a woman there who said she had a friend in the FBI lab in Washington who might know the answer," Oram recalled. "It is one of the best forensic labs in the world. I rang there, and to my surprise this man she mentioned answered the telephone. He said that all you had to do was get some red cells and do a straight typing, and it would work. It was incredibly simple. I knew there had been a good deal of hemorrhage in Tami Lynne's lungs, so I took some lung tissue which had been kept in Formalin and squeezed it. Out came the red cells. They were brown and muddy, so I washed them in a salt solution, put them under a microscope, and found they were perfectly preserved. I gave them to the chief of our blood bank for an analysis, and he found they were Type A."

It was a great disappointment. Marybeth was a Type A, too, the commonest blood group in the Schenectady area. So Harley Spooner's blood group was no longer relevant because the child had inherited that particular gene from her mother. There were more sophisticated tests to determine paternity, but for those it was essential to have fresh blood.

At that, John Poersch decided against having Harley Spooner testify. Several of his aides, especially Alan Gebell, who had worked for months putting the prosecution's case together, disagreed with this decision. "They were all jumping around about it, and I thought Gebell was going to commit suicide," Poersch commented afterward. "Young people are so enthusiastic, they would have the trial go on for five months and make a play out of it. But it isn't a play. The case was coming to an end the way I wanted it to end. I think my gut reaction not to put Harley on the stand was right. It would have muddied the waters." He didn't explain how.

This trial was about to go into its sixth week, and Poersch had his own family vacation planned, on Block Island, where he went every year. It was midsummer and the Schenectady weather was uncomfortably hot. Sitting in the closed atmosphere of an air-conditioned courtroom, day after day, was a physical and emotional strain upon the jury, and Judge Harrigan was keenly aware of this. Furthermore, the longer the trial continued, the greater the backlog of his other cases became. A prolonged trial is out of the run of business for a semirural country courthouse and can create a confusion which takes months to clear up. The trial of Marybeth Tinning had reached that stage.

In the district attorney's office it was decided to bring Harley Spooner into the courtroom the following Monday morning and to make sure that Marybeth saw him. This would serve as a warning to her that the prosecution knew about, and might use, this man's claim to the the father of Tami Lynne.

As Harley described the incident, "By then the trial was almost over. Her mother-in-law had just testified. Then they called this doctor from England. One of the D.A.'s assistants asked me to come to court that day, and he put me in the press seats. After a while he said, 'We are going to move you to the table in front of her if you think you can handle it.' I said, 'Yes', and I sat there for several minutes; then they moved me again.

"I could see Marybeth getting scared and nervous. She was trying to write things down but kept turning pages. Then she said she wanted to talk to her lawyer. She took him outside and was trying to act like I wasn't there. I didn't want to face her myself because I felt like killing her."

The death of this baby had a strange effect upon him, one he had not anticipated, even deeper than his desire for revenge. He who was so short on sentiment that he hadn't wanted to cradle her in his arms went to the Most Holy Redeemer Cemetery one day and put flowers on the Tinning family plot. He didn't like flowers and felt foolish carrying them. But with unexpected tenderness he laid them on the ground by a marker, which as he remembered it, bore Tami Lynne's name and the dates of her brief life.

He had actually gone to the wrong cemetery, and his subsequent recollection of the grave marker was flawed. Tami Lynne was not buried at Most Holy Redeemer with the first seven Tinning children. That plot had already been filled by them. Her body was interred in a Protestant cemetery near Duanesburg, next to Michael's, in a grave site which belonged to Joe's parents. And at the time of the trial, eighteen months after her death, her name had not yet been inscribed on the headstone.

There was one other potential witness for the prosecution: Dr. Kevin D. Barron, Chairman of the Department of Neurology and Professor of Pathology at Albany Medical College. Dr. Oram consulted him after Dr. Arnulf Koeppen surprised the court by stating that Jonathan had Werding-Hoffman disease and that Tami Lynne might also have suffered from it. At Oram's request Barron looked at the slides of Tami Lynne's autopsy and reported that what he saw there did not constitute evidence of this fatal condition. Oram asked if he would repeat this on the witness stand. It was a delicate situation because Barron and Koeppen were colleagues, but after some consideration Barron agreed. His message reached Oram on Monday, July 13, the same day that Harley Spooner was first brought into court. Barron was not available to testify until that Wednesday. But on Wednesday the case went to the jury, and it was too late for any more evidence.

THIRTY-TWO

You know, of course, that I didn't do it.
                                    —*Marybeth, in prison*

There is a wisdom about the way some juries work which, early in their deliberations, can bring complex testimony to the level of a common understanding. On this Wednesday afternoon, faced with one another and the decision they had to make, most of the Tinning jurors decided that a lot of the medical evidence was irrelevant. They reminded themselves that they were not there to determine whether or not Tami Lynne had a genetic disease, only whether or not her mother had killed her. As they talked about this, they agreed that one of the most persuasive witnesses had been Cynthia Walter. Her daily observations of Tami Lynne—as a nurse, a neighbor and a mother—carried more weight with them than the ways in which different doctors interpreted the autopsy slides. They were impressed by Cynthia's description of Tami Lynne as a healthy, normal baby who was lively and kicking a few hours before she died. They reasoned that Edna Tinning's description of how this baby cried and wanted to be held sounded like nothing worse than the passing fretfulness of teething.

This led to a consensus that even if Tami Lynne did have Werdnig-Hoffman disease, she was a long way from dying of it. Therefore, there had to be a presumption of murder, and Dr. Oram's conclusions about suffocation had been very convincing. Ironically, most jurors agreed that if Callahan had presented a simple SIDS defense instead of all that complex medical testimony, it would have been much harder for them to decide that this baby died unnaturally. With a SIDS defense, Callahan could also have avoided reference to other Tinning babies.

Early in their discussions they had a secret ballot. On the first vote seven of them thought Marybeth was guilty; five were either undecided or in favor of acquittal. What bothered the five was the validity of her confession. Discussion centered on whether the police had intimidated her into making it. If the jurors agreed she was coerced, they would have to disregard it, and that might have left insufficient evidence for a conviction.

Two jurors felt strongly that the police may have bullied Marybeth into confessing, and as they talked about this, it was evident that their views were influenced by their life experiences. Rodney Van Ness, the younger of the two black men, seemed mistrustful of authority and was therefore more willing to believe Callahan's charges of police coercion. Joan Montanye, who had recently retired from the telephone company, could not forget how her first husband had been badly injured in an altercation with the police. She felt their treatment of him to have been brutal and unjustified; from that frame of reference it was easy for her to see Marybeth as another victim. Also, she was not convinced by the prosecution's case. Every night during the trial she noted in her diary, "Still no real proof."

After discussing this back and forth, the jurors voted a second time. Three who had been uncertain now decided that Marybeth was guilty, making nine in favor of conviction. After a supper break they returned to the long, narrow room behind the courtroom and talked about the medical evidence, particularly Dr. Oram's. Judge Harrigan had not allowed them to take notes—a frequent judicial ruling, made in the belief that jurors should concentrate all their attention on the witnesses—which left gaps in their collective memory.

They asked for the transcript of Dr. Oram's testimony to be read to them, and as they filed into the courtroom, there was a stir among the reporters and the few lingering spectators. Had they reached a verdict? But as the official court reporter, Linda Cafarelli, reeled off Oram's testimony with impressive speed and accuracy, it was clear that they had much left to consider. The last vote of the day was ten for conviction, two for acquittal.

Judge Harrigan had arranged for the jurors to be sequestered throughout their deliberations. At about 9:30 P.M. they were taken to Schenectady's Holiday Inn, barely two blocks away. After twelve hours indoors, they would all have welcomed the refreshing walk; instead, they were shepherded on to a bus and guarded by court officials. Most of them went straight to their hotel rooms, feeling like prisoners.

All through the next day, Thursday, there was no shift in the vote. Every time the jury foreman, Norman Small, took a count it was still ten to two. There was no longer any secrecy that the dissenters continued to be Joan Montanye and Rodney Van Ness, both still concerned that Marybeth's confession may have been made under duress.

The jurors had been given copies of the confession in its original question-and-answer form. If Paul Callahan had not introduced the medical testimony about Jonathan, all mention of other Tinning children would have been edited out of the document before it went to the jury. Instead, Judge Harrigan explained that he had allowed Marybeth's admission to suffocating Timothy and Nathan to remain in evidence "for the sole purpose of showing intent." He warned jurors to steel themselves against the temptation to use this knowledge to give additional weight to Marybeth's statement that she also killed Tami Lynne. In short, they were allowed to know that she had confessed to other murders but not to take these into consideration.

They were also shown some of Tami Lynne's autopsy photographs—the least gruesome ones, taken before Dr. Oram made his first incision, showing a perfect and very pretty baby who was obviously dead. They were passed around the jury table in silence. "We were all so moved," a juror commented afterward. "It brought home to us that we were not dealing with an abstract case but with the death of a child who should have lived."

There was much more they would like to have known. They had watched Marybeth almost every day for almost six weeks, sitting beside Callahan, looking interested and alert, paying attention to all the testimony, making notes, but never showing deep emotion, never telling her side of the story. It had been impressed upon them that she had a right not to testify and that this should not influence their judgment of her. But they couldn't help speculating about what she might have said on the witness stand and whether it would have done her harm or good.

There were two alternate charges in the indictment, both of

second-degree murder. The first was the familiar charge that Mary-beth had caused the death of Tami Lynne with the intention of doing so. The second, less common, was known as the depraved indifference to human life charge. It alleged that Marybeth reck-lessly engaged in conduct which put her daughter's life in jeopardy, fully aware that the child might die as a result of it. "This is much more serious than a charge of reckless conduct and it raises the crime to murder in the second degree," Judge Harrigan explained. If Marybeth were found guilty, it had to be on one of the two counts, and the jury must decide which. Essentially the choice was a legal technicality, since the sentence would be the same for each.

At intervals on that Thursday the jurors sent messages to the judge which gave some indication of the way their discussion was going. They wanted the charges read back. They wanted a legal definition of the word "intimidation." They wanted the full text of the Miranda warning. They wanted to hear Joe Tinning's testimony again, then the testimony of the police investigators.

Marybeth sat tensely through all this, often with her head down and her hands in front of her, fingertips touching. She might have been praying. There was no more need for her to take notes, and her briefcase which looked so new and slender when this trial began was on the desk in front of her, closed and bulging.

During the midmorning break she and Joe had coffee and ciga-rettes together in the courthouse cafeteria. She chatted amiably with a woman journalist who remarked that this must be a terribly difficult wait for her. Marybeth gave her familiar smile—a flash of even white teeth, slightly projecting. "I'm not a patient person," she replied. "And I tend to look on the black side of things. If I'm going out for the day and there is a mist that morning, other people will look at it and say that the weather will clear up and be sunny. But I am always convinced it is going to rain."

Avoiding the obvious question, the journalist asked Marybeth about her childhood in Duanesburg. "There was nothing to do there," she replied. "It was a great treat to go into Schenectady for shopping or a movie." She was being very friendly and seemed to want to talk. "Young people nowadays have much more freedom," she observed. "They travel around a lot more."

This was so like any other exchange of pleasantries between strangers that it was easy to forget the circumstances in which the conversation took place, easy also to find Marybeth friendly and likable, and, since likable, to begin doubting the charges against her. Suddenly the incomprehensible became understandable: how intelligent women like Cynthia Walter and Sue Lencewicz had so warmed to Marybeth that they trusted her with their children, even knowing that she had lost so many of her own; how neighbors, nurses, doctors and employers had felt so sorry for her that they had gone out of their way to help her; how slow they were to suspect her; how defenseless and misunderstood they assumed her to be.

She made another remark during that coffee break which was to be recounted among the courthouse staff for many months afterward. Several news photographers had followed her into the cafeteria and were vying for pictures of her. Responding like a celebrity, she remarked to one of the waitresses: "If you ever want to redecorate this place, you could paper the walls with all my photographs."

As the wait for a verdict went on into the afternoon, the small group of court watchers grew larger. There was nothing for them to do but hang around and wait, but the longer this went on, the more determined they were to stay to the finish. None of them had a compassionate word to say about Marybeth. The two former waitresses who could not bring themselves to wish her well had not missed a session in these last few days. There was also an ex-photographer who said he had a professional interest in seeing the expression on her face when she heard the verdict. During the afternoon a very large woman with cropped gray hair joined the group. She wore a bright red T-shirt with lime green polyester pants, stretched to their limit. There were tattoos on her brawny arms, one in the shape of a dagger, the other with the message "Death is certain. Life is not."

"I hope it's a guilty verdict," she said. "Anyone who can do that to a baby deserves it."

Behind the double doors of the deliberation room the jurors were talking about Joe Tinning. His testimony had impressed them almost as much as Cynthia Walter's. They were aghast at his lack of emotional response but struck by his honesty. "He was not capable of lying," a woman juror commented. "He had no energy left for invention." What they remembered most about his testimony was that he heard Marybeth say, "I killed Tami." Twice.

By 8:50 P.M. they had talked themselves out, and the vote was still ten to two. None of them was ready to tell the judge they had reached a stalemate, which was what made this jury extraordinary. They all were prepared to wrestle with this problem for as long as it took to resolve it. The youngest juror, Jacqueline Hutchins, made it very clear that her weekend plans for a large twenty-fifth birthday party were entirely secondary to her willingness to stay with this task.

They went back to the Holiday Inn for a second night, facing the possibility of a hung jury. Susan Bokan, the real estate developer, went to sleep praying that this wouldn't happen. Bernard Gerberg, the recently retired engineer, slept badly and dreamed that it did. At breakfast next morning Joan Montanye quietly remarked to Gerberg, "I think we may have some trouble with Rodney." What she was really saying was that overnight she had decided to change her vote. "It was just a gut feeling," she explained.

In the two days of discussion Gholson Howard, the older of the two black jurors, had impressed the others enormously. He was not a highly educated man, but he was what Bernard Gerberg called a mensch, a Yiddish word which expresses the most compassionate and humanitarian of personal qualities. Howard knew exactly why the younger black man had so many reservations about convicting Marybeth, and after breakfast, as the jurors were waiting for the courthouse bus, he made a memorable gesture. He reached in his wallet, took out a photograph of a little girl, and showed it to the group, Van Ness in particular.

"Isn't she beautiful?" he remarked. "That's my granddaughter, and I think the world of her." It was all he needed to say.

As they settled in the deliberation room, Rodney Van Ness was still struggling with his decision. He did not vote when Norman Small took the first count of the day. The other eleven votes were for convictions. Van Ness said he wanted to think a while longer. Some of the jurors talked to him about Marybeth's confession and the letter she had written to her brother.

"How would you feel if she were free and had another baby?" one juror asked.

Another put the question: "Would you trust your own child with her?"

Rodney Van Ness had four young children. He muttered, "I'm being pressured."

After that the others left him alone. He sat with his head in his hands, then paced up and down. Some jurors passed the time playing cards while others leaned out of the sash windows, chatting quietly as they gazed across the rooftops of Schenectady's business district. There was a lot of tension in the room, but no animosity.

Susan Bokan suddenly had a brilliant idea. Marybeth's confession had given all of them difficulty. They had read it through twice in its dialogue form and had found it hard to get a feeling of the atmosphere in which it was made.

"Why don't we read it out loud like a play?" Susan suggested. Turning to Van Ness, she said, "Rodney, you assign the parts."

Susan was a graduate of New York University's drama school, which made her the natural choice to play Marybeth. Van Ness named four other jurors to play Investigator Karas, Investigator Imfeld, Investigator Barnes and Margot Bernhardt, the court stenographer who had taken Marybeth's statement.

"I put all I had got into that reading," Susan said afterward. "It may have been the performance of my life." She was of the same generation as Marybeth, but more educated, more vivacious, and much more sure of herself. In the next twenty minutes she tried her hardest to enter into the personality of this woman whom she had watched day after day but never heard talk. When the reading was finished, at least five minutes elapsed before anybody spoke.

Susan Bokan knew intuitively what they were all thinking. "At first several of us had thought that the police were harsh and bullying, but when we read the transcript, it just didn't play like that. There were no Gestapo-like tactics. If there had been, it would have come across in the reading."

One by one, around the table, the jurors described their feelings about the confession, about the trial, and about the experience of working together. All of them spoke of their respect for the others. Bernard Gerberg added, "But if we have a hung jury, I feel that, collectively, we shall have failed in our job."

On the other side of the double doors which separated them from the courtroom, Judge Harrigan spent some of the waiting time hearing minor cases. An assault. A burglary. A couple of arraignments. Such is the normal business of a county court like this one, and it had to go on. While it did, Marybeth, Joe, the lawyers, the press, and the determined Marybeth watchers moved to the back and sides of the courtroom, waiting. At the noon lunch break the jurors asked to have sandwiches sent in. Word went around that they must be close to a verdict.

Meantime, the television reporters rushed outdoors, as they did at every break in the proceedings, to be photographed in front of the Greek Revival courthouse while they breathlessly told viewers about the latest development in the Tinning trial. At this Friday lunchtime all they had to say was that there was nothing new to say; nevertheless, the crowd that gathered to watch them was larger than usual.

Paul Callahan returned from lunch with a vanilla ice-cream cone in his hand. Always a smart dresser, he looked particularly elegant in a silver gray suit, lilac shirt and plum-colored tied. As he walked up the courthouse steps, he muttered, between licks of ice cream, "I don't like Friday afternoon jury decisions." He was obviously worried. Reporters asked how his client was coping with the long wait. At this stage, he replied, she was "very hyper."

She had reason to be. In the deliberation room, at just about this time, Norman Small was taking the last vote. It was 12—0. There were gasps of surprise but no rejoicing. The atmosphere in the room was one of intense sadness mingled with enormous relief.

At 1:40 P.M. the jurors filed back into the courtroom with a request but no hint of agreement. Could the judge explain once more the difference between the two murder charges? Marybeth stiffened. The implication of the question was clear, yet she could still hope that the jury might reject both charges and find her innocent.

Judge Harrigan went over the murder counts carefully. For the first, the jury must determine beyond reasonable doubt that Marybeth caused Tami Lynne's death by smothering her with a pillow, fully intending to kill her. He added: "It is not necessary to find that the intent to kill was in the mind of the defendant for some time before the death. It is sufficient to show that it was in her mind when she did it."

The second count was more complicated. For the depraved indifference to human life charge it was necessary to show that Marybeth deliberately put her daughter's life in jeopardy, in circumstances that were brutal and inhuman. "The risk to life must be of such a nature that the disregard thereof constitutes a gross deviation from normal conduct. For it to be reckless she must know that a risk of death exists, and she must disregard that risk."

The jurors went back to the deliberation room. While everyone else waited tensely, the judge heard two more brief cases. A middle-aged man was put on five years' probation for a robbery and treated like a gentleman. ("You have a right to appeal within thirty days, and good luck to you, Mr. Klein.") A sullen-looking young man was arraigned for burglary in the third degree and scolded. ("Have you ever tried mowing a lawn? A lot of ladies out there would be glad of a strong back like yours.") At 2:35 P.M. Judge Harrigan announced: "Let the record reflect that I have a note from the jury indicating that they have reached a verdict." Suddenly the courtroom was filled with people.

For the last time the jurors filed in. All of them looked somber; some had been crying. They had reached their final verdict fifteen minutes earlier but had needed to compose themselves before sending their message to the judge. As they settled in their places, none of them glanced at Marybeth. Sitting between her attorney and her husband, she clutched at the fine gold chain around her neck. She was wearing one of her familiar outfits, dark red slacks with a short-sleeve pink blouse, and she seemed to be shrinking into it. The foreman was asked the verdict on the first murder charge.

"Not guilty," replied Norman Small.

"Not guilty," they echoed, one by one.

Paul Callahan and Marybeth exchanged smiles. They had assumed that if there was a conviction, it would be on this first charge. Marybeth relaxed visibly.

Judge Harrigan asked about the second charge. Norman Small hesitated for an instant, then said, "Guilty."

"Is that unanimous?"

"Yes."

Again the judge asked each juror to repeat the verdict. When it came to Rodney Van Ness's turn, he nodded.

"You have to say your verdict for the record," Judge Harrigan reminded him.

Another pause. Then, very quietly: "Guilty."

Susan Bokan glanced across at Marybeth. To her embarrassment, Marybeth was looking straight at her. Susan caught a flash of anger in the dark eyes. As she translated it, the look said, "I counted on you, and you let me down." It was as though Marybeth had known intuitively that Susan had played her part, had tried to understand her, and then, in her view, had failed her.

As the last juror said, "Guilty," Marybeth's face reddened. Joe put his right hand over her left one. She bowed her head and began to sob quietly. Soon her body was shaking convulsively. Embarrassed, everyone concentrated on the judge as he thanked and dismissed the jurors, sparing them the continued sight of Marybeth's agonized weeping. Throughout the last six weeks she had seemed as detached as if this were someone else's trial. Now, perhaps for the first time, she realized her situation and was appalled.

Minutes later it was all over. Barney Waldron, the sheriff, led her across the covered bridge from the courtroom to the cells of the county jail. She went quietly, tears still streaming down her face. There was no farewell embrace with Joe, who continued to sit at the defense counsel's table as though expecting something else to happen. The reporters had rushed out of the courtroom after Marybeth; barred from following her, they rushed back and started hurling questions at her husband,. "Were you surprised at the verdict?" they asked, flashbulbs popping in his face.

Another man might have ignored them or expressed anger. Joe Tinning answered politely. "Definitely."

Then the unfailing question: How did he feel about it?

"I think the jury were hard on her. They didn't really think about it. They did their job, but they have a different view from mine."

Over three days the jurors had, of course, thought about it a great deal. After deciding that Marybeth was guilty, they agreed that the second murder charge—that of depraved indifference to human life—was more appropriate than the count of intentional murder. It also seemed less stark and condemnatory. Gholson Howard made the point that it might lead to her getting more psychological help in prison. The rest of them readily agreed, hoping this was true.

After the verdict they went back to the deliberation room to collect their belongings. They all were shaking. Some began to weep. Some embraced. The experience of working together under stress had brought this disparate group of people very close and had given them an understanding of one another which no one else, not even their loved ones, could ever quite appreciate. In the end they all felt they had made the right decision, but none of them had any joy in it; some were even offended when the district attorney came into the room to congratulate them. But there was an underlying feeling of satisfaction that they had been able to reason together and reach unanimity.

Susan Bokan, who had been anxious to serve from the beginning, said she found the experience very impressive. "I had always hoped it was true that the jury system really works, but I was never sure of it before. The role of leadership kept shifting, and although we had some shouters, myself included, they were always ready to give center stage to the quiet, thoughtful ones like Bernie Gerberg. Even when there was only one holdout, the other eleven were still willing to be convinced that Marybeth Tinning was innocent if it could be backed up by evidence."

Virginia Famularo was the last juror to leave the building. After the farewells she had gone into the ladies' room to have a good cry. She was a middle-aged housewife who had provided some amusement to court officials, badly in need of light relief, on account of the messages she kept asking them to relay to her husband, "Remind Sal to feed the monkey," a pet who was kept in the basement of their house. Virginia had arrived at her guilty verdict after hours of anguish and doubting and was emotionally drained. The last person she wanted to meet at this moment was Paul Callahan, but as she returned to the deliberation room, she came face to face with him. She was still tearful.

"I'm sorry," she said lamely.

He put a hand on her shoulder. "It's all right," he said. "You did your job."

On the floor above, in the district attorney's office, John Poersch was giving a press conference. His mood was buoyant. "I can assure you that this is only round one, and I shall see Mrs. Tinning on the defense again," he announced. "Certainly if I have anything to do with it."

What would be the charge? "The two other children mentioned in the confession."

Why hadn't he charged Marybeth with these two murders at the same time as Tami Lynne's? "Because it's to my advantage to try them one at a time." He did not explain.

When would he bring these charges? "Well, not right now."

If he had been the defense attorney, would he have pleaded

insanity? Poersch evaded that question. "Callahan had to make certain judgments. I really don't know his client. What I might say would be only supposition."

Where would he rank this trial? "Up there with Lemuel Smith, and that was a tough one." It was still the yardstick by which he would measure all other murder cases.

And what did he think was Marybeth's motive? "The motive was obvious. She said she did it because the baby was crying, and she thought she was a bad mother."

That weekend, as Marybeth waited in the county jail for her sentencing hearing, John Poersch left for his Block Island vacation, Paul Callahan drove to Boston to watch the Red Sox play Oakland, Norman Small played golf, and most of the other jurors—restrained from mentioning the case while they were living with it—stayed home with their families and talked and talked about Marybeth.

THIRTY-THREE

You're killing me, you're killing me.
—*Marybeth, as she was being taken to Bedford Hills*
Correctional Facility

Eleven Weeks later a very different Marybeth was brought back to court for sentencing. She had lost weight dramatically. Her hair had been cropped into a masculine shape and was now blond only in places; the rest of it was her natural dull brown. Her skin without makeup blended with her shirtwaist dress, which was the color of porridge. Prisoners from Schenectady's county jail were encouraged to wear their own clothes for court hearings to help them feel more comfortable and dignified, but what Marybeth had chosen did nothing to enhance her. She was a study in beige, all spirit drained away.

John Poersch demanded the full prison sentence, a minimum of twenty-five years. "This woman knew the consequences of her acts, but they were of no interest to her," he said. "She is a wicked woman. Her deeds were done for her own personal reasons, and under those circumstances I would suggest that the severest penalty be given to her."

Paul Callahan argued that she had no previous convictions and that her behavior during more than a year on bail had been exemplary. Since then, in the county jail, she had been helpful to other prisoners. This statement may have been colored by Marybeth's own recollections. She had made it known to Callahan, and he had passed this on to the local newspapers, that she had been teaching one fellow prisoner to read and making a baby blanket for another who was pregnant. Belatedly Callahan was trying to present his client as maternal and compassionate. Inside sources at the jail claimed that there was only a grain of truth to these stories, that it was a prison matron who was giving the reading lessons, and the "baby blanket" was a blue afghan which Marybeth was crocheting for her mother-in-law. When the stories appeared in print, Marybeth said she didn't know where they came from.

The report from her probation officer contained the comment: "With the exception of the severity of her present offense which mandates incarceration, the defendant does not impress as a likely candidate for state prison."

Callahan cited it to emphasize his point that she should have the lightest possible sentence. Not that Judge Harrigan had much discretion in this case. In recent years New York state judges had been severely restricted by the legislature's sentencing statute which mandated the sentences for major crimes. A first offender found guilty of murder in the second degree could not be given fewer than fifteen years to life imprisonment or more than twenty-five years to life.

Before passing sentence, the judge asked: "Mrs. Tinning, do you care to make a statement?"

"Yes, your honor, if I could indulge the court,' she replied, and proceeded to read from her own handwritten notes on lined yellow paper. She spoke so quietly that she could barely be heard.

"I want you and the people in this courtroom to know that I am very sorry that Tami Lynne is dead. There is not a day that goes by that I don't think of her. I miss her very much. I just want all of you to know that I played no part in the death of my daughter, Tami Lynne. I will try to hold my head high and accept the punishment that society and the law requires for the crime I was convicted of. I did not commit this crime but will serve the time in prison to the best of my ability. However, I will never stop fighting to prove my innocence. The Lord above and I know that I am innocent, that one day the whole world will know that I am innocent, and that maybe then I can have my life back again, or whatever is left of it." She looked up, then added softly, "That is all."

Judge Harrigan's sentence was almost as much of a shock to her as the jury's verdict: twenty years to life, to be spent in the state's prison for women at Bedford Hills. "It is my feeling that the severity of the incident requires such a punishment," he explained.

He did not call for a psychiatric report, and considering the way the New York statute worked, there was not much point in doing so. Even if psychiatric treatment were to be recommended, Harrigan could not commit Marybeth to an institution for the mentally ill because her lawyer had not entered an insanity plea. The most the judge could do would be to recommend some psychiatric treatment in prison, with no assurance that she would get it.

From the beginning of her dealings with Paul Callahan, Marybeth had insisted that she had not killed Tami Lynne, and this had dictated his conduct of her defense. She said, "I didn't do it," so often that despite her earlier confession, she herself believed it. Inevitably the denial was repeated in her prepared statement to the court, and yet there was something odd about its phraseology— that remark about accepting the punishment which society and the law require—as if conceding that punishment was deserved. Most people in her place would have used a word like "sentence."

"Punishment" is not in the vocabulary of most prisoners. It acknowledges guilt, and prisoners usually protest innocence. Yet it was the word Marybeth used, over and over, not only now but immediately after her arrest. "They're going to punish me, they're going to punish me," she had sobbed, huddled on her prison cot like a frightened child. And only after that: "I didn't kill Tami Lynne." While she was in the county jail she did not speak of her other children.

She was sentenced on the same day that Joe's parents quietly celebrated their fiftieth wedding anniversary. They were still very defensive of Marybeth and had visited her several times in prison, taking her religious books. They also arranged for a Protestant minister to visit regularly and counsel her. Both they and their son Joe resisted any other kind of professional help. "I'm leery of psychiatrists," Joe told an Albany newspaper. "They maybe offer to help you but it'll take years." He felt his wife would find more solace in the Scriptures, and evidently she agreed. ("They all take a turn for religion in jail; you never saw anything like it," a prison matron observed.)

Except for Joe, none of Marybeth's relatives was in court for the sentencing. The rift between the generations had deepened ever since Carol and Andy had given a television interview on the day the trial ended to say they were satisfied with the verdict. "We did it because we wanted people to see that there were some normal, caring members of this family who were truly distressed about what happened to those children," Carol explained.

She had asked a reporter to telephone her after the sentencing with news of the judge's decision. When told that her sister-in-law would spend the next twenty years in prison, she made no comment. Embarrassed by the silence at the other end of the telephone, the reporter remarked that in court that day Marybeth had looked terrible. Without a moment's hesitation Carol responded: "So did those babies when she was done with them."

THIRTY-FOUR

She was an unwanted child who never grew up.
                                               —*A former friend*

It all began with Jennifer, so the police and others believed, and this seemed a logical explanation. They reasoned that the balance of Marybeth's mind became disturbed by this baby's unexpected death and that when subsequent children were born, she tried to resolve her feelings about the tragedy by reliving it.

The truth was more complex, and some of it did not begin to emerge until after the trial. Fragments of information, significant but tantalizingly incomplete, came from people who had been afraid of her, or, rather, afraid of what they knew about her and had kept to themselves. The former waitress who heard Marybeth say, "And God told me to kill this one, too," finally summoned the courage to call the district attorney's office and describe the conversation which had haunted her for years—but not until Marybeth had been safely delivered to a maximum security prison a good three hours' drive from Schenectady.

This woman was not alone in her fears. Over the fourteen years in which all nine Tinning children died, the people who had the most consistent relationship with Marybeth, other than her family, were her fellow waitresses. Neighbors and friends were exchanged every two or three years, but Flavorland employees kept coming back to the same jobs between babies, as Marybeth did. They were pragmatic, reliable women, quick in their reactions and not easily fooled, and every one of them who worked with her was eventually traumatized by Marybeth.

When the trial was over, Sue Normington told how, several years earlier, she had a strange compulsion to buy a baby doll because it reminded her of Mary Frances. It was at a time when she was deeply troubled by her suspicions about Marybeth but had not known what to do with them. She saw the doll for sale in a flea market and felt she had to have it, without knowing why. The doll had the strawberry blond hair and fair complexion of Mary Frances, the same innocent smile on her porcelain face, and she was dressed in a pink knitted outfit very like the one the baby was wearing when her mother brought her into the restaurant and carelessly set her down on a high stool by the counter. Holding the doll reminded Sue of how she had picked up Mary Frances and cuddled her, the last day she saw the baby alive.

In trying to explain her purchase, she said: "I was going to give this doll to Marybeth and tell her—I don't know what I was going to tell her, but she would have gotten the message that she couldn't get away with it. But I could never find a way to do it." Instead, she reported her suspicions to Social Services. From time to time she would take out the doll from the drawer where she kept it, and feel all the old pangs of sorrow and misgiving. Only after Marybeth was found guilty did these feelings begin to resolve themselves. "Then I put the doll away with the newspaper report of the verdict, and I have not thought about it since. I was relieved. I had carried it around in my heart for so long."

There were other fragments of memories which went much farther back, to long before Jennifer. They came from men and women in their forties who had gone to school with Marybeth, who remembered her first as a timid little girl with "odd ways about her" who came from a lonely little house on the outskirts of Duanesburg where there never seemed to be any laughter. She had developed into a tiresome child clamoring for attention on the school bus, but not getting it, then into a friendless teenager who made so little impression in high school that despite her later notoriety, some of her former teachers had a hard time remembering her.

"I cannot recall anything good or bad about her," one of them said after her arrest. "So far as I am concerned, she was almost a nonentity."

Eventually it was her turn to be a school bus monitor. "She did not handle authority well," a contemporary recalled. "She would scream at the smaller children and push them around, and she would get into shouting matches with kids who were too old for her to boss. Before long she had alienated every child on the bus."

It was a difficult period for an adolescent girl who didn't fit in. A woman who had been her classmate talked about this sympathetically. "Back then only the popular girls dated, and she was not one of those. The popular girls went around in cliques, and they could really hurt the others. There was the clique that would be trying out for cheerleader, there was the basketball clique, and there were the girls and guys who were hotshots. To be a hotshot, you had to dress to a certain standard—black and white saddle shoes and full-cut flannel skirts with poodle designs appliquéd on them, or knee-length crinolines—and you had to hang around smoking in corners. Smoking was the big thing then, not even drinking, certainly not drugs. The hot girls wore their hair long and rolled up, or in sausage curls when they dressed up for a date. And if you weren't in one of these cliques, you were nobody.

"Marybeth was very plain, and she dressed plain. She is more attractive now than she was in high school. She didn't have a pretty face. She had projecting teeth and a pouting expression, and most of the time she wore her hair short and straight. She was not part of a clique, and was never likely to be. Not that she was a bad person in school. I don't remember her getting into trouble or being sent to the principal. But she was different. She had a lot of mood swings. There were times when you would see her smiling; times when she would walk through the halls expressionless. And you could never be quite sure whether she was telling the truth. I wouldn't call it lying, but she would tell exaggerated stories to make herself look important.

"She never spoke about her father. I have a feeling that he was a bad part of her life."

Another of Marybeth's classmates shared the feeling that "something went wrong in her childhood, like being a victim of some kind of abuse. I think she had a lot of anger." This woman recounted one of the stories that Marybeth told in high school: "It's going back a long time, so I may have forgotten some details, but it was something about her having to go to Connecticut for the weekend to testify in a court case about an accident she was supposed to have witnessed. We all knew it was fantasy because courts don't sit at weekends."

Marybeth was always the heroine of her own fantasies, whether she was being an important trial witness or, later in life, delivering a stranger's baby in a shopping mall. There was only one recurring story in which she was the victim, and it was undoubtedly true: the tale of the child who was hit with a flyswatter and locked in her room, a tale told so often that the hurt must have run deep. She was justified in thinking that her younger brother was their father's preferred child. Buddy never got locked in his room. "I don't have to hit your brother," he remembered his father telling Marybeth. "He can learn from your mistakes."

With the father long dead, the daughter's recollections unreliable, and the mother declining to talk about it, there is no way of knowing whether this was child abuse or old-fashioned blue-collar discipline. "Back in those days we all had strict parents," one of Marybeth's contemporaries observed. "Mr. and Mrs. Roe seemed to be nice people." But no one in the village knew much about them.

Marybeth Roe was graduated from Duanesburg Central High School in 1961. She was an average student with vague ambitions for college which were probably unrealistic. There was nothing distinctive about her school record; she never won any prizes, played on a team, or sang in the choir, but she did serve as president of Future Homemakers of America in her junior year. The school's 1961 yearbook had a significant comment to make about Marybeth. In preparing the book, a committee of her peers listed a Mark of Distinction for every student, and these ran the gamut from wavy hair and freckles to gullibility and a sense of humor. Marybeth was summed up in one word: "temper."

She hung around the house for a few weeks after graduation until her father nagged her into going out to work. She seems to have taken the first job which came her way, that of a nurse's aide on the pediatric ward at Ellis Hospital, but there may have been more choice than chance about it; she felt a strong attraction to babies even then. Twenty-five years later officials at Ellis Hospital anxiously searched through the records to see if there were any unexplained infant deaths while she was working there, but found none. In her personal file her superior had given an affirmative answer to the question "Would you hire her again?"

There are other recollections, about this time, of a baby conceived but never born, a story which cannot be confirmed but which Marybeth told to enough people to be credible. "They made me do it,' " she said to one friend, referring to the abortion. She did not explain who "they" were. Abortion was not legal at that time (although there were known to have been one or two good "abortion mills" in Schenectady), and as a Catholic Marybeth would have been brought up to think of it as murder. Were the deaths of all those subsequent babies related to this traumatic experience in girlhood?

In one version of the story a father was mentioned. It was a fanciful tale with a Marybeth touch at the end of it. She said that she had been seduced by an Episcopal priest and that many years later she made a long journey to his deathbed, where there was a reconciliation. The person who heard this tale did not believe the priest part of it and wondered whether Marybeth invented him because the real father was someone she found it too painful to talk about, to whom she may never have become reconciled.

Joe Tinning may have been unaware of all this. He knew very little about Marybeth before he met her on that blind date and was not the type to ask probing questions. When they married, he was in General Electric's apprenticeship program and she was still working at Ellis Hospital. Ruth Roe was said to have warned her new son-in-law not to give in to her daughter's crying spells, meaning the tears that Marybeth would use to get her own way. Joe was never assertive enough to follow this advice, and the childish tears persisted through their marriage; however, the first few years seem to have been happy enough. It was at the time of Marybeth's third pregnancy, the one which became Jennifer, that terrible things began to happen.

The first of these—and it may have a great deal of relevance to everything that followed—was the sudden and untimely death of Marybeth's father. It is extremely difficult for a woman to cope with a bereavement when she is about to give birth. Even in the most supportive of families, the emotional stress is so overwhelming that she may concentrate, sometimes to the point of obsession, upon one or the other. Either she will put all her psychic energies into her pregnancy and delay mourning until after her baby is born, in which case she may suffer a severe postpartum depression, or else she will become so emotionally involved in the bereavement that she may almost forget the coming baby.

Marybeth followed the latter course. She had always felt ambivalent toward her father: angry and afraid of him because he disciplined and discriminated against her, yet striving hard to be like him, or at least to please him, because his forceful personality was so much more appealing to her than that of her diminutive, ailing mother. Physically she resembled him and, so one keen observer noted, sometimes seemed jealous of her mother for occupying his attention.

She was almost seven months pregnant with all these conflicting feelings unresolved when Alton Roe, Sr., had his fatal heart attack. In the several days that it took him to die at Ellis Hospital she must have hoped for some word of reconciliation, perhaps like the deathbed scene which she wove into her story of the abortion. This does not seem to have happened. It must have made her feelings of grief and guilt and anger—always inextricably intermingled in any bereavement—so much more pronounced and painful.

There was yet another lasting hurt. As he was dying, Marybeth's father asked a favor of his son. Promise me, he said in effect, that if you ever have a son you will give him our name: Alton Lewis Roe. At that time Buddy (who eventually carried out the promise) was several years away from being a father. Marybeth was only ten weeks away from being a mother, but in her father's scheme of things her baby was secondary. It would be her brother's child, yet to be conceived, who would perpetuate the family name. Even fecund and grieving, Marybeth couldn't measure up to the expectations of this dying man.

He was buried in October, and at Christmas Jennifer was born. To a Catholic mother in a Catholic hospital Christmas is a special time to have a baby, a time when the woman's own birth experience becomes linked in a significant and touching way with the miracle of the Christ Child. Marybeth took the imagery even farther than that. Still obsessing about her father, she confided to some of the St. Clare's nurses that this baby was her Christmas gift to him. She would give this grandchild an importance, whether he had thought of it or not. She even spoke of Jennifer's birth as necessary for her father's soul to be memorialized, even immortalized, in pure new human form. In her troubled mind this act of birth seems to have been an expiation for the wrongs of the past, but it was not the new baby she kept talking about. It was her dead father. "She went on and on about him," one nurse remembered.

Among former nurses at St. Clare's Hospital strange stories were told about the birth of Jennifer, but not until after Marybeth was convicted. Some of these women knew things about Marybeth which had not gone into her medical records, things which they felt they shouldn't be talking about even now—or perhaps should have talked about sooner, depending upon how they viewed the conflict between respecting patient's confidentiality and acting in her best interests.

What a few of them eventually revealed is unsubstantiated, but it fits the puzzle so perfectly that it is almost certainly the missing piece. It was known on the maternity ward that Marybeth tried to induce the birth of Jennifer so that this baby would be born on Christmas Day, the reincarnation of her father in heaven. This was such a bizarre event that sixteen years later some of the former nurses clearly remembered it, and how Marybeth kept talking about bringing her father back to life through the spirit of this child. A clumsily induced labor would explain the kind of infection which is the commonest cause of brain abscesses and meningitis in a newborn, the condition which was fatal to Jennifer. She was born on December 26 and died eight days later.

No one seems to have questioned Marybeth, as is understandable, in light of her extreme grief reaction to this baby's death: the attempt to take Jennifer's body to bed with her, and to cover them both with a sheet. Instead, Marybeth was released from the hospital to arrange the first of nine elaborate funerals, every one of them making her the focus of love and sympathy such as she had never experienced before.

Even when her other two children died within the next two months, no suspicious questions were asked. The rest was predictable. After her arrest Marybeth's brother expressed the opinion that if she had not been charged with Tami Lynne's death, she would have moved to yet another place where she was not known, a move she had in fact already planned, and "there would have been more babies."

Pregnancy seems to have been more significant to Marybeth than its outcome. In a childlike way she liked the idea of babies, she enjoyed dressing them up and showing them off, she even "played with" Tami Lynne (her own words) shortly before smothering her. But she did not enjoy being a mother, certainly not the diaper-changing, burping, colicky, up-all-night part of it. Her greater satisfaction came from the gravid state of feeling so much more fulfilled and important than the lonely, inadequate person she other-

wise was. The promiscuity of her later years may have been motiv-
ated by her psychological need for yet another pregnancy, at a time
when the romance had gone out of her marriage, as much as by an
urge for sex. All her life there had been this terrible emptiness,
and she knew only one way to fill it.

She did not mourn her babies or keep their memories alive in
the way that other mothers do, by bringing them into her conversation and reminiscing about how old they might have been. But
when she was living in Duanesburg, between the death of Michael
and the birth of Tami Lynne, there was a troubled teenager whom
she spoke of (never to her face) as "my daughter," to whom she
showed some of the affection she might have given a child of her
own, if only one had lived.

They met when, as a member of the ambulance team, Marybeth
helped take the girl's grandfather to the hospital. Several days later
she paid a kindly call on the family to inquire how the patient was
doing. There she met the granddaughter, learned of this girl's
unhappiness in her own parents' home, and took an interest in her.

They had long conversations in unlikely places, like Giovanni's
Hilltop Tavern and the Duanesburg ambulance station, where
Marybeth helped her "daughter" with her homework and discussed
her personal problems. She encouraged the girl to stay in school
when she was tempted to drop out, and as an occasional treat took
her to a restaurant in Schenectady. "I know she loved babies," the
"daughter" remembered, "because one time when we were out
together there was a woman with a baby sitting at the next table,
and Marybeth was playing with it." The girl assumed she had never
had children of her own. In all this time, at least two years, Marybeth had not mentioned them.

After she left Duanesburg, Marybeth kept up the contact. "She
called me during the trial to ask if I was feeling better. I had been
in the hospital, and she seemed really concerned. I asked her how
she was doing, and she said she was holding up. She sounded
good." The "daughter" was twenty-two by then and living away
from home. She heard no more from Marybeth after her conviction.
"But if she would write to me from prison, I would still like to
keep in touch. She is a good person, and I will never believe she
killed those babies."

POSTSCRIPT

Marybeth's appeal was filed in July 1988, one year after her conviction. It was prepared by Schenectady County's public defender, Martin Cirincione, who had replaced Paul Callahan as Marybeth's counsel after she applied for legal aid. She maintained that the costs of her defense had left her indigent, which meant that both sides of the appeal had to be paid out of Schenectady County's limited funds.

Unless he could present dramatic new evidence, which apparently he couldn't, Cirincione was restricted in his appeal to testimony given at the trial. He seized upon two aspects of this. He argued that despite Callahan's mention of other Tinning children, the judge erred in letting the jury see Marybeth's full confession without deleting her admission to smothering Timothy and Nathan. This was a fine legal point, arguable both ways, about Judge Harrigan's interpretation of New York State's Molineux ruling which related to the admission of evidence of prior crimes.

Cirincione's other argument was more difficult for District Attorney John Poersch to counter. In his closing speech to the jury Poersch had made a serious blunder. "When you read those statements and when you look at the other evidence I'm sure you'll find that Marybeth Tinning here murdered her three children," he had told the jury. He meant only one child, of course. But then he repeated the assertion. Both times Callahan objected. On the first occasion the judge sustained his objection; on the second her overruled it. Now, as a basis for his appeal, Cirincione argued that

Poersch's prejudicial remarks alone justified a new trial. He described what took place as "a trial in which Mrs. Tinning, although charged with killing only one child, was prosecuted for the deaths of all nine of her children." In a responding brief, Poersch denied that any actions of his or of the judge had prejudiced the jury.

During the year since Marybeth's conviction Poersch had publicly repeated his promise to reopen his investigation into the other Tinning deaths. He had also stated that some people had come forward with new information which he expected would lead to further criminal indictments against Marybeth. He promised "a complete investigation, from beginning to end, into the deaths of these children."

This is what state police authorities had urged him to do in the first place. In local law enforcement circles there had been considerable criticism of Poersch's failure to assemble enough evidence for Marybeth to be charged with the three murders she admitted, and not just with that of Tami Lynne. Before she was brought to trial, there were police concerns that the prosecution could lose this case if she was charged with only one murder. With three indictments against her a conviction was much more certain, and much less likely to be overturned on appeal. Having missed out on this, Poersch was still being urged to bring other charges to ensure that Marybeth would not gain an early release from prison. However, when the New York State Court of Appeals began consideration of Marybeth's appeal in November 1988, there was still no news of the promised investigation by the district attorney's office. By that time John Poersch had become preoccupied with troubles of his own.

Of the three major towns in New York's capital district, Albany, Schenectady, and Troy, Schenectady had long had the worst reputation for criminal activity. In the city's poorest neighborhood, Hamilton Hill, drug trafficking and drug-related prostitution had been a scandal for years, and it was widely suspected that organized crime had too much influence in high political places for effective action to be taken.

In May 1988 a private citizen, Gail Podrazik, formed an activist group named Clean Sweep United with the aim of eliminating Schenectady's drug trade. The district attorney's office was one of Clean Sweep's early targets. Alleging that Poersch was not vigorously prosecuting the violators, group members followed him around town for several weeks, documenting the time he spent in taverns and in restaurants with liquor licenses. Sometimes while they watched him in these places they would telephone his office and ask to speak to him. According to Ms. Podrazik, the most frequent response was that he was in a meeting.

Her charges against the district attorney were publicized by the Schenectady television station WRGB, and Poersch responded by calling a press conference. He allowed no questions but made a rambling statement in which he talked proudly of his conviction rate. "I've accomplished a fantastic record and I think I'm the best D.A. the county has ever had,' he asserted.

He looked shaky and was sweating. He acknowledged that he did visit taverns and restaurants but argued that he worked irregular hours and was on call for twenty-four hours a day. "What I do between the time I get up in the morning until I go to bed at night is my business. And I will do what I wish to do from now until that date when I retire, if I do retire."

He had been district attorney for eleven years and was under mounting pressure to resign from a prestigious appointment which brought him $82,000 a year. Suddenly it became a priority for him to bring dealers to justice, rather than to initiate fresh charges against Marybeth Tinning.

While he was preparing her appeal, Martin Cirincione had several long prison visits with his new client. He became very sympathetic to her, and seemed to like and trust her. He also became convinced that she had not had a fair trial. Given the fact that she was charged with only one murder, he felt the jury had been prejudiced by frequent references to the untimely deaths of all her other children. He argued that even Dr. Oram's conclusions about the cause of Tami Lynne's death were influenced by his knowledge of the family history.

"Mrs. Tinning has been very straightforward with me," he stated. "She comes across as extremely sincere, genuine, normal and rational. She has always maintained to me that she did not kill Tami Lynne, and so far as I know she has not said anything different to anyone at any time, except when she made her statement to the police. And what she said about being coerced into making that statement is certainly believable."

In his brief to the court of appeals Cirincione requested a new trial and, failing that, a reduction of Marybeth's twenty-year-to-life sentence, which he described as "harsh and excessive." Privately, he commented: "The American judicial system has regressed in the past twenty years to the point where retribution is the prime motivator for society, and the courts' reasons for punishment. Twenty years ago all the constitutional rights came to the fore. Since then there has been a slow erosion of those rights, not only by the U.S. Supreme Court but also by the way in which lower courts have interpreted the law."

After Cirincione submitted his appeal, Marybeth let it be known that she was willing to grant an interview for this book, with her new lawyer present. Previously she had refused to have any formal conversations with the author or with any other reporter. Shortly before the interview was due to take place Cirincione canceled the appointment. "She would really like to tell her story, but is concerned about how it will be perceived," he explained.

Joe Tinning continued to make long and regular visits to Bedford Hills prison where he was often seen taking down lengthy notes at his wife's dictation. Some strange stories about Marybeth's behavior in jail reached state police officials. One was that in conversations with fellow prisoners she had described the deaths of some of her children in what was said to have been self-incriminatory detail. Another report concerned her reactions to babies. At Bedford Hills women who are pregnant when they are sentenced are allowed to keep their infants in the jail's nursery for up to a year. Marybeth was often seen hanging around near that nursery. And women who had babies there said they were afraid of her.

On December 29, 1988, her appeal was denied by five justices of the New York State Supreme Court's Appellate Division. Their decision was unanimous and so unequivocally expressed that the chances of its being overridden by a higher court seemed almost negligible. The justices rejected Marybeth's contention that she had been coerced into admitting to three murders and upheld Judge Harrigan's decision to send her full confession to the jury. Although they found the district attorney's closing remarks to have been "improper," they ruled that he made "a harmless error which was not enough to counteract the overwhelming evidence of guilt."

EPILOGUE

Murder is murder. A mother who kills her baby should
be prosecuted to the full extent of the law.

It is wrong for American courts to imprison mothers
who kill their babies. They suffer from a mental illness.
                    —*From letters to the editor of* Time *magazine,*
                                        July 11, 1988

Infanticide is more common than most people care to acknowledge.
It is the dark side of the crib death statistics, the ultimate form of
child abuse, the crime with no clear motive or rational explanation.
It is the form of murder which most perpetrators lie about, claiming
that the baby was simply found dead or even kidnapped, and they
are likely to be believed; of all capital crimes, it is the least prosecuted and most overlooked. Almost any medical examiner's office
in a major city is aware of many suspected infanticides which never
reach the courts. In their most frequent form—suffocation with a
soft object—they are virtually impossible to distinguish from natural death, and there is usually only one material witness, the mother,
and she has blanked the whole thing out of her consciousness. Only
when the crime is bizarre enough, or repeated often enough, are
these cases prosecuted. Then society is astounded to learn that there
are women like Marybeth Tinning.

The outrage can be extreme. Many people retain a biblical attitude toward infanticide, demanding the harshest punishment for a
crime which seems so heinous and contrary to nature that in their
view, justice should not be tempered with. Those who were there
will long remember the woman who stood outside the Schenectady
County Courthouse on the afternoon of Friday, July 17, 1987,
waiting for a rush of reporters down the steps which would signify
that the jury had reached a verdict. "What is it?" she asked anxiously, running after them. As soon as she heard the word "guilty",

she stopped in her tracks and jumped up and down with delight, right there in the middle of State Street.

Those who were closer to the trial—jurors and court officials—were left with troubled feelings which persisted long after Marybeth began to serve her sentence. They had listened to quantities of expert testimony without gaining any insights into the woman who was accused, let alone an understanding of what had brought her to this place. Most jurors were distressed that the law did not permit them to recommend the psychiatric treatment which they felt was overdue. In a most unusual move they met together several times over the ensuing months to talk about the case and wonder aloud what they might have done differently, if only they had been given the evidence and opportunity. Schenectady's trial of the decade left its scars, not all of them on Marybeth.

She continues to be an enigma. In an attempt to understand her, several eminent psychiatrists and psychologists were consulted during the preparation of this book. This kind of research is both rewarding and frustrating because none of these experts was able to examine Marybeth, also because aberrant behavior rarely follows a near textbook pattern. The symptoms are subject to a variety of interpretations depending upon the way they present themselves at a particular time, the way they are viewed in relation to the patient, and the professional background of the specialist who is viewing them. Thus there may never be a simple explanation for the complexities and anomalies of a life like Marybeth's. All the experts agreed, however, that this woman appeared to have either a severe personality disorder or a clinical disorder back to childhood. Several of them expressed surprise and dismay that this was not part of her defense.

Interviewed after she was sentenced, one of the expert defense witnesses, Dr. John Emery, commented that in his view her case could have been presented differently to the court. "If I had been in charge of it, I would have insisted on her being seen by a psychiatrist who knew the subject. If she did kill her child, the chances are that she is mad in a particular sort of way, and to treat a woman who has a mental disease as a criminal is an inhuman approach.'

In the British system, more familiar to Dr. Emery, the quaint time limit of a year and a day after childbirth has been established as the period in which a woman may not be judged criminally liable for killing her child. The law has determined that during this period she may not have made the necessary emotional separation from the baby to be completely rational in her attitude toward it. She may still see it as part of herself, and if she kills it in a fit of anger, despair, or self-hatred, she may symbolically be committing suicide. Significantly, eight of the nine Tinning children died within six months after Marybeth gave birth, although not always to the child who died. The only exception was the adopted son, Michael.

Joe Tinning spoke of his wife's frequent mood swings, which struck several experts as likely manifestations of a manic-depressive condition. Much of Marybeth's other strange behavior fits this diagnosis: the lying to make herself seem important; the petty thievery and compulsive spending; the buying and hoarding of things she didn't need; the grandiosity; the smoldering anger which could turn to violence or threats of violence when she was thwarted. During one argument with Joe she kicked in their television set (so she admitted to a Flavorland colleague); after another there was his overdose of phenobarbital. Such extreme reactions might well explain why he avoided disagreements with his wife forever after. It could also account for the chilling effect she had on those around her who sensed that beneath her friendly and trusting manner, she was capable of uncontrollable rage. After Marybeth was sentenced to a twenty-year prison term, some of his workmates said that Joe Tinning had the air of a man from whom an enormous burden had been lifted.

Women who are prone to manic-depressive disease are potential victims of postpartum psychosis, a mental state in which they are likely to kill their babies. It is a severe psychiatric disorder occurring in only one or two out of every thousand births, and this means that most obstetricians never see a case. Therefore, it can easily escape diagnosis in the short time that a woman spends on the maternity ward, or be passed off as the "baby blues," the relatively mild and transient depression which afflicts many new mothers. If the infant later dies at home, the event is likely to be certified as a crib death, especially when a doctor notes the mother's profound distress and how well her child was cared for. Victims of postpartum psychosis are unlikely to batter their babies. They look after them, then they may kill them and blank out the memory. In the meantime, they do not bond to them. Typically Marybeth did not breast-feed her babies and often turned away when a nurse brought her latest newborn into her hospital room.

"These women see the new baby as the bad part of themselves and they want to get rid of it," according to Dr. Stuart S. Asch, Professor of Clinical Psychiatry at New York Hospital-Cornell Medical Center, who has made a study of postpartum psychosis. "It is a form of suicide. The woman wants to have a baby but then becomes overtaken by the psychotic idea that the baby is evil and must be done away with. Somewhere within herself she knows what she is doing, but there is great denial."

The psychosis can be triggered by a traumatic family crisis, such as the death of a parent during pregnancy. If the relationship with that parent has been ambivalent, especially if the new mother felt that she herself was unwanted as a child, she may transfer her anger to the baby and kill it. Depressed people have a great deal of anger which makes them feel unlovable and worthless (Marybeth's frequent statement that she was a bad mother is characteristic), and the psychotic woman's compulsion to kill her baby stems from the hope that if she gets rid of this bad part of herself, she will be loved again. When she finds she isn't, she may try to get pregnant once more because pregnancy fills the void of loneliness and makes her feel whole. "It is a cyclical repetitive disease in which the conflicts are never resolved," said Dr. Asch. "Without treatment it is likely to recur after subsequent births."

Religious fantasies often play a part in postpartum psychosis, so that in the euphoria of pregnancy a woman may think of her unborn child as a divine being, and of herself as a chosen instrument for bringing it into the world. When the child is born with all the usual human frailties, the letdown can be overwhelming. If Marybeth did equate the birth of her third child with the Nativity, she must have been disillusioned by the outcome. The baby was a girl, born a day after Christmas, and imperfect. From then on none of her babies lived long, and she became very tense as Christmas approached, and she was on the evening of December 19, 1985, when she returned from the shopping trip with Cynthia Walter, a few hours before she suffocated Tami Lynne.

There may be other explanations. One psychiatrist suggested the Marybeth may have had a dissociative disorder, with the result that she could have developed two or more distinct personalities as a defensive reaction to a severe trauma. This is a rare condition in which each of the multiple personalities functions like a self-contained individual, usually unaware of the existence of the others. Each personality will have different behavior patterns and memories, and at different times one or the other of these will be dominant. Often they are complete opposites from one another. Over the years several of Marybeth's associates noted extreme variations in her demeanor, from that of the frightened child to that of the manipulative seductress, which could have been evidence of this. It was also observed that sometimes she seemed to be "off in a twilight zone."

The most frequently documented cause of a dissociative disorder is sexual abuse in childhood. Often the memory of this is so deeply buried that none of the personalities the child created to cope with the trauma will have any clear recollection of it. Skilled psychoanalysis is, of course, necessary to make the diagnosis and to provide treatment. If indeed Marybeth did have a dissociative disorder, there could be a question of her fitness to stand trial since the Marybeth whom the jurors saw may genuinely have had no memory of the Marybeth who smothered Tami Lynne. Or there may be a simpler explanation for the many faces of Marybeth: that in an attempt to overcome her own feelings of inadequacy, she learned to adapt to various roles which she felt would impress others. Most people do that to a certain extent. Marybeth seems to have been expert at it.

This is the considered opinion of the Reverend Burnham Waldo, the only professional who is known to have counseled her in depth. He, too, was struck by the different parts she would play and saw them as contrived attempts to make herself acceptable, rather than as manifestations of different personalities. In a detailed memorandum to the author he described his reaction to the Marybeth he came to know, and tried to help, over a three-year period between the death of Michael and her pregnancy with Tami Lynne, a time when he was in charge of a Methodist church on the outskirts of Duanesburg, and a fellow member of the Duanesburg Volunteer Ambulance Corps. He wrote:

> The most consistent thing about her was her inconsistency. She seemed to lack a cohesiveness to her personality. Even before she told me about the loss of her children I felt she held

some deep personal tragedy which was sometimes expressed in anger. As I got to know her better I realized that her personality dysfunctions came from her nearly total lack of self-esteem, due to having been put down and rejected from the time she was a child. It seems as if every opportunity to achieve success and build self-confidence only left her with feelings of inadequacy and failure.

Her compulsiveness seemed to stem from a subconscious drive to work out her inner self-hatred. Her imitative behavior can be seen as attempts to get attention, acceptance and affection. I saw her as someone who, filled with self-hatred, desperately tried to be somebody, anybody, rather than the nothing which she had been led to believe she was by the people who mattered most to her.

This inner drive to be accepted caused her to assume roles and personality characteristics which she felt would please others. I am sure that while she was in a particular role—and this included the fabrication of events—she firmly believed she was the person she was trying to be. As soon as people tired of her story or seemed not to believe her, she would change the story, drop the role, and behave in a childlike way, even using tears and anger to regain the sympathy of the listener. At these times her "dominant person," the little girl desperately trying to be grown up and not knowing how, asserted itself.

Like several others who eventually crossed her, Waldo admitted to being traumatized by his contact with Marybeth—angry that she told lies about him and tried to ruin his reputation but regretful that he was not able to help her more. He was hard on himself about this: "I tried to get her to see a mental health professional, but I did not try hard enough." Still, the closer he got to persuading her to face up to her illness, the more she reacted by threatening him—if not overtly, then by spreading malicious gossip which could undermine his position in the community. When he finally told her that he could not see her anymore and that she needed a psychiatrist, her reaction was so strong that he felt in personal danger. More than anything else it was the look in her eyes which horrified him. It was the same look that others described as a look of the devil—shocking enough to set him wondering about the physical presence of evil in the world, about whether, without even wanting this to happen, a person could become captive to its destructive power. He was reminded of certain biblical passages and of dark tales he read years ago.

"I am going to the library to reread Thomas Hardy," he remarked when it was all over.

As for Marybeth's crime itself, surprisingly little is known. Back in 1968 Dr. Asch had stated in a medical paper* that in his opinion a large percentage of "crib deaths" were actually "infanticides, perpetrated by the mother as a specific manifestation of postpartum depression." It was a most unpopular opinion to express at that time; consequently, very little American research has since been done on infanticide. Motherhood was regarded as too sacred to be demeaned by the suggestion of murder; as Hedda Gabler said of her hero's suicide, people don't do such things. So while medical institutions have spent considerable sums researching the possible causes of Sudden Infant Death Syndrome, one cause has consistently been overlooked because no one in authority was ready to suspect the unthinkable and investigate the obvious. Dr. Asch had to abandon a study of the causes of infanticide begun in the 1960's because the opposition was overwhelming. Medical authorities refused to cooperate, he felt isolated professionally, "and then the police department wanted the names of the mothers and I refused."

British law is kinder to the Marybeths of this world. At the same time it permits the kind of research on infanticide which might be impossible in the United States, even if the climate was right, because in America it might be seen as illegal invasion of privacy. As a result British doctors have been able to learn a lot about how mothers kill their babies by actually watching them prepare to do so. Women suspected of multiple infanticide have been put into test situations, left alone with their babies in hospital rooms while, unknown to them, their actions were observed and photographed, always with medical staff on hand to rescue the babies if necessary. The researchers' findings dispelled the widely held belief that women who repeatedly suffocate their babies do so spontaneously

* "Crib Deaths: Their Possible Relationship to Post-Partum Depression and Infanticide," Stuart S. Asch, M.D., *Journal of Mount Sinai Hospital*, New York City, Vol. 35, 1968.

and unthinkingly because they can't stand the crying any longer. What they saw was a much more calculated crime.

Dr. Roy Meadow, professor of pediatrics and child health at St. James's University Hospital, Leeds, who has been in the forefront of this research, commented: "I do not think the suffocation is done spontaneously in a moment of exasperation. It is very difficult to do, particularly in terms of the force required, and that force has to be sustained for about two minutes. There is always a struggle. Even with a tiny infant there is a lot of threshing of arms and legs. When we have watched these mothers through videos, we have seen them carefully looking over their shoulders to make sure a nurse isn't watching, then waiting awhile and looking again before going up to the baby with a soft object and preparing to put it down on the child's face with considerable force. It is a premeditated act. Afterwards these mothers manage to black out what has happened because they do not want to remember."

Having coined the term "Munchausen syndrome by proxy" for people (usually mothers) who get a perverted satisfaction from making others (usually children) ill and then rescuing them, Dr. Meadow has since found similar characteristics in women who were suspected of repeated infanticide. Most of the British women who were investigated had long-term stable marriages to men who constantly deferred to them but gave no emotional support. Often they had held jobs on the fringes of the medical profession and enjoyed being involved in the daily drama of hospital life. They tended to hang around the wards for more hours than was necessary, making themselves useful to the nurses, and comforting other mothers— gestures which made them feel important. Some of them stole hospital equipment.

"They love playing with the stuff," Dr. Meadow said. "They become hooked on things medical in all kinds of ways." Also, when challenged about harming their babies, "most of these mothers will not admit to all the things they have done and have a lot of trouble with their stories because they cannot tell you the whole truth." There was an element of all this in Marybeth Tinning.

A few other factors may be relevant. According to Dr. Asch, women who are prone to postpartum psychoses are just as likely to express anger toward an adopted child as toward their own, their disease being emotional rather than hormonal in origin. Initially such a woman wants to adopt a child but then feels woefully inadequate because she herself did not give birth to it and because it can never fulfill her unrealistic expectations. In a psychotic state she may also kill older siblings. Again the most frequent method is by suffocation, which, of course, requires much more force to succeed with a child then with a baby. A psychotic mother may well panic when her child starts convulsing from lack of oxygen, rush it to hospital for resuscitation, then later repeat the act.

These women are intolerant of their children's demands because there was not enough nurturing in their own childhoods. Typically they cannot stand the sound of their babies crying. The three babies whom Marybeth confessed to killing were all crying or "making a funny noise" when she put a pillow over their faces. She was unusually sensitive to noise, beginning with her negative reaction to her father's loud voice, permanently raised because as a punch press operator at General Electric he was used to shouting over machinery. Throughout her adult life she became agitated by disagreeable noises, and in the Schenectady County Jail she had a violent reaction to a fellow prisoner singing gospel songs in a true but loud voice. Other women prisoners were enjoying the performance when Marybeth turned to a guard and remarked with some annoyance: "Duct tape. That's what we need."

"Duct tape?"

"Yes." And in an unmistakable gesture, she pointed to the singer, then drew a forefinger across her own mouth. Suddenly fearful, the prisoners exchanged looks, remembering what happened to Tami Lynne.

INDEX

acute pulmonary oedema, 67, 114
Albany Medical Center, 143, 144
Albany Medical College, 259
Albany *Times Union*, 309, 313
Allen-Bruni, Eileen, 295
American Heart Fund, 60
Andrew, Courtland, 59, 61
aneurysms, 171, 175
anoxia, 85, 292
Archives of Disease in Childhood, 312
Arthritis Foundation, 60
Asch, Dr. Stuart S., 365, 368–369
Asher, Dr. Richard, 216
aspirin, baby, 81

"baby blues," 364
baby brokers, 121
Baden, Dr. Michael M., 214, 229,
    256, 257, 260, 311
Barker, George, 157
Barker, Sara, 104, 107, 115
Barnes, Investigator William W.,
    184–185, 229–236, 238,
    239–249, 266, 267, 268, 288,
    290, 297–298, 340
Barron, Dr. Kevin D., 333
battered baby syndrome, 218
Beckwith, Dr. J. Bruce, 212

Bellevue Maternity Hospital, 92, 93,
    133
Bender Laboratory, 303
Berenberg, Wlliam, 132
Bernhardt, Margot, 238, 239, 249,
    268, 269, 340
Bernstein, Charles G., 216
Bokan, Susan, 276, 339, 340, 342,
    344
Boston Children's Hospital, 132,
    137, 139, 141, 142, 144, 247,
    305

Cafarelli, Linda, 335
Callahan, Paul, 222–223, 258,
    263–266, 267, 268, 276–277,
    278–279, 282–324, 334–335,
    336, 341, 342, 345, 346–347,
    348, 358
cancer, 22, 79
cardiopulmonary arrest, 67, 68, 128,
    142, 145, 246
cardiopulmonary resuscitation
    (CPR), 37, 40, 240
Christman, Dr. Janet, 131
Cimma, Dr. Richard, 143
Cirincione, Martin, 358–359
cirrhosis of liver, 139
Clark, Mary Higgins, 104, 106, 114

Clean Sweep United, 359–360
congenital heart disease, 42, 147
Connie (widow), 181, 205
Cooley, Dr. James K., 164–165
Coons, Moira, 115–117
Crofts, Raymond, 89, 90
Cunningham, Dr. James F., 255

Daly, Lawrence H., 59–62, 116, 117,
    136, 280–281
Daly, Susan, 58
Daly Funeral Home, 58, 62, 97, 107,
    115, 117, 132, 157, 259
Daoud, Dr. Assaad, 144
Davies, Dr. Jack N. P., 258–260,
    291, 292, 299–303, 307–309,
    310, 311, 314, 318–320,
    322–323
Day, the Rev. Roger, 58–59, 62, 262
Days of Our Lives, 222
DiMaio, Dr. Vincent J. M., 216, 217
Duanesburg Volunteer Ambulance
    Corps, 164, 168–172, 177,
    194–198, 202, 227, 267
Dubb Transportation, 202

Ellis Hospital, 50, 84, 93–94, 110,
    124, 129, 167, 314, 331
Emery, Dr. John L., 11–14,
    310–314, 315, 316, 318–320,
    331, 363

Famularo, Virginia, 344
Figliola, Joseph, 49
Ford, Dr. Bradley, 30–31, 70, 221,
    284–285

Gebell, Alan, 230, 256, 268–270,
    271, 277, 324, 332
Gerberg, Bernard, 339, 340, 344
Giovanni's Hilltop Tavern, 181, 197,
    286
Gospé, Dr. Sidney, Jr., 317, 318

Harding, Madeline, 202
Harrigan, Judge Clifford T., 261,
    264, 270–271, 275, 280, 283,
    285, 286, 289, 298, 301, 304,
    311, 323, 330, 332, 335, 340,
    341–342, 347–348, 358
Haven of Schenectady, 179–180
hemorrhagic meningitis, 79
hepatitis, 139
Hovey, Michael, 103, 110, 111, 113
Howard, Gholson, 339, 343
Hutchins, Jacqueline, 339
hypospadias, 137

Imefeld, Investigator Robert, 55–57,
    222–225, 228, 232, 234, 236,
    238, 256, 266, 267, 284, 288,
    296, 340
infanticide, 313, 362–370
Irish, the Rev. Harold, 155, 191

January, Dr. Virgil, 225–226
Jewett, Sharon, 63
Jewett's Poultry Farm, 165, 190
Jorgensen, Dr. Grace, 92
Journal of Forensic Sciences, 215

Karas, Investigator Joseph V.,
    109–110, 112, 222–228, 232,
    234, 236, 238–244, 256, 266,
    267–268, 289–290, 296–297, 298,
    340
Karpowicz, Dr. Kevin, 68–70,
    157–158, 202–203, 204
Kathy's Motel, 181, 191, 197, 205,
    267, 277
kidney abnormalities, 137
King, Stephen, 104
Knapp, Douglas, 154
Koeppen, Dr. Arnulf, 301–309, 314,
    323, 333

Lencewicz, Brian, 23, 26, 30, 44,
    241, 252

Lencewicz, Dennis, 26, 43
Lencewicz, Susan "Sue," 23, 24,
    25–28, 30, 43, 44, 203, 204,
    241, 251, 252–253, 338
Lionarons, Judy, 150
liver diseases, 139
Lobovits, Dr. Alan, 131–132
Looney, Captain Gerald E., 75, 229
Lou Gehrig's disease, 305

McBreen, Patricia "Trish," 125,
    126, 142, 145, 148
McCarthy, Gary, 256, 325
McGiffin, Steven, 196, 203
Mannix, Colleen "Betsy," 55–57,
    65–66, 70–71, 222, 256, 284
Meadow, Dr. S. Roy, 216–217, 369
Mele, Dr. Dominick, 113, 124–125,
    126, 127, 130, 131, 132, 135,
    138–140, 141, 221, 302, 308
Miranda warning, 266, 288, 337
Mohawk Mall, 171
Molineux rule, 271, 358
Montanye, Joan, 335, 336, 339
Most Holy Redeemer Cemetery, 27,
    64, 333
Munchausen syndrome by proxy,
    216–217, 369
Munson, Barbara, 170
Muscular Dystrophy Association,
    309

Nelson, Police Chief Richard, 75,
    253
Normington, Suzanne "Sue," 45–48,
    64, 66, 103, 104, 122, 350–351

O'Connor, Investigator Daniel,
    49–50, 70, 72, 74, 132, 256,
    296, 298
Oneida County Jail, 253, 254, 255,
    263, 285
Oram, Dr. Thomas F. D., 50–55,
    85, 159–160, 209–219, 224,
    258–260, 290–292, 301, 302,
    303, 314, 323, 330–331, 335,
    336, 360
Our Lady of Fatima Church, 163

Pilcher, Patricia "Pat," 125–127,
    129, 135
Podrazik, Gail, 359
Poersch, John, 49, 74, 230, 256–257,
    263, 264–265, 276, 279–324,
    325, 332, 344–345, 346,
    358–360
Poersch, Mathias P., 279
polygraph tests, 222, 224, 231, 234
Posluszny, Dorothy, 147–148, 150,
    159, 161
postpartum depression, 53, 354
postpartum psychosis, 364–370
Princetown Reformed Church, 63,
    64, 149, 151, 190, 267

Ray, Charles "Chuck," 118–120,
    122, 129, 130, 132, 133, 134,
    140–141, 146, 149–150,
    154–156, 161, 188, 205–206
Ray, Janet, 118, 132, 133, 141, 146,
    149, 155, 161, 205
Resusci baby, 194–195, 198, 227
Reye's syndrome, 22, 67, 80, 81,
    84–85, 87, 210, 266
Roe, Alton L., Jr., "Buddy," 19, 27,
    88, 101, 150, 182, 194, 231,
    253, 263, 353, 355
    testimony of, 285, 286–287
Roe, Alton L., Sr.:
    death of, 21, 27, 82, 89, 183–185,
    231, 235, 297, 352, 353, 354
Roe, Ruth, 22, 27, 89, 254–255,
    262–263, 353, 354
Roe, Sandra "Sandy," 27, 32–33, 88,
    97, 101, 134, 140, 150–151, 152,
    158, 189, 194, 225–226, 247, 253,
    285–286

Rolling Greens Bowling Lanes, 32
Ross, Sandra "Sandy," 140,
153–154, 160, 165–166

St. Clare's Hospital, 41, 42, 50, 70,
107, 110, 111, 112, 123, 124,
128–131
St. Clare's Hospital Building Fund,
60
Sanders, Stuart, 49–50, 51, 52,
55–56, 66
Sanderson, William, 52–53, 55
Schenectady Department of Social
Services:
child abuse complaints
investigated by, 47, 55, 64, 143
Child Protective Unit of, 115, 126,
150, 159
Schenectady Gazette, 21, 60, 66, 68,
114, 118, 159, 196, 205, 309
Schenectady Memorial Park, 64
Schwenk, Dr. August, 93, 121
Scopes trial, 256–257
septicemia, 55
Sim, Dr. Young J., 50, 52, 54, 55,
159
Small, Norman, 336, 339, 341, 342,
345
Smith, Lemuel, 264, 345
Spooner, Harley, 325–333
Sprague, Investigator William
"Bill," 256, 296
Stazak, Richard, 67
Sudden Infant Death Syndrome
(SIDS):
aborted, 123
asphyxia vs., 85, 130, 145,
209–210, 212–214, 368–369
as diagnosis, 22, 40, 54, 62, 67,
80–81, 94, 113, 123, 124,
131–132, 145, 218, 221, 266
Tami Lynne and, 212–213, 257,
292, 302, 303, 311, 315–317,
334–335
Sudden Infant Death Syndrome
Foundation, 60
Sullivan, Dr. Robert L., 73–74, 94,
114, 157

Three Faces of Eve, The, 105
Tinning, Amanda, 44, 121
Tinning, Andrew J. "Andy," 44, 92,
93, 94, 95, 98, 99, 100, 101, 103,
120–121, 174, 225, 228, 254, 263,
348–349
Tinning, Barbara Ann, 22, 27, 53,
81, 84–86, 88–93, 133, 139, 210,
227, 244–245
Tinning, Carol, 25, 26, 30, 43–45,
86, 94–96, 97, 98, 99–103,
120–121, 140, 158, 174, 203, 225,
228, 252, 254, 263, 287–288, 310,
348–349
Tinning, Edna, 36, 64, 82, 103,
120–121, 133, 148–149, 151–152,
158, 161–162, 163, 168, 178, 185,
189, 190, 194, 255, 263, 320–321,
334
Tinning, Jennifer, 22, 27, 53, 60, 79,
81–83, 91, 131, 210, 214, 245,
260, 308, 350, 354–356
Tinning, Joel, 93, 95, 99, 100
Tinning, Jonathan:
apnea monitor for, 142
autopsy on, 144, 309
birth of, 137
death of, 60, 69, 70, 74, 141–145,
148, 157–158, 202, 236, 245,
246–247
funeral of, 146, 176
grave of, 27
hospitalization of, 141–144, 247,
303, 305
illness of, 141–144
kidney problems of, 143

Tinning, Jonathan (*Cont.*)
  Marybeth's reaction to death of,
    144
  medical problems of, 137–138
  name of, 27
  as premature, 137–138
  signs of Werdnig-Hoffmann
    disease in, 303–309, 318, 323,
    330, 333
Tinning, Joseph "Joe"
    (grandfather), 64, 163–164,
    168, 170, 178, 198, 205,
    254
Tinning, Joseph A. "Joe" (father):
  Andy and, 98, 100, 101, 103
  bowling as pastime of, 34, 37, 96,
    177, 251
  at children's funerals, 115, 155
  court appearances by, 343
  as General Electric employee, 24,
    161, 175, 200–202, 275, 276,
    354
  honesty of, 233, 294, 299
  investigaton of Marybeth and,
    222–223, 229, 232–237,
    248–249, 269–270
  marriage of, 24–25, 83, 91,
    96–103, 119–120, 179, 182, 185,
    231–232, 235, 248, 326, 327,
    354
  Marybeth dated by, 185
  Marybeth's arguments with 96,
    97, 161, 228
  Marybeth's arrest and, 249,
    251–252, 254
  personality of, 25, 120, 233–234,
    251
  poisoning of, 98–102, 116, 226,
    228, 231, 234, 252, 267, 294,
    364
  police questioning of, 228,
    232–234, 269, 296–298
  religion of, 179, 233

  salary of, 29
  testimony of, 269–270, 294–299,
    308, 337, 338
  trailer bought by, 188
  vasectomy considered by, 133
Tinning, Joseph A., Jr. "Joey"
    (son):
  death of, 53, 60, 83–84, 245
  funeral of, 85
  grave of, 27
  personality of, 90
  Reye's syndrome and, 81, 84, 87,
    210
  seizures of, 139
Tinning, Marybeth Roe:
  abortion as viewed by, 137, 203,
    214, 283, 353–354
  as abused child, 91, 105, 184–185,
    225, 353
  in ambulance corps, 164, 168–172,
    177, 194–198, 202, 227, 267
  ambulances called by, 111, 243,
    244, 246–247
  apartments rented by, 19,
    106–107, 161
  apnea monitors used by, 113
  appeal by, 358–361
  arrest feared by, 56–67, 65
  arrest of, 62, 238, 249, 250–252,
    261, 289, 329
  as arson suspect, 189–192, 196,
    202, 231, 267, 327
  attention needed by, 91–92, 178,
    203–204, 214, 217, 218, 231,
    261, 351–352
  as baby-sitter, 26, 28, 252, 279
  bail raised for, 254, 255, 346
  Ballston Spa home of, 206, 220,
    236, 255, 261
  as bus driver, 202, 326
  as Catholic, 41, 48, 106, 129–130,
    132–133, 191, 354

Tinning, Marybeth Roe (*Cont.*)
child abuse complaints about, 47, 64, 66, 69–70, 115–117, 125–127, 143, 157–158, 160
childhood of, 21, 91, 105, 163, 184–185, 225, 337, 351
children's deaths as explained by, 22, 109–114, 171
at children's funerals, 115, 146, 155, 226
children's graves tended by, 27
confession by, 109, 111, 171, 184–185, 219, 235–249, 254, 256, 258, 261, 262, 263, 264–270, 280, 288–290, 295, 304, 309, 322, 335–336, 340, 348, 358
confidential information on, 66–69, 70–71
conscience of, 174
at counseling center, 179–180
court appearances by, 266, 276–278, 288, 291, 295, 310, 336
criminal investigation of, 49–57, 61, 71, 72, 73–75, 84, 210, 218–219, 225, 248, 256
crying of babies and, 112, 240, 242–243, 345, 369–370
crying spells of, 183, 354
"daughter" of, 357
in Duanesburg, 161–166, 197
education of, 163, 353
as "evil person," 192
exaggerated stories told by, 22, 26, 92, 172, 178, 179–180, 183, 194, 216, 352–353
eye contact avoided by, 123, 125, 138
failure of system in case of, 65–70
family's support for, 148–149, 163–168, 254–255
fear of, 191–192, 321–322

first aid known by, 80, 113, 246
as foster mother, 86, 87–89, 90, 121–122, 134–135, 215
funeral benefits collected by, 97
"genetic incompatibility" of, 22, 54, 61, 69, 121, 123, 126, 127, 137, 139–140, 141, 142, 148, 160, 212, 213, 258, 290, 303–309, 317–318, 325, 334
gossip about affairs of, 180–182, 205, 325–333
guilt of, 251, 252–255, 262, 269, 285, 287, 298, 299, 348
guilty verdict on, 67, 105, 321, 334–345
gun owned by, 193–194, 222, 286
inadequacy felt by, 109, 167, 184, 234, 240–241
incarceration of, 249, 253–254, 263, 361
innocence of, 252–255, 262, 347, 348
insanity plea of, 263
insecurity of, 20, 149, 183
instant gratification needed by, 167
jury in trial of, 271, 275–277, 288, 302, 323, 332, 334–345, 363
lack of emotion shown by, 146, 159, 226
letters written from prison by, 253–254, 285, 339
marriage of, 24–25, 83, 91, 96–103, 119–120, 179, 182, 185, 231–232, 235, 248, 326, 327, 354
"Marybeth touch" of, 171, 178, 186, 215
maternity dresses worn by, 44–45, 91
media coverage of, 21, 114–115, 250, 261, 271, 275–276, 279, 285, 309–310, 321

Tinning, Marybeth Roe (*Cont.*)
  medical history of, 53–54, 73–75,
    79, 92–93, 94, 113, 123–125,
    131–132, 157, 250, 304,
    334–335, 360
  metabolic defects in children of,
    258, 292, 308
  as mother, 31–32, 37–38, 53, 109,
    125, 167, 184, 204, 227,
    235–236, 241, 283, 345
  neighbors of, 147, 161, 220
  nightspots frequented by,
    180–181, 197
  "not guilty" plea of, 264
  as nurse's aide, 80, 87, 167, 245,
    353
  obituary notices by, 114–115
  paranoia of, 56–57, 65, 174
  personality of, 21, 71, 91, 92, 97,
    105–106, 119–120, 123, 167,
    203–204, 225, 231–232, 234,
    241, 284, 363–368
  physical appearance of, 20–21,
    91–92, 352
  playacting by, 277
  police questioning of, 109–110,
    112, 222–249, 266–270,
    288–290, 296–299, 323, 337,
    360
  pregnancies of, 19, 30, 44–45,
    81–82, 91–92, 106, 118, 122,
    136–137, 147, 203–205, 255,
    328, 355–356
  pretrial hearing for, 184, 266–271,
    329–330
  prison sentence of, 253, 346–349
  prosecution of, 219, 230, 256–257,
    332
  as Protestant, 149, 151
  psychiatric reports on, 255, 263
  psychiatric therapy for, 102–103,
    174–180, 186, 234, 343,
    347–348, 363

  public opinion on, 115, 250–251,
    253, 321
  pulp fiction read by, 104–106
  rights read to, 223, 226–227, 234,
    238–239, 265, 266, 267, 269,
    288, 296
  as robbery suspect, 96, 97–98,
    107, 146
  Schenectady as home of, 23–24,
    199–201
  self-hatred of, 183
  social life of, 19–25, 118–120, 178,
    201, 211
  Social Services records on, 65–66,
    87–88, 90
  spending by, 34, 96–97, 120, 182,
    228
  strangeness of, 21, 90–92, 104,
    123, 125, 138, 170
  suspicions about, 47, 68–73, 85,
    93–94, 105, 106, 115–117, 125,
    142, 145, 157, 158–159,
    189–193, 218, 351
  Task Force on, 71, 73–74, 84, 210,
    225, 248, 256
  tenseness of, 32–34, 165, 223
  testimony given by, 266–268
  trailer fire and, 188–192, 196, 202,
    231, 267, 327
  trial notes taken by, 278
  trial of, 113, 261, 263–266, 271,
    275–345
  tubal ligation of, 133, 136–137
  Valium taken by, 98
  as viewed by nursing staff,
    123–127, 142, 145–146
  as waitress, 35, 46, 89–91, 92, 96,
    103–106, 107, 115, 120, 137,
    204–205, 275
  as witch, 192–193
  Woods case compared with,
    215–218, 256, 271

Tinning, Mary Frances:
  apnea monitor for, 128
  autopsy on, 74, 130–132
  baptism of, 132–133
  death of, 47, 60, 64, 72, 74,
    128–134, 140, 142, 144, 235,
    245–246, 351
  grave of, 27
  hospitalization of, 123–127, 132,
    137, 139, 144, 247, 309
  life support for, 129–130
  Marybeth's reaction to death of,
    128–134, 245–247
  medical history of, 131
  pneumonia of, 131
Tinning, Michael Raymond:
  adoption of, 44–45, 74, 121–122,
    148
  autopsy on, 54, 69, 157, 159–160,
    211
  Charles Ray's relationship with,
    140–141, 146, 149–150, 154,
    155–156
death of, 35, 47, 54, 67, 69, 70, 74,
    152–156, 157–161, 165–166,
    173, 202, 225–226, 235, 247,
    248, 357, 364
  funeral of, 63, 156, 176, 191
  grave of, 27, 64
  head injury of, 150–151, 158
  health of, 134–135
  hernia of, 135, 148
  Joe's relationship with, 148, 154
  Marybeth's reaction to death of,
    152–154, 160
  race question and, 134, 148
  sickle-cell anemia test for, 135
  viral pneumonia contracted by, 22,
    45, 54, 67, 69, 74, 155, 160,
    210, 247, 258, 308
Tinning, Nathan:
  apnea monitor for, 113, 125
  autopsy of, 114

  birth of, 107
  as brain-dead, 111
  death of, 60, 74, 107, 109–113,
    114, 116, 121, 134, 236,
    241–243, 248–249, 290, 304,
    336, 358
  exhumation of, 256–260
  funeral of, 115
  grave of, 27, 259
  Marybeth's reaction to death of,
    109–113, 227
  physical appearance of, 107
  resuscitation attempts for, 111,
    114
  signs of asphyxia in, 114
Tinning, Tami Lynne:
  Apgar score of, 316
  apnea monitor for, 30, 70, 285
  autopsy on, 50–55, 159, 209–219,
    291–293, 299–300, 301–320,
    334
  baptism of, 41–42
  birth of, 23, 204–206, 316, 328
  blood type of, 330–331
  crib for, 36–37
  crying by, 31, 38, 227, 239,
    240–241, 286, 310
  death notice for, 60, 66, 70
  death of, 19, 36–57, 72, 112, 171,
    206, 221, 222–223, 232, 234,
    235, 249, 256, 259, 263,
    282–324, 366
  diaper rash of, 32, 55, 292
  feeding of, 31–32, 286
  funeral of, 46–48, 57, 58–64, 262,
    283
  grave of, 64
  health of, 30–31
  hyperammonemia and, 139, 209,
    212, 214, 302–303, 304, 308,
    311, 315
  Joe and death of, 37, 38, 40, 41,
    42, 43, 239, 285, 295–296

Tinning, Tami Lynne *(Cont.)*
  last hours of, 39–43, 62–63,
    282–283, 317, 320–321
  Marybeth's attitude toward, 29–36
  Marybeth's fears about, 22–23
  Marybeth's reaction to death of,
    39–48, 56–57, 65, 283
  Marybeth's versions of death of,
    36–48, 56, 226–227, 239–241,
    266
  medical records of, 56, 70, 210
  memorial contributions for, 60
  name of, 23
  physical appearance of, 29, 227,
    282–283
  political aspect of case on, 71–73
  resuscitation attempts for, 227,
    240, 282–283
  signs of asphyxia in, 70, 209–220,
    229, 240, 292, 313, 316, 334
  Sudden Infant Death Syndrome
    (SIDS) and, 257, 292, 302, 303,
    310–311, 315–316, 334–335
  Walter, Cynthia, reaction to death
    of, 39–41, 62–63, 227,
    282–284, 317–318
  Walter, Cynthia, relationship
    with, 22, 31–32, 36
  Werdnig-Hoffmann disease and,
    305–307, 308–310, 312,
    313–314, 317–318, 334
Tinning, Timothy:
  birth of, 93, 133
  death of, 60, 74, 109, 112, 115,
    140, 235, 241, 242, 243–244,
    248–249, 290, 304, 336, 358
  exhumation of, 257–260
  funeral of, 94, 95
  grave of, 27, 259–260

  Joe and death of, 94
  Marybeth's reaction to death of,
    94
Toms, Dr. Mary Eleanor, 141

urea cycle defects, 139, 212

Valdes-Dapena, Dr. Marie, 315–316
Van Ness, Rodney, 335, 336,
  339–340, 342
vitreous humor, 211

Waldo, Ann, 174, 182
Waldo, the Rev. Burnham H.,
  Marybeth counseled by, 169–170,
  171, 172, 173–180, 182–183,
  186–187, 188, 192, 366–368
Waldron, Sheriff Bernard "Barney,"
  116–117, 157, 193, 343
Wall, Pat, 172–173, 175
Walter, Aaron, 19, 23, 31, 34, 40,
  41–42, 62–63, 220–221
Walter, Cynthia, 19–25, 26, 29, 30,
  31–32, 33–36, 37, 39–41, 58,
  62–63, 191, 204, 220–221, 227,
  239, 251, 253, 282–284, 317, 334,
  338
Walter, Mark, 20, 34, 39, 40, 41, 58,
  251
Werdnig-Hoffmann disease,
  303–309, 312, 313, 316, 317, 318,
  323, 330, 333
Where Are the Children? (Clark), 104,
  106, 114
Williams, Colonel Henry F.
  "Hank," 71, 75, 257
Woods, Martha, 215–218, 256, 271

Zampella, Investigator John, 72, 74,
  94, 132